AMERICANA LIBRARY

ROBERT E. BURKE, EDITOR

SAN FRANCISCO'S LITERARY FRONTIER

by

FRANKLIN WALKER

With a New Introduction by the Author

UNIVERSITY OF WASHINGTON PRESS

SEATTLE AND LONDON

TO

GEORGE R. STEWART

FOREWORD

DURING the generation that elapsed between the discovery of
gold in California and the completion of the transcontinental
railroad, San Francisco was the heart of an isolated frontier,
unique in many ways. One of its more unusual attributes was
the rapid development of a literary culture that not only produced an interesting school of journalism but formed the tastes
and methods of several writers later to attain prominent positions in American letters. My purpose in this volume has been
to trace in detail the experiences of these writers while they remained on the west coast, to analyze and evaluate their early
writings, and to reconstruct the background of their work. A
logical concomitant of these objectives has been the construction of a literary history of San Francisco from 1848 to 1875,
with emphasis upon the sixties.

In the first place I have built up a group biography in which
I have dealt with eight major characters, including four well-
known figures, Bret Harte, Mark Twain, Ambrose Bierce, and
Joaquin Miller, and a quartet of less prominent writers, Ina
Coolbrith, Charles Warren Stoddard, Prentice Mulford, and
Henry George. In addition I have dealt sketchily with the lives
and writings of some forty minor writers.

In my critical approach I have concerned myself with showing how the personality and interests of each subject was reflected in his journalism and how the time and place influenced
each writer during the years under discussion. To this end I

made a chronological survey of all the writings by the eight
major figures to appear in the West between 1848 and 1875
and in addition covered much of the work done by the twoscore
minor figures. Naturally, most of this survey was made in the
files of the journals to which these writers contributed. Basing
my conclusions on this examination, I have attempted explicitly
to outline the nature and value of the writings of Harte and his
friends during their days on the Pacific Coast and implicitly to
estimate the influence of their Western sojourns on their later
careers. In only two cases have I carried the detailed account
beyond 1875: I have followed Henry George through to the
completion of *Progress and Poverty* in 1879 because the work
had been initiated much earlier and its conception was a result
of observations of a pioneer society; and I have described the
writing of H. H. Bancroft's histories, completed in 1890, because they constitute in spirit and fact a fitting record of the
Pacific Coast frontier.

In addition to the group biography, I have presented by
sample and summary a detailed picture of journalistic and literary activity in San Francisco during its early days. I have
neglected the fifties and stressed the sixties for three reasons:
the book would be too long if both decades were treated exhaus-
tively; the sixties produced much more literature of lasting importance than did the fifties; and, most important, the major
figures in the book did not mature until the sixties. The tech-
nical problem of combining social history and group biography
demanded a choice between two methods: a chronological account of the development of literary schools, based upon the
fortunes of the principal journals, such as the *Era,* the *Californian,* and the *Overland Monthly;* and the sequential pres-
entation of each individual writer's development. I have chosen
the social-history approach, preferring an inclusive continuity
to a series of more or less detached biographies; I hope that the

advantages of such a plan will outweigh any confusion arising from the shuttling of figures in and out of the story.

I have concentrated on a study of literary activity in San Francisco rather than in the entire West because during the generation following the gold-rush San Francisco was the focal point, and to an unparalleled degree the literary capital, of a huge frontier territory. As San Francisco alone had the wealth, reading public, and facilities to publish literary journals and books, almost all the important writers west of the Rockies, from Oregon to Arizona, sooner or later became identified with its literature. Because of its rapidly attained sophistication and its unusual financial prosperity, the city provided a means for expression to the frontiersman while the frontier was still in existence. An examination of its literary output, therefore, adds to the rapidly growing body of information dealing with the influence of the frontier on American life and letters.

Acknowledgments to institutions and individuals, a list of the sources consulted, and an appendix of notes and references will be found at the end of the volume.

CONTENTS

LIST OF ILLUSTRATIONS

INTRODUCTION

THE editor of the Americana Library has asked me to write informally on my present evaluation of *San Francisco's Literary Frontier* now that it is being reissued just thirty years after its original appearance in 1939. My major reaction is that I still consider it a good book and am heartily pleased to see it back in print. Almost as strong is my feeling of relief and satisfaction at being able at last to correct a number of errors in fact which crept into the earlier edition, much to my surprise and chagrin. Though these errors were minor, I was intemperately pleased when the University of Washington Press informed me that it was possible to make the corrections which I had indicated. After three decades of embarrassment at having put Promontory Point in Nevada—however did *that* boner creep into my manuscript and evade the editorial readers?—I can now sleep peacefully, knowing at last it is where it belongs, in Utah. I continue to be amazed when errors of this sort appear after words have been fixed in cold print; surely a gremlin must be at work to bother writers.

To larger matters. It is not too surprising that the perspective provided by the passing of a generation has failed to bring me any major change of heart or shift of attitude toward the ideas in this book, for the work is not primarily concerned with a thesis nor is it particularly controversial. With the passage of time my evaluations of the writings of the various characters who weave their ways through the story have not materially changed nor do

I see any marked alteration in the accepted views of the social and cultural scenes reflected. Thus, in this discussion, I am forced to resort to remarks which can be classified as marginalia, or obiter dicta.

The aspect of the book which has most annoyed me—and this annoyance has not decreased with the years—is the title. *San Francisco's Literary Frontier* is academic, in its worst sense, stuffy, and to some degree misleading. Yet when I wrote the book I was not able to think of a better name, wisely spurning a friend's suggestion that I call it "They Wanted to Sleep with Ina Coolbrith" in order to be in step with current titles. Nor have I been able to think of an appropriate title since then. I'm afraid that catchy labels are not my forte; I *did* suggest that my *A Literary History of Southern California* (an even worse title than *San Francisco's Literary Frontier*) be called by a phrase borrowed from Margaret Mead, "Hoar Frost on New-laid Eggs," but my publishers felt that some Southern Californians might be offended by my flippancy. When I recently titled my account of the early Carmel literary colony *The Seacoast of Bohemia,* utilizing a quotation from Shakespeare in time-honored fashion, I was satisfied that I had at last found an appropriate and catchy title. After the book came out I discovered to my dismay that not only had the phrase been used as a title several times before but that a popular novel had been published in the same month as my book under the same title. Apparently I can't win when it comes to choosing titles.

The loose alignment (accentuated by its title) of *San Francisco's Literary Frontier* with Frederick Jackson Turner's theory about the influence of the frontier on American character, political institutions, and cultural attitudes may possibly have been unfortunate. With the swing of the pendulum away from the frontier as a major or *the* major germinal factor in American life, writings which stress the frontier influence tend to depreciate in value. Historians who feel that Turner (or at any rate the many followers of Turner) has overemphasized the role of the frontier have pointed persuasively to other influences molding national character and history—such as the "melting pot," the movement from the country to the city, and developing technologies—which they feel have been as influential as the advancing frontier or the tug of virgin land. Today the argument seems to have quieted down, with the frontier still being considered a major shaping influence in our society. Certainly, whether or not the term "frontier" adequately applies to the San Francisco of the 1860's, the spectacular growth of the affluent city, together with its isolation, had much to do with its unusual cultural flowering.

The emphasis in *San Francisco's Literary Frontier* is on the writers who played their parts in this nearly unique social setting. Thus, the book is a group biography rather than a treatise. Paradoxically, it started not as a study of frontier letters but as a portrayal of the American writer in Europe; thus, the chapter titled "From Gold Gulch to Parnassus" represents my initial orientation toward the subject, the germ from which the rest developed. As a student of English literature at Oxford, I first became interested in American writers because of their appeal to my English classmates. Not only did they see the bizarre in the writings and behavior of men like Mark Twain, Walt Whitman, and Herman Melville, but they felt that a literature was coming from across the Atlantic which was essentially different from British writings. Particularly they looked to the Far West in their conversations with me, possibly because I had spent my childhood and youth in that area and, even more to the point, was a Rhodes scholar from Arizona, the home of all that was tough and woolly. Accordingly, when I returned to the United States and enrolled at the University of California to work for my Ph.D. degree, I began a study of certain writers—specifically Bret Harte, Mark Twain, Joaquin Miller, and Ambrose Bierce—

who had gone to England to widen their audience after gaining a reputation in the Far West. I put this study aside for a dissertation on Frank Norris but returned to it later, finding that my project grew the richer as I examined the growth of these writers in a pioneer society.

The lasting importance of the four writers whom I chose to be the central figures in *San Francisco's Literary Frontier* has been attested to by the continued interest in them during the thirty years intervening between the first edition of the book and its reissue. New biographies of each of the four have appeared, with a particular enrichment of details in the cases of Mark Twain and Ambrose Bierce.[1] In addition, the relations between Bret Harte and Mark Twain, which started amicably in San Francisco but turned very bitter at a later period, have been thoroughly examined by a scholar who has successfully defended Harte against many of the charges made by Mark Twain late in his life.[2] Joaquin Miller has received little attention from scholars, but a doctoral dissertation has been written comparing his contributions to the western local-color story with those of Harte.[3] Moreover, Miller has been added to the list of writers treated in an excellent monograph series put out by the Twayne Publishers.[4] Interest in Bierce still runs strong with the general reading public; there have been reissues of the best of his short stories and of his *Devil's Dictionary,* and "The Occurrence at Owl Creek

[1]Richard O'Connor, *Bret Harte* (Boston: Little, Brown, 1966); DeLancey Ferguson, *Mark Twain* (Indianapolis: Bobbs-Merrill, 1943); Justin Kaplan, *Mr. Clemens and Mark Twain* (New York: Simon and Schuster, 1966); M. M. Marberry, *Splendid Poseur: Joaquin Miller* (New York: Crowell, 1953); Paul Fatout, *Ambrose Bierce* (Norman: University of Oklahoma Press, 1951); Richard O'Connor, *Ambrose Bierce* (Boston: Little, Brown, 1967).

[2]Margaret Duckett, *Mark Twain and Bret Harte* (Norman: University of Oklahoma Press, 1964).

[3]Roger P. Walterhouse, "Bret Harte, Joaquin Miller, and the Western Local-Color Story" (Ph.D. dissertation, University of Chicago, 1937).

[4]Orcutt William Frost, *Joaquin Miller* (New York: Twayne, 1967).

Bridge" has been turned into a successful art movie. A much-needed scholarly analysis of his fiction has appeared,[5] and a complete edition of his letters is under way. An additional sign of the continued interest in Bierce is the reissue of Carey McWilliams' excellent biography, which has long been out of print.

Of the four major writers in the book, Mark Twain has received much the most critical attention, just as he has unquestionably attracted the most readers. Critical attention to Mark Twain and his writings has turned into a major industry, and the years he spent in Nevada and California have not been neglected. Several works have added to our knowledge of his activities in the Far West. Many details concerning his Virginia City experiences that were not known thirty years ago were made available by the discovery of a scrapbook containing many of Mark Twain's contributions to the *Territorial Enterprise*, the files of which have totally disappeared. These have been ably edited by Henry Nash Smith and Frederick Anderson,[6] who have also been largely instrumental in opening the Mark Twain Papers to general use. New light on Mark Twain's San Francisco days has not been so plentiful as that shed on his Nevada sojourn, although a more nearly complete edition of his signed San Francisco writings has appeared,[7] and a scholar who has ably analyzed his writing up to 1867[8] is in the interesting process of identifying and annotating his unsigned contributions to the San Francisco *Morning Call*. Also Mark Twain's letters to the

[5]Stuart C. Woodruff, *The Short Stories of Ambrose Bierce* (Pittsburgh: University of Pittsburgh Press, 1965).

[6]Henry Nash Smith and Frederick Anderson (ed.), *Mark Twain and the Enterprise* (Berkeley and Los Angeles: University of California Press, 1957). Also by the same editors, *Mark Twain: San Francisco Virginia City Territorial Enterprise Correspondent* (San Francisco: Book Club of California, 1957).

[7]Bernard Taper, *Mark Twain's San Francisco* (New York: McGraw-Hill, 1963).

[8]Edgar M. Branch, *The Literary Apprenticeship of Mark Twain* (Urbana: University of Illinois Press, 1950).

Alta California have been collected and edited; these include the letters sent in on his way to New York and his return to his home in Hannibal as well as the originals written on the *Quaker City* trip which formed the basis for *The Innocents Abroad.*[9]

Of the lesser quartet of characters who play major parts in the book—Charles Warren Stoddard (Pip Pepperpod), Ina Coolbrith, Prentice Mulford, and Henry George—little has appeared to supplement or alter the accounts given of them in *San Francisco's Literary Frontier.* Of the four, Henry George has been the most discussed, particularly by economists and social reformers, who have been more interested in his theories than in the influence of the frontier upon him; among other treatments, he has been the subject of a new biography, has been considered in one of the Twayne monographs, and has even elicited a complete concordance to *Progress and Poverty.*[10] A doctoral dissertation was completed on Stoddard in 1939 but has unfortunately never been published.[11] Ina Coolbrith has, on the other hand, evoked little interest among the scholars, but the active Ina Coolbrith Society keeps her memory green. Her role as niece of the founder of the Mormons has been generally accepted. Almost dead without a trace is the Diogenes of the Tuolumne, Prentice Mulford, but even he has his partisans, as I discovered one pleasant evening when a visiting art historian looked me up to discuss the Mulford whose writings had played such an important part in his youthful days in Germany.

[9]Franklin Walker and G. Ezra Dane (ed.), *Mark Twain's Travels with Mr. Brown* (New York: Knopf, 1940); D. M. McKeithan (ed.), *Traveling with the Innocents Abroad* (Norman: University of Oklahoma Press, 1958).

[10]Charles A. Barker, *Henry George* (New York: Oxford University Press, 1955); Edward J. Rose, *Henry George* (New York: Twayne, 1968); Helena M. McEvoy, *Complete Concordance to Progress and Poverty* (Chicago: Ability Press, 1959).

[11]Carl G. Stroven, "A Life of Charles Warren Stoddard" (Ph.D. dissertation, Duke University, 1939).

The journals to which the San Francisco writers contributed in the early days have also received both scholarly and popular attention since this book first appeared. *The Golden Era* and *The Overland Monthly* are the subjects of doctoral dissertations, and an extensive treatise on California magazines from 1850 to 1950 was completed in French at the University of Paris.[12] Not long ago an attractive compendium of articles and illustrations from *Hutchings' Illustrated California Magazine* appeared under the title *Scenes of Wonder and Curiosity from Hutchings' California Magazine*.

Of the precursors in the fifties whom I included in *San Francisco's Literary Frontier* Alonzo Delano (Old Block) lies quietly in his grave, possibly with his famous nose protruding; if further attention has been given to George Horatio Derby (John Phoenix) other than his inclusion in studies of American humorists I am not aware of it, although I understand that George R. Stewart's definitive *John Phoenix, Esq.* may soon be reissued. The influence of John Rollin Ridge on the Joaquin Murieta legend was further explored by the late Joseph Henry Jackson.[13] An excellent trade edition of *The Shirley Letters* was published by Alfred Knopf, and a leading California historian has been

[12]Lawrence E. Mobley, "The *Golden Era* Magazine, 1852-1866" (Ph.D. dissertation, Michigan State University, 1961); Thomas J. Macdonald, "*The Overland Monthly*, 1868-1898" (Ph.D. dissertation, Stanford University, in progress); Reine Kruh, "Un Siecle de magazines Californiens, 1850-1950" (unpublished manuscript, University of Paris, 1962).

[13]Joseph Henry Jackson, *Bad Company* (New York: Harcourt, Brace, 1949).

[14]John Walton Caughey, *Hubert Howe Bancroft* (Berkeley and Los Angeles: University of California Press, 1946); Alfred Riggs Ferguson, *Edward Rowland Sill* (The Hague: Martinus Nijhoff, 1955); Thurman Wilkins, *Clarence King* (New York: Macmillan, 1958).

[15]Richard H. Dillon, *J. Ross Browne, Confidential Agent in Old California* (Norman: University of Oklahoma Press, 1965).

[16]David Michael Goodman, *A Western Panorama* (Glendale, Calif.: Arthur H. Clark, 1966).

working for some time on a biography of their writer, Louise Amelia Knapp Smith Clappe.

Among writers who played minor roles in the later chapters of the book, Hubert Howe Bancroft, Edward Rowland Sill, and Clarence King have to my knowledge been the subjects of detailed biographies,[14] and John Muir continues to be a lodestar among lovers of mountains and exploration. There probably are many other studies of early San Francisco writers, particularly in article form, that I have missed. I have not tried to make an exhaustive survey of these writings; I merely have hoped to indicate by citing the ones that have come to my attention that the field is still a vital one. I will conclude these informal remarks by pointing out the rather extensive attention that has been paid to one additional minor figure, J. Ross Browne. A surprising amount of his fugitive journalism has been brought out in fine printing editions; one art press in Southern California puts most of its effort into publishing Browne items. Recently two lengthy biographies have appeared, one stressing his role as a confidential agent for the federal government,[15] the other emphasizing his skill in presenting a panorama of the Far West in his journalism.[16] I have left him for dessert in this discussion because he is much in my mind at the present time. The pleasurable research and travel which I have undertaken as a preliminary to writing an account of the reactions of Ross Browne, Mark Twain, and Herman Melville to journeys to the Holy Land have quite occupied my attention of late and have taken me far from San Francisco, even though the thoughts and behavior of two of my three victims constantly bring me back to the frontier.

FRANKLIN WALKER

Oakland, California
January, 1969

SAN FRANCISCO'S LITERARY FRONTIER

CHAPTER I

A PRECOCIOUS FRONTIER

THE *Golden Era* appeared a day early that week so that its issue would commemorate the driving of the spike which would mark the completion of the transcontinental railroad. On Saturday, May 8th, 1869, San Francisco was buzzing with excitement, making her preparations for " the greatest and brightest day " in her annals. Plans were completed for the longest parade in the history of that parade-loving city. The guns at Fort Point were loaded and primed — set to volley when the big moment arrived. Bells were rigged up to peal when the momentous taps were transmitted over the telegraph from Utah. Judge Nathaniel Bennett, orator of the occasion, was rehearsing his speech, ready to deliver it to the portion of the crowd that would be able to elbow its way into the Mechanics Pavilion, the largest hall in the city. The honorable Frank Soulé was prepared to declaim the poem of the day. The Reverend Dr. Cox had memorized his invocation.

Then came the news that the train bringing the delegation of the Union Pacific to the end of the track in Utah had been delayed by floods and creditors and that the East would hold up the West for two more days. For a moment San Francisco hesitated. Then, refusing to be disappointed — such enthusiasm could not be bottled up much longer — she went ahead with her celebration, three days and three nights of it. She held her parade, she assembled for the speeches, she shouted till she was hoarse. Then she dispersed to the Occidental, to the Lick House, to the Merchants Exchange, and to a hundred other bars for a three-day spree. San Francisco was all set to celebrate. Why wait for the stuffed shirts to perform in Utah? The railroad meant little to Promontory, where native Piutes mingled with a temporary population of Irishmen, Chinese, and silk-hatted promoters. It meant everything to San Francisco. Gone forever were the days of her isolation. Twenty years gone were the days when it took three months to round the Horn in a clipper ship, a full summer to cross the plains and mountains in a Conestoga wagon. Twelve years gone was the time when the people had to wait three weeks for the news of a presidential election to reach them by way of Panama and the Pacific Mail. Eight years had passed since the period when the pony express took ten days to rush news-sheets printed on tissue paper from St. Jo to the Pacific. Tomorrow San Francisco would be as close to New York as St. Louis was fifteen years ago. Trains would shuttle across the continent in seven days, bringing mail, newspapers, magazines, and books cheaply and quickly; bringing steel, clothes, and machinery from the East and carrying back gold and grain from California, silk and spices from the Orient; bringing visitors and settlers to a sunny land and taking nostalgic pioneers home on visits. Why should San Francisco wait to celebrate? Celebrate Saturday, celebrate Sunday, celebrate Monday — keep on celebrating in frenzied joy at the vision of prosperity and growth.

When Monday came, the dignitaries speechified at Promontory Point. They bumbled sententiously as they drove in the silver spike donated by Nevada, the alloy spike donated by

Arizona, the two gold spikes donated by California. Leland Stanford of the Central Pacific held forth last; then, with telegraph wires adjusted to record his three blows on the golden Last Spike, he swung the silver-headed maul and missed. Thomas C. Durant, representing the Union Pacific, missed in turn out of courtesy. But over the wires sped the three clicks which told that the thing was done. At that moment Omaha rang its bells and blew its whistles. At Chicago the three dots started a parade four miles long. In New York a massed choir sang the *Te Deum*, in Philadelphia the great Liberty Bell was tolled, in New Orleans a carnival was inaugurated, in cities and villages throughout America the people rejoiced simultaneously at the beginning of a new era.

In San Francisco the three clicks set loose all the noise that was left after the celebrations on Saturday and Sunday. Twenty guns boomed from the old red fort; artillery barked from the hills where it had been stationed; the bells of the city pealed out; and the hoarse citizens let loose once more and then took another drink. In the evening there was a parade with many illuminations speaking the thoughts of San Francisco. The letters spelled out by flickering candles and flares announced that San Francisco was to be the largest city in the world. The feeling of isolation, the fears of those days in '61 when no one knew whether California would stay in the Union or become a Pacific republic, were over. From the biggest transparency glowed the words: " The Pacific Railroad, Uncle Sam's Waistband — He would burst without it."

The beginning of a new era is always the end of an old one. To the San Francisco citizens who celebrated the completion of the transcontinental railroad, isolation had meant separation from loved ones, and the putting up with a thousand inconveniences of daily life. The railroad would end these; it would also bring more people, and more people would surely bring more prosperity. The railroad would make San Francisco more like St. Louis, more like Chicago, more like Philadelphia, more like Boston. Thus San Francisco looked forward to becoming like other cities, readily relinquishing, despite platitudes of man's love of individuality, the circumstances which nourish that individuality, regretting little the end of an experiment in civilization that to later generations was to appear unique.

Few men appreciated the American frontier until the American frontier disappeared. In the year that the Federal Census announced its disappearance it was discovered by the historians, and during the half-century that has passed since its end the reading public has grown increasingly interested in its social record and in its literature. Of all American frontiers, none has attracted the attention of the curious and intelligent more persistently than the Far-Western society created by the forty-niners. And, for reasons inherent in its economic and social development, no frontier community has appealed to the imagination as much as has San Francisco. It was a civilization created overnight, grown articulate enough in the days of its youth to speak while frontier conditions still existed.

The growth of this western land had been unprecedented. Nothing like it had taken place east of the Rockies. Whereas small streams of pioneers had flowed down from the Appalachians along the Ohio River Valley, and trickled along the Great Lakes, and seeped across the plains, a tidal wave hit the Pacific slope and filled it up in two decades. And this unusual growth centered in San Francisco; in 1848 it was a village with two hotels, two wharves nearly completed, and eight hundred inhabitants — not enough to fill a good-sized theater. Twenty years later it was the capital of a vast territory, a financial competitor of New York and a cultural rival of Boston. Furthermore, whereas the farmers of the plains had always been in direct touch with the established civilization immediately behind them, these Argonauts traveled into an isolated territory and started a new country from scratch. The society they created was far more complex than that of the agrarian frontier.

Several aspects of this new frontier made it more promising as a cradle of culture than those that had come before it. In the first place, its population was much more heterogeneous socially and racially than that of the usual agrarian frontier. Instead of being made up almost entirely of farmers, it drew men of every profession. Politicians like Gwin and Baker came west hoping to rise quickly in a country which would surely offer at least six new senatorships and possibly the presidency of a new republic. Physicians like Dr. Clappe saw the advantages and adventure of practicing medicine on the fringe of civilization. Editors like Noah Brooks crossed the Rockies because they knew hundreds of newspapers would sprout overnight in the new country. It has been said that San Francisco in its early days had a greater percentage of college graduates than any other city in America. The large number of well-educated men, members of the white-collar professions, promised Western society support for the arts.

The existence of the Pacific Ocean assured a cosmopolitan population to San Francisco. California was a frontier that faced two ways; the sea approach in particular brought men from vast distances and many lands. Unlike the frontiers of the Great Plains, filled slowly by traders and farmers pushed forward by the creeping agrarian advance, the population along the Pacific, attracted by the tug of gold — so much stronger than that of free land — came from all over the world. Superimposed upon the slight Spanish-Californian stock was a new population from Australia, England, Ireland, France, and Germany. Mexicans came up from the south, Russians drifted down from the north, and Kanakas and Chinese crossed the seas from the Orient. The American immigration was divided between the Yankee from Massachusetts and the Pike County man from Missouri, between the politician from New York and the ranger from Texas, between the farmer from Pennsylvania and the fire-eating " gentleman " from South Carolina.

The many voices of this polyglot frontier soon became articulate in newspapers published in German, Italian, French, Swedish, Spanish, and Chinese. Dumas's *Gil Blas in California* was evolved from the journal of a French resident of San Francisco; one of the first novels to come out of the West was by a German in the German tongue; the Chinese figured as characters in the earliest Californian children's stories; and the Spanish-Californians and Mexicans nourished the West's most famous legend, the story of Joaquin Murieta. More significant, however, than the appearance of a French newspaper or a Spanish story was the stimulation produced by a score of national cultures coming in contact with one another in a new and plastic society. The singularity of the outlook of the pioneer was increased by his everyday contact with the many varied cultures.

Heterogeneous in cultures, social classes, and racial stocks, the society of this Far-Western frontier was unique in its sex and age. Most of the Argonauts were male and young. Although the scarcity of women during the gold-rush has furnished a favorite theme for many stories, few readers realize how disproportionate the relation between the sexes remained long after '49. Actually, the proportion of women to men among the immigrants increased from one twelfth in 1850 to only one third in 1880. Births within the state, in spite of the " fecundity of certain portions among the inhabitants " noticed by Bancroft, failed to balance the sexes before the end of the century. And, naturally, most of the men who ventured across the plains were young men; more than half of them were, in fact, between the ages of twenty and thirty. Even in 1860 two-thirds of the population were still under fifty. Thus in upsetting the established order of a patterned world, it was youth without women that welcomed adventure and new ways of doing things. The dynamite of California was composed of one part vigor and one part unsatisfied passion.

Another unusual feature of this Far-Western land was its reluctance to follow the ordered development of the typical frontier. Most frontiers insisted on settling down; this one refused to. Its development was not so much progressive as repetitive. San Francisco became the mother of a score of daughter frontiers, listening to each in turn, expressing the experiences of each to a curious world. The miners were always on the move: they rushed to Coloma, they rushed to Sonora, they rushed to Bidwell's Bar, they rushed to Gold Lake. When they made a strike, they returned to San Francisco and lost it there; when they failed to make a strike and went broke in the mines, they trudged back to San Francisco, labored for a while at good wages, and got enough money for another grubstake. In the winter, when the floods covered the placers, and the snows froze men who tried to exist in thin huts, most of the miners returned to the city. The few that sailed home were soon replaced by many more.

Moreover, the process did not stop when, in the early fifties, the placers began to play out. The miners simply went farther; they swarmed out of San Francisco in search of pots of gold under more distant rainbows, but they continued always to return. The Fraser River rush in 1858 took 23,000 men north to British Columbia, but the disappointed gold-seekers were back in the city in three months, with little gold, but many experiences to yarn about. Two years later the Comstock Lode — the richest of all bonanzas — was discovered just across the line in Nevada; San Franciscans built Virginia City, stripped

Mount Davidson of its fabulous wealth, and then returned to the bay to live on Nob Hill. The men who opened up the Bill Williams and Mowry mines in Arizona, the Salmon River and Boise strikes in Idaho, and the Alder Gulch and Last Chance diggings in Montana looked upon San Francisco as their home. It was the center of Western population, the port into which their mining machinery was shipped, the headquarters of their engineers and consultants, and the natural outlet for their product. Economically, the states between the Sierras and the Rockies were colonies of California. For the present only a handful of men took root in these soils; the greater part, mobile as quicksilver, restless and adventurous like all the West, abandoned their short-lived towns and returned to the city by the Golden Gate.

But mineral wealth was not all California had to offer. Had it been so, the miners might have returned to their homes as soon as they had expected to when they left them; and even with the continual opening up of mines in the frontier watersheds, San Francisco might eventually have become a ghost town had there been no agricultural frontier to nourish a stable populace. The coastal plains had yielded no more than tallow and hides during the Spanish-Californian occupation, but when thousands who came to the mines had to eat, they soon found that it was unnecessary to bring food from the antipodes, with rich soil covering their own valleys. As placer mining became less remunerative, newcomers began to raise potatoes and other vegetables indispensable to a people living on a salt-meat diet. Many of the men from Pike were homesick until they got back to the soil; what they wanted was good land, especially grass-land — near woods with wild game. When they found it, they forgot about their claims. The shrewder ones found that cereals, particularly hard barley, were easily grown, and that the large interior valleys, condemned as barren by the natives, would yield fortunes in wheat. By 1854 the state was producing most of its own food. By 1860 there were nearly twenty thousand farms within its borders. Thus cattle, grain, and fruit-growing formed three more successive frontiers, supplementing the mining activity.

If the recurrent rushes for metal in the fifties and sixties had failed to keep frontier conditions alive, if the addition of agrarian front-lines had failed to add new elements to the ferment, the extraordinary situation of California during the Civil War would have prevented the society from settling early into a mold. From the war-torn East and South, where brothers were killing brothers, men escaped over the mountains to the Pacific Coast, glad to get away from a world they could not stomach. Samuel Clemens was only one of tens of thousands who became pioneers because there was no fighting west of the Rockies. Restless, disillusioned men, some of them deserters from the Union army, others from the Confederate forces, some transporting their families to a peaceful soil, others leaving their families forever, they ranged over the mountains from mining camp to mining camp, squatted on the sandy land which had been ignored by earlier farmers, or drifted into the city to find employment.

These are some of the reasons why San Francisco remained rough and grew sophisticated at the same time. Provided a life of adventure and change by the recurrent mineral and agrarian frontiers, the city at the same time grew receptive to art, music, and literature. While its editors, its publishers, and its writers were becoming socially mature enough to describe what they saw around them, a steady stream of frontiersmen was constantly being pumped in and out of the heart of the West.

The factor that counted most in the production of Western literature, however, was wealth. The Far-Western frontier was fortunate in that, from its earliest days, it was able to support a prosperous rather than an impoverished society. In New England the colonial settlers, with little wealth and an absence of cheap labor, had been forced to use all their energy in fighting a stubborn wilderness. The pioneers in the Mississippi Valley and on the Great Plains had faced the same problems, with much the same results. The typical farmer could not afford to hire help; he worked long and late to keep himself alive, and he rarely freed himself from debt. Under such conditions it took as much as a century to build up enough wealth to provide for colleges, libraries, and public schools. Luxury and leisure were unknown for several generations, and a scar was left on the cultural life of the people.

The Westerner, instead of borrowing money, loaned it; instead of enslaving himself to the mortgage-holder, he supplied the wealth which strengthened a nation and affected a world. After 1850 Western mines were producing an average of fifty million dollars' worth of gold a year. By the time California gold had begun to thin, Nevada silver had taken its place. As one result of this rich mineral production, Californian merchants were able during the Civil War to buy from the East in greenbacks and sell at home in gold, assuring themselves of boom days during the sixties.

Of course not every man in California was free from poverty. The fact that the average yield of the miner after the lucrative days of '49 was little more than two dollars a day shows that many barely struggled along; others were in dire want. In contrast to the bizarre picture of a Rufus Lockwood skipping twenty-dollar gold pieces on the water off Meiggs Pier as idly as an urchin skips stones on a mill-pond, is the gloomy vision of a thousand disappointed men committing suicide in the city each year. However, while the miners worked day after day in ice-cold water up to their knees, with the sun blistering their backs, while they searched for enough dust to buy bacon and meal at exorbitant prices, the middlemen bought the dust from them and made two dollars on every ounce that passed through their hands. Nor were the gamblers the only ones that handled the gold when it reached the city; high law fees were paid, fine clothes and carriages were purchased, blocks of buildings were rented, and real estate boomed in the market. Churches, theaters, and libraries appeared overnight. The society as a whole was well off; wages were higher than in any other spot in America, interest rates were good, money flowed freely, and the wealth per capita was the highest in the nation.

Such a sudden production of wealth as the West saw in the fifties and sixties naturally resulted in many excesses. Miners carried gold watches that weighed a pound apiece; gamblers sported the largest diamonds they could buy; the Bella Union glittered with imported cut-glass chandeliers. Courtesans paid fabulous prices for imported gowns; twelve-course dinners with terrapin and *plombières* cut short the life of the epicure; and barouches and landaus, lined with satin and drawn by the best horses money could buy, rolled along the plank road to the Mission. The Westerners boasted that " New York dresses better than Paris, and San Francisco better than New York." The average consumption of European products was much greater than on the Atlantic slope. The Californian used more than twice as much sugar and coffee and three times as much tea as his brother in the East. He consumed seven bottles of champagne to every one drunk by the Bostonian.

Not all of the wealth, however, went into luxuries. Schools, the first essential in creating a reading public, grew rapidly. The Public Institute was opened in Portsmouth Square in San Francisco before gold was discovered, and in 1849 the California State Constitution made provision for an elementary-school education free to all. Three years after the gold-rush there were seven public grade schools in San Francisco; four years later there were twenty-four and in addition a public high school. In 1855 the College of California, later to become the State University, was founded across the bay by Henry Durant. The interest of San Franciscans in reading prompted the establishment in the mid-fifties of three public libraries — the Mercantile Library, the Mechanics' Institute Library, and the Odd Fellows' Library. Other social institutions such as fraternal organizations and societies of special purpose grew like weeds. The Odd Fellows and the Masons, organized in '49, were followed by the Sons of Temperance, the Swiss Benevolent Society, and the Hibernian Society. Hebrews, English, Germans, Scandinavians, Slavs; mechanics, seamen, and soldiers; merchants, printers, and stevedores; doctors, writers, and churches clubbed together to draw up constitutions and bylaws and to hold picnics. The most ambitious of these societies was the California Academy of Science.

The capital of the West supported in abundance journals through which its writers could get their training and reach their public. As early as 1850 there were fifty printers working at their trade in the fast-growing city. San Francisco boasted that in the mid-fifties it published more newspapers than London, that in its first decade it published more books than did all the rest of the United States west of the Mississippi. Whatever voice the Western frontier might develop was sure of expression in its many literary organs, among which the *Pioneer*, the *Golden Era*, the *Hesperian*, the *Californian*, and the *Overland Monthly* could compare with the best Eastern journals. Wealth to produce and education and leisure to read such journals alone made them possible.

This New Atlantis upon the shores of the Pacific was by no means a typical frontier, but the acme of all frontiers, the most concentrated of quickly flourishing societies. With its hetero-

SAN FRANCISCO IN 1848 AND 1849.
Contrasting pictures to show the growth of San Francisco during the first year
of the gold rush.

Courtesy of California State Library

SUNDAY IN THE MINES.

A painting by Charles Nahl.

Courtesy of E. B. Crocker Art Gallery

THE GOLD RUSH AS LONDON SAW IT IN 1849.

A cartoon from *Punch* dealing with the stampede of adventurers from many countries after gold was discovered in California.

Courtesy of the University of California Extension Division

geneous population, with its constant renewal of pioneer conditions, and with its wealth far above the subsistence level, this
precocious civilization learned to talk while it was still young.
Thus during the quarter-century that followed the gold-rush
frontier literature was actually written by eyewitnesses — participants in the drama which they described. These interpreters
of life had an unparalleled opportunity to see it in rapid flux,
moving swiftly from trader's hut to Palace Hotel, from Poker
Flat vigilantes to state supreme court, from a mining stake for
every comer to a commercialized society with a stock exchange
in which millionaires gambled while poor men rioted on Nob
Hill.

Inevitably, the literature of El Dorado stressed the novel, the
picturesque; in fact, it nearly missed the deeper significance
of the scene in picturing its external trappings. Lawlessness
rather than the growth of law; gambling rather than the building of a fortune; the prostitute with the heart of gold rather
than the pioneer mother were given the limelight.

Yet the frontier contributed something more fundamental
than its peripheral excitements to its most thoughtful interpreters. Men do not often get such a view of themselves as they
were then furnished. Ordinarily they live with eyes dulled by
habit, unaware of how they are made, ignorant of how they
look and act. The adolescent boy leaves home for college and,
on his return, discovers his family. The traveler comes home
from a summer in Europe to see his village for the first time.
The people of a nation, after disturbing the set order of their
lives in a war, look about and examine themselves in surprise at
what they find. Since time began, writers have sought ways of
scaling the cataracts of habit from their eyes; and the Far-
Western frontier offered an unparalleled opportunity to see
clearly and vividly. Between 1848, when James W. Marshall

discovered gold at Coloma, and 1869, when San Francisco celebrated the building of a railroad that ended its isolation, a people lived through a condensed version of the world's economic
and cultural growth. To this phenomenon the writers of El
Dorado owe their distinction and Western literature its absorbing interest.

CHAPTER II

THE FIFTIES

WHEN California was taken from the Mexicans in 1846, the sandy, wind-swept peninsula on which San Francisco was to be built was nearly as barren as the day on which Ortega had first seen it nearly eighty years before. The dilapidated Presidio overlooking the Golden Gate housed twelve ragged men and a sergeant; three miles away among the sand dunes the secularized Mission Dolores gave refuge to eight native men and women. During the three centuries that California had been held as an outpost of empire by Spain and Mexico, it had added little to the culture of the world except a pastoral myth which chambers of commerce would later exploit during real-estate booms. The one book of importance that had been stimulated by its easygoing life had been written by a Yankee who had spent a year loading hides in California to recover his health, sacrificed to studies at Harvard. In *Two Years before the Mast* Richard Henry Dana described a Spanish-Californian society whose members were little more likely to create a distinctive literature than the native Indians, who lived on acorns and dried grasshoppers. The Spaniards in California had not developed a frontier; they had merely held it for fear someone else would get it.

Half-way between the Presidio and the mission, on Yerba Buena cove, was a small settlement of gringos, less than two hundred in number, which was the nucleus of the city to come. This handful of traders saw the American flag raised in the Plaza, when Captain John B. Montgomery arrived to cut short the *opéra bouffe* of the Bear Flag revolt and annex California to the Union. Two years later a slightly larger group saw Sam Brannan run along the Calle de Fondacion, excitedly waving a bottle of gold dust above his head while he shouted that gold had been found near Sutter's Fort. Although within a few days those gringos almost to a man had departed for the scene of the discovery, the days of modern San Francisco had begun. The next year Bayard Taylor, standing on the deck of a clipper ship in the bay, saw the lights of myriad tents glowing on the hillsides like a host of Japanese lanterns. The canvas settlement reminded him of " the cities of the magic lantern, which a motion of the hand can build and annihilate." But the canvas changed to wood and stone, and when Dana returned in 1859 to the cove in which twenty years before he had seen but three wretched shacks, he found a metropolitan city which dazzled him with its gay shops and thriving industry.

Much that was dramatic and bizarre accompanied that rapid growth. Five times the wooden buildings burned to the ground and five times the city was rebuilt overnight. Twice the people, after neglecting civic problems in their rush for money, took the law into their own hands and hanged the nearest offenders. After the output of gold began to fall off and a panic was upon the city, the vigilante bell rang a third time and a citizen's committee ruled from Fort Gunnybags during the summer of '56. Not many days later Alderman Casey shot editor James King of William, and soon the bodies of Casey and Cora dangled from ropes above the heads of a silent and earnest populace.

The modern reader has long been assured that San Francisco during the fifties was an extraordinary place. A year before gold was found, John Russ of Stevenson's regiment bought two lots in Yerba Buena for thirty dollars; ten years later he sold them for enough to build the largest hotel in town. John Parrott imported the stone for the Parrott Building from China in blocks cut and numbered so that the Chinamen he imported with them could fit them together in San Francisco. A cow disappeared in the bog where the city hall was to be erected, and Market Street was a high ridge of sand, sixty feet above its present level. The city's drinking-water was brought over in barrels from Sausalito across the bay, and soiled linen was sent all the way to China to be laundered. The steam paddy moved the sand hills into the bay, thus pushing the waterfront six city blocks past the wharves. A Frenchman named Limantour turned up with a Mexican grant for all of San Francisco and had the people eating out of his hands until his papers were proved to be forged.

Palatial gambling saloons like the Bella Union and the El Dorado flourished, and the denizens of the Barbary Coast invented shanghaiing. Duels were fought openly, some advertised in advance, with excursion steamers carrying the crowds of spectators across the bay to the field of honor. The belief in the Anglo-Saxon's destiny was strong, and filibusters recruited many San Franciscans to accompany them on attempts to grab off portions of Mexico: Count Gaston Raoul de Raousset-Boulbon led a band of adventurers on an ill-fated junket into Sonora; William Walker gave up his editorial job to sail down and capture Baja California, but failed to hold his gains; and Henry A. Crabb of Tennessee, in a disastrous foray into Sonora, was the third and last to find Mexico too much for him. By the mid-fifties it was clear that the palmy days of filibustering were over; Houston had succeeded in Texas, Frémont had carried his bluff in California, but de Raousset-Boulbon, Walker, and Crabb died failures.

The melodrama of the fifties was but the glitter covering steady civic development of a less spectacular nature. While volunteer fire-brigades were drilling, the art association was being formed. While vigilantes were policing the town, streets were being paved with planks of Oregon fir. While editors were fighting duels, the *Golden Era* and the *Pioneer* were struggling to give the people something worth while to read. A score of churches were built; private, public, and parochial schools were provided; and the state suspended the anti-lottery law so that funds could be raised for the Mercantile Library. While Doc Robinson, the Chapmans, and Lola Montez extertained enthusiastic audiences, the local opera was not afraid to attempt the most recent continental successes. Although the city was gamboling with a flourish and a huzza, it was growing in a manner that promised an early maturity.

Though most of the creative writers during the fifties came from the ranks of newspapermen, by no means all of the newspapermen were creative writers. The demand for papers antedated the demand for literature, and many of the editors were opportunists seeking a break in politics or even dabbling in blackmail. The most legitimate sources of revenue for the dailies and weeklies were the war-chests of the political parties and the public funds, which supported at least one journal in each county with routine government advertising. With these revenues, advertisements came first, editorials second, and news third. Most of the papers were one-man journals, the editor dividing his time between composing fiery leading articles and condensing the month-old news that arrived by steamer. Surprisingly little effort was made to report local items, except po-

litical ones; rather, the editor filled in space indiscriminately
with articles on customs of the early Britons and legends of the
digger Indians. In addition, contributions by local writers were
always welcome, and usually did not have to be paid for.
The editors were of necessity men of action. Walter Colton,
who started the first California newspaper, the *Californian*, in
Monterey on August 15, 1846, had been the chaplain of an
American frigate and the editor of the Philadelphia *North
American*. While acting as alcalde in Monterey, his chief judicial problem was to devise adequate means of inflicting penalties
with no jail at his disposal. His eccentric and breezy comments
on the results he expressed in his *Three Years in California*. His
partner in the *Californian* was Robert Semple, a dentist, physician, printer, and adventurer from Kentucky who had been a
ring-leader in the Bear Flag revolt and who was to become a
member of the first legislature. In printing their weekly journal on an old Spanish press, they ran short of both paper and
type, leaving curious issues on coarse yellow paper normally
used for cigar wrappings. As the Spanish font contained no
w's, genuine double *v's* were used instead.

Shortly after the inauguration of the *Californian*, the *California Star* was founded in San Francisco by Sam Brannan, a
Mormon who had brought a boat-load of his followers to the west
coast in the hope of setting up an independent Mormon state.
With the discovery of gold Brannan grew fabulously wealthy,
partly, it is said, by collecting tithes from the Mormon miners;
he led the first vigilante movement, and he eventually lost his
money through drink and speculation almost as fast as he had
made it. The editing of his mouthpiece he left to others. After
a sporadic career the journal united with the *Californian*, which
had moved up from Monterey, and became the first genuine daily
in the West, under a new title, the *Alta California*, and the
youthful, vigorous editorship of Edward C. Kemble.

By the time the *Alta* celebrated its fifth birthday, there were twelve other dailies in the city, and several times that number of weeklies; nearly every small town in the state also had a local journal, many with picturesque names like the *Wine, Women, and Song Journal*, the *Miner's Spy Glass*, and *Satan's Bassoon*. Bancroft estimated that over a thousand men were occupied in journalism during the fifties, and that Californians supported more newspapers per man than any other people in the country. The spectacular side of the game continued: Edward Gilbert, editor of the *Alta*, was killed in a duel similar to many others fought by Southern editors with hair-trigger tempers; James King of William, disgruntled at losing his money, founded the *Bulletin* to attack his enemies and incidentally to " clean up the city "; James Casey, ward politician and editor of a rival journal, shot him down like a dog and precipitated the most spectacular of all mob uprisings; and William Walker, the gray-eyed man of destiny, edited a daily while he searched for volunteers to help him annex Mexico or found an empire in Nicaragua.

Out of the newspaper files accumulated during the first five years of San Francisco journalism, gleaned from the columns of the *Californian*, the *California Star*, the *Alta California*, and the *Herald*, came *The Annals of San Francisco*, probably the best book ever written about the city. This volume, which appeared in 1854, was compiled by Frank Soulé and James Nesbit, newspapermen who had come west with the gold-rush, and Dr. John H. Gihon, an early settler who built the first house on Rincon Hill. Its eight hundred pages were divided into three parts: a history of California during the Spanish and American occupations; the most interesting section, a year-by-year, sometimes day-by-day, account of the city's social history from '46 to '54; and a final part including detailed, vigorously penned descriptions of special local institutions, such as the Great Fires,

Steamer Day, and the Hounds, and ending with sixteen short biographies of old-timers, giving the sole clue to the publication's indebtedness to the Society of California Pioneers, which apparently sponsored it. *The Annals*, which disappointed some contemporary readers because it did not emulate Gibbon or Macaulay in tone, has pleased later generations because it is full of interesting details recounted in a breezy and enthusiastic style. It has been drawn on so frequently as a source book that it is no exaggeration to say that our modern conceptions of early San Francisco, from prodigious rats to Chinese prostitutes, from the hanging of Jenkins to the record voyage of the *Flying Cloud*, are based ultimately on the work of Soulé, Gihon, and Nesbit.

Though the newspaper editors did not establish a uniformly high reputation for honesty, learning, or originality, though the material they printed served chiefly to fill space or to further some personal end or prejudice, the great amount of publishing resulted in keeping the people in the habit of reading and in providing an outlet for any writing of merit that might appear. The men who were to contribute to the magazines or write the books of the sixties almost invariably did their apprentice work on the small-town or metropolitan newspapers.

In addition to the dailies, many weekly publications catered to special interests among Californian readers. Several of them were no more than newspapers; a number were published in foreign languages, particularly French, Spanish, and German. Some, like the *Christian Observer* and the *California Christian Advocate*, were issued by religious denominations and confined their writings to special fields; others, like the *Illustrated Times* and the satiric broadsheet *Hombre*, were too short-lived to be of importance. The first weekly of literary pretensions to survive over a number of years was the *Pacific*, started in 1851. It called itself " A Religious and Family Newspaper," with the slogan: " First Pure then Peaceable — without Partiality and without Hypocrisy." Edited by a Reverend Mr. Douglas, it carried a small amount of secular material in addition to such items as " The Power of Prayer " and " The Swearer Rebuked by the Child." Occasionally original poems appeared in the traditional Poet's Corner; signed articles on the Indians, mining, and scenery were printed; and, as the paper flourished, engravings were added. The editor apparently did not care for fiction.

More definitely literary were the *Golden Era*, and its rival for a few years, the *Wide-West*. The *Golden Era*, the most important journal ever published on the Pacific slope, flourished from the day it started, December 19, 1852. Within a month its city circulation alone was 2,000; and shortly after, announcing 1,100 subscribers in the northern mines, it boasted: " Our circulation finds its way into every city, town and mining district in the state. The miner, after his hard week's toil, seated in his rude hut in the placers, finds the *Era* a welcome visitor, full of intelligence, fun, news, and incidents." Its crowning glory was a highly decorative masthead with the title printed with letters carved out of quartz; the novel type weighed over eight pounds and carried seventeen pennyweight of gold to the pound. The success of the paper was due principally to the enthusiasm and foresight of its two young editors, J. Macdonough Foard and Rollin M. Daggett. Foard ran the paper, while Daggett, in red shirt and top boots, tramped through the mines selling subscriptions and writing the mining letters. One day he was held up by a Mexican bandit, who, after relieving him of his hat, boots, and a hundred and eighty dollars in gold collected for the *Era*, returned six dollars, which he politely stated was the price of boots in those parts.

The *Era* was a chatty, informal journal, carrying poetry and fiction, summaries of the news, an occasional signed article, and columnist chatter by the earliest of its many pseudonymous writers, Vide Poche, Dow, Jr., and Cadiz-Orion. Its four pages were about equally divided among fiction and poetry, editorial and news digest, and advertisements. As the journal outdistanced its rivals, familiar names began to appear — sketches by Old Block, poems by Yellow Bird, or learned treatises on such subjects as the progress of civilization during the last quarter-century by J. S. Hittell. Although the paper rarely paid more than five dollars a column for prose and nothing for poetry, local writers came to look to it as their readiest market. In the correspondents' column the editors gave advice to aspiring writers from Arizona to Oregon.

In 1854 Ferdinand C. Ewer announced that he hoped San Francisco had matured enough to support a monthly magazine carrying the work of those who were " desirous of distinguishing themselves in Poetry, Belles Lettres, and the more flowering paths of literature." His faith was almost miraculously borne out when the *Pioneer*, unaided by advertising, illustrations, or fiction, appeared regularly for twenty-four months, before the financial depression of the vigilante year put an end to its useful life. The *Pioneer* openly patterned itself on the *Knickerbocker Magazine;* its aim, like that of its popular Eastern model, was to " avoid heavy twaddle and to seek to entertain." The intellectual level of San Francisco readers must indeed have been very high to have found light entertainment in " The Anglican Arrangement of Churches, in Connection with the Medieval Prototype," in " Hints on the Moral Influence of the Commercial Spirit of the Age," or in " An Epitome of Goethe's *Faust*." To balance these, however, Ewer presented burlesques by John Phœnix, chit-chat by Jeems Pipes, mining letters by Dame Shirley, and monthly gossip by the editor. Many verses by local writers were printed, and Edward Pollock, the poet laureate of the fifties, contributed a learned paper on " Thoughts towards a New Epic," in which he discussed a poem that he did not live to write.

The most celebrated article to appear in the *Pioneer* was one telling of communication with the dead, an account which purported to be true, but was nothing but an elaborate hoax. Because of the policy of the magazine to eschew fiction, Judge J. C. Edmonds, New York spiritualist, was perhaps justified in taking Ewer's " The Eventful Nights of August 20th and 21st " seriously — so seriously that he reprinted it in the *Sacred Circle* as the most astounding confirmation of spiritism that had ever come to his attention. He should have sensed a joke when a Western editor wrote of how a corpse communicated with him by mysteriously causing his hand to write backwards. But the East had not yet grown wary of the guffaws of a Dan de Quille or a Mark Twain, the artificial thrill of a Caxton or an Ambrose Bierce. It had still to learn that the Western air bred hoaxes. Ewer was not writing another " Case of M. Valdemar " ; he was just baiting his public.

The tall, erect editor of the *Pioneer*, with his straight, black hair and goatee that gave an appearance of length to his massive face, was a thoroughgoing atheist when he wrote " The Eventful Nights." He had come to the frontier to find himself ; he might well have become a Roman Catholic like Stoddard or a spiritualist like Mulford, for he had lost the religion of his youth and was searching for something to take its place. Of Unitarian-Quaker stock from Nantucket Island, trained in civil engineering at Harvard, he dabbled in journalism in California during the transition period when he denied the existence of a God. For the moment his intense nature found activity in editing the *Pioneer*, but shortly after that venture was over, the thirty-year-old atheist became such an ardent believer in Episcopalianism that he was ordained and made assistant to the local bishop, William Kip. Another year saw him rector of San Francisco's Grace Church; shortly thereafter he was put in charge of Christ Church in New York, where he was noted for his " dazzling eloquence and substantial qualities of mind." Then he grew to be an ardent Anglo-Catholic, shocked his congregation with his love of ritual, angered the nation with eight sermons on " Protestantism a Failure," broke with his congregation and founded a church of his own, and, as a climax, collapsed with a cerebral hemorrhage in a pulpit in Montreal. At his funeral tall candles burned above his purple velvet pall, and in the casket the medal of the Convocation of the Blessed Sacrament rested upon his breast.

No native Californian wrote books in California during its frontier period. The Pacific Railroad arrived but twenty years after gold was discovered, when the children of the pioneers had not yet grown to maturity. For that reason the literature of the fifties is uniquely a literature created by writers translated in their youth from staid social groups to a chaotic society; the writing was all done by outsiders, men born in Nantucket, or Sag Harbor, or Albany, or Philadelphia, or Hannibal, or London, or Dublin. There was a surprising number of such men who later made minor or major reputations for themselves in literary pursuits, men of action, who did their shift in the mines and then turned to more sedentary occupations.

Benjamin P. Avery, John S. Hittell, and J. M. Hutchings were typical of the emigrants who developed literary aspirations; twenty-three, twenty-four, and twenty-five respectively, they came to the mines to make their fortunes and remained in the West to edit journals and write books. Avery, who sailed with the men of means round the Horn, was from New York; delicate and quiet-spoken, he suffered through six years of mining and prospecting, often destitute and ill, before he started a weekly newspaper in a village in Nevada County. Hittell, born in Pennsylvania of Bavarian stock, trained at Miami University in the " Latin-Scientific Course," started west with an ox train and walked twelve hundred of the miles to Horsetown, where he failed to pick up the golden pebbles that he had been told of. Back to his books he went and was shortly lecturing in San Francisco on phrenology. He supported himself with a job on the *Alta* while he prepared a plea for pantheism and a cultural history of mankind, and collected enough statistics on California to make him an authority. Hutchings, of England, also sweated in the mines for a couple of years before there came to him the brilliant idea of writing a new set of ten commandments for the miners and circulating the novel decalogue on the back of a letter-sheet. His *Miner's Ten Commandments*, which led off with " Thou shalt have no other claim than one," sold nearly a hundred thousand copies in a year. Its author put away his pick and spent the rest of his life exploiting the scenery of California in his writings and the magazine he edited. Anticipating the rush for Yosemite, he settled early in the valley, opened the first hotel there, and for years had almost a monopoly on the tourist trade.

Rollin M. Daggett was only eighteen when he set off across the country with a knapsack, a gun, and a dog. Somewhere on the trail he stumbled upon a camp where the dead of cholera lay unburied while two small children cried for their parents. He took charge of the children and their cow, who furnished them with milk, joined a decrepit Pike outfit, and started across the Sierra in the late fall. As the party climbed the cliffs above Donner Lake, the oxen weakened and would have given out had they not been aided by a huge, sturdy bull that loomed up out of nowhere, dragged them over the summit, and then disappeared as mysteriously as it had appeared. Daggett was never sure whether it was a real bull or a hallucination. He later told the story in his novel, *Braxton Bar*, as well as many other yarns about his days in the mines. Two years of mountain life, and he was in the city, founding the *Golden Era*.

Hubert H. Bancroft, bookish and twenty, mined with his father near Sacramento in '52. A few weeks were enough for him; he became a merchant in Crescent City, soon opened a book-store in San Francisco, and developed a consuming interest in records that later were to be incorporated in monumental histories. From Dublin came J. Ross Browne, an inveterate wanderer ever since he had run away with a special, and then esoteric, knowledge of shorthand. When Senator Gwin got him the job of reporting the State Constitutional Convention at San Jose, he was given ten thousand dollars for his labors. He strayed away again, but he eventually settled down in Oakland in a huge Chinese pagoda. Another wanderer was Stephen Massett, showman and jack-of-all-trades, a florid, goateed, urbane Englishman, who presented a curious likeness to a crested bantam rooster, a benignant human chanticleer. On June 22, 1849, he gave the first theatrical entertainment in San Francisco, in which he sang some of his own melodies and impersonated three characters from Shakespeare. He then dabbled in real estate, his principal venture being Pipesville among the sand dunes near the Mission Dolores. His amusing accounts of his dwelling there earned him the name of Jeems Pipes of Pipesville, by which he came to be known to readers throughout the world.

The four most interesting figures of the fifties were Dame Shirley, Old Block, John Phœnix, and Yellow Bird. Of the four John Phœnix was the only one to make more than a local reputation, but each was a pioneer in a type of writing later to become famous and each had a merit which deserves to be better known. Characteristic of the fifties was the fact that these writers were all better known by their pseudonyms than by their real names and that they all wrote as an avocation. Though they were identified as much with rural California as with San Francisco, their works reached the public principally through such metropolitan journals as the *Golden Era* and the *Pioneer*, as did the cream of the writing throughout the West. Dame Shirley gave the best account of the mines, Old Block offered the most interesting reflection of mining philosophy, John Phœnix was the first of the Far-Western humorists, and Yellow Bird gave body to the best-known California legend.

The most detailed and vivid picture of mining life during the gold-rush period was written not by a miner turned literate, not by a journalist visiting the Mother Lode, but by a small, fair, golden-haired bluestocking from New England, a dainty adventurer with a sturdy soul who was wearing her yellow curls down to her shoulders when she stepped from the *Manila* after rounding the Horn in '49. Although the fragile-looking pioneer was only thirty years old when she came west, she had already had more than her share of hard knocks. In her New Jersey birthplace Louise Amelia Knapp Smith had lost her father when she was a baby, her mother before she finished her teens; she had had to substitute for normal home-life attendance at boarding-schools, finishing off at Amherst Academy; and she had found her closest friend in a man old enough to be her father. Alexander Hill Everett, elder brother of Edward Everett, and himself a noted writer and diplomat, had become the father confessor of his " *chère* Louise " — had guided her footsteps and perhaps, as she grew older, had possessed her heart. When he died suddenly in China, whither he had gone as his country's first commissioner, Louise suffered intensely. A year later the lonely girl married Dr. Fayette Clappe, who soon afterwards came to San Francisco to practice medicine. In hotel rooms and in canvas shacks, through fires and mob law, she stayed by him in the city; then she went with him to one of the most inaccessible and rough-

OLD BLOCK'S CABIN.

Alonzo Delano, or Old Block, is sitting on the keg in the foreground, enjoying the luxuries of a miner's life. From *Old Block's Sketch Book*.

OLD BLOCK HAS A NIGHTMARE.

Old Block pictures his entrance into heaven in a fantasy included in *Old Block's Sketch Book*. The writer's famous nose is much in evidence.

THE MINERS' TEN COMMANDMENTS.

A broadsheet written and published by James M. Hutchings.

Courtesy of California State Library

est of the gold camps, where she kept her good humor during a
bitter winter and a summer of violence which ended with the entire community going broke and abandoning the diggings. Her
marriage failed to bring happiness in spite of her loyal support
of her improvident husband, and on April 5, 1857, the *Alta
California* carried the notice that Louise Clappe had obtained
a divorce from Fayette Clappe. From that day Shirley was
alone; she, who loved children but had borne none, spent many
years teaching in the old Denman Grammar School, mothering
her niece, encouraging the more brilliant of her students to
write, and delivering lectures on art and literature to the members of her " salon."

The Shirley Letters, twenty-three in number, were written by
Mrs. Clappe, or " Dame Shirley," to her sister, Mary-Jane
Smith, who was living in the East. They tell of Shirley's experiences in going to the mines in September 1851, and cover her
life in Rich Bar and Indian Bar on the Feather River during a
little more than a year, ending with the general exodus from the
region after the first snow of '52. Although Shirley apparently
had little expectation of publishing the letters when she wrote
them, she made them as literary and objective as if she had intended them for the world at large. They were so inclusive in
their details and chronology that when Ewer of the *Pioneer*, one
of Shirley's friends, read them, he was pleased to feature them
in his magazine as they stood. Much of their quality was the
result of Shirley's interest in the " epistolary art." A relative
of Julia Ward Howe, a friend of Emily Dickinson, and an ad-
mirer of Margaret Fuller, she had been trained in the best New
England tradition and wrote her letters with as much care as if
she had been composing poetry. When she arrived at Rich Bar,
she wrote to her sister: " I am bound, Molly, by promise to give
you a true picture (as much as in me lies) of mining life and its
peculiar temptations, nothing extenuating, nor setting down

aught in malice." Reflective, even-tempered, remarkably observant, she managed to stay feminine and yet face the crudities of pioneer life without flinching. She changed a good deal between the time she exclaimed over a pretty squaw's " limbs, as round as an ' o,' " and the day she at last reluctantly admitted that bloomers were a fit costume for Western females. She never consented to wear them, however.

When Shirley reached Rich Bar, she stayed for a few days in the canvas-fronted Empire Hotel in a camp with a thousand men and two tough-fibered women. Then the Clappes moved into a log cabin round the bend of the river, at Indian Bar, a small community composed of cabins and huts made from calico shirts and pine boughs which clustered on a bar " as large as a poor widow's potato patch, walled in by sky-kissing hills." There she " saw the elephant " in its entirety. Unflinching, far removed in spirit from the other girl in Indian Bar, who fainted when she saw blood on a miner's shirt, she lived through a winter in a spot where there were " no newspapers, no shopping, calling, nor gossiping, little tea-drinkings ; no parties, no balls, no picnics, no tableaux, no charades, no latest fashions, no daily mail (we have an express once a month), no promenades, no rides or drives ; no vegetables but potatoes and onions, no milk, no eggs, no *nothing*." And then, in the dead of winter, the potatoes and onions ran out. For weeks the only food was hard, dark hams, unpenetrable to the sharpest knife, barrels upon barrels of rusty pork, and " quintals of dreadful mackerel." Yet she was still able to chuckle on the day the pack train brought in supplies : the miners rushed to pay forty cents a pound for potatoes and within fifteen minutes the smell of frying onions was rising from every cabin in the diggings.

As the winter wore on, she learned to look upon profanity as at times " grotesquely sublime," relaying to her sister such expressions as " I will use you up so small that God Almighty

Himself cannot see your ghost." Although she considered drink
and gambling as the twin curses of mining life (the only prostitutes in town had been run out just before she arrived), she
found herself sympathizing with the men when, after weeks of
forced idleness during the flood season, the entire male populace
went on a three-week drunk — a saturnalia which ended only
when everyone was prostrate. Finally, when spring came and
the men grew more restless under their long idleness and the
knowledge that the bar was not to yield the golden harvest anticipated, violence broke out. She saw one man tried by the
mob, convicted of stealing four hundred dollars, given thirty-
nine lashes, and deported. Then she saw another thief, who had
stolen eighteen hundred dollars, executed by the impromptu
jury that had convicted him. " The whole affair, indeed, was a
piece of cruel butchery, though *that* was not intentional, but
arose from the ignorance of those who made the preparations.
In truth, life was only crushed out of him, by hauling the writh-
ing body up and down several times in succession, by the rope
which was wound round a large bough of his green-leafed gal-
lows." The worst element in the camp got drunk and shouted,
as if the spectacle were offered for their particular amusement.

The storm broke when the citizens of Rich Bar, round the
bend, passed a law that no foreigners could mine in their diggings. As a result the Spaniards and Mexicans came to Indian
Bar. Soon a Yankee stabbed a Spaniard who tried to collect an
honest debt, and a Spaniard knifed an American in retaliation.
A Sabbath-day riot resulted. The Spaniards were rounded up
and tried by the committee, two were whipped, and all were
forced to abandon their property and leave the bar. A little
later Shirley wrote: " We have lived through so much excitement for the last three weeks, dear M., that I almost shrink from
relating the gloomy events which have marked their flight. But
if I leave out the darker shades of our mountain life, the picture

will be incomplete. In the short space of twenty-four days, we have had murders, fearful accidents, bloody deaths, a mob, whippings, a hanging, an attempt at suicide, and a fatal duel." Thus the camp, which the sun reached but two hours each day, worked the dark winter out of its system.

Peace had returned to the camp when the Fourth of July came round. Shirley helped in the celebration by making a flag out of red calico, cotton cloth, and faded drillings from the Bar hotel, with a gold star glittering in the middle of a field of faded blue. There was a grand banquet, an eagle-screaming oration, and then the poem of the day, preserved by the fair listener:

Ye are welcome, merry miners! in your blue and red shirts, all.
Ye are welcome, 'mid these golden hills, to your nation's Festival;
Though ye've not shaved your savage lips, nor cut your barbarous
    hair —
Ye are welcome, merry miners! all bearded as ye are.
. . .
For now the banner of the free is in very deed your own,
And 'mid the brotherhood of States, not ours, the feeblest one.
Then proudly shout, ye bushy men, with throats all brown and
    bare,
For lo! from 'midst our flag's brave blue, leaps out a golden star!

In November Shirley sat upon a " segar-box " in the chimney corner of her dismantled cabin, gazing out upon the piles of gravel, the calico hovels, and the shingle palaces of a camp thickly peppered with empty bottles, oyster-cans, sardine-boxes, and fruit-jars, the harsher outlines of which were softened by the thinnest possible coating of radiant snow. Only twenty men were left at Indian Bar. The flume which the men had taken so long to build, which had cost them over $3,000, had turned the river aside to reveal only $41.70 worth of gold. Shirley was about to leave for San Francisco. " My heart is heavy at the thought of departing forever from this place. I *like*

this wild and barbarous life; I leave it with regret. The solemn
fir trees, ' whose slender tops *are* close against the sky,' the
watching hills, and the calmly beautiful river, seem to gaze sor-
rowfully at me. — Yes, Molly, smile if you will at my folly, but
I go from the mountains with a deep heart of sorrow. I look
kindly to this existence, which to you seems so sordid and mean.
Here, at least, I have been contented."

In his postscript to *Chips off the Old Block*, Alonzo Delano
spoke wistfully of the mission he had just completed — a mission which he undertook at the request of a circle of ragged,
half-starved miners sitting about a fire on a cold night in the
Sierra, wishing that someone would tell the world of the trials,
perils, and disappointments that they had suffered in California. While newspapers and guide-books talked of " big
strikes, rich leads, and lucky hombres," these men had worked
with little success; had lived on pork and bread, when they could
get them; had slept on the hard ground in fair weather and
foul; and had suffered from scurvy, cholera, and the bloody
flux. They wanted someone to tell the world of the difficulties
and disappointments of pioneering.

Old Block was the man to write the account, for he had " seen
the elephant " in its worst form. After being educated in Illinois
and " polished " in Indiana, he had left wife and child to join
the wild-goose chase to California. After an arduous trip with
his ox team across the Rocky Mountain plateau, he was persuaded to cross the Sierra by the Lassen or " Greenhorn " cut-
off. On this route he ran into no end of grief and learned to eat
hawks, crows, rats, " and other nutritious vegetables." When
he at last lay in the grass at Sacramento, he thought for the moment that fortune seemed to be smiling on him, at least " from
a small corner of her vacillating mouth." He borrowed money
from a friend, bought a stock of goods, and set out to sell them

in the mines. But a hard winter was upon him; he recovered from the fever in time to come down with the bloody flux; his cattle became mud-bound in a flood that drowned thirty men in the vicinity; and when he at last reached the mountains with a pack train, he lost six of his mules over a cliff. Ever resourceful, in the spring he was earning a living by sketching portraits, " including the whiskers," at an ounce a head. Everywhere he met disappointed miners, sick miners, nostalgic miners.

The predicament of most of the men he knew came forcefully home to him when he was strolling through a deserted camp where men had built a wing dam in vain. In an old shack he was startled to see the effigy of a man propped upright against the wall. The wretched dummy, rigged out in an old shirt, tattered trousers, and what was left of a pair of boots, wore on his breast a paper which bore the following epitaph:

" Californians! O! Californians! Look at me. Once as fat and saucy as a privateersman; but now — look ye — a miserable skeleton. In a word, a used up man. Never mind, I can sing away, notwithstanding:

> O, Californy! this is the land for me,
> A pick and shovel, and lots of bones,
> Who would not come, the sight to see?
> The golden land of dross and stones!
> O, Susannah! don't you cry for me,
> I'm *living dead* in Californ—ee!

Living dead in a land of gold and bones, and yet able to sing. There was a theme for you!

A year later, after Old Block had set himself up in business on Long Wharf in San Francisco, as " a dealer in squashes and cabbages; a sort of Wharf Rat," he delivered the first whittling from his penknife to the office of the *Pacific News*. When he laid his offering on the desk of Jonas Winchester with the comment: " There's something you can use if you like it or think it worth printing," Winchester was not too favorably impressed by his visitor's appearance. Old Block was a compact, wiry, keen-eyed man of medium height and spare frame, dressed shabbily, but evidently self-possessed. His outstanding feature was his nose, which rivaled that of Cyrano de Bergerac. One of his friends summed up that nose when he wrote: " He is famous for one of the largest noses in California. Indeed, he seems rather to belong to the nose than the nose to him." Old Block always maintained that it was the itch of that eagle beak that led him westward. As time passed, a host of stories grew up around it. Its owner once remarked: " See here, stranger. Will you kindly brush that mosquito off the end of my nose? You are nearer to it than I am." And a fellow writer suggested that if Old Block were to be buried in a shallow grave, his nose could be used for a tombstone!

Old Block's articles in the *Pacific News* proved to be very popular with the readers. In them he described the greenhorn, the miner, the trader, the gambler, and other Western types with just the right combination of realism, homely philosophy, pathos, and humor. He was, in fact, a direct descendant of Laurence Sterne, with Yorick's own tricks of breaking off sentences with a whimsy, of merging pathos into humor, of sprinkling his realism with sentimental passages. These articles, when collected in 1853 into a book entitled *Chips from the Old Block*, sold over fifteen thousand copies in California. A second series published three years later, entitled *Old Block's Sketch Book*, was almost as popular. For the Eastern public, Old Block, under his legal name of Alonzo Delano, wrote *Life on the Plains and among the Diggings;* in this book he dropped his playfulness and devoted himself rigorously to a realistic account of the gold-rush. Though not so popular as many romantic books dealing with that theme, it found favor with the many who desired a truthful, restrained picture.

Part of the reason for the success in California of Old Block's sketches was his collaboration with Charles Nahl, most famous of early California arists. This German lithographer and physical-culture enthusiast, who had turned up in Rough and Ready in '49 with a suit of chain armor, a collection of halberds and swords, and a plentiful supply of sketch-books, became locally famous, before a winter had passed, for his forceful pictures of mining life. Though the famous illustrator was ordinarily lacking in humor, when he worked with Old Block, who possibly made the preliminary sketches, he furnished drawings that went as well with Old Block's quaint style as did Phiz's with that of Dickens. To the two may possibly be ascribed the verse and drawings of *The Idle and Industrious Miner*, a Hogarthian pamphlet rich in its homily on mining life.

Though Old Block wrote no fiction, he presented some of the characters he had known in the hills not only in his sketches but also in a play which he entitled *A Live Woman in the Mines*, an ordinary enough melodrama with a few amusing touches of local color. Here one meets Pike, his girl, High Betty Martin, and a reprobate named Old Swamp, who is full of sermons and stories about his courtin' days. Old Swamp's proposal was done with a flourish. " You and me will settle down for life, like two tame turkeys over a pig-stye. Will you go the caper? " Pike, who lives " up in the mountains, where you have to dodge to keep out of the way of the sunrise," is a riproarer when it comes to poetry. He considers his best lines to be:

> O, Carolina Betty's yaller hair
> Has laid my heart and innards bare.

High Betty Martin, who wears men's clothes and totes a gun, is ready for a shooting at any moment, though she has a woman's heart beneath it all, God bless her. In the action of the play the two themes that receive the most hilarious attention are the excitement attending the arrival of a woman in the diggings and the methods by which the miners avoid starvation. When the heroine — not High Betty, but a fluffy bit of innocent femininity — approaches the mines, the members of the advance guard borrow her petticoat, which they call " a woman's skin," and take it to the camp in advance to prepare the boys for the advent of a *live* woman. Starvation also appears to be a great joke to the miners. After the meat is gone, they eat rats and put whisky in the hot-cakes to liven them up. They also tie the last piece of pork to a string, whereupon each man swallows it, pulls it out, and passes it on. Finally they eat their boots, which are not cooked too tender, for in their tough state they stick better to the ribs.

Although Old Block contributed many sketches to the *Pacific News*, the Sacramento *Union*, the *California Farmer*, and the *Golden Era*, he was not primarily a writing man. He always said that if he had nothing to do but write for the papers, he considered himself out of a job. After a San Francisco fire drove him off Long Wharf, he moved to Grass Valley, where for years he was in charge of the Wells, Fargo and Company Banking and Exchange Office. Ultimately he established a bank of his own; he used all of his earnings to develop quartz mines in the vicinity; and he was one of the most enthusiastic of Grass Valley's promoters. His active life hid a series of personal misfortunes, however, for he not only buried his first wife in her youth, but carried on to support a son, bed-ridden from childhood, and a daughter who became insane shortly after coming to California. When he died in 1874, the flags were hung at half-mast, and all business at Grass Valley was suspended to honor a leading citizen. The New York Hill bonanza paid his creditors, but the death mask that was to preserve the outlines of his prodigious nose was destroyed in a fire. The sketches of Old Block, long forgotten, today are appearing in handsome reprints and are gaining more readers every year.

It was inevitable that Old Block and John Phœnix should meet sooner or later. Although they had exchanged a few letters, substituting for regular addresses on the envelopes the profiles of a large nose and a ragged soldier respectively, their plans to get acquainted did not materialize until chance brought them together on a boat sailing from San Francisco to Oregon. Old Block was taking a sea voyage to recuperate from the effects of an attack of fever; however, as the vessel cleared the Heads, he regretted his choice of a cure as he leaned against the rail, munching some biscuit and cheese to combat seasickness. At his greenest, he saw the captain approach, accompanied by a lieutenant of the United States army. The latter's heavy blue military jacket, with its brass buttons and epaulets, made the wearer almost as broad as he was tall. Bright blue eyes twinkled in his square-cut face, which ended in a close-cropped beard, and his long, dark hair was plastered diagonally across his forehead. The captain presented Lieutenant George H. Derby to Alonzo Delano. Old Block, caught off his guard, but ever mindful of the hospitality of the Westerner, offered a biscuit in one hand and a piece of cheese in the other. John Phœnix said: " Thanks, I've had my dinner." And then he added: " By Jove, Old Block, you *have* got a big nose."

During the remainder of the journey Old Block forgot his fever and John Phœnix the roads he was to build in Oregon, while the two chatted like long-lost friends. What tales did Derby tell? What execrable puns did he make? What hoaxes did he play? As the meeting came near the end of Phœnix's sojourn in the West and as Old Block was full of questions and an eager listener, we may assume that the humorist's career was thoroughly canvassed.

John Phœnix may have begun at the beginning and told how, after an irresponsible boyhood in Massachusetts, he attended West Point and graduated seventh in a class of fifty-nine. Perhaps he joked of the story that his high record resulted from the answer he made when asked what he would do if he found himself in charge of a besieged fort with enough provisions to last for only forty-nine days: the solution was to abandon the fort and then besiege the enemy till the food ran out. Or he may have denied the tale that Jeff Davis, then Secretary of War, exiled him to the Pacific Coast in '49, when he was only twenty-six, because he sent to the War Department a facetious report recommending, in military terms, an addition to the regulation uniform. This was a three-inch ring to be attached securely to the seat of the private's trousers, there to serve several purposes, illustrated in the accompanying sketches: the infantry sergeant could check the flight of the retreating soldier by deftly passing a hook at the end of a long pole through the ring; the cavalry officer could keep his seat without difficulty by hooking the ring to the saddle; and, in the artillery, cannon could be hauled up a hill by hitching several men to the carriage by means of the rings. The report further suggested that oranges should replace pompons on the dress hats, and that demountable hairbrushes would prove more useful than ordinary epaulets.

It is quite possible that a man with as irrepressible an urge towards hoaxes as John Phœnix had should get into trouble with his superiors by mixing humor with business. Throughout his published works are sprinkled burlesques of military matters, such as the one described above, reprinted in the Caxton *Phœnixiana*. With pen and pencil (for his bump of humor expressed itself as readily in drawing as in writing) Phœnix showed the advantages of arming the " dark " infantry with pepper-boxes and bulldogs, especially effective in night attacks, and he illustrated a report on the " Manners and Customs of the Coyote " with views of " front, side and rear elevations."

The most elaborate of his parodies of official documents was his " Official Report of Professor John Phœnix, A.M., of a Military Survey and Reconnoissance of the route from San Francisco to the *Mission of Dolores*, made with a view to ascertaining the practicability of connecting those points with a Railroad." Possibly aimed at Jeff Davis' proposal for a transcontinental railroad survey, this report gives in full detail the hazards and trials encountered by Professor Phœnix in laying out and measuring a line three miles long, passing through the heart of the city, adjacent to all the best saloons, and subject to such great peril from the natives that each man was armed with four Colt revolvers, a Minié rifle, a copy of Colonel Benton's speech on the Pacific Railroad, and a mountain howitzer carried on a wheelbarrow. Full scientific data is given on accomplishing triangulation without a heliotrope; on the performance of the go-it-ometor, which failed to serve its purpose of measuring the route because its wearer, under the influence of five glasses of lager beer, danced four of the miles that were found in the total; and the results of geological surveys made in the layers of *sulphuretted protoxide of hydrogen*, etc., that covered the old plank road.

During the early days of John Phœnix's service in California, his wit was known only to a limited audience. Coming up from the isthmus on the *Panama* in 1849, he had amused Jessie Benton Frémont with his mock trials, even when she was worrying about reports that her husband had lost a leg in the Rockies. At Monterey he had continued his amateur theatricals, and, while idling at Benicia between surveys in the interior, he had amused himself by writing for San Francisco newspapers under the name of John P. Squibob (" Squibob — a Hebrew word, signifying ' There you go, with your eye out ' "). Later, San Francisco became his headquarters, and he satirized many of the local institutions, from the California Academy of Arts and Sciences to the Ladies' Relief Society. But the incident that made him famous throughout the West occurred during his stay in San Diego, whither he was sent in '53 to build a diversion dam on the San Diego River. Time hung heavy on his hands in the quiet settlement until chance brought him amusements of an unusual nature.

When Judge John Judson Ames, editor of the San Diego *Herald*, left for the north to solicit funds for his weekly newspaper from the Democrats' campaign chest, he left his friend John Phœnix in charge. The humorist at once saw great possibilities: " I'll send you the paper next week, and if you don't allow that there's been no such publication, weekly or serial, since the days of the ' Bunkum Flagstaff,' I'll *craw fish*, and take to reading Johnson's Dictionary." He pepped up the journal with mock news-items, mock editorials, even mock advertisements. He turned a page of the *Herald* into *Phœnix's Pictorial, and Second Story Front Room Companion*, with illustrations made from little advertising cuts — houses for sale, cattle with brands, and ships to charter. The same small house served for the mansions of Phœnix, Shakespeare, and Bigler, the ships illustrated the Battle of Lake Erie, the cattle were used to represent Prince Albert as well as a view of a California cattle ranch by Landseer. But the fun really started when he switched the political support of the paper from Bigler, the Democratic candidate for governor, to his Whig rival, Waldo. When a copy of his journal reached Ames in San Francisco, the editor was furious and the joke spread like wild-fire; all of California talked of the successive issues of the *Herald*, where, throughout the heated campaign, Phœnix hurled diatribes at Bigler and sang the praises of Waldo. As the *Herald's* sustenance came principally from the Democratic Party, the audacity of Phœnix's shift was the subject for Gargantuan laughter.

After the election was over and Bigler won out, Ames returned on the steamer *Goliah,* ready to mete out punishment. Phœnix's account of the interview that followed is a masterpiece of Western humor. He describes that moment of suspense when " the Judge " towered six feet two over his victim, and follows with a series of asterisks which he felt alone could do justice to the terrific conflict. The climax comes at last: " We held ' the Judge ' down over the Press with our nose (which we had inserted between his teeth for that purpose), and while our hair was employed in holding one of his hands, we held the other in our left, and . . . shouted to him, ' say Waldo.' " It was all over, except for the discovery that a copy of the advertisements in the current *Herald* had been struck off on the back of the Judge's shirt while he was being held over the press.

After the *Herald* excitement John Phœnix returned to San Francisco, where he became a leader among the group of writers that assembled at Barry and Patten's saloon. He wrote many amusing articles for Ewer's *Pioneer* and contributed, as the spirit moved him, to various California papers. His forgiving friend, Judge Ames, collected many of his sketches and published them in *Phœnixiana,* and the humorist's widow added to these in *Squibob Papers,* issued a few years after his untimely death. Although these books have preserved the best of Phœnix's journalism, a reading of their contents only partly captures the spirit that so amused the Californians. Phœnix managed to create a prodigious reputation which even in his lifetime approached the legendary. The stories that went from mouth to mouth about him were in some ways more important than his writing. Many of them were lost because they were unprintable, for Derby loved the off-color joke even more than Mark Twain. Others remain as weak puns stripped of their build-up. But even after nearly a century has passed, men still chuckle over the time Phœnix stopped the driver of the Golden Eagle Bakery wagon to confound him with an order for " three golden eagles, baked brown and crisp "; or the time he asked if he could leave his wife at the Delaware Women's Depository, even if she was from Maryland; or the time he introduced his mother and his wife after assuring each privately that the other was very deaf. They raised a terrific hullabaloo while he stood by delighted.

John Phœnix left California in 1856, shortly after his conversation with Old Block. He served a few years building lighthouses on the Gulf Coast before he suffered a sunstroke. After a lengthy period of suffering, he died of softening of the brain in 1861. The West, which had stimulated his fancy, cherished his memory.

The twelve-year-old boy lay trembling on his bed, peering through the window down into the moonlit yard. He was terrified, for he had just seen a band of armed men dash up to the house, quickly dismount, and call to his father to come out. The boy realized that these men were determined to kill his father, for the Ross faction among the Cherokees had been fomenting trouble ever since his father and grandfather, chieftains of the tribe, had signed the papers at New Echota which had relinquished the tribal lands in Georgia and had provided for migration of the Cherokees across the Mississippi to Indian Territory. That act was four years past; but the move which Major Ridge had believed inevitable had been declared a sacrilege by a band of young Cherokees who felt that only blood would atone for abandoning the burial grounds of their ancestors. The small boy feared that that blood was now about to flow. He heard his father talk to the armed men for a moment, hoping to make them see reason. Then John Ridge cried to his wife: " They will kill me; it will do no good to say a word. Keep still," and stepped quietly through the door. The next moment the boy heard his mother plead for a quick death for her husband. Bowie-knives flashed in the moonlight; a score of blades plunged into the yielding body of John Ridge; one man thrust twenty-nine times before his lust was sated. The deed did not take long, but long enough for the faces of several of the assassins to be burned upon the mind of the boy who looked through the window.

John Rollin Ridge was never to forget the sight of those flashing blades, of that blood oozing through the sheet wound about the body of his father. Throughout his life he was to hear his white mother sobbing over the body of her husband and his Indian grandmother calling to the Great Spirit to avenge the death of a hero. When, later that same night, messengers brought the news that Major Ridge also had been murdered by assassins, the grandmother's stoical chant grew fiercely vindictive at the loss of both her husband and her son. The boy learned that the avenging spirit of a noble line of savages was bequeathed to him that night. The deed darkened his mind with an eternal shadow; retribution for that deed remained his chief purpose in life.

Before that fateful 22nd of June in 1839, the boy had led a comparatively happy life. When he was born on his grandfather's estate in Georgia, Major Ridge not only was accorded the loyal tribute due to a hereditary chief of the Cherokees, but had acquired the wealth and manners of a prosperous Southern planter. He had a large house, many servants, and a reputation for learning and sagacity. When he went to Connecticut to attend his son's wedding, he wore a coat trimmed with gold lace and rode in the finest carriage the small town of Cornwall

GEORGE HORATIO DERBY (JOHN PHŒNIX) IN 1846

Courtesy of Mr. George R. Stewart

JOHN ROLLIN RIDGE (YELLOW BIRD).

Courtesy of Society of California Pioneers

had ever seen. He had gone to see his son marry a white girl against his wishes and against the wishes of her parents. When he had sent his son to obtain a white man's education at the Cornwall Indian School, he had not foreseen that his heir would fall ill, that for two years he would be nursed back to health by Sarah Northrup, the daughter of the principal, and that at the end of that time John would be pining away for Sarah, and Sarah for John. After the couple were married, Connecticut editors wrote indignantly about the union, an enthusiastic poet composed an idyll about the lovers, and the school closed its doors. But Sarah and John moved into a two-story house in Georgia, and a visitor from Cornwall was astonished at Sarah's seventeen servants. " She simply said to this one, go, and he goeth, and to another come, and he did so. She dressed in silk every day."

Soon after John Rollin Ridge's birth in 1827, trouble with the whites in Georgia became acute. They coveted the rich soil of the Cherokees and drove thousands of Indians from their homes. They were haled into court on false charges, convicted on suspicion, and frequently hanged for violating laws they did not understand. When oppression became intolerable, the Ridges led the movement to accept proposals of the Federal government and migrate to Indian Territory. In the most tragic of Indian migrations, the Cherokees moved across the Mississippi. As the new land was not so fruitful as the old and the tenure for the Indians seemed insecure, the group who had opposed the migration took their anger out on those who had advised it. The Ridges were massacred and John Ross became leader of the Cherokee nation.

The full account of John Rollin Ridge's experiences during the eleven years that elapsed between the massacre and his arrival in California will probably never be told. For some time he continued his education, first at a public school in Arkansas, then in college in New England. But when he was still in his teens he was writing to his cousin Stand Watie for " an article which I wish extremely you would get for me — a Bowie knife " and confiding that " there is a deep-seated principle of Revenge in me which will never be satisfied, until it reaches its object." Shortly thereafter he returned to Indian Territory and allied himself with James Starr, who was leading a guerrilla war against the Ross faction. Apparently Ridge killed one of his enemies in self-defense; but, because he was on the losing side, he chose to flee to avoid trial by Cherokee law. Having found the task of avenging his father too great for his frail hands, he came to California in 1850, hoping to make his fortune. Some day, however, he intended to return to the Cherokees and finish his task.

One evening while he was sitting on the gallery of Hay's Pavilion in San Francisco, Ridge, warmed by a few drinks, grew confidential with one of his fellow editors. After telling once again the story of the massacre, he said that he had noted each of the thirty-six men who had driven their knives into his father's body; he had remembered their faces and had learned their names. Since then the number of assassins had diminished, one by one, until only four of them remained alive in 1861. Some were slain in altercations peculiar to the border, others were found dead by the wayside, still others had disappeared. Ridge was not ready to assume responsibility for their deaths, but he was sure that he knew how each had come about. He had not given up hopes for the remaining four, and some years before had gone all the way up to Weaverville to investigate the tale that in a local saloon a man had boasted membership in the Ross faction.

The tall, handsome John R. Ridge known to Californians in the fifties and sixties was an upright, law-abiding citizen. Many who met him hardly realized he was half-Indian, for he had a fairly light complexion, regular features, and large, dark eyes; only his wiry, jet-black hair indicated his racial heritage. His early experiences on the coast were not unlike those of his friend Old Block. After meeting with little luck in the mines, he started on a writing career when the New Orleans *True Delta* offered him eight dollars apiece for a series of articles on crossing the plains. Later, while politics and newspaper editing claimed most of his time, he contributed many articles and poems under his nom-de-plume, Yellow Bird, literal translation of his Indian name, to the *Golden Era* and the *Hesperian*. His conventional but somewhat attractive poetry will be discussed later, as well as his unusual newspaper career during the Civil War. But to the fifties belongs his *Life and Adventures of Joaquin Murieta, the Celebrated California Bandit*, a book that played a unique part in Western literature.

The ascertainable facts about the bandit known today as Joaquin Murieta are meager in the extreme and tell of a petty brigand little more romantic than the countless other bandits of Latin-American societies. The early fifties in California were marked by continual brigandage — partly an accompaniment of the unrest in the mines following the decline in gold output, when the Mexicans and Indians were blamed for acts of violence whether they were guilty or not; and partly the expression of the last flare-up of Mexican nationalism, resulting from the iniquitous mining tax on " foreigners " and the growing conviction that the conquered Spanish-Californians were not to receive the fair play promised them by the treaty of Guadalupe Hidalgo.

In the spring of 1853 a succession of bold robberies in the mining communities of Calaveras, Tuolumne, and San Joaquin counties were attributed to an unidentified bandit who was known by the very common Mexican name Joaquin. The principal traits of Joaquin and his band were that they exterminated Chinese like coveys of quail and that they seemed to be ubiquitous, moving from one section to another with great rapidity. Because the robberies varied so widely in locality, many of the skeptical-minded held that one mysterious operator was being blamed for the depredations of a number of bandits; accordingly, when it was first proposed to the legislature that a reward of five thousand dollars be offered for Joaquin's head, the committee on military affairs reported against the motion, objecting that " dozens of heads similar in some respects to that of Joaquin might be presented for identification." That a reward and salaries in advance for an irregular group of rangers headed by Captain Harry Love were eventually voted seems to have been the result of pressure from interested parties. The reward was not open to the public at large, but was payable only to Love, an adventurer who was so vicious that he was ultimately shot while mistreating his wife, and his band of so-called " rangers," as disreputable a group of thugs as ever killed under the law.

Not knowing just what man was wanted, the legislators named five Joaquins, with different surnames, any one of which would do. What was one dead Mexican, more or less? Under the circumstances, it was almost certain that Love and his rangers would bring back a head. On July 25th, 1853, they surprised a small group of Mexicans in the wild region west of the Tulares, and when one of the rangers, named William Burns, said that he recognized the fabulous Joaquin, they riddled the fleeing Mexican with bullets. A second corpse turned out to be that of none other than " Three-Fingered Jack." Three days later Love's rangers arrived in Stockton with the head of the supposititious Joaquin and the mutilated hand of his lieutenant (Three-Fingered Jack's head had putrefied past the point of identification under the hot San Joaquin Valley sun). To forestall the doubts of the skeptical, various people who said they had known Joaquin hesitantly identified the head, already pickled in alcohol and soon to be exposed in a show-case in San Francisco, where it would be a sight for the curious for years to come. Sardonically humorous was the fact that one of the identifiers was a prostitute from San Andreas named Salome, although it is not recorded that the head was brought to her on a platter! Ten years later William Burns, the ranger who had " recognized " Joaquin, was boasting openly in a Virginia City saloon that Joaquin " would have to be killed just once more to entitle him to burial " and that " one pickled head was as good as another if there was a scar on the face and no one knew the difference."

Had it not been for the notoriety of the Love gang and the exhibition of the pickled head, Joaquin might have become no more a subject for legend than such of his contemporaries as Valenzuela, Claudio, Garcia, Sato, Senate, or a dozen others. The deeds attributed to him differed little from those of the rest of his breed of strange-humored cutthroats. But the conditions were ripe for the creation of a good romantic Robin Hood story. Miners had been impressed by the proud spirit of many Mexicans like the one described by Dame Shirley who, after being unjustly lashed by a drunken mob in Rich Bar, " swore a most solemn oath, that he would murder every American that he should chance to meet alone " for subjecting him to a punishment which he considered worse than death. Rumors that the deposed Spanish-Californians were banding together for an attempt to retake California had been common since the first days of the gold-rush. And the very absence of information about Joaquin, who was supposed to ride relays of horses so fleet that no one ever saw him plainly enough to identify him, gave room for legend to create a romantic, heroic figure.

In 1854, less than a year after Love's triumph, Yellow Bird published a detailed account of Joaquin's life and adventures which not only fixed to the bandit the surname Murieta but provided the substance for every subsequent retelling of the Joaquin legend. Couched in the language of the penny dreadful, with occasional passages of impressive rhetoric and macabre humor, the narrative laid claim to being based upon research: " In the *main*, it will be found to be strictly true." The author openly asserts, however, that his purpose in writing is partly that of the propagandist: he wishes to do justice to the Mexicans, for " no man who speaks the truth, can ever deny that there lived *one* Mexican whose nerves were iron in the face of death." As a preface to a miscellaneous account of Joaquin's hold-ups and his death, he presents, as the most forceful part of his story, an interpretation of the robber as a wronged man whose early career was essentially heroic. He says Joaquin was a handsome young Sonoran, of pure Spanish blood, who was both honest and hard-working when he came to California accompanied by his sweetheart, Rosita. In the mines he suffered great indignities at the hands of the Anglo-Saxons; first ruffians beat him and raped Rosita before his eyes, then another group hanged his half-brother on a false charge and, tying Joaquin to a tree, publicly disgraced him with the lash. At this greatest of insults " he cast a look of unutterable scorn and scowling hate upon his torturers, and measured them from head to foot, as though he would imprint their likenesses upon his memory forever." He was transformed from a peaceable citizen into an outlaw whose soul was filled with revenge; he meted out justice to each of the men who had ravaged his sweetheart and also to those who had whipped him. Having turned criminal for justice, he was forced to remain highwayman for spoil. Like most bandit heroes, he confined his activities to heroic deeds and left the butchery to his lieutenant, Three-Fingered Jack, who had a passion for slitting Chinamen's throats. Like all good folk-heroes, Joaquin was grateful to those who aided him, was gallant to pretty women, and was social-minded in robbing the rich and letting the poor go unmolested. Finally, he planned to raise his career above the level of banditry by espousing the cause of his people and leading a revolution against the gringos.

Most of the romantic features of the Joaquin story as told by Yellow Bird are common to the legends of outlaws, popular ever since man began to find pleasure in vicarious adventure. Several novel features of Ridge's account, however, speak eloquently of the author's experience and philosophy. In this goriest of outlaw sagas the hero's favorite weapon is not the gun but the knife — the knife which Ridge had used among the Cherokees and was by common gossip his favorite weapon of defense in California. Moreover, in supporting the Mexican cause, the cause of the down-and-outer, he was supporting the minority cause of his fellow Indians, whom he had seen mistreated and driven from their lands when he was a boy. In telling of Joaquin's plans to strike a blow for his people, he was expressing his own lifelong hopes to help the Cherokees regain their place in the sun. And, finally, in having Joaquin achieve his revenge by wiping out his degraders one by one, Ridge was vicariously blotting out each of the assassins who had driven their knives into the body of his father. Since the fateful day of the massacre, his one thought had been to get his enemies and reassert the leadership of his family among the Cherokees. He put into his book all of the feelings that lay below the surface of the civilized editor.

As the first detailed account of Joaquin's career, Ridge's book was accepted as history and became the basis for all later versions of the legend. During the decade after its appearance it was pirated in the San Francisco *Police Gazette*, with minor changes and accretions. It was also expanded into an anti-Catholic play by a San Francisco dramatist and was given nation-wide circulation through retelling in De Witt's fifteen-cent novels. H. H. Bancroft and Theodore Hittell used Ridge's account almost without change in their histories. It drifted down into Mexico and South America and across the ocean to France and Spain, reappearing in many guises. One version of the story, written in Spanish, translated from the French, and published in Santiago, Chile, asserted that Joaquin was a Chilean. Recently, just as the Arthurian stories returned from the continent to England, the legend has returned to America and has been used extensively in biography, in fiction, and in the cinema. Always the basic story is the story told by Ridge, although many minor incidents have been added throughout the years. Thus the massacre of an Indian on the Cherokee reserve colored the most vital of Western folk-tales.

CHAPTER III

APPRENTICE DAYS

THOSE who were to be the principal writers of San Francisco of the sixties were but youngsters when Marshall found gold in the tail-race of the mill at Coloma. The oldest, Prentice Mulford, was fourteen. He was just finishing his schooling in Sag Harbor, Long Island, and was planning to become the captain of a whaling vessel. In Hannibal, Missouri, thirteen-year-old Sam Clemens was already working at a trade as printer's devil on the *Missouri Courier*, for his father's death had brought an end to schooling as well as to his adventures as Tom Sawyer. Francis Brett Harte, one year Clemens's junior, was a sensitive, sickly schoolboy when gold was discovered. He was about to go to work in a lawyer's office to help a resourceful mother. But he lived in New York rather than beside the Mississippi, and, as " a dreamy lad thirsting for information concerning the world," sought this world in books, reading Shakespeare at six and publishing a poem on *Autumn Musings* at eleven. Never a Tom Sawyer, he longed to be a Robinson Crusoe.

Joaquin Miller, christened Cincinnatus Hiner Miller, probably eleven years old at this time, was moving from cabin to cabin with his parents as they drifted through the Miami Reservation and up along the Wabash and Tippecanoe rivers. He was supplementing a rudimentary education obtained from his father by an intimate contact with the lore of the frontier. Nine-year-old Henry George had just entered Mount Vernon Grammar School in Philadelphia, but, already growing restive under compulsory Sunday-school attendance, he was haunting the waterfront, building toy boats, and planning to sail before the mast. Ambrose Bierce, the six-year-old youngest in a family of twelve, had been ushered into life at a religious camp ground called Horse Creek in Meiggs County, Ohio, handicapped by parents who gave each of their twelve children names beginning with *A*. And the baby of the group, Charles Warren Stoddard, had spent the five years of his life in Rochester, New York, blissfully unaware that religion and love and the burden of living would keep him a nervous wreck during most of his years to come.

During the fifties Harte, Mulford, Miller, Stoddard, and George arrived in California by way of the sailing ship, steam packet, and covered wagon, and lived through experiences which were to furnish much of the material for their later writings. These were their formative days, when they were finding their way from the mining claim to the editor's desk. On the other hand, the later-comers, Clemens and Bierce, remained in the Middle West during this decade, the former serving apprenticeships in type-setting and journalism before he realized a long-cherished ambition and became a Mississippi river pilot, and the latter suffering the horrors and restrictions of the child of an unsuccessful farmer as his father drifted with his large family from the Western Reserve to Elkhart, Indiana. His feeling about his childhood was expressed in the lines he wrote about it:

> With what anguish of mind I remember my childhood,
> Recalled in the light of a knowledge since gained;

The malarious farm, the wet, fungus grown wildwood,
The chills then contracted that since have remained. . . .

The earliest member of the clan to arrive in the West was not, however, one of these young men, but a girl who came to be looked upon as the sweetheart and heroine of the group. Ina Donna Coolbrith was known by all of the writing men of the sixties; she contributed to the *Golden Era* and the *Californian* and the *Overland Monthly;* she was the confidante and, if we are to believe gossip, the sweetheart of Harte, Stoddard, Clemens, and Miller. Why did she never marry? The beautiful young woman with dark auburn hair and gray eyes, classic profile, and lithe figure, held men at arm's length, willing always to be a companion but never a wife. She was a mystery to all her acquaintances, a heroine with a secret tragedy in her past. The few intimate friends who knew something of her story loyally kept their lips sealed, while rumor whispered about the strange circumstances of her birth and the blighted romance of her girlhood. Her biography, pieced together from old letters, rare books, and community records, is as bizarre as the plot of a romantic novel.

Joseph Smith was only twenty-two years old when, in 1827, he was directed by the angel Moroni to the spot on a hill near Palmyra, New York, where he dug up the golden plates of the Book of Mormon. Three years later he organized the Church of Jesus Christ of Latter-Day Saints, basing his creed on revelations obtained by translating the " reformed Egyptian " inscriptions which covered the plates. Aided by the extraordinary enthusiasm for new religions which marked the first third of the nineteenth century in America, the Mormons grew rapidly in numbers; and shortly they moved to Kirtland, Ohio, where Agnes M. Coolbrith enters the story.

Agnes Coolbrith, a young convert from Maine, boarded in the Smith household and was cared for by the prophet's mother,

Lucy Smith, who recorded that Agnes " devoted her whole time to the making and mending of clothes for the men who were employed on the temple." That she should have been so active in the church is not strange, for all the members of the Smith household were devoting their talents to the cause: the prophet's father, who had been made Patriarch, had as his principal duty the giving of blessings for ten dollars each, while Lucy Smith was caretaker of the museum of relics, which included, in addition to mummies and papyri, " the leg of Pharaoh's daughter, the one that saved Moses." The brothers of the prophet had been made elders in the church. The youngest, Don Carlos, though but a lad when the sect was started, was ordained at once and sent out as a missionary, playing the double role of preacher and agent for the Book of Mormon. Returning home from one of his journeys, he fell in love with Agnes Coolbrith.

Don Carlos Smith and Agnes Coolbrith were married on August 1, 1836. Within five years they had three children, whom they named Agnes, Sophronia, and Josephine. Before the third child was born, however, the couple had gone through many troubles. Hardly was the temple completed before the prophet found it expedient to abandon the Kirtland settlement and go west into Missouri. There the Mormons suffered great terror and hardship, for the Missourians fiercely persecuted them, resorting to the use of fire, lashings, tar, and bullets. As Don Carlos was away much of the time on missionary work, Agnes was unprotected from the attacks of the mobs; on one bitter cold night angry men burned her house and turned her out of doors with two-year-old Agnes and Sophronia, then a babe in arms. She fought her way for three miles through snow and waded waist-deep through the Grand River before she reached shelter.

A little later the Mormons recrossed the Mississippi and established their colony at Nauvoo, Illinois, but, as the new community was built on swampy land, many of the people suffered severely from malaria. When Don Carlos set up the printing press which had been buried during the trouble in Missouri, he was forced to issue the *Times and Seasons* from a cold, damp cellar, through which ran a stream of icy water. He soon became violently ill, and although he recovered sufficiently to play for another year his parts of President of the Quorum of High Priests and Brigadier-General of the Nauvoo Legion, he succumbed to pneumonia in his twenty-fifth year. Four months before his death, on March 10, 1841, his third child was born. She was christened Josephine D. Smith, but she later adopted the name of Ina Donna Coolbrith.

To this point the story of Agnes Coolbrith and her children is well recorded, for as the wife of Don Carlos Smith and the sister-in-law of the prophet, she appears in the official memoirs of Lucy Mack Smith, the prophet's mother. From this source we also know that she remained with the Mormons at least until the fall of 1843, for on October 3 of that year " Sophronia, second daughter of Don Carlos, died of the scarlet fever, leaving her widowed mother doubly desolate." That she had not entered into a second marriage, as was the custom among widows of the sect, may have been the result of her distaste for the new doctrine of polygamy introduced in this year by the handsome, six-foot-two Joseph Smith, who had for some time practiced " plural marriage " in private. When before his death Don Carlos had heard rumors that the prophet was contemplating this step, he had cried out: " Any man who will teach and practice spiritual wifery will go to hell, no matter if he is my brother Joseph." Disaster in this world followed quickly on the heels of the prophet's announcements of the doctrine of polygamy and of his intention to run for president of the United States. In June 1844 he and his brother Hyrum were massacred by a mob in the near-by town of Carthage.

Two years of external persecution and internal dissension passed before Brigham Young succeeded in starting the Mormons on their long trek to Salt Lake. Agnes Coolbrith, antagonized by the doctrine of polygamy, disheartened by the schisms in the fold, left the Mormons at this time and took her two little girls to live in St. Louis, where she soon married William Pickett, a printer on the St. Louis *Republican*. Two years after the gold-rush the Pickett family migrated to California.

The arrival of Ina Coolbrith in California is associated with still another figure well known in frontier annals, the famed hunter, squaw man, and raconteur James P. Beckwourth. She is said to have been carried before him on his saddle, the first white child to cross the Sierra Nevada over the Beckwourth Pass. If this story is true, and there is little reason to doubt it, the time of the crossing was the summer of 1851, for it was then that Beckwourth discovered the low-lying pass leading from the Truckee River to the headwaters of the middle fork of the Feather River, a few miles from the camp where Dame Shirley was " seeing the elephant." In fact Beckwourth in his autobiography tells of meeting a wagon train of tired emigrants at the Truckee and escorting them safely over the mountain. His description of their condition explains why Ina Coolbrith and her family were so glad to see him.

" At the close of day, perhaps amid a pelting rain, these same parties heave wearily into sight: they have achieved the passage of the Plains. . . . The brave show they made at starting, as the whole town hurrahed them off, is sadly faded away. Their wagon appears like a relic of the Revolution after doing hard service for the commissariat: its cover burned into holes, and torn to tatters; its strong axles replaced with rough pieces of trees hewn by the wayside; the tires bound on with ropes; the iron linch-pins gone, and chips of hickory substituted, and rags wound round the hubs to hold them together, which they keep

continually wetted to prevent falling to pieces. The oxen are
held up by the tail to keep them on their legs, and the ravens and
magpies evidently feel themselves ill treated in being driven off
from what they deem their lawful rights."

Probably the Pickett wagon, carrying Ina, her older sister,
her mother and stepfather, and the two Pickett boys born in St.
Louis, presented just such a forlorn appearance. The family
had been in constant danger of attack from the Indians in Utah
Territory, they had suffered terribly from thirst and fatigue
during the long pull through the Humboldt sink, and they felt
that they would never reach the green meadows beside the sparkling Truckee. As they looked at their half-starved, stumbling
cattle, at their now wretched wagons, then at themselves, tired-
eyed, drawn-faced, gaunt, thin as the miserable oxen, the Sierra rising up abruptly in front of them seemed as insurmountable as the Himalayas. Beckwourth, with his offer of aid over
an easy pass, was to them a true *deus ex machina*. Ina remembered him as " a dark-faced man, something like a mulatto,
with long braided hair reaching down to his shoulders, dressed
in beaded buckskin, with mocassins and no hat." When he saw
her and her little half-brothers, he exclaimed: " God! they're
the sweetest things in life! " After giving them some candy, he
asked the pretty ten-year-old child with the dark hair and gray
eyes to ride with him as he led the way. She ever after romanticized him as a hero.

Hero he was, but hardly of the stamp the girl imagined. A
mulatto born in Virginia, he had led the strenuous and unprin-
cipled life of the typical fur-trapper, scout, and dispatch rider.
When he lived as chief among the Crows, he kept a large retinue
of squaws, and when he was not fighting hostile Indians, he was
selling the friendly ones whisky. He did not hesitate to boast
about scalping his enemies, and maintained that he once bashed
in the head of his favorite squaw because she disobeyed him.

Like his kind, he was fond of telling tall tales, such as the one about the time he entered a cave naked on a wager and killed a grizzly with his bare hands. Though it contains many such exaggerations, his *Life and Adventures of James P. Beckwourth*, which he dictated to T. D. Bonner in 1855, is the most satisfactory story of a mountain man in American letters. We should like to know more about T. D. Bonner, the far-sighted newspaperman, who took down his story. It has been suggested that he was the " Squire " of the *Shirley Letters*, and that he used to ply the old scout with rum to get a better story as they sat through the evenings in a saloon at Rich Bar. " The more they drank, the more Indians ' Jim ' would recall having slain, his eloquence increasing in inverse ratio to the diminishing rum supply, and at last he would slap the ' Squire ' on the knee and chortle, ' Paint her up, Bonner! Paint her up! ' And Bonner painted her up for the joy of posterity."

Ina spent a few weeks in Plumas County, where William Pickett tried his luck at mining, and then went down to Marysville, where the winter was made wretched by both fire and flood. After a short stay in San Francisco, the Picketts moved again, this time to southern California. Though Ina spent her teens and early twenties in Los Angeles, in later life she was almost as secretive about her sojourn in the south as she was about her birth and parentage. Certainly for an observant child there was much to see in the Anglo-Mexican pueblo, queen of the cow counties, and toughest town in California, so vividly described by Horace Bell in his *Reminiscences of a Ranger*. Yet the few remarks she left indicate an uneventful youth. She attended classes in the first schoolhouse to be opened in Los Angeles and played games on the hot, dusty plain; when she blossomed into a young lady, she was honored by being chosen to open a gala ball on the arm of ex-Governor Pio Pico; she began writing verses when she was eleven and soon saw them published in the local pa-

THE IDLE AND INDUSTRIOUS MINER.

Two pages from the Hogarthian series drawn by Charles Nahl and accompanied by verses attributed to Old Block. One shows the idle miner in the clutches of the gamblers; the other, the industrious miner reading the Bible before his cabin on a Sunday morning. Bret Harte wrote that he was inspired by these sketches to write his California tales.

Courtesy of the Huntington Library

The Miner's Song.

WORDS BY J. SWETT.   MUSIC BY JAS. C. KEMP.

The east-ern sky is blushing red, The distant hill-top glowing, The riv-er o'er its rock-y bed In i--dle frol-ics flow-ing; 'Tis time the pick-axe and the spade Against the rocks were ring-ing, And with ourselves the golden stream A song of labor sing-ing.

The mountain air is fresh and cold,
Unclouded skies bend o'er us;
Broad placers, rich in hidden gold,
Lie temptingly before us.
We need no Midas' magic wand,
Nor wizard rod divining;
The pickaxe, spade and brawny hand
Are sorcerers in mining.

When labor closes with the day,
To simple fare returning,
We gather in a merry group
Around the camp-fires burning,
The mountain sod our couch at night,
The stars keep watch above us,
We think of home and fall asleep
To dream of those who love us.

THE MINER'S SONG.

A native Californian ballad written by John Swett, later famous in developing California's public schools. This simple hymn to labor was published in Hutchings's *California Magazine.*

Courtesy of California State Library

per, the Los Angeles *Star*. Examination of the files adds the information that the *California Home Journal* of San Francisco also printed many of her Los Angeles poems, signed with her nom-de-plume, Ina. When, in 1861, she wrote a memorial poem for T. S. White, the editor of the *Star* announced that she had " already obtained almost a world-wide reputation."

The reason that Ina Coolbrith said so little about her early life in California was that there was a secret connected with that apparently idyllic period just as there was with the stormy days of her birth. Perhaps she had this secret in mind when she refused to write her autobiography: " Were I to write what I know, the book would be too sensational to print; but were I to write what I think proper, it would be too dull to read." She wished to forget Los Angeles as she had tried to forget Nauvoo.

On the 9th of September 1858 Josephine D. Smith married Robert B. Carsley, partner in the Salamander Iron Works and erstwhile player of the bones in the first minstrel show in Los Angeles. The seventeen-year-old bride did not long enjoy the happiness she had anticipated, for her husband apparently proved to be an unreasonably jealous and temperamental mate. Three years after their marriage he left for San Francisco in a fit of rage, only to return a few weeks later to harass his wife with importunities, accusations, and threats. He followed her to her stepfather's home, where she had taken refuge, accused her of infidelity, called her " a whore " and names of similar import, threatened her life with a carving-knife and a six-shooter, and took one shot at her with a rifle. In an attempt to protect his stepdaughter, William Pickett so wounded Carsley in the hand that it became necessary to amputate it. When Josephine Carsley brought suit for divorce on the grounds of extreme cruelty, her husband abandoned his plans to contest the case, and Judge Benjamin Hayes granted a divorce on December 30, 1861.

Though the legal papers in the suit leave many questions un-
answered, the evidence as recorded and the attitudes of the ref-
eree and judge indicate that Ina was the victim of a patho-
logically jealous man. There is no way of ascertaining what
grounds he had for accusing his wife of infidelity; certainly his
blackguardly conduct hardly encouraged trust in his word.
Shortly after her marital tragedy Ina moved to San Francisco.
By combining her nom-de-plume, Ina, with her mother's maiden
name, Coolbrith, and by breaking all associations with the
pueblo in the south, she hoped to get a new start. In the mid-
sixties, when her poetry for the *Californian* brought her recognition as a writer of promise, she was accepted by the San Francisco journalists as the virginal Ina Coolbrith, highly respected
by all who knew her. Possibly because they had secrets of their
own, they co-operated in keeping the door closed on the skeleton
in her closet.

On an early spring day in 1854 a slender seventeen-year-old
boy, with curly black hair, slight silken mustache, and an aquiline nose that barely suggested his quarter strain of Jewish
blood, stepped onto a San Francisco wharf from the paddle-
wheel steamer *Brother Jonathan*. He had come out by way of
the Nicaraguan crossing to join his mother, who the year before
had journeyed to Oakland to marry an old friend, Colonel An-
drew Williams. Francis Brett Harte had come west, not to mine
gold nor to seek adventure, but to be with his family. And yet,
during the years of his early manhood, he was to find both gold
and adventure — not in the hills, but behind the editor's desk.

Just as the bizarre pioneer society portrayed in Bret Harte's
stories came in time to be accepted as more genuine than the real
one, so the romantic tradition established by his fiction has created for the world a man who never existed. The public generally has accepted the picture of a wild and woolly Harte, who

washed gold in the mines, held off bandits as a gun-guard on the top of stagecoaches, and risked his life fighting Indians. Recently old-timers, jealous of his popularity or annoyed by his picture of themselves, have tried to replace the red-blooded Harte with a yellow-blooded one, a snob, a dilettante, a dude who wore corsets, a deserter of his family, a man who never paid his debts. Few lovers of the dramatic have been interested in the truth: that Harte was primarily a writing man who saw the wilder side of Western life as an artist rather than as a hardened participant and then extracted the core of drama from his observations for his writing.

During his first six years in California Bret Harte was finding himself. Three of those years he spent in Oakland, with a few excursions into the interior, the remaining three in the little town of Union, up on Humboldt Bay. At the end of the first period he was sending sugar-and-water poems to the *Golden Era;* at the end of the second he bravely wrote an editorial that caused him to be driven from the community for speaking the truth like a man.

Shortly after his arrival in California, he began to collect impressions which he later used in his fiction. A short fallow period spent in the sleepy little village across the bay from San Francisco, with its sheep and cows in the street and its lingering air of Spanish pastoral life, was followed by a few months of school-teaching in a Sierra mining town, probably La Grange. Here surely the germ of *M'Liss* was planted. When the school closed down because the miners moved away, Harte set off on a forty-mile tramp into the Mother Lode country, wearing patent-leather shoes and carrying a morocco dressing-case. For defense (or was it to complete the costume?) he carried a second-hand revolver, which " insisted on working around and dangling, embarrassing and unromantic, right in front." One views with skepticism his story that when he reached his destination, he ran into a gun-fight in the first saloon he entered and a wandering bullet shattered the whisky glass in his hand. After running across some friends, he spent several weeks, or possibly months, in the " perpetual picnic " of mining, but had such little success that when he left he had to walk up to Jackass Hill and borrow twenty dollars from Jim Gillis in order to get back to Oakland.

After intermittent tutoring, working with an apothecary, and writing verses in the cupola atop the Williams house, Harte followed up his experience as an amateur in the mines with a second romantic episode, a " brief, delightful hour " as an expressman on a stage line. Although Harte in an interview many years later is quoted as saying that his predecessor in the position had been shot through the arm and his successor killed, it is not likely that there was much danger associated with his job. The days of stage hold-ups had not yet arrived, and if there had been any bandits, there were many more experienced gunmen than Harte to defend the coach. He was apparently a novice at both mining and express riding, magnifying the romance of these occupations only after many years had passed. At the time he was more like Miniver Cheevy, who longed for " the medieval grace of iron clothing " when he found only commonplace khaki close at hand; in one of his earliest articles he described the fifties as a " hard, ugly, unwashed, vulgar, and lawless era."

Certainly Harte's *juvenilia* completely failed to reflect the raw frontier. In the summer of 1857 the *Golden Era* published his first writings, inconsequential, sugary poems signed by Bret, and entitled " The Valentine," " Lines Written in a Prayer Book," " Love and Physic," " The Fountain of Youth," and " The Student's Dream." One was submitted " after Longfellow," and all echoed facile popular verse of the sort that appeared in the anthologies designed for the parlor table, in the

Knickerbocker Magazine, or in the poet's corner of the *Golden Era.* One or two were adolescently humorous, but even these were better than the " really poetic " ones, when the poet got homesick for the old homestead barn or waxed enthusiastic about Jessie:

> Oh, the blessed, oft caressed,
>> Flowing, glowing, auburn tresses,
> Or the fairy shape impressed
>> In the gracefulest of dresses.

This sticky tone, typical of effusions by sentimental amateurs in the West, was also present in Bret's early prose — for instance, in a sketch in which he described the emotion which stirred a companion when he found a baby's shoe in the surf. " A child's shoe! a tiny worn-out and patched morocco gaiter — that was all! . . . Of the group two were fathers, and one had passed a long exile from a happy hearth thousands of miles away. As *he* took up that little bit of leather and prunella, do you think he saw only the long, white beach, and the vacant expanse of sky and water? Or did his fancy conjure up a misty, tearful vision of sunny curls, love-lit eyes, graceful figure, and fairy feet rising out of that little shoe, as the genii rose from Solomon's casket, in the Arabian story? "

When this sketch was written, young Harte had just moved to the village of Union, now Arcata, on the northern California coast, where he could stay with a married sister. There, on New Year's Eve, he wrote in his diary: " Ah! well did the cynical Walpole say that life is a comedy to those who think — a tragedy to those who feel. I both think and feel." He may have been thinking and feeling intensely, but he was doing little of anything else. Try as he would, he could find no job for which he was fitted in the frontier village. Accordingly, he drifted, alternating fence-building, teaching in a private school, and running a drug-store, with courting the hotel-keeper's daughter, loafing languidly, dressing fastidiously, and growing Dundrearies. As a friend put it: " He was willing to do anything, but with little ability to help himself. He was simply untrained for doing anything that needed doing in that community. . . . He seemed clever rather than forcible, and presented a pathetic figure as of one who had gained no foothold on success."

This depressing state of affairs ended, however, when a newspaperman named Colonel Whipple started a weekly paper called the *Northern Californian* and hired Harte as his printer's devil. The smell of ink steadied the young Werther, although it curbed rather than cured his romantic urges. In a short article for the paper he started by admitting that a printer was " a mechanical curiosity, with brain and fingers," but went on to say: " Think not that the printer is altogether a machine — think not that he is indifferent to the gem to which he is but the setter — but think a subtle ray may penetrate the recesses of his brain, or the flowers that he gathers may not leave some of their fragrance on his toil-worn fingers." In spite of the flowers, however, the regular task of setting the type, rolling the forms, and operating the hand press kept him down to earth and was good for him. And when his employer began to use him as his assistant in collecting news items and writing leaders, he was really contented.

For a year Harte inked his fingers and wrote locals; he even indulged in a word battle with the editor of the *Humboldt Times*, published in Eureka, at the other end of the bay. He learned to look for interesting details in the life about him, and he rapidly developed an efficient and readable journalist's patter to describe what he saw. Moreover, as the " junior " on the town journal, he now carried himself as a man of some importance. His day in the sun came in February 1860, when Colonel Whipple made a trip to San Francisco and left him in charge of the paper. The absence of his editor proved to be as important to Harte as a similar experience had been to John Phœnix, but the results were of an entirely different nature. A group of the local riff-raff chose that moment to enact the most inexcusable massacre of Indians of California's history. At four in the morning of February 26th they visited an Indian rancheria located on a spit of land in Humboldt Bay, where with hatchets and axes they butchered sixty Indians, most of them women and children. Their attack was without provocation, for, although the Indians a hundred miles back in the mountains had been causing trouble, the coast tribe had given no offense. The pioneers were merely carrying out the principle that any dead Indian was a good Indian. And although the ruffians of the community had done the deed, the better class of citizens were supposed to keep their mouths shut.

Harte, however, was too outraged to play the coward and ignore the incident. The lad whom the villagers had considered effeminate and undetermined took a stand that showed he had his principles and was brave enough to maintain them. In the next issue of his journal he attacked the murderers in an article headed: " Indiscriminate Massacre of Indians — Women and Children Butchered." He did not mince words: " We can conceive of no palliation for woman and child slaughter. We can conceive of no wrong that a babe's blood can atone for." As might be expected, the temporary editor found himself dangerously unpopular after his stand. Although he had the tacit support of the better citizens, the mob that used the rope was against him. There is probably some truth in the story that he was told to choose between the noose and leaving town; it is certain that shortly after the incident he was aboard the *Columbia* bound for San Francisco. He had had a taste of the genuine frontier, and, at twenty-three, as he began his writing career, he was in a mood to describe it in realistic terms.

Among the strange sights noted by Prentice Mulford when he sailed into San Francisco harbor in 1856 was an old whaling brig, entombed in the mud below Clay Street, where it was being used as a warehouse. Her ignoble fate was to him a symbol of the decline of Sag Harbor, Long Island, her home port and his birthplace. When he was born, Sag Harbor was one of the most active whaling ports on the Atlantic, and as a small boy he had watched many a bluff-bowed ship set out to pursue Moby Dick in the South Pacific or in the Arctic. Before he was well in his teens he had seen the whaling industry decline with the development of new oils to displace blubber. When he came of age he found himself one of a generation of " Sag Harbor aborigines " with their heritage turned to dust. Many of his companions, seeing no future at home, had rushed to California in '49, and, though none had returned with fortunes, the migration continued during the fifties. In his twenty-second year Mulford had at last given up trying to earn a living in the land of his forefathers and was ready to see what he could find in the West.

Ever since he was a lad circumstances had been against Mulford and had early convinced him that he was a failure. His father bequeathed him trouble by leaving him a store and hotel to run in the decaying village. In four years he was bankrupt — a bad beginning for a shy, eighteen-year-old boy. With a growing sense of unfitness, fostered by townsmen who were quick to call him a ne'er-do-well, he tried one job after another, but always either luck or his natural ineptness was against him. By the time he obtained a job on the sailing ship, the *Wizard*, bound for a voyage round the world, his self-confidence was pretty well gone. A rough voyage under a bullying captain did not help matters; a badly infected finger added to his natural ineptness; and on reaching San Francisco, he was not surprised to be discharged with the remark that he was not cut out to be a sailor. As he left the boat, he wondered if there was anything in this world that he could do properly.

While waiting for something to turn up, Mulford took stock of his new surroundings. San Francisco seemed to him to be mostly fog in the morning, dust and wind in the afternoon, and the Vigilance Committee the rest of the time. He drifted down to the Market Street wharf, where he mourned over the decaying hulks of sailing ships in " Rotten Row," waiting to be picked to the bones by Chinamen in the employ of Hare, the wrecker. He loitered in the barren, wind-swept Plaza, where Chief Burke exhibited gangs of sneak-thieves, tied two by two by their wrists to a rope — like a string of onions. And when he had nothing else to do he wandered about the garret of his lodging-house, where he found the belongings of scores of lost and strayed Long Islanders, many of whom had gone to the mines and had not returned. It was like groping around in one's family vault.

When all of his money was gone, Mulford got a job sorting the sea-bird eggs that were brought in from the Farallone Islands to be sold to coolies and proprietors of cheap restaurants. During the early days of the gold-rush, when San Francisco was a canvas city containing more miners than hens, these eggs had brought as much as a dollar apiece; the story goes that Doc Robinson, a well-known actor, had got his start by braving the swells for a whaleboat-load of eggs, which he sold at a fabulous figure. The romance of the profession disappeared, however, when egg-collecting settled down, under the monopoly of the Farallone Egg Company, to a steady crop of 16,000 dozen a year. As the islands were systematically cleared of all eggs, rotten as well as fresh, sorting them when they reached the mainland was an important but not a pleasant task.

Mulford was able to quit this malodorous job when he cooked an Irish stew for the captain of the *Henry*, which was " hove down " at North Point; the captain was so pleased with the stew that he hired Mulford to cook for his crew on a whaling trip down to Lower California. When they found that the new cook's culinary knowledge stopped with Irish stew, the members of the crew were disgruntled and almost mutinied during the three months he was learning to make edible bread, lobscouse, and plum duff. With growing resentment they rebelled at his salt-water coffee, his putty-like pudding, and particularly his " involuntary meat pie," created when a mouse fell into the biscuit dough. But this time he couldn't be fired, for there were no other cooks on the vessel. Eventually he won approval from the men with his sea mince pie, made of salt beef and dried apples. By the time he returned from the ten months' cruise he was a full-fledged second-class cook, with no grumbles from his companions when he received his fifteenth lay, amounting to $250.

His painfully acquired art did him little good, however, for he was discharged from his next cooking position before the vessel left port. His earnings from the *Henry* cruise were soon exhausted, San Francisco had nothing new to offer him, and as a last resort he went to the mines. In 1858 he turned up at Hawkins' Bar on the Tuolomne with seven dollars in cash and a trunk containing several vests, all that remained of the suits he had brought from the East. In that year Hawkins' Bar was having somewhat of a boom, but a premature rain washed out the arduously developed river claims, and the output began to decline. Mulford, after traveling half-way round the world, had merely stepped from one decaying village into another.

Mulford mined for three years in the Mother Lode country, learning to use the various methods with little success. Hawkins' Bar saw him wash gold with the pan, graduate to the rocker, and try his hand at the pocket. Then he " twisted his anatomy out of shape in crevassing," drawing forth the long-lodged dust of ages, spoonful by spoonful, hauling out the little residuum of gold at the end of the crack with an iron scraper bent at one end. Finally he moved upstream to the new diggings on the left bank of Swett's Bar, where he and his three partners tried to make a fortune out of a placer claim in the river-bed, diverting the water so that they could expose the gravel streak at the base of the bank. For two years he stood in the ice-cold water with the sun beating on his head during the day, he ate his bread and beans alone in his cabin in the evening, and he joined the loungers in the saloons at Red Mountain Bar on Sunday.

Mulford found that gold-mining meant hard work and little returns, for he and his fellows were gleaning the leavings of '49 in an area which had once been fabulously rich but was now played out. Old-timers told of many a strike and occasionally a lucky man hit a rich pocket, but for the most part the miners averaged no more than two or three dollars a day. This was just enough to support a man in the mines, but not enough to take him out. There were, however, compensations for the hard work; no man could tell you what to do, and you could wear your flannel shirt outside your trousers if you pleased. Who was better than the next man, when anyone might strike it rich tomorrow? If a community drunk had not precipitated Mulford into a writing career, he might have spent the rest of his life pocket mining in the Tuolumne country.

Growing up was even more painful for Charles Warren Stoddard than it had been for Prentice Mulford, but for very different reasons. He was born in Rochester, New York, in 1843, of a New England family which included such different members as Jonathan Edwards and Aaron Burr. When he was twelve, in 1855, he came to San Francisco with his father, mother, two sisters, and an elder brother who was in very precarious health. Here for two years he spent a happy time. He chased goats on Telegraph Hill, he melted tin cans for the solder they contained, he thrilled over the parades of the fire-brigades with their silver trumpets and gaudy uniforms, he peeped into garishly ornamented saloons where beautiful women in strange attire took dust from the miners. He attended the first public school in California, where Dame Shirley decided he was a talented boy and did her best to develop his genius. Even the violent happenings of early San Francisco thrilled rather than depressed him: sheer drama was the moment when he stood thirty feet from Casey as the latter shot James King of William; and no nightmares followed the sight of Casey and Cora hanging from the roof of Fort Gunnybags as King's funeral cortege wound up the road to Lone Mountain. All in all he found it an exciting life, even a gay one, and he himself was an excited, carefree boy.

In his fourteenth year, however, he went through some trying experiences which were to make him aware for the first time of his neurotic tendencies. His brother had become so ill that the doctors insisted that a long sea voyage was the only remedy that might save his life, so the parents determined to send the two boys east. In January they left San Francisco on the *Flying Cloud*, the finest clipper ship of the day, to go round the Horn to New York. The ninety-day voyage was indeed a long one for the sensitive lad, whose only companions were his dying brother, four years older than himself, the kindly wife of the captain, and an elderly man also traveling for his health. But finally it ended and he joined his grandparents in upper New York State, where he was soon to suffer more than the loneliness of the preceding three months.

The grandparents were ardent, evangelical Protestants, stern-living, duty-bound, hell-fearing people, leaders in the periodical revivals held in their church. Stoddard tells in his remarkable spiritual autobiography, *A Troubled Heart*, how this religion frightened him: "the blackness of darkness . . . flooded the fearful night of my infancy." Once he was taken from boarding-school to attend a revival meeting in which the emotional force of a praying congregation drove him to the "anxious seat," terrorized at the prospect of burning forever in hell. "I was threatened with nervous prostration, and every hour I grew more feeble and excited. At night, as I lay in my bed, in a small chamber under the gable roof, where the frosty stars seemed to blink at me with cold, sharp eyes, I wondered why so miserable a sinner as I was permitted to live unpunished." The final ordeal in this strict religious training came when he was taken, for discipline, to the funeral of a boy his own age, that he might realize the mutability of life and the necessity of being always prepared for death. Never thereafter could he forget the mingled odors of fresh varnish and tuberoses. These were fearful experiences for a young, nervous boy to suffer; it is strange that the grandparents remained blind to the obvious havoc they were producing in the delicately adjusted mechanism.

When Stoddard returned to his family in San Francisco in 1859, he was so high-strung that routine tasks seemed impossible for him. As he could attend school only spasmodically and then was interested in nothing but writing poetry, his parents agreed that he might better try to find congenial work. Accordingly he decided to get a job and write poetry on the side, for the return of his first poem by the *Waverly Magazine*, "Helen the Forsaken," modeled on *Evangeline*, had not destroyed his ambitions to become a poet. A week in a clothing-store and a month in a toyshop brought on nervous exhaustion, followed by typhoid fever, and taught him that forcing himself to maintain a too strict schedule was indeed likely to affect his health seriously — the harder he attempted to discipline himself, the surer were his nerves to rebel at such treatment. Nevertheless, when he recovered, he got another job, this time in a bookshop belonging to one C. Beach, who advertised both his business and his bad taste by hanging a crude painting of a sea beach above his door. Here Charlie earned his twenty dollars a month by sweeping the floor, dusting the books, washing the windows, and waiting on the few customers. Sometimes he tried to amuse himself by reading the tracts which lined the walls of this Western headquarters of the American Tract Society or by browsing in one of the Bibles that lay on the counter; but he hated the tracts and had almost memorized the Bible. More often he hid behind his feather duster, where, with one eye out for the possible approach of Chilion Beach, he scribbled verses.

On an evening not long after he went to work in the bookstore, seventeen-year-old Charlie Stoddard, who, with his slender figure, his rather girlish good looks, and his spiritual manner, reminded one of Shelley, spent what seemed to him an eternity walking back and forth on the south side of Clay Street just below Montgomery. Each time he passed a box fixed on the side of the building which housed the *Golden Era* offices, he hesitated, darted shy glances up and down the street, then hurried on. The bright light which lit the wooden sidewalk just at that point was to him a searchlight drawing the eyes of San Francisco to him. At last, after an hour's nervous vigil, the street was empty; the boy dropped an envelope into the box hastily, fumblingly, and fled in a cold sweat.

When the *Golden Era* appeared the next Sunday morning, Charlie quickly obtained it, and there, with his father, mother, and two sisters in the room, eagerly, almost fearfully glanced through it. How difficult it was to seem composed as he scanned the eight pages of close-printed columns! The journal burned in his hands when he discovered, tucked away in the correspondents' column on the fifth page, a poem signed by Pip Pepperpod. Just a slight quatrain in imitation of Tennyson, but how important it was! And underneath it was a comment by the editor that Pip's effort was appreciated, that the verse was well written, that more by the same hand were solicited. The boy was so pleased that he could hardly keep back the tears. Only a few months before, recovering from typhoid fever, he had written the quatrain " Upon Emerging from the Shadows of Death "; now he was stimulated by the thought that he might indeed be on the way to becoming the lyric poet of the Pacific.

Each week he slipped a contribution into the box on Clay Street; each Sunday the *Era* carried a poem by Pip, now printed in more and more favored locations in the journal. Editor Joe Lawrence even commented on the promising new contributor and suggested that he come out from behind his mask. With growing confidence Charlie told one or two friends, sworn to secrecy, that he was young Pepperpod. He had chosen the odd nom-de-plume because of his admiration for Pip of *Great Expectations*, adding the Pepperpod through love of alliteration.

A few months after the appearance of the first verse, a man came into the shop, to find young Charlie behind the duster as usual. The youthful poet had never met this man, but he knew well enough who he was: Starr King, the eloquent, luminous-eyed orator, who was called by his friends the bantam rooster of the Unitarian Church and by his enemies " that damned Poodle-eyed Yankee." He looked at the boy and said, as he thrust a clipping before him: " Charlie Stoddard, did you write that poem? "

" Yes, I did, sir."

" It's a good poem and I hope you will write many more." With still more encouraging words, he left the shop, while Charlie clutched in his fist season tickets for King's popular lectures on the American poets. Charles Warren Stoddard was launched on his career.

Shortly before Henry George came to California in 1858, he solemnly recorded in a notebook his findings as an amateur in auto-diagnosis: " A Phrenological Examination of Head by Self." In a long list of traits measured by his cranial bumps, he underscored four that he felt were specially revealing of his character: his combativeness and his amativeness were both much larger than normal, and, while his mirthfulness was small, his bump of hope was of generous proportions. Though he cautiously noted that he looked upon the science of phrenology with some skepticism, he was struck with the confirmation it gave to his previous knowledge of himself.

Combative he had always been, sometimes to his advantage, sometimes to his loss. After five months in high school in Philadelphia, he had told his father firmly that he wished no more schooling, and his father, acquainted with his temperament, did not waste time opposing him, but instead hunted him up a job. Two years later, when his son swore he would go to sea, the father found him a place on the *Hindoo*, captained by a family friend. During a year's sailing on the East-Indiaman Henry toughened his sinews, talked with disappointed gold-seekers in Australia, and learned to be callous about the corpses floating in the river at Calcutta. When he returned to Philadelphia, his father once more found him employment, this time as a typesetter in a printing firm. His triple purpose was to keep his son at home, to give him a trade, and to teach him to spell — George had a talent for mis-spelling like that of Charlie Stoddard, who thought that " stuff " should be spelled s-t-o-u-g-h. Before the year was out, however, the pugnacious lad had disagreed with the foreman of the job-room, saying that he would not quietly submit to the latter's " impositions and domineering insolence." In later life Henry George was to quarrel many times with his employers, even when the loss of a job meant going without food. As he grew older, the combativeness of the boy was augmented by the aggressiveness of a short man sensitive about his height.

The boy's " amativeness " was given little opportunity of expression in a strongly puritanical family where playing-cards were taboo, it was a sin to ride on a public conveyance on Sunday, and such worldly books as *The Scottish Chiefs* had to be read on the sly. After his year aboard an Indiaman, Henry became a mild rebel against his family taboos when he helped his pals to form the Lawrence Literary Society, for which the requisites for membership were " to drink Red Eye, sing good songs, and smoke lots of cheap cigars." If the members of the fraternity added youthful philandering to their other sins, no record of it appeared in George's notebook. It is more likely that the boy's erotic urges found expression in a tendency to fall in love easily, a failing which apparently got him into no serious trouble. At twenty-two, however, it caused him to elope with Annie Fox, when he had neither job nor money to support her. With his usual impulsiveness, he married the girl and trusted to luck he could take care of her; his luck not only justified his faith but provided him with an excellent wife.

The small amount of mirthfulness in Henry George's make-up is apparent to anyone who reads his journals and letters. From the earliest entries in his diary, which concern themselves principally with the direction of the wind, to his remark in his letter home that " California is sadly in want of missionaries and I think it would be a good notion for the Sunday school to send out a few, provided that they be gold-fever proof," he reveals himself as earnest, curious, at times observant, but never playful. He was concerned with how to get on, and he does not seem to have enjoyed himself overmuch in the getting. He was the sort of person who would get an idea and expand it until it became in his mind a panacea for all ills, and after it reached that stage he had enough of the preacher in him to proselyte for his gospel. If he had had a sense of humor, he would never have died campaigning for the single-tax; but if he had had a sense of humor, he probably would never have been sufficiently tenacious and single-minded to develop his theory so forcibly.

The fourth of the phrenological traits, hope, is the most important tool in the equipment of a crusader, and George had it in abundance. In his youth, that hope was nearly always centered on making a fortune, and although he lost job after job through bad luck or his pugnaciousness, he was always expecting something good to turn up. In his diagnosis of himself he had written: " Desires money more as a means than as an end, more for its uses than to lay up; and pays too little attention to small sums." He was at heart, moreover, a gambler, biding his time for the turn of the card which would bring the big win, discouraged not a whit at small losses. It was his bump of hope that brought him west when he was nineteen; as the *Shubrick*, the lighthouse steamer on which he was working his way as steward, put into the Golden Gate, he had only the most nebulous plans, but he was sure that somehow he would make a fortune.

In this frame of mind George was an easy victim to the fever accompanying the most disastrous of all gold-rushes, the stampede to the Fraser River mines that was just beginning when he arrived. Word that gold had been discovered in British Columbia, some hundred miles north of the Canadian border, nearly emptied San Francisco that summer of 1858. In the vanguard of the ships that sailed north was George, working his way to Victoria on a topsail schooner, sure that his fortune was just round the corner. But, along with the disillusioned thousands, he discovered on arrival that the Fraser River was far too high to allow mining. Moreover, when an acquaintance with some knowledge of mineralogy assayed a bit of " pure gold " from up the river, he found it to be principally tin and lead. (It was rumored that the samples that brought on the Fraser rush were chosen carefully and introduced into San Francisco by the steamship companies.) George stayed in Victoria for a while, earning his food by working in a store owned by a relative, and then, characteristically, he fought with the relative. In November he was back in San Francisco from the " terrible Fraser," stone broke.

It took one more trial to convince him that he was not to shake a fortune from the grass-roots. After a winter working at weighing in a rice-mill and type-setting, a winter spent at the What Cheer House, a temperance hotel for men only, where the absence of women and liquor was partially compensated for by a library which contained Adam Smith's *Wealth of Nations*, he set off for Placerville to take his chance at prospecting. He had no intention, however, of digging his pittance a day, like Prentice Mulford; on the contrary, he intended to discover a rich lead and hold it for speculation. The future single-taxer planned to grow rich off the unearned increment of his strike! His hope was stronger than his physique, however, although he wrote home that he was growing tough in the West: " I have not changed much except that I am even uglier and rougher looking. You thought I looked hard when I came home from Calcutta, but you should have seen me in Victoria." Having no money, he set out on foot, slept in barns, and earned his food working for farmers. But with his slight build he was not strong enough for such a life. For two months he plodded on towards the Mother Lode, and then, without reaching the foothills, he turned about and came back to the city.

Typesetting once more supported him, though, as he was less than twenty-one, he could not collect printer's wages. For a year he worked on the weekly *Home Journal*, published by Joseph C. Duncan; and on September 2, 1860, when he came of age, he was advanced to foreman of the shop at thirty dollars a week. In the autumn, while he still had a job, he fell in love with

Annie Fox, a pretty orphan from Los Angeles. And in the winter San Francisco received new life with the discovery of silver in Nevada. Henry George felt that he was on the upturn of the wheel of fortune. " If Washoe only equals the expectations entertained of it by sober, sensible men, times will be brisk . . . and everyone will have a chance for ' a gold ring or a broken leg.' " A steady job, a pretty girl to love, and a fortune in the offing. What more could a man with a large bump of hope ask from the world?

When Joaquin Miller, the " poet of the Sierras," came into prominence in England during the early seventies, he immediately sensed the sales-value of an adventuresome boyhood spent in the wildest portions of western America. With the same skill as a showman that suggested his wearing a red shirt, high boots, and a broad sombrero on Piccadilly and that prompted him to illustrate frontier manners by smoking three cigars at a time, biting the ankles of squealing debutantes in Mayfair drawing-rooms, and emptying a hatful of rose leaves over the pretty head of Lillie Langtry, he dramatized his accounts of his early days until the Englishmen believed he was a cross between Davy Crockett and Mike Fink. According to his stories, he was a crack pistol-shot, a daring horseman, even an expert with the tomahawk; he had fought desperate battles against the Indians, had turned about and outwitted the whites as a renegade, and had faced many perils as a filibuster. Just as he borrowed the name of the West's most famous bandit for his nom-de-plume, he borrowed the events of the dime novel for his past. He saw to it that he was everything the Englishman expected of a frontiersman. As a result, the unraveling of the thread of fact in the tangle of romantic fiction created by the poseur is an almost impossible task.

He was born in a farmhouse near Liberty, Indiana, on September 8, 1837, the first son of Huling Miller, a hard-working, earnest man who had failed as a merchant and was barely supporting his family as a school-teacher. He was christened Cincinnatus Hiner Miller, the Hiner after the doctor who had delivered him, the Cincinnatus after the " patrician farmer and Roman dictator." As a boy he knew the feel of puncheon floors and homespun garments and joined in singing " Money Musk," " Zip Coon," and " Ol' Dan Tucker." Before he was eight he had helped build the log cabin and erect the fences for a new home on the Miami reservation. His father paid for the land by teaching school, often taking his fees in barter, but no sooner was the land clear than he mortgaged it to a wily Yankee peddler for a wagon-load of clocks. Soon thereafter the wagons were again packed and the family drifted westward to another clearing.

The Millers took eleven years to reach the Pacific slope. The longest trek came in 1852, when, with two wagons, the family joined a train crossing the plains and Rockies over the Oregon trail. The seven months' journey, like most emigrant crossings, was more tedious than dangerous. Huling Miller traveled unarmed, for he believed that his Bible should be his only weapon, and that cholera was a graver threat than Indian arrows. The only accident was the loss, over a cliff near South Pass, of the lighter wagon, filled with the Connecticut clocks.

In September the family settled on an Oregon homestead located on the upper reaches of the Willamette, where Huling Miller was to spend his remaining thirty years wresting a living from stubborn ridgeland. Little " Nat " Miller, as the boy was called, worked on the farm, stopping at the end of each row of corn to read an exciting passage from Frémont. He maintained later that not until he was well along in his teens did he have an opportunity to play ; he says : " In truth, I never had been a boy like other boys ; never had a ball, marble, top, or toy of any sort, but now I began to be inflamed with a love of action, adventure, glory, and great deeds." Perhaps it was a result of his growing-pains that in the late fall of 1854 he ran away from home. He planned to make his fortune in El Dorado and then dramatically to return to pay all of his father's debts. When he reached the divide in the Siskiyous from which he could see the land of promise, he felt weak but willing: " I was alone, a frail, sensitive, girl-looking boy, almost destitute, trying to make my way to the mines of California . . . on a little spotted Cayuse pony."

If we are to take Miller at his word, the four following years in northern California were packed full with adventure and romance. Even of his less exciting occupations, such as working as a cook for the miners, mining a bit for himself, and helping run a trading store, he tells interesting experiences. In his *Life among the Modocs* he told of three mountain men who befriended him and made his life adventuresome: James Thompson, the gambler, who was the " Prince of Tigre " incognito; Joseph De Bloney, the " California John Brown," with whom he attempted to form an idyllic Indian republic on the slopes of Mount Shasta; and Indian Joe, a scout who had come west with Frémont and knew the entire frontier. Often in his later writings Miller boasted that for a considerable time he led the life of a renegade, won over to the Indians' side because they were so persecuted by the whites. The heart of his romance, forming the theme of several of his poems, was an erotic adventure: he won the heart of a beautiful Indian maiden, the daughter of a noble chief, and lived with her in an Arcadia on the slopes of Mount Shasta. She it was who saved his life when he got in trouble with the white men in the valley.

He asserted that, in addition to wooing a copper-skinned princess and aiding in setting up a new state among the Indians, he made long trips into Arizona, Colorado, and Mexico,

rustling horses with Indian Joe; and he would have us believe
that he even found time to join William Walker on his filibustering expedition to Nicaragua. His saga includes taking part
in several battles, sometimes on the side of, sometimes against,
the Indians; and the wounds he received troubled him throughout his life — even affecting his handwriting. Of one of these
battles he gives a characteristically vague account: " When the
Modocs rose up one night and massacred eighteen men, every
man in Pitt River Valley, I alone was spared, and spared only
because I was *Los Bobo*, the fool. Then more battles and two
more wounds. My mind was as the mind of a child and my memory is uncertain here." With Miller's memory far too active at
times and conveniently uncertain at others, there is little hope
of getting at the truth in his autobiographical writings. In half
a hundred places he touches on these experiences, contradicting
himself, misplacing events, shifting allegiances, admitting in
one line that he was humbugging and continuing the game in
the next. His deception is to be much regretted, for in the four
years spent in one of the wildest parts of California, he had a
more intimate contact with the frontier than did any of his fellow writers. An exact account of his life would probably be
more interesting than all of his fictions — at least, it would be of
more value to the social historian.

Records which can be used to check Miller's romancing show
him as much less of a hero than do his own tales. The accounts
of old-timers who knew him in Shasta City, Yreka, and Dead-
wood belittle him as delicate, effeminate, useless — an affected
youth, who wore his yellow hair down to his shoulders, read
newspapers with his gloves on, and let a squaw rustle his food
for him. Unsavory also are the reactions of one or two mountain men who assert that it was a mistake that he escaped lynching. The accounts verify the fact that he cohabited with an Indian woman in Squawtown — an act which may have appeared

romantic to his youthful fancy, but aroused the disapprobation and contempt of the members of the community who were not doing likewise. And the illegitimate child of the union, named Cali-Shasta, lived to curse her romantic father for bringing her into the world.

There are also papers in the Shasta County Court House, telling of the arrest of the poet for horse-stealing in 1859. It is clear that he was captured and jailed for taking a horse (he claimed that he borrowed it for legitimate reasons); that he escaped from the jail with no great difficulty (he wrote a poem telling how his Indian mistress liberated him); and that he departed the region with no intent to return.

But especially are Miller's romantic tales exploded in a diary which he kept at the time, and later gave to Ina Coolbrith with the warning that to divulge its material would ruin his reputation. Its recent publication has proved of interest to scholars interested in Miller, but has hardly startled the general reading public. With only a few gaps, it tells of Miller's life day by day from 1854 to 1858, from the time he arrived in California until he returned to Oregon to enter Columbia College. (He must have returned to California to steal the horse a year later.) It minimizes the parts played in Miller's life by " The Prince " and De Bloney and opens the question whether the two may not have been the same person. It offers no evidence that Miller was involved in any attempt to form an Indian republic, although it does prove conclusively that he lived on the best of terms with the Indians for nearly a year, and that he was practically cut off from contact with other white men during this period. It established the fact that he did fight and was actually wounded in the Battle of Castle Rocks, and that later he took part in the Pitt River War. And it shows definitely that he did not go to Nicaragua and, for that matter, was not south of Shasta City during this period of his life.

Of particular interest is an entry in the diary which settles at last the date of Miller's birth; the evidence proves conclusively that he was born September 8, 1837, four years before the date which he wished the world to accept. Thus he was seventeen when he came to California, twenty when he first became a father, and twenty-two when he stole the horse. The best explanation for his untiring attempts in later life to show that he was a mere boy during his Shasta days is that he wished to appear sufficiently immature to be free of all moral blame.

The entries in the diary range from terse comments such as "Prospected Made 000" and "Went to Shasta City and saw A. Higgins executed for the crime of murder," to rambling, unpunctuated summaries of performance in the past and resolutions for the future. After one such outburst, he confessed: "I have dug and tugged starved and economized the winter through and I could not this day raise the miserable sum of twenty-five dollars. Yes here I find myself in this damed [*sic*] hole of Squaw town in poor health . . . no money to leave the place on and no prospect of making any." Into the diary also went copies of personal letters and snatches of verse, of which the following stanza is representative:

> O how I wish I a goin was at home
> In the valley of the old Willamette
> And never again I'd wish to roam
> Ile seal the assertion with damn it.

Perhaps the most interesting entries are those which comment on his stay with the Indians. At one point he remarks: "Yes I the high minded proud souled Hiner Miller join in a digger Indian dance for a change in weather," and again he describes himself as a sort of Crusoe among the natives. "This is indeed a lovely day. My Indian has gone a hunting with the break of day. My squaw is out digging roots my dog is lying at my feet my rifle is by my side my pipe is in my mouth a dozen or more naked Digger Indians that follow me . . . are stretched out around in the bright sunshine." This was the material which went into his later romances.

His wildest days behind him, Miller graduated from the provincial Columbia College in Oregon in 1859, and the next year was teaching school in a village near Vancouver, in Washington Territory. Although he had scribbled many verses in his diary and had written his class poem in college, he was to wait twelve years before publishing his *Songs of the Sierras*.

Such were the apprenticeships that Ina Coolbrith, Bret Harte, Prentice Mulford, Charles Warren Stoddard, Henry George, and Joaquin Miller spent in the West during the fifties. In 1860 they were still very young; twenty-six-year-old Mulford was the veteran and seventeen-year-old Stoddard was the youth of the group. With the exceptions of the girl and the youth, all had had some experience at mining, though the only one to stick to it was Mulford. When the sixties opened, Ina Coolbrith was living in seclusion in Los Angeles; Bret Harte had just returned from Uniontown and was about to become a compositor on the *Golden Era;* Prentice Mulford was still digging his two dollars a day in the mines; Charles Warren Stoddard was working as a clerk in a book-store in San Francisco; Henry George had found a job as a printer after going to British Columbia and the San Joaquin Valley in pursuit of gold; and Joaquin Miller was teaching school in Washington Territory. To date neither Mulford nor George had shown any interest in writing; Coolbrith, Stoddard, and possibly Miller had scribbled a few verses of no importance; and Harte had been publishing prose and poetry for three years. With the latecomers, Samuel Clemens and Ambrose Bierce, these six were to produce the best of the literature of the Far-Western frontier.

CHAPTER IV

WASHOE SILVER AND THE CIVIL WAR

THE LUSTY city of San Francisco came of age in the early six-ties. There had been a moment during the most distressing days of its adolescence when its future looked very doubtful. Not only had the nation-wide panic of '57 been felt in the West-ern city, but the output of gold from the Mother Lode had fal-len off appreciably, real-estate speculation had been checked by a collapse in prices, and, as a final blow, nearly twenty-five thou-sand San Franciscans had stampeded to the Fraser River. But by Christmas of '58, when most of them had returned swearing never again to leave " God's country," the corner had been turned.

No longer did the croakers prophesy that San Francisco would dwindle to the size of Vallejo or become a ghost town in the midst of a territory gutted of its mineral wealth. The steam paddy, which had stood cold for six years, fired up and set about removing more sand hills and dumping them into the bay. The vexatious Santillan land suit was dropped, opening up the southern and western parts of the city to purchasers and build-ers; overnight Happy Valley and Rincon Hill became preten-tious residential sections. In '59 thirteen thousand newcomers arrived as compared with five thousand the year before, and during the following three years San Francisco more than doubled its population as well as its assessed valuation. It constructed buildings at the rate of two thousand a year, including such well-known structures as the Russ House, the Lick House, the Occidental Hotel, and the Metropolitan Theater. In 1863, with a population of 115,000, it contained 41 churches, 105 schools, 12 daily papers, and 231 dealers in whisky.

San Francisco's rapid growth in the early sixties was largely the result of two forceful stimulants: the mining of Nevada silver and the Civil War. The war, which meant agony and destruction elsewhere, was an almost unmitigated blessing to the people living west of the Rockies, as it furthered home industry and built up population; while the precious metals dug from the Comstock Lode at Virginia City brought wealth to San Francisco at the rate of six to twenty million dollars a year. In fact, the value of Washoe silver was so great that it did much to finance the Union cause and even brought on a post-war boom throughout the nation. In addition to affecting San Francisco's material growth, Nevada silver and the Civil War influenced the city's literature, for Virginia City supplied both fresh ideas and capable writers, while the war naturally left its impression on the oratory, poetry, and journalism of the period.

When the rush to Washoe started late in '59 many old-timers were skeptical. They had already been taken in by the Gold Lake, the Gold Bluff, the Fraser River, and the Kern River stampedes. Many times they had reached the pot at the foot of the rainbow only to find it empty. Yet once again the call was stirring in their blood: "Let us be off! Now is the time! A pack mule, pick and shovel, hammer and frying-pan will do. You need nothing more. Hurrah for Washoe!" Of course they succumbed. That winter, until the passes were closed by the snow, an almost continuous line of pack trains, mule-drawn wagons, horsemen, and men on foot climbed painfully over the Sierra by way of Placerville and Lake Tahoe and then entered the alkali valleys of Nevada. They were not to be disappointed again. This time it was not a fiasco. This was the biggest strike of all.

Nevada silver yielded so plentifully and the inhabitants of Virginia City lived so intensely that accounts of the Washoe boom slip easily into exaggerated fustian. Wealth and wildness are the main ingredients of the story ; as Dan de Quille put it : " Gold coins jingle in the pockets of all the city," and " a man before breakfast " was the watchword of the day. The printer runs out of exclamation marks and dashes in setting up books about the Comstock Lode, and even Mark Twain in *Roughing It* loses for a moment his characteristic drawl. The unornamented facts are as dramatic as one could wish. From the inside of a mountain in the midst of a desert were taken over four hundred million dollars' worth of silver and gold, and on the side of that mountain flourished for three decades a city larger than any in the West except San Francisco and Salt Lake City.

About one hundred miles east of Sacramento, barely across the Sierra Divide, in Washoe County, Nevada, stands this fabulous Mount Davidson. Half-way up its farther flank, at an altitude of six thousand feet, miners discovered an outcropping of blue rock which assayed richly of silver accompanied by gold. The vein, which dipped far into the mountain, shelving off nearly parallel to its face, was named the Comstock Lode after a worthless sheep-herder who had long maintained that the mountain was full of wealth and was at hand to lay claim to a share in the first strike. In the canyons and on the side of the mountain, clusters of shacks which soon sprang up were called Silver City, Gold City, and, over the center of the lode, Virginia

City, named after a drunken prospector, James Fennimore or "Old Virginny," who lost his whisky but christened the town when he fell upon its stones.

Virginia City soon outdistanced its rivals and had acquired during the first bonanza twenty thousand inhabitants, churches, and theaters, ministers and prostitutes, a water shortage, and other signs of civilization. Its initial bonanza ended in 1864, when wasteful methods in mining, "wild-catting" of stock, and continuous litigation almost put an end to silver-production. A few years later it produced again, but this second or "big bonanza" left no mark on Western literature; it was the less settled, more individualistic flush times of the early sixties that fostered the famous *Territorial Enterprise* school, in which Mark Twain got his start.

The side of Mount Davidson was about as bad a place to build a town as one could find. No wood was to be had for fuel or building; the little water available was evil-tasting and evil-acting; and the wind blew with the ferocity of the sirocco on the south coast of Sicily. Ross Browne, who could stand only a month of Virginia City when he visited it in '60 (but who anticipated Mark Twain's *Roughing It* in his amusing account of his visit), summed it up as "a mud-hole; climate, hurricanes and snow; water, a dilution of arsenic, plumbago, and copperas; wood, not at all except sagebrush; no title to property and no property worth having. . . . The Washoe mines are nothing more than squirrel-holes on a large scale, the difference being that the squirrels burrow in the ground because they live there, and men because they want to live somewhere else."

Most of the men on the Comstock were burrowing in the ground that they might live on Nob Hill, overlooking the Golden Gate. When Mark Twain, as he lay awake imagining himself a millionaire, told his bedfellow that the first thing he

was going to do with his money was to build a castle in San
Francisco, he was expressing succinctly the close relationship
between Washoe and the metropolis of the West. Virginia City
was built by San Franciscans: its capital, its banks, its law-
makers came from San Francisco; its every scrap of iron and
bolt of cloth was brought in from California. Three stagecoaches daily connected Virginia City with its parent, and Piper's Opera House on the Comstock regularly billed the leading
actors and lecturers from over the mountain. The silver bars
poured into their forms in the Comstock were consigned to the
mint in San Francisco, and the fortunes made on the Comstock
were spent in San Francisco, bringing prosperity to that city.
Naturally, the writers in Virginia City looked upon San Francisco as their literary headquarters; they were nearly all from
the bay city and most of them returned when the flush times
were over.

The Virginia City *Territorial Enterprise* was an offspring of
San Francisco's *Golden Era*. Joseph T. Goodman and Denis
McCarthy, its owners and editors, were both from the *Era* staff,
where they had served their apprenticeships as printers and
writers. Rollin M. Daggett, the local editor, was that co-
founder of the *Era* who had canvassed the Sierra mining camps
in his red shirt and high boots. Though Goodman brought both
Dan de Quille and Mark Twain out of the sagebrush, once he
had put them to work they became contributing correspondents to the *Golden Era* and Mark Twain joined the *Golden Era*
in San Francisco as soon as he left Virginia City.

All accounts agree that the men on the staff of the *Territorial
Enterprise* were brilliant and congenial — and that they had a
good time in spite of alkali hell and high wind. Mark Twain
called Virginia City the city which afforded him the most vigorous enjoyment of life he ever experienced. Dan de Quille

loved it so much that he stayed in it till it died beneath his feet.
Joe Goodman expressed his love for it in a poem, of which one
stanza reads:

> In youth when I did live, did love
> (To quote the sexton's homely ditty),
> I lived six thousand feet above
> Sea level, in Virginia City;
> The site was bleak, the houses small,
> The narrow streets unpaved and slanting,
> But now it seems to me of all
> The spots on earth the most entrancing.

The mainsprings of the journal were Goodman and Mc-
Carthy, who had picked up the *Enterprise* at a bargain soon
after their arrival, had turned it into a daily, and had found a
horde of subscribers at two dollars a month and advertisers at
almost any figure asked. McCarthy ran the press-room, while
Goodman wrote the editorials; both were handy with their guns
and were able to back up any hoaxes played by their assistant
editor, Daggett, or their locals, Dan de Quille and Mark Twain.
Daggett, now grown plump and cynical (he even crowed when
the Indians massacred Custer), cultivated a sinister reputation
which went well with the scar over his left eyebrow. De Quille,
whose real name was William Wright, was a quiet worker who
was both an expert on mining engineering and a very amusing
humorist. Steve Gillis, bantam fighter from Mississippi, was
the liveliest soul in the composing-room. In print their opponents in journalistic feuds but in real life their bar-room companions were the writers on rival Comstock journals, such as
Tom Fitch, " Unreliable " Rice, and C. C. Goodwin.

Daggett often remarked on the impression Sam Clemens cre-
ated when he walked into the *Territorial Enterprise* office one
August day in '62 and announced that he was the new reporter.
" He had been living on alkali water and whang leather, with

SAN FRANCISCO IN 1849.

From a painting in the Golden Gate Park Museum.

Courtesy of the University of California Extension Division

VIRGINIA CITY IN 1861.

Courtesy of Mr. Harry T. Peters

THE GRADE TO WASHOE.

A drawing by J. Ross Browne showing the perilous route over the Sierra to Nevada during the early days of the Virginia City boom. Reproduced from *Crusoe's Island*. *Courtesy of California State Library*

RETURN TO SAN FRANCISCO.

J. Ross Browne's picture of a disappointed miner returning from the diggin's. From *Crusoe's Island* *Courtesy of California State Library*

only a sufficient supply of the former for drinking purposes, for several months, and you may imagine his appearance when I first saw him." Daggett and his companions, misled by Clemens's drawl and slouchy gait, concluded that he was abnormally lazy. They were only partly right; Mark Twain had a goodly share of the loafer in his nature, but his languor at the moment was more the result of an indeterminate state of mind than of laziness. For a year and a half he had been drifting, floundering about without knowing where he was going. He had at last accepted a job writing for the *Enterprise* largely because his enthusiasm for mining had played out and he had to earn a living some way or other.

His period of unrest had started when the Civil War put an end to Mississippi River traffic. He had been unusually contented as a pilot; for four years he had worked to master every curve and snag of the river and at the end of that arduous training had become an expert in a profession that combined romance with utility. Then the Southern states seceded, the river was blockaded, and the river boats let their fires go cold, never to heat them again.

Clemens, like most of the river pilots, found himself divided in sympathy when the conflict broke out. He had been brought up in Missouri, a border state which hovered between secession and loyalty; many of his friends on the river went with the North and many with the South; and, although he was anti-slavery in sympathy, he was not sufficiently concerned with the abolitionist's cause to start gunning for his acquaintances in New Orleans. The result was that he drifted, leaving his fate to circumstances. He joined a home-guard unit in Hannibal, an impromptu organization without official connection with either side, although the sympathies of the group were primarily Confederate. During the fortnight or so that he spent in the guard, he went through all sorts of inconveniences; he had his hair cut short, he developed a boil, he nearly drowned in fording a river, he fell out of a hay-window when a barn caught fire. The end of the " campaign " found him in bed with a sprained ankle and an intense dislike of war. As soon as he was able to be about, he joined his brother, Orion Clemens, who was about to leave for Nevada to become secretary to the Territorial Governor, and on July 26, 1861 he set out for the West, where there was no fighting. He was very glad to get away.

During the year between his arrival in Carson City and his joining the *Enterprise* staff Clemens spent most of his time mining. First in Unionville, in the center of Nevada, and later in Aurora, down by the California border near Mono Lake, he worked feverishly at silver leads, certain that he would become wealthy if he had any sort of luck. In addition to laboring in the mines, he used every cent he could scrape up or borrow from Orion to invest in silver stocks. Each period of excitement was followed by depression; the shaft yielded worthless, stubborn shale, and the stocks devoured assessments. In stagnant backwashes following fits of energy, he loafed on the streets of Carson City, he made an exploration trip to Mono Lake, he camped on the shores of Lake Tahoe. Short of cash, he wrote some sketches and sent them up to the *Enterprise;* using the name of " Josh " he penned the first of many articles on decrepit and perverse horses, he burlesqued a Fourth of July celebration, he described a movable claim that followed a mountain slide. His offerings were printed, and when Dan de Quille asked for a year's vacation to visit his home in the States, Goodman wrote to Clemens suggesting that he sub for the local editor during his absence. Sam Clemens did not know what to do; he had reached the end of his patience and resources as a silver-miner, but journalism was not very tempting to him. After many days of indecision he set out for Virginia City on foot, disheartened, indifferent, but ready to try the new field.

It was not long before his attitude towards his work shifted to enthusiasm. It was good to have a regular income; it was good to live in a virile city after months in the sagebrush; it was good to be able to write successful sketches; it was good to be a man of importance. Even the horseplay initiation that "the boys" put him through could be tolerated for these advantages. They hid his candle to hear him swear and they tricked him into giving a heart-felt speech of thanks for an imitation meer-schaum pipe, and he still loved them.

His own hoaxes were confined to his column; handicapped by the popularity of Dan de Quille's elaborate "quaints," includ-ing the latter's famous magnetic rocks and air-conditioned hel-mets, he was hard pressed to establish his own reputation as a literary liar on the grand scale. The first big success came with the Petrified Man story, in which he penned a grave scientific account of the discovery of a petrified man thumbing his nose at posterity. Six months after he joined the staff, he used the name Mark Twain for the first time; by the end of his year he was the most popular journalist on the Comstock and his arti-cles were being reprinted in San Francisco papers. He was no longer plagued with lassitude, for he had found a congenial profession.

Mark Twain was only one of thousands of men who came west in the early sixties to get away from the Civil War. Disillu-sioned by the struggle, unconvinced of the necessity of shedding their brothers' blood, they brought their families to a land which offered reasonable assurance of peace and security. In the second year of the war a San Francisco journal estimated that almost a hundred thousand people entered California to escape the conflict. The West welcomed these war emigrants be-cause they included women and children and assured the found-ing of stable homes. It had seen enough of the transient adventurer. " An influx of males is rather a locust plague, to a land overflowing with milk and honey. They gorge themselves and are off. They return to whence they came, to lay their spoils at the feet of waiting femininity. Of those who gorge to repletion and fall off . . . we have had enough." The new-comers settled on the land and produced rich crops; they also supplied labor for the fast-developing home industries, made necessary by the closing of Eastern factories and the establish-ing of the Confederate blockade. While the rest of the nation bled, California prospered.

The peace which Californians enjoyed during the Civil War might not have been theirs if the group of Southern politicians headed by Gwin and Terry had had their way. But the plans of this group to swing California for the Confederacy, or, fail-ing that, to declare for a Western republic, were soon defeated by a Union sentiment strong enough to avert civil conflict within the state. Though California's politics had been con-trolled by Democrats from the day that statehood was granted, the sympathy of the majority of the populace had been swing-ing towards the cause of abolition ever since Terry killed Brod-erick in their famous duel. The latter, though a questionable politician while alive, gave inestimable support to the anti-slav-ery party by dying a martyr. When the golden-tongued Baker played the part of Mark Antony and gave the cry for liberty while he pointed dramatically at the body of the slain, he drove his listeners straight into the arms of the Republicans. Thus San Francisco shuddered a little incredulously when it heard the news of the firing on Fort Sumter, but it paraded and united in a huge Union mass meeting as soon as it realized the war was on. There was never any serious question as to its stand after that, although there were many Confederate sympathizers within the state, particularly in the south, and during the campaign for Lincoln's re-election peace sentiment ran strong and Copperheads came out into the open. Except for a few occasions during the war when feeling ran high, hysteria was confined to the minority and most of the people of the state went about their business, glad that they could do so in peace.

Though California remained peaceful, the War of the Rebellion was amply reflected in Western literature, particularly in the speeches of its orators, the verses of its poets-of-the-day, and the leading articles of its editors.

No frontier institution furnished the early humorists with better material for burlesque than the orators' practice of twisting the lion's tail and making the eagle scream on every patriotic holiday. The flowery orations often contained such ridiculous passages as Tom Fitch's reference to the planets as " the auger holes of heaven " or Newton Booth's apostrophe to the Union: " Baptized anew, it shall live a thousand years to come, the Colossus of the nation — its feet upon the continents, its scepter over the seas — its forehead among the stars." Yet not all orators were flamboyant and not all orations were ridiculous. In the early days in California, when speakers played prominent roles in community life, they were often quite worth listening to. Moreover, the art of oratory as displayed by men like Edward Baker and Starr King, or even Tom Fitch, Edmund Randolph, and Frank Pixley at their best, was a more polished, more formally developed art than any other to be found on the frontier. As it is an art that has almost completely passed away, the propaganda-conscious modern fails to realize its worth in the day when it flourished. As the best orations were printed after their delivery, they form an integral and important part of frontier literature.

Edward Dickinson Baker and Thomas Starr King spoke so effectively during the days when California seemed to be hanging in the balance that their followers have started another civil war about which one saved the state for the Union. The economic-minded historian denies that either did so, but he admits that first Baker and then King did much to make the state's decision quick and definite, and thus perhaps avoided bloodshed and damage to property.

Early San Franciscans remembered three occasions at which Baker appeared a very demigod in forensic strength. They talked often of the speech the tall, strikingly handsome, gray-haired orator delivered in 1858 when, after months of waiting, they received the news that the Atlantic had been successfully spanned by an electric cable. Even more impressive was his speech at Broderick's funeral. After the militia, the fire-brigades, and the fraternal orders marched past the bier, Baker rose to stir them with his silver voice. During a long, impressive silence he stood at the head of the coffin, gazing at the body until the tears ran down his cheeks. Then he delivered an oration which, according to the admiring J. S. Hittell, " surpassed any in Demosthenes, Cicero, Burke, Mirabeau, Brougham, Webster, Sumner, or Gladstone."

A year later Baker, now called the Gray Eagle of Republicanism, was elected Senator from Oregon, the first Republican to represent a Western state in Washington. Though not an Oregonian, he had been drafted by the Free-Soil Party to defeat the Democrats in Joseph Lane's own stronghold. He was an experienced politician, as he had served a term in Washington as Representative from Illinois. Aided by his reputation and eloquence and the votes of the Douglas Democrats, he succeeded in carrying the state by a narrow margin. Before leaving for the East, he delivered his third memorable oration in the Metropolitan Theater in San Francisco, which was able to pack in only one third of the twelve thousand people who clamored to hear him. The time was auspicious, as the eve of the great conflict was at hand. That day Baker's purpose was to strike a deciding blow for his old friend Abraham Lincoln, the Republican candidate for president. His peroration was a stirring plea for freedom. His audience hung on his words as his voice rang out: "We are a city set on a hill. Our light cannot be hid. As for me, I dare not, I will not be false to freedom. Where the feet of my youth were planted, there, by freedom, my feet shall stand. I will walk beneath her banner. I will glory in her strength. I have watched her, in history, struck down on a hundred chosen fields of battle. I have seen her bound to the stake; I have seen them give her ashes to the winds. But when they turned to exult, I have seen her again meet them face to face, resplendent in complete steel, brandishing in her right hand a flaming sword, red with insufferable light. I take courage. People gather round her. The Genius of America will at last lead her sons to freedom." As he spoke of the sword with the insufferable light, he made as if to pull his own from the scabbard. At that instant a young man leaped upon the stage, waving a huge American flag. The audience went wild, cheered themselves hoarse; the crowds outside the theater took up the cheer. The Gray Eagle had accomplished his purpose; the impossible happened a few months later when Lincoln carried California by a few thousand votes.

Baker's work as orator for the Union cause was carried on by Starr King, who arrived in San Francisco in 1860 to fill the pastorate of the First Unitarian Church. King's rise had been very rapid. Without distinction by birth, he had made his way in the conservative Boston Unitarian circles largely through his speaking-ability, coupled with a pleasant personality. When he yielded to his impulse for adventure and decided to go west, his Boston friends were frankly horrified, but Horace Greeley, who had just returned from his Western tour (and his ride with Hank Monk), praised his decision: "You will be fascinated by it, except San Francisco, which I think has the worst

climate, and is the most infernal hole on the face of the earth."
Though King and his wife found San Francisco better than
infernal, they suffered a good deal of homesickness for New
England; the best that King could say of the " decrepit-look-
ing city " with its streets " bilious with Chinamen " was that the
future might see it " stretched out on its desolate hills rubbing
the dust out of its eyes and washing the fleas off its feet in the
great Pacific basin."

But King was no man to linger over homesickness when there
were things to be done. Dynamic and ambitious, he filled his
days with pastoral, literary, and patriotic activities. Although
some members of his congregation objected that he gave too
much of his time to social reform and politics, to benefits for
the Home of Inebriates and the Dashaway Temperance Society, or to sermons on Civil War issues rather than on God's relation to his Servants, they were forced to admit that King
never slighted his obligations to his pastorate. During his four
years on the coast he not only built up the membership of the
church but promoted the financing and construction of an excellent new building. Nor did he stop with his routine duties.
Following a precedent among the Unitarian clergy, he made his
contribution to belles-lettres, and, although he never composed
poetry, as did Baker, he was capable enough at writing sketches
of California society and scenery. In his series of letters to the
Boston *Evening Transcript* he was at his best in his descriptions of mountain scenery, for he was a mountaineer of long
standing and had already published a volume on the White
Mountains of New Hampshire. In addition to these essays,
King wrote a number of carefully planned and smoothly
phrased discourses on American poets and statesmen, which he
presented in lectures and later published. One of his reasons
for coming to San Francisco was to aid in raising the cultural
level of the community.

But most of King's seemingly unlimited supply of energy was expended on the campaign for support of the Union. At first he helped to arouse Northern sentiment through his lectures on American statesmen; then he threw himself into furthering the collections for the Sanitary Commission, the Red Cross of the Civil War. His campaign was eminently successful, for Californians gave over a million dollars, a fourth of the national total. San Francisco contributed about half of the state donation, more than five dollars per man, woman, and child.

This crusade throughout the state to raise money for the wounded soldiers appealed to King's impassioned nature. And as he campaigned for the money, he fought the cause of the North with every ounce of his one hundred and twenty pounds. As his dark, luminous eyes grew fiery, his hearers were reminded of his boast that, although he was a bantam, when he was angry he weighed a ton. Indeed, his love of a fight was far from Christlike, and his bitter attacks on the enemy reflected little spiritual toleration. Even his sermons were turned into political harangues under such titles as " The Choice between Barrabas and Jesus " and " The Treason of Judas Iscariot." In the mining camps the men cheered his fighting spirit and declared he took every trick. When Southerners hissed him at Stockton, he gave them " cracks in return," exclaiming: " There are only two kinds of animals that express themselves by a hiss — the goose and the snake. . . . Behold the Copperhead! " When he spoke of the Confederates, he spoke of children of darkness, although it was but a few months since he had called them his brothers. Jefferson Davis was in league with the devil. " His cause is pollution and a horror. His banner is a black flag. I could pray for him as a man . . . but as president of the seceding states — pray for him! As soon as for antichrist! Never! " There was right on only one side of the Civil

War. " The Rebellion — it is the cause of Wrong against Right. It is not only an unjustifiable revolution, but a geographical wrong, a moral wrong, a religious wrong, a war against the Constitution, against the New Testament, against God! "

King's fighting energy, even more compelling when coming from one of his size and homely appearance — his long, lank hair, pudgy nose, and wide mouth had earned him the nickname of " Yankee poodle " — his incandescent language, his pledge that Jehovah was behind his very intolerance, made him wield a tremendous force for the Northern cause. Southerners hated him intensely and reviled him bitterly. In Sonora, a Confederate stronghold, the editor of the *Union Democrat* wrote what many felt: " Starr King made a tour of the southern mines in the interest of the miner's cause. And this clerical charlatan, hypocrite, and double-distilled humbug is still repeating his threadbare lecture on patriotism. . . . Starr King is a fair representative man of the rabid, fanatical, godless Boston school of political preachers. Their cry is now nigger, nigger, blood, blood! The peace doctrine of the meek and lowly Jesus, who taught peace on earth is scouted as treasonable by those fanatical mountebanks of the clerical school."

His strenuous, almost humorless nature must have made him a better exhorter than companion. He inspired men, but he hardly made them comfortable. An anecdote oft-repeated by King will illustrate his temperament. While he was making a boat trip on the Columbia River during his campaign in Oregon, he discovered among the passengers a man whom he could not stir into excitement over the war. Uninterested in King's semi-public monologue, he stood solitary by the rail. King walked over to him and said: " Have you no interest in the tremendous events now convulsing the country? "

" None at all," was the reply ; " all I want is to be left alone."

" Do you realize that the life of the Republic is hanging in the balance, and that your countrymen are dying by the thousands? "

" I have lost no one. All I want is to be left alone."

" Have you no love of country? No appreciation of the blessings that have been yours all your life under the flag and the splendor that it represents? "

" No, I just want to be let alone."

When he told the story in his lecture, King at this point would straighten himself and, in a voice that thrilled all who heard it, cry: " And that abject, cowering wretch sat there, though Mount Hood in its majesty was towering above him, and the Columbia was rolling at his feet. I should have thrown him overboard, only the water was pure."

Perhaps the majority of readers will agree with the thousands who cheered at this moment, but a skeptical few will sympathize with the man who wanted to be let alone.

No man of King's physical endowment could long keep up the pace that he was going. During his fourth year in California the exhausted minister was an easy prey to diphtheria. However, he lived to see his new church completed, to find his own debts paid through an adventurous investment in Washoe silver, and to see that the North was winning the war. And when he was told the end was at hand, he said farewell to wife and child, bade the church elders clear off the mortgage, and expired reciting the Twenty-third Psalm. San Francisco mourned his passing as a major catastrophe. The newspapers carried heavy black borders, flags hung at half-mast, and at his funeral he was accorded a military salute by minute guns in Union Square and heavier cannon on Alcatraz Island. Bret Harte, who had lost his dearest friend, expressed the mood of the city in his tribute, " Relieving Guard ":

Came the relief. " What, sentry, ho!
How passed the night through thy long waking? "
" Cold, cheerless, dark, — as may befit
The hours before the dawn is breaking."

" No sight? no sound? " " No; nothing save
The plover from the marches calling,
And in yon-western sky, about
An hour ago, a star was falling."

" A star? There's nothing strange in that."
" No, nothing; but, above the thicket,
Somehow it seemed to me that God
Somewhere had just relieved a picket."

In the West, as throughout the nation, the Civil War was
the subject of a great many poems, most of them very bad, but
a few worth remembering because of their emotional force or
timeliness. The laments for the dying soldier, the songs following Union victories, and the rhymed invectives directed against
the Confederates which filled the poets' corners of the newspapers were as a whole less effective than the stirring poems declaimed at war rallies and Fourth of July celebrations by well-
known poets-of-the-day. That Bret Harte should have excelled
the horde of journalistic versifiers, ranging from the squeaking
Pip Pepperpod to the frenzied Eliza Pittsinger, was to be expected; but that, as an obscure type-setter on the *Golden Era,*
he should overcome his natural reserve and for the moment steal
the limelight at political meetings from such old hands at elocu-
tion as Frank Soulé, John Swett, and William H. Rhodes can
be explained only as a paradox created by war excitement.

Harte's sudden emergence before the public eye came about
principally through the intervention in his career of Jessie Benton Frémont, a brilliant and energetic woman who was aptly
described as " a she-Merrimac, thoroughly sheathed, and carry-

ing fire in the genuine Benton furnaces." This daughter of Senator Thomas Hart Benton of Missouri, who had married John Charles Frémont at seventeen, had already shown her mettle by countermanding the orders of the War Department so that her young husband could make his fame as the Pathfinder, by bolstering up his courage in the hours of his court martial for bungling a revolution in California, and by campaigning for him when he ran as the first Republican candidate for president. When the Frémonts returned to California after the unsuccessful campaign, Jessie became mistress of the huge Mariposa estate in the Mother Lode foothills, which her husband had bought for the small sum of three thousand dollars shortly before gold was discovered. The many visitors to the estate, among them R. H. Dana and Horace Greeley, duly approved the colonel's stamp-mills, but reserved their enthusiasm for the ability of his charming wife to serve them meals worthy of the best French chefs.

Shortly after Bret Harte returned from Union, Jessie Frémont, on a journey from Mariposa to San Francisco to escape the summer heat, read one of his articles in the *Golden Era* and decided that the young journalist showed promise. Greatly interested in writers and writing — she herself published a novel and several volumes of sketches — she invited Harte to her home in the city. She praised his work, discussed his plans with him, and presented him to her friends. A bit diffident at first, Harte was soon so much at home at the Frémonts' that he was dining every Sunday at Black Point. There he met Baker; there he met Starr King; and there he found himself swept into the current of Republican activity. Probably around the Frémont dinner-table was hatched the plot to have Harte wave a flag on the stage of the Metropolitan Theater at the climax of Baker's speech for Lincoln. It was his first public appearance.

Harte had enjoyed writing poems supporting the Union cause, but after a few distressing experiences on the platform he rebelled against reciting at public meetings. On at least one occasion he failed to turn up when he was announced. This failure was only one of the disappointments which marked the celebration of July 4, 1863. Enthusiasm for the war had apparently died down. First the parade did not turn out as well as advertised. The ranks of the fraternal organizations showed many gaps, and a beer truck decorated with weeping willows struck a dismal note. The Metropolitan Theater was only partially filled, and when John Swett read the Emancipation Proclamation, the hisses and boos of the Copperheads went unchallenged. In doleful cadence the audience sang the "Battle Hymn of the Republic." Finally, after explaining that Harte was ill, Starr King read the absent poet's verses for the day, which contained many stanzas in this vein:

> Far better the tempest than yon lurid glow
>   That lights, while it mocks, the deep gloom of the sky —
> Far better the lightning that smites with one blow,
>   Than the Copperhead's crest uplifted on high!

The *Golden Era* records that after the meeting there were fireworks but no drunks!

All together Harte wrote more than thirty Civil War poems, ranging from lyrical pleas for Union support to satirical attacks on the enemy. Some of these poems, like "The Wrath of McDawdle," were of general interest, while others, such as "Semmes!" were merely verse comments on local reactions to the war. Thus San Franciscans were greatly excited when the Confederate privateer *Alabama* captured the California-bound *Ariel;* although Captain Semmes treated his prisoners with great courtesy and sent them on their way unharmed, Harte was unforgiving and wished him raised "In exaltation . . . And high saltation, From some yardarm." The humorist also got full value from the ludicrous fate of the *Camanche*, an iron monitor shipped in sections to the west coast, where it was to be assembled to defend San Francisco from possible attack. It was never bolted together, however, for the ship which carried it sank at the pier's end and San Francisco was once more without a navy.

The writers who were most concerned with the Civil War were the newspaper editors, partly because they voiced the hopes and fears of the public, partly because the war intensified the political issues which accounted so largely for their support. The few months separating Lincoln's election and the defeat at Bull Run brought a sweeping realignment of opinion among these journalists. During the presidential campaign the press had been strongly Democratic: of the California newspapers, twenty-two supported Breckenridge and the Southern chivalry group, twenty-four held for Douglas and compromise, and only eight backed Lincoln and a clear-cut anti-slavery decision. The election of a Republican and the secession of the Southern states changed everything. As the war fever spread, more and more editors became " loyal," and after the dark news of mid-summer arrived, the most active Democratic journalists confined their remarks to state politics. But as the war dragged on interminably, many Californians came to favor an armistice and recognition of the Confederacy. The anti-war spokesmen grew very aggressive, particularly in the southern part of the state and in the San Joaquin Valley. And in the campaign of '64 between Lincoln and McClellan, though the Democrats, then openly labeled Copperheads, were beaten, they polled more than a third of the state vote.

On the Union side the two papers most ardent in their support were the Sacramento *Union* and the San Francisco *American Flag*. Because of its firm anti-slavery stand, the *Union*, for

years the most influential newspaper in the state, is said to have
been worth more to the Northern cause than Starr King or an
army corps. More spectacular and also more hysterical was
the *American Flag*, the mouthpiece of Calvin B. McDonald,
"The Thunderer," who was quite willing to fight the war by
himself. To many San Franciscans he was a brave man who
fought alone without political alliance, a hero as he strode
through the crowd outside the *Flag* office, ready to kill or be
killed at any instant for his loyalty to his country. To others
he was an intemperate fire-eater, who attacked the innocent citizen who disagreed with him as viciously as he did the spies of
the Confederacy working within the city.

His vituperative, rhetorical style gave rise to amusing parodies, as follows: " The man who dares stand up in the face of
the terraqueous universe, and charge me with being addicted to
whiskey, is a mephitic pachyderm, to whom the infanticidal
swine that gulps down her own offspring yet warm from the
womb, is a cooing turtle-dove." Contemporary remarks show
that McDonald exceeded his fellow editors in bombast during
a period when competition was very keen.

More interesting than the Unionist editorials, however, was
the persistent campaign of the minority opposition. Readers
of Western journals grew accustomed to veiled or even open
pleas for the Confederacy and usually accepted them tolerantly
and with good humor. Thus they were amused by G. B. Densmore's melodramatic serial in the *Golden Era* telling of the ne-
farious machinations of the Knights of the Golden Circle, a
secret Confederate order operating in their territory, or they
chuckled when they read that a saloon in Auburn had concocted
a new drink called " Gilmore's Greek Fire," which was guaran-
teed to be death to Copperheads. When Florence Fane joined
the *Golden Era* staff as a columnist, she did not hesitate to speak

THOMAS STARR KING.

BRET HARTE SHORTLY AFTER HIS METEORIC RISE TO FAME.
Courtesy of California State Library

a good word for the South, nor did Adah Isaacs Menken hide her sympathies (or much of anything else) when she was playing *Mazeppa* on the coast. Rowena Granice Steele, who had written sensational stories for the *Era* in the fifties and had collected them in one of the earliest volumes of California fiction, *The Family Gem*, received much publicity when she christened her baby Jefferson Davis Lee Stonewall Jackson Steele. The editor of the *Era* suggested that the Southern Confederacy be added to the name. And, in the best of humor, the same editor published a poem sent in by a Copperhead which contained an acrostic spelling " Hurrah for the South "! He turned the laugh on the contributor by substituting first words beginning with *N* and *R* in the thirteenth and fifteenth lines, adding a footnote: " Bad luck this time, Johnny Rebel. Try again."

But during the tenser moments of the war Johnny Rebel's remarks were not so easily tolerated. Secesh editors like John R. Ridge, who not only attacked the administration policies in his Grass Valley *National* but caned the publisher of the local Unionist journal, were under constant surveillance by the military authorities. In Ridge's case, the government was not only interested in the outspoken Cherokee's hostile journalism but apprehensive of his activities in the Knights of the Columbia Star, a secret organization devoted to resisting " the re-election of Lincoln by all possible means, including force of arms."

When the military commander in the West felt it necessary, he suppressed opposition journals. Thus on September 16, 1862 General Wright ordered that the Stockton *Argus*, the Stockton *Democrat*, the San Jose *Tribune*, the Tulare *Post*, and the Visalia *Equal Rights Expositor* be excluded from the mails. In spite of this move the Visalia paper continued to give trouble until its presses were destroyed and its type pied by an angry mob. There was, in fact, no keeping the secesh editors quiet, and it was not long before a Mariposa editor was again calling Lincoln " a traitor to God and humanity, his hands dripping with the blood of his countrymen."

Among the editors who ran into difficulty with the government was Joaquin Miller, who, after abandoning school-teaching for a brief period of studying law and riding a pony express in Idaho, had settled temporarily in Eugene City, Oregon, as editor of the *Democratic Register*. In his editorials he expressed the grievances of the Democrats. He fought the proposed conscriptions laws, saying: " The drafting of troops in this State we shall oppose to the bitter end." He also objected to the Confiscation Law, he condemned the introduction of greenbacks, and he called the Sanitary Fund " a species of pious swindling got up by men in the East." After three months of these attacks on Union policies the *Democratic Register* was suppressed by command of General Wright. Owner Nolton and editor Miller then resorted to a common subterfuge practiced by Copperhead editors; they started another paper with a new name, the *Review*, printing it on the same press and circulating it among the same subscribers. General Wright's orders had been carried out, however; the Eugene City *Review* was less than the *Democratic Register* with a new masthead, for its fangs had been extracted.

There was nothing in Miller's antecedents to explain his becoming a secesh editor. As he was born north of the Mason-Dixon line, one would expect his sympathies to have been with the Union. Possibly the owner of the *Democratic Register* dictated the policy of the paper and the editor wrote what he was told to, but lack of courage to stand up for his own ideas was not one of Miller's failings. As a matter of fact, his sins against the Union were hardly enough to deserve anything so drastic as government suppression. In opposing greenbacks and the draft he was but following majority opinion in both Oregon and California. Miller was probably telling the truth when he said that he got into trouble because he was a pacifist. In his poem " Only a Private Killed, They Say," written for the Eugene City *Review,* he expressed his feelings on this subject and also revealed his poetic immaturity.

> Only a private killed, they say, he is dead among the trees:
> We pause, we pitty [*sic*], but alas! alas!
> Not all for the dead on the dewy grass,
> But for wounds that no eye sees.
> Another can fill their places away, away where brave men dare,
> But who the hearts of the sisters, the brothers?
> Who the love of the widows, the mothers
> Can fill, in the quiet cottage these?

While the orators stirred the people's feelings, while the editors wrote for union or secession, many Westerners desired action on the field of war. They could get into the fighting only through following one of three devious courses: they could make their way through the Southwest or Mexico and join the Confederate forces, they could volunteer to serve with Eastern units of the Union army (many even paid their passage to the recruiting point), or they could join the companies that were detailed to prevent trouble in the Southwest. In spite of these unattractive openings, many Californians fought for the South, and 16,000 of them served under Union colors.

The percentage of literary men among the Westerners who joined the army was probably not much lower than that among writers throughout the nation. Ambrose Bierce, who was later to be associated with the West, served as a Union officer, was cited for bravery, and became one of the first American writers to portray war realistically. Samuel Clemens of Missouri played at soldiering for a few days in a Confederate home guard, decided he didn't like it, and escaped to Nevada. Edward D. Baker left his seat in the Senate to lead the California

Brigade and died a hero at Ball's Bluff early in the war. John C. Cremony, journalist, served as a captain with the Southwest detail. The experiences of the last named were the most representative of the fate of Western volunteers.

Most of the men who volunteered for action and spent four years in Western garrison posts or on Indian duty came home disappointed. Captain Cremony was an exception, for service in the Southwest was very much to his liking. The newspaper job he was holding in San Francisco when the war broke out was not exciting enough for this hardened adventurer from the West Indies, who as a boy had run away to sea, had fished for everything from mackerel to whale, had seen something of both piracy and slave-trading, and had lived as a captive among the Patagonian Indians of South America. He was interested in the Southwest because he had campaigned there during the Mexican War and had served as the interpreter for the boundary commission which surveyed the southern border from Texas to the Pacific after that war was over. As captain of cavalry during the Civil War he did more than help hold the Southwest for the Union, escort cattle across the desert, and keep the Indians quiet; he continued his study of the Apaches, compiling a vocabulary of the Apache tongue and making notes for the book he was later to write on these picturesque Indians.

To the slight war records of Western writers should be added an account of a belated gesture by Henry George. It reflected the romantic temperament of San Franciscans who had become excited over such incidents as the firing upon the British cruiser *Sutlej*, when it was mistaken for a Southern gunboat, and the discovery of plans to turn the *Chapman* into a Confederate privateer. In keeping with theatrical practice, a short after-show or farce followed the main drama of San Francisco's war days. Now that the rebels had been disposed of, the romantic-minded victors decided that something ought to be done to support the

Monroe Doctrine. While the United States had been busy with the War of Secession, Napoleon III had invaded Mexico and had created a throne for a Habsburg below the Rio Grande. No red-blooded American could sit idly by while Maximilian remained in Mexico City, even if this bewildered monarch was doing his best to rule in a liberal manner. In 1865 Juárez, the Mexican President who was holding out against Maximilian in the north, found many an American ready to aid his cause. In New Orleans a society which called itself the " D.M.D.", or Defenders of the Monroe Doctrine, openly violated neutrality laws by furnishing arms and men to the Indian leader. In New York the " Mexican Patriots " were busy floating a loan, with Baja California offered as security. Inevitably San Francisco, the cradle of many a filibuster movement, took a hand in organizing societies to help " the cause of Mexican liberty." After a great conflict the war fever dies slowly.

In the midst of these activities was Henry George, the incurable romantic. Long disturbed in mind because he had not enlisted for service with the Union, he felt that it was not too late to strike a blow for liberty. Twice he was checked in the midst of a dramatic flourish. As a lieutenant aboard the *Brontes*, with ten thousand rifles in the hold and desperate if not competent leaders in charge, he groaned when a revenue cutter put an end to the dash out of the harbor. Undaunted, within a few weeks he and his plucky wife were kissing the republican flag of Mexico and swearing an awful oath on a bare sword as they were initiated into the fraternal order of the Monroe League. Under the leadership of a newspaperman named Lithicum, they were to join Juárez at San Luis Potosí. But nothing came of it. Nothing was ever to come of romantic escapes for Henry George.

CHAPTER V

THE *GOLDEN ERA*

DURING the sixties the *Golden Era* continued to be the most important, if not the most pretentious literary journal published in San Francisco. Just as it had outlived the *Pioneer*, the *Wide-West*, the *Hesperian*, and *Hutching's Illustrated California Magazine*, it was to prove of tougher fiber than the *Californian*, *Puck*, or the first *Overland Monthly*. Its occasional engravings appeared crude beside the colored fashion plates imported by the *Hesperian* directly from New York; the paper upon which it was printed was scratch-pad compared to the elegant sheet of the *Californian*; and at no time did its contents pretend to the literary finish of the *Overland Monthly*, which could easily be taken for one of the best Eastern magazines. One of the virtues of the *Golden Era* was that it could not easily be taken for another magazine; in its earthiness, its informality, its naïveté; in its " puffs," its sensation novels, and its advice to unfledged poets, it was distinctively a product of the frontier, not sufficiently concerned with imitation to lose its character. Its indigenous nature gave it strength. Although " M'liss " was perhaps the only item appearing in its pages to gain more than local fame, it did more to develop writers on the

Pacific Coast than any of its rivals. Nearly everyone served his apprenticeship on the *Era*.

During its eight years of publication in the fifties, the *Era's* founders, Rollin M. Daggett and J. Macdonough Foard, had succeeded in making it indispensable to the miners and farmers in the hinterland. The enterprise of its owners made up for any lack of quality in its contents, composed principally of " selected " material — short stories, poems, bits of knowledge, and old jokes clipped from other journals. As it was limited to résumés of stories that had grown stale before reaching the isthmus, supplemented by local rumors and gossip, it offered little in the way of news. But though the editors paid nothing for poems and rarely more than five dollars a column for prose, they obtained a surprising amount of local writing. Such popular figures as Steve Massett, " Old Block " Delano, and John R. Ridge, though not " regular " contributors, were represented frequently with poems and sketches. Youngsters like Harte and Stoddard chose the *Era* as the most likely journal to publish their first efforts. But the paper needed a staff with literary ability to give it tone. Before the sixties its sketches and stories were supplied, on the one hand, by men in other professions who looked upon literature simply as an avocation and, on the other, by hacks who would write for the journal for the pittance which it had to offer.

Of the former, William H. Rhodes was a notable example. Rhodes might have been a typical member of the Southern " chivalry " had his interest in writing not given him distinction. Born in South Carolina, he naturally upheld the political and social ideas of this group of Southerners. After schooling at Princeton and Harvard, he practiced law in Galveston, Texas, where he met the future Judge Terry and accompanied him west during the gold-rush. But when Rhodes became a member of the great Vigilance Committee, he broke with his

companions and even had to sit in judgment on the importunate
Terry, who had knifed one of the committee's marshals. When
it looked as if Terry would be condemned to death, Rhodes did
his best to save his friend's neck. After his victim's recovery
Terry escaped to kill Broderick and marry Althea Hill, but he
never forgave Rhodes for joining the Northern rabble. At outs
with his political confederacy, Rhodes struggled along with a
law practice which barely supported him; his interest lay in
writing, a folly which he could not resist. Under the name of
Caxton he wrote many poems, urbane, correct, but uninspired.
His institutional odes were popular, however, especially the one
written for the Masons, starting:

> O sacred spirit of Masonic love!
> Offspring of heaven, the angels' bond above.

He also wrote a play about Joseph Smith called *The Mormon
Prophet*, which was never acted but sometimes was read to appreciative audiences. His many short stories in the Jules Verne
manner, dealing with such subjects as the telescopic eye, a trip
to the center of the earth, and the man who discovered a formula
to burn up the ocean, added to his local reputation. His contemporaries knew him as a tall, elegant-looking man, with genial, kindly countenance, who not infrequently lost a client, unwilling to trust a man whose hand was in law but whose heart
was in literature.

Men like Caxton contributed to the *Era* because they loved
to write; hacks like Elbert Gerry Paige clung to a job to keep
from starving. When Paige came to the *Era*, he was almost a
famous man. After getting the New York *Sunday Mercury* off
to a successful start, he had earned a reputation as the " American Tupper " by writing for its pages a weekly sermon under
the name of Dow, Jr. These sermons contained little of the fire-
and-brimstone atmosphere of the famous revivalist Lorenzo

Dow, however, for they were essentially humorous, loaded with just enough homely wisdom to make them therapeutic as well as palatable. Hardly had Dow, Jr., published a book of these sermons before he began to slip; he took to drinking heavily; and somewhere along the path downward he lost his wife and child. Seeking a new start on the Pacific slope, he joined the *Era* staff as a compositor and writer and continued his little sermons in that journal. It took him just five more years to drink himself to death. In his obituary notice in the *Era*, the editors felt it necessary to explain to the public that, far from letting Dow, Jr., die from starvation as rumor had it, they had kept him alive as long as possible largely through sentimental attachment. His periodical sprees had made him useless as a compositor and undependable as a writer. His story could probably be duplicated more than once from the annals of those who tried to support themselves during the fifties by writing.

In 1860 Joseph E. Lawrence and James Brooks bought the *Golden Era* from Daggett and Foard. Foard had other newspaper and political ventures in mind, and the restless Daggett, nomadic by nature, joined the rush to Virginia City, where he became a member of the *Territorial Enterprise* staff.

The new editor, " Colonel " Joe Lawrence, was a marked contrast to the old. Daggett was a swarthy, heavy-set man who seemed sardonically cheerful but could become as savage as a trapped bear when angered. Rough, energetic, a pagan opportunist who had his ruthless moments, his place was on the fringes of civilization. Joe Lawrence was as bland and urbane as Daggett was importunate and uncouth. Of Long Island extraction, remarkable in his youthful days for neatness of dress and " personal beauty," he had been working inconspicuously as a newspaperman in California since '49. As he had been none too successful on the editorial staff of the *Times and Transcript*, he had chosen the running of a literary weekly as more suited to his easy-chair, sunshiny disposition than the daily press. Everyone who left a record of Lawrence speaks of his geniality, his full brown beard, his meerschaum pipe, his easy-going ways. He was tolerant, honest, gentlemanly, they say; we know from his performance that behind his affability were a good business head and energy which moved like a well-oiled piston rather than a jerky hand-pump. As soon as he took over the *Era*, Lawrence gave it distinction.

Lawrence used a double-barreled policy on the *Era*, aiming on the one hand to retain or even increase its popularity in the rural districts and on the other to improve its contents sufficiently to satisfy the city. For the first he had tradition to back him; the farmers and miners throughout the Mother Lode country, in Nevada, even in Arizona and Oregon, had come to look upon the Sacramento *Union* and the *Golden Era* as institutions. These two journals penetrated the wilderness as persistently as canned oysters. One miner expressed the sentiment of thousands when he wrote: " Many times the *Era* has gladdened my heart amid the rude mountains of the Sierra, in early days, when the whoop of the Digger-Indian, the growl of the fierce grizzly, or the screams of our emblem bird, the Eagle, were more frequent and familiar sounds than those of church bells." Lawrence planned to retain this audience by continuing the departments on mining and agricultural intelligence, the many clipped items of miscellaneous information, and, above all, the chatty tone of the " Correspondents' Column."

It was the last department, lying in the heart of the journal on the left side of the editorial page, that did more than anything else to keep the *Era* a friendly sheet. No inquiry was too humble or too fantastic to be ignored here. A baked-bean recipe was given for Mary Ann of Pike County. A request for a physical description of Jesus was answered with a learned dissertation and citations from ancient books. During the Civil War quite a discussion raged in the column on why soldiers lost four times as many left as right legs, and more than one complaint was published attacking the " squirters," tobacco-chewers who on streets or in restaurants were careless with their shots.

This column also served to publish poems which were not good enough to reach the regular pages. Whenever a miner sitting by his fire on the Yuba felt called upon to compose a line or two, he could feel sure that the correspondents' editor would at least acknowledge its receipt, with some suggestions for improvement if it were too hopeless to print. A little rough, some of these comments, but all in good fun. An enthusiast for Burns who had sent in a Scotch ballad entitled " To a Flea " was advised: " The first stanza is very Scotch, the next is slightly Scotch, the next is Scotchless, and all the rest are *nix* Scotch. It is a pity you did not imbibe more Burns before you burst." Duly Scotched, the poem was returned and printed. Just as bad were the verses in Chinook contributed by an Oregonian, and the trifle on a humming-bird and bumble-bee which ran:

> The humming bird and bumble bee
>   One Summer's day got on a spree;
> They guzzled together with floral licker
>   Till they got sicker, and sicker, and sicker.
>
> The bird pecked at the bumble's thighs
>   The bumble whacked her in the eyes;
> And then they fit and fit and fit,
>   Until they couldn't get up and git.

Such departments would hold the rural public. Lawrence's principal task was to supply reading-matter which would appeal to a city that was rapidly growing self-conscious about its culture. First, he needed good columnists, regular writers on his staff who in their theater reviews, town gossip, and literary comment would wield a definite influence. Second, he needed good contributors; his journal should offer the best available market for the cream of local talent and the most distinguished of visiting celebrities. To get the first he hired young men of promise: Bret Harte, Charles Henry Webb, Charles Warren Stoddard, Ralph Keeler, Prentice Mulford. He not only gave them free rein to develop their ideas, but, with the largest circulation of any paper on the coast, he was able to pay them for their work. He was notably generous, and as long as the money held out, the journal's coffer was a bank for the staff. Then he snared his distinguished visitors by establishing himself in the Lick House (and later in the new Occidental Hotel), where, with the aid of his own charming manners and an excellent bar run by none other than Professor Jerry Thomas, inventor of the Blue Blazer and of Tom and Jerry, he had the newcomers promising articles without a protest. Everyone from Mark Twain to Adah Isaacs Menken succumbed to his campaign of geniality and gin; the bar was the battlefield (except for *la* Menken, who had her drinks in her room), and the captives were taken in the *Era* office, which, under the reign of Colonel Lawrence, became the literary club of San Francisco.

In format the *Era* was more like a newspaper than a magazine. Though each issue contained but eight pages, the amount of printed material was surprisingly great, as each page, measuring fifteen by twenty-two inches, carried six columns printed in seven-point type. Thus a page of the *Era*, in printing nearly nine thousand words, contained as much as thirty pages of a normal-sized modern book. After deducting the two and one half pages used for advertising, one computes that the *Era* each week carried as many words as a current issue of the *Atlantic Monthly*.

Ordinarily the weekly was published without illustrative adornment other than its masthead, which showed an Indian standing on a promontory, hand to brow, looking towards the setting sun, underlined by the caption: " Westward the Star of

Empire Takes its Way." Occasionally, however, a spirited drawing by Nahl or some lesser artist accompanied the novel on the front page. In addition, the *Era* advertisements contained enough " boiler-plate " cuts to create an enlarged edition of John Phœnix's pictorial. To the modern reader these advertisements are often as interesting as the text. They range from current theater programs and maritime notices of clipper ships, with all the romance evoked by the names of Lola Montez or the *Flying Cloud*, to advertisements for New Codfish, Balsam for the Lungs, Extract of Sarsaparilla and Stillingia, or the omnipresent Squarza's Punch. In one column the virtues of patent overspring pianofortes were extolled, while in another the makers of Lyon's Flea Powder took advantage of the miner's passion for rhyme:

> In summer when the sun is low,
>   Come forth in swarms the insect foe,
> And for our blood they bore, you know,
>   And suck it in most rapidly.
>
>   . . .
>
> But fleas, roaches, 'skeeters — black or white —
>   In death's embrace are stiffened quite,
> If Lyon's powder chance to light
>   In their obscure vicinity.

The *Golden Era* offered its large bulk of reading-material and advertisements for one bit a copy or four dollars a year.

Even when Lawrence was obtaining a maximum of local writing, a large portion of the *Era* was still made up of selected material. In this respect it represented the typical magazine-newspaper throughout the nation. Entire departments such as those titled " Gossip Abroad," " Lights and Shadows," " Surface Diggings and Siftings," and " The Farm, Garden and Household " were obviously borrowed from Eastern journals or obtained through some agency resembling the modern syndicate. There were no copyright laws to prevent free use of European fiction; many current novels such as Dickens's *Bleak House* were printed serially, presumably without thanks, and often articles and stories translated from the French or German were used. Even more eclectic were the encyclopedic articles titled " Julius Cæsar," " Josephine's Ring," " Cures for Insect Bites," " Was the Moon ever a Comet? " and " Positions in Sleeping."

The upper left-hand corner of the front page of the *Era* was occupied by the " Poet's Corner." If an acceptable poem by a local writer was at hand, it was printed here; if not, one by a more famous bard was used. Thus, " Evelyn Hope " by Robert Browning and " The Great God Pan " by Elizabeth Barrett alternated with " Satin Slippers " by S. DeWitt Hubbell of Nevada City and " It Might Have Been " by Rose Maple of Vacaville. Here the favorite Western themes of homesickness, praise of mountain and sea scapes, and tributes to nature's flowers — botanical or human — were treated over and over again by aspiring lyricists.

For fiction the *Era* specialized in the " sensation novel," usually reprinted from Eastern or European sources, but occasionally written by a Westerner. Though the veterans in sensation-novel writing, M. E. Braddon, Pierce Egan, Mrs. Henry Wood, and Ned Buntline, accounted for most of the *Era* serials, there were a number of hacks at home who could turn out fairly good ones. Mark Twain ridiculed their formula in *Roughing It* when he told of the composite romance which he helped write for the short-lived *Weekly Occident* of Virginia City. Its characters included a heroine who was " virtuous to the verge of eccentricity," a young French Duke " of aggravated refinement," a mysterious Rosicrucian who consorted with the devil, and an Irish coachman with a rich brogue; its action included a quarrel between the devil and the Rosicrucian, a marriage between the blonde heroine and the coachman, and a recognition by means of a strawberry mark on the left arm. Some of the Western serials were " The West, a Story of California," by Urbano; " The Deserted Shaft: a California romance," by William Simpson; and " The Pitt-Smythes, or life in England, Utah, and California," by Mrs. Amelia Griffith. These stories combined the devices of the penny dreadful and the excesses of the sentimental romance, using Western names and settings with little realistic purpose.

When one attempts to separate the original from the selected material in the files of the *Era* and other journals of the early West, one constantly runs into difficulty caused by the universal use of nom-de-plumes, a practice which had long been common among the journalists of England and America. Beginning writers usually experimented with several of these, finally settling down to the one that pleased them most; but only after they had attained a wide reputation, and not always then, did they use their legal names. The uninitiated must conclude that the *Era* was written by Riding Hood, Pip Pepperpod, Iago, Banquo, Diana Doolittle, Whittlestick, and a score of other alliterative geniuses. Perhaps the writers hid their identities because they loved high-sounding or fanciful names, but it is more likely that the custom went to extremes in the West because the editors wished to make their contributors appear more numerous than they really were.

In addition to its other departments, the *Era*, being a combination newspaper and literary journal, ran one or two columns of news. Before 1860 the " Eastern intelligence " was condensed from newspapers that had come by water by way of the isthmus or across the country by stage; then for a year the journal carried a by-line with the thrilling announcement that its news was arriving by pony express. The *Era* no longer featured news from the States after the transcontinental telegraph was completed, however, because the immediacy of wire releases made a weekly summary redundant. Strange to say, local news, which should have abounded in interest, was collected in a haphazard fashion and reported almost laconically. Occasionally the columnists made some use of local color, mentioning street characters such as Emperor Norton, describing the death and elaborate funeral of his dog Lazarus, commenting on Hank Monk's arrival in Carson with his spindles smoking, or reporting the parades and demonstrations during the war. But their accounts of acts of violence that would be played up as sensational stories in the modern press were usually short and succinct. Customs in headlines also differed a great deal from those of the present day; it is hard to take an item seriously when it is headed " Horrible! Most Horrible! " even if it tells of a fire in which three lives were lost. More forceful, however, than modern news-stories are these grim vignettes:

" One of the pioneers of Washoe, James A. Rogers, blew his brains out, September 2nd. Cause: discouraged."

" Mr. Marshall, of the old circus firm of Lee and Marshall, was badly shot, lately, at Walla Walla, whilst endeavoring to prevent the mob from hanging one William Peoples."

" Died, suddenly, at Centerville, July 2nd, W. Harry Thomson, formerly of New Jersey, aged 32 years. 'Gored to death by a bull.' God hold thee and thy stricken ones, friend Harry. 'Hail and Farewell!' "

But the *Era's* most impressive news-story was one told without words; a national tragedy was expressed through the heavy black border that surrounded the pages and separated the columns of the issue of April 16, 1865, following Lincoln's assassination.

The *Era* would have remained a casual magazine if it had not been given substance by the work of a number of staff contribu-

The Golden Era.

SAN FRANCISCO, CALIFORNIA, SUNDAY, DECEMBER 7, 1862.　VOL. XI.—NO. 1.

THE *GOLDEN ERA.*

The most active of the early San Francisco literary weeklies.

Courtesy of California State Library

PRENTICE MULFORD.
Courtesy of California State Library

tors, noted for their columns of comment, their short stories, and their poetry. Of the customary departments, the foreign correspondence, usually featured in frontier journals, was the least effective; although the *Era* had arrangements with representatives in New York, Washington, London, and Paris, their observations were spasmodic and did not equal in interest the foreign comment in the local newspapers. Also the departments devoted to reviews of the theater, of music, and of books were uneven in quality — at times they were written with force, at other times they lagged desultorily. By many degrees the most interesting of the weekly departments was the column of local comment called at different periods " Table and Town Talk," " The Bohemian Feuilleton," " Lucubrations," " Things," and " Inigoings." The principal columnists were Bret Harte, Charles H. Webb, Frances Fuller Victor, Ralph Keeler, Prentice Mulford, and, late in the decade, Charles Warren Stoddard.

During the period that Bret Harte was playing a conspicuous part as a Civil War poet, he was serving on the staff of the *Golden Era*, first as a compositor and then as a columnist and general utility writer.

His *Wanderjahre* ended with his return from Union to San Francisco; he was now ready to devote himself to writing in earnest. The stain of ink was on his fingers, the lessons of casual journalism had been absorbed during three years of concocting leaders and fill-ins for a country newspaper, and, with sensitive and intelligent advice, Harte was rapidly slipping into the groove which leads to artistic performance. The *Era* gave him unlimited opportunity to experiment. The files contradict Foard's statement, made long after he left the *Era*, that Harte was " nothing but a poor hanger-on," an indifferent compositor, and a contributor of occasional sketches. On the contrary, starting late in April 1860, a steady stream of articles, sketches, short stories, and poems appeared under his pen-name, Bret, while at the same time he wrote " Town and Table Talk," later titled " The Bohemian Feuilleton," under the names of The Bohemian, Jefferson Brick, J. Keyser, and Alexis Puffer.

Harte's work as a columnist for the *Era* was unimportant but shows steady improvement in writing skill. The early papers were filled with the man-about-town's observations on city life, exhaling the musty odor of Bohemianism from the contents as well as the title of the department. Thus he squeezed the juice over-vigorously from such topics as the Bohemian comments on Sunday in San Francisco, on Russ Gardens; the Bohemian " does " the agricultural thing, the cheap shows; the Bohemian discourses on muscles, on " ferocious wild beasts," and on female gymnastics. He lingered over the forlorn condition of the Plaza as well as the smiles of the flirtatious damsels at the fair. He wrote whimsically on the question of whether short dogs oscillated their tails more rapidly than long ones.

Not all of the Bohemian's contributions were idle chatter or weak burlesque, however. Harte was learning how to write a very acceptable brand of informal essay, and as experience brought self-confidence in his work as a columnist, he gained effectiveness if not vitality. His " Bohemian Papers," later included in *The Luck of Roaring Camp and Other Sketches,* are the pick of the lot. In them his defense of John Chinaman forecasts his pleas for the social outcast in many a story, and his account of Boonder, a dog who was killed because of his conservative dislike of progress in the form of street-cars, is told with the genuine charm that accompanies all of his sketches of pets and children. Finally, his growing interest in local color is reflected in his realistic portrait of the decayed Mission Dolores, with " its ragged senility contrasting with the smart spring sunshine, its two gouty pillars with the plaster dropping away like tattered bandages, its rayless windows, its crumbling entrances, and the leper spots on its whitewashed wall eating through the dark adobe."

The score of short stories which Harte wrote during his first year on the *Era* range from the insipid " My Metamorphosis " to the forceful " M'liss," published in four parts under the original title of " The Work on Red Mountain " late in 1860. When he told a yarn about a youth who, when approached by tittering damsels while bathing naked, escaped detection by pretending to be a Greek statue, Harte could not be worse. When he portrayed pioneer life in Smith's Pocket, alternating with consummate skill between humor and pathos, Harte could hardly be bettered. In " M'liss " he sensed for the first time the value of the observations he had made in the mining country, and as a result he wrote better than he had ever done before. The effectiveness of the story lay in the vivid descriptions of the Sierra foothills and the mining society, the touches of humor, such as Melissa Smith's farewell note to her master, and the moments of pathos — acceptable if you are in the mood of the narrative — in such passages as that which tells of the suicide of M'liss's father, old drunken Smith, whose rich lead had turned out to be a shallow pocket. And not a small excellence of " M'liss " is that it ended without the traditional sacrifice which fixed itself like a leech on the Harte method after the success of " The Luck of Roaring Camp."

In the best of these early sketches Harte worked with the touch of a genuine artist. Portions of " Notes by Field and Flood," of " High Water Mark," of " A Night at Wingdam " make the reader aware of an excellent reporter working on malleable and very promising material. If he could only learn to picture the life around him and forget his books. If he could only refrain from bringing in a reference to Homer or Bucephalus when he is talking about a society of flannel-shirted miners washing a living from the red earth. And, above all, if he could only let himself go, and be natural. Even in these early sketches, in addition to the gingerbread, the musty bookishness, the too deliberate squeezing of the tear gland or tickling of the ribs, there is a restraint bred of an excess of self-consciousness. It accounts for the patronizing tone which mars his portraits of both honest miner and kind-hearted whore, and which finds its most distasteful expression in his introductions to *Outcroppings* and to the *Luck* volume, where he runs himself down almost as if he expected the reader to come to his defense.

One is tempted to make theories, to look for the literary blight deep within the root of personality. Harte's meticulous carefulness as a writer was a proverb among his acquaintances. G. B. Densmore remembered with despair that his co-worker wrote and rewrote a few pages while he was dashing off a novel, and yet when Densmore was done, he had nothing but vapidity, while Harte had a pruned and finished product. Another friend said that Harte once filled an entire wastebasket in his efforts to achieve just the right answer to an invitation. Add to these the reports of Harte's taciturnity during evening parties at San Rafael and of his dainty aloofness, his cordiality without warmth, with which he greeted men like Mark Twain and Prentice Mulford. One cannot make the charge that Harte missed the significance of the scene around him; rather, he was the first of Western writers to sense its possibilities. What one does regret is that ever hampering sense of cautiousness, that overdeveloped critical attitude which put fetters on his feelings as well as his writing. Bret Harte at the very beginning of his career showed that he was a victim of a fastidious critical faculty and did not have the creative urge to break it down. He did not trust himself to feel deeply.

Harte's inhibitions are magnified by comparing his early journalism with that of Mark Twain. Mark Twain pruned not at all, but said what he had to say and, as a result, frequently said it very badly. He cursed when he felt like cursing, and he raved when he wanted to rave. Bret Harte felt the gloved hand of his restraining angel constantly on his shoulder, reminding him that his fellow writers were second-rate, telling him that his own efforts were full of crudities. Moreover, the two men laughed in a very different way. While Mark Twain burlesqued the world and himself, he had a jolly good time doing it. The world was a joke, sometimes a tragic joke, but Mark Twain was never little about it. Harte did his more effective humorous work when he satirized the methods of other writers in his " Condensed Novels."

It is not surprising to find that Harte, even during his early twenties, was feeling gingerly for the safety-rope. As he worked diligently on achieving form, on bettering the phrase and improving the tint, he fell under the kindly patronage of Jessie Benton Frémont. She took him under her wing, read his manuscripts, directed him wisely to look for subjects in his immediate environment, and, at the same time, encouraged him to clothe his stories in the diction of yesterday, and of what one should read in the most polite circles. Financially she was his guardian angel; spiritually she was no more than another voice from an orthodox world. She realized that a writer could not do the proper amount of revision and live on what Colonel Lawrence had to offer his contributors. So, *dea ex machina*, she arranged before she left for Washington to have her protégé taken care of by getting him a job in the Surveyor General's office in San Francisco. When Bret Harte was relieved from the deadly task of journalism, he devoted himself on the one hand to writing for the *Atlantic Monthly* an Irvingesque legend about seeing the devil on Mount Diablo and on the other to composing poems on state occasions for Starr King and his Sanitary Commission.

Harte had in the meantime assumed responsibilities which

made him more dependent than ever on a regular salary. In Starr King's choir was a young lady five years Harte's senior who sang sweetly and managed some way or other to lead the erstwhile Bohemian to the altar in 1862. With added responsibilities, Harte again took up his writing for the *Golden Era*, after being absent from its columns for a year. His chit-chat came now to reflect the disadvantages of an uncultured neighborhood, the difficulty of growing anything but hollyhocks in the garden, and the adventures of a youthful vagabond named Melons, viewed sardonically (but a bit wistfully). The " Condensed Novels " were inaugurated effectively with a take-off on Victor Hugo titled " Fantine." And, at the request of Colonel Lawrence, " The Work on Red Mountain " was rewritten, lengthened, and changed in title to " M'liss."

In the fall of '63 Bret Harte succumbed to the promptings of his marital and paternal instincts (or obligations) and took a job in the Mint which would keep a married genius in funds. At the same time he turned his back on the *Golden Era*, which he had concluded was a journal too provincial and not sufficiently cultured to suit his taste, and joined with C. H. Webb in founding the *Californian*. The *Californian* was planned to appeal to the sophisticated taste of a more mature San Francisco, and was, as we shall see, to neglect the portrayal of the rough and smelly frontier almost entirely.

Bret Harte, however, could not become a genuine Bohemian simply by changing the name of his column to the " Bohemian Feuilleton." He did not have the temperament to become the San Francisco representative of a cult that specialized in literary hoaxes, vitriolic criticism, and loose living. He was not the man to carry out the tradition " of making taverns into rendezvous of arts, and of dying drunk and delirious in a gutter, an attic, or the back room of a saloon." Harte lived comfortably in a suburban flat instead of starving in an attic; he obeyed a conventional wife instead of keeping a tubercular mistress; he put new wallpaper on the front room of his house instead of painting the town red. Not until Charles Henry Webb arrived in town on April 20, 1863, was there in the West a *bona fide* representative of the Bohemianism which had created such a furore in the East.

Though of a mild variety, Webb possessed many of the attributes of the true Bohemian. He had the essential romantic background, for in his youth he had run away to sea and had spent four years whaling in the South Seas and in the Arctic. Moreover, he liked the ladies, and, with his red hair, heavy mustache, and slight lisp he managed to make them like him. Although he was a bachelor and free to live in a garret, he chose the Occidental Hotel, where life was fast rather than fretful. Finally, Webb came direct from the headquarters of America's Bohemia; he was a Pfaffian and a contributor to the *Saturday Press* and *Vanity Fair*. The Pfaffians had earned their name by gathering nightly in New York at Herr Pfaff's tavern, below the sidewalks of 653 Broadway, where they found good company, literary ideas, and the flavor of the Bohemianism introduced in Paris a decade before by Henry Murger.

After giving up whaling for journalism, Webb wrote a column titled " Minor Topics " for the New York *Times*. Gifted in punning and the spawning of quite passable light verse, he found no great difficulty in reaching the pages of Clapp's *Saturday Press* and Artemus Ward's *Vanity Fair*. His conviviality and his conversational ability — made more effective by the tantalizing impediment in his speech — stood him in good stead in the gatherings at Pfaff's. The war, which broke up the Pfaffian coterie, found him lukewarm for conflict; a period of observation as a journalist at the front did not add to his liking, and he was glad to come to San Francisco as a correspondent for the New York *Times*. He also served as literary editor for the San Francisco *Evening Bulletin*, and he joined the staff of the *Era* at a salary which exceeded any previously paid by that journal. Under his writing names of Inigo and John Paul (was there a predilection for Jones in his blood?) he soon became one of the most popular journalists on the west coast.

Webb's department in the *Golden Era* called " Things " was, for consistent performance, the best column to appear in that journal in the sixties. He early conceived the idea of writing his column as a letter addressed to various leading men in the city, judiciously mixing his wit with a good amount of civic advice. One week he chatted with General Wright, military commander of the West, about the low nature of the shows at the Melodian; another week he addressed Bishop Kip of the Episcopal Church, touching lightly on the condition of the Chinese white slaves in San Francisco; again, he wrote intimately to Manager Leland of the Occidental Hotel, pointing out that though Adam Smith defined man as the only animal who made bargains, San Francisco had two dogs, Bummer and Lazarus, who also fitted the definition, for did they not exchange bones in the market place? Webb was an inveterate punster; he proposed to open a Western epic with the line " arma virumque Washoe "; he told Bishop Kip, in his letter describing Adah Isaac Menken's strip act in *Mazeppa*, that, though Adah was great in her line, " her line is not a clothesline, Bishop," and he referred to Sam Brannan, the local Crœsus, as " a thing of booty and a bore forever."

But Webb was not always light-hearted; his wit frequently turned to satire with an edge that knew no blunting. His attacks were the result of an irritable disposition rather than a social conscience, however, and usually he wrote in the vein of the orthodox Western humorist, easing his mind on the " puffers " only when he received notice of another assessment on his mining stock. For Webb, like other Western journalists, used the money made with his pen to speculate in mine holdings. His specialty was Mexican mining. In the good company of Judge Stephen J. Field and a number of other notable gentlemen he helped to support what he called the Humbuggio Mining Company and El Tigre Colorado of Sonora and Sinaloa. Their silver and gold remained in the mountain (there was no doubt about its being there) while he sank ten thousand dollars in assessments without returns. But such is nearly always the fate of Bohemians, whose goddess jealously guards them from the conventionalizing effect of great wealth.

Much of the routine writing for the *Era* was done by women. Apparently the women of California, not too busy with family duties to neglect the arts, were more conscious than the men of the value of decorating the frontier with home-grown flowers. H. H. Bancroft has stated rather scornfully that the many busybody women who wrote poetry or described dresses or even wrote novels in the sixties were by nature second-raters who might better have employed their time in looking after their husbands. Although his strictures are partially justified, the feminine journalism of the frontier was no worse than that produced today by the itch to " create " among penwomen and members of culture clubs. In the midst of the effusions of sappy poets and gushy columnists one runs into the firmer works of an Ina or a Florence Fane.

West-coast lady novelists followed the school of Mrs. Henry Wood and May E. Braddon in producing a good deal of sensational trash: " The Heiress' Revenge " by Alice Mason, " The Fortunes of Pop Donovan " by Margaret Hosmer, and " Minnie Hall's Envy " by Mary Morris Kirke reveal their natures in their titles. The poetesses were even more prolific than the sensation novelists, but they wrote the most conventional of verses. Similarly uninspired were the columns on dressmaking, society, and gossip, written by Occasia Owens, Sally Sorrell, and Diana Doolittle; today we do not even know the real names of those who wrote them.

The prose of Hagar, Alice Kingsbury, and May Wentworth was more interesting. These three women had in common not only their work for the *Era* but their decision after a short period of writing to retire from public life into domestic oblivion. Hagar (Janette H. Phelps), she of "the calm eye but passionate nature," sounded loud and clear the call to arms for women; she wrote heated editorials on the EQUALITY OF WOMEN, which evoked scurrilous, sardonic attacks from the men. For a while she answered back and then was silent. Alice Kingsbury was an English actress who came west to look for a long-lost brother; the records do not reveal whether she found the brother, but they do note the fact that she made a decided hit playing the part of Fanchon in *Fanchon and the Cricket* at Maguire's Opera House. She left the stage, however, and for a while devoted herself to conducting a rather "cute" column in the *Era;* she also wrote a book of advice to bachelors and a collection of stories for children entitled *Ho, for Elfland.* In time, children absorbed all the other interests in her life; her creative urge expressed itself in the plastic arts when she modeled lovely cupids from her babies, in maternal lines with the production of a brood of twelve children. May Wentworth (Mary Richardson Newman Doliver) also wrote books for children, using the California scene in her *Fairy Tales from the Gold-lands.* During the sixties she was a most active journalist, writing an interesting column for the *Era* on town topics and spiritualism, and composing many poems as well as editing an anthology, *The Poetry of the Pacific.* Her period of activity appears to have fallen between the loss of her first husband and the appearance of her second.

There was one woman columnist on the *Era*, however, who turned out to be a genuinely able writer and scholar. Frances Fuller Victor came to California with some literary reputation already attained, for, with her sister, Metta Fuller, she had published a book of poems in 1851 which received a good share of critical approval. The two sisters not only printed their poetry together but they married brothers. In spite of their close ties, Metta Fuller Victor and Frances Fuller Victor soon drifted apart, both in place of residence and in nature of writing. Metta remained in the East to write lurid fiction for Beadle's dime novels, including such titles as *Who Owned the Jewels? Born to Betray*, and *Parke Madison; or Fashion the Father of Intemperance, as shown in the life of the Senator's son*. Frances came to California and eventually became the " Clio of the Northwest "; Ella Sterling Cummins summed up her career by saying that she did " some of the strongest work in historical research yet attempted by any woman writer."

When her husband, a naval engineer, was assigned to San Francisco in 1863, Frances Fuller Victor experienced no difficulty in finding literary pursuits in her new home; she was soon writing city editorials for the *Evening Herald* and poems, short stories, and a weekly column for the *Golden Era*. Her nom-de-plume on the *Era* was Florence Fane, and her column covered a multitude of subjects, from society comments to book reviews. Never slipshod or careless, in her reporting of the news of the week she sometimes reflected the ability at observation which is to be found in a few of her short stories and in most of her historical studies.

After two years in San Francisco her husband was transferred to Oregon, and the *Era* lost one of its best columnists. Oregon, however, gained a historian. Entranced with the terrain and the people, she set herself the task of telling their story. Her volume on Joe Meek persuaded H. H. Bancroft that he needed her on his staff, and as a result she became an important cog in the remarkable machine that produced the Bancroft histories.

One evening in the spring of 1864 Charlie Stoddard proudly escorted Ada Clare, " the Queen of Bohemia," recently arrived from Pfaff's in New York, to a charity ball. The outstanding attraction of the evening was the dancing of a dapper young man with a head a little too large for his slender wiry body — a nervous, pale young fellow with dark eyes, longish brown hair, and neat mutton-chop whiskers. In the cotillion he tripped among the dancers as airily as a puff of thistle-down, and occasionally gave a toss of the toe that must inevitably have dislocated the halo of his partner, had she worn one. The petite Ada's insistence that she meet the agile dancer brought her an immediate introduction to Professor Ralph Keeler, teacher of languages in a fashionable private school on Rincon Hill. Conversation revealed that Keeler was two things dear to all Bohemians — a genuine vagabond and an actor.

Keeler's vagabond days had begun at ten, when, after running away from his guardians — his parents had long since died — he had got a job as a pantry boy on a Great Lakes steamer. Before he was fifteen he had roamed all over the Middle West, working on boats, on trains, or just bumming it. Then he decided to start a minstrel troupe. He bought a banjo, had pennies screwed on the heels of his boots, and practiced *Jordan* on the former and *Juba* on the latter, until his landlady told him to leave. Just then a stroke of luck came his way. In the cholera-ridden city of Toledo he entered a bar and ordered a drink to fortify him, with the caution: " None of your instant-death kind, either." The urchin's request amused the onlookers, among them Johnny Booker, the famous minstrel, who was getting together a troupe to go on the road. Learning from a friend that Keeler could dance, he tried him out on the spot, hired him, and soon the boy was appearing as the " Juvenile Phenomenon," one of the best-known *Juba* dancers among the minstrels that played the Midwest.

As troupes went broke even in those days, Keeler's fortunes went up and down with several companies. Finally he joined the Mitchells, who ran two show-boats on the Mississippi and Ohio. The boats traveled together; on one was presented the show in which he did his jig and wench dances, and the other housed a museum of waxworks. He became quite fond of the " stuffed hyena, hilarious alligator, Tam O'Shanter, and the Twelve Apostles," but best of all was the stolid, blue-eyed lady with long black lashes and pink cheeks who had been bought with an odd lot from an old collection at Albany, and, attired in cheap gauze, labeled " The Empress Josephine."

One day, when Keeler was eighteen years old, the *Floating Palace* and the *Raymond* passed a college on the banks of the river. Suddenly it struck the boy that he wanted to be something more than an end-man. He forthwith left the show, and by working his way, borrowing, and skimping he went to college for four years. Then, after in some way acquiring $181 in greenbacks, he sailed third-class to Europe and enrolled in the famous Prince Rupert University at Heidelberg. This incredibly small sum, augmented with a scant hundred dollars earned by writing for newspapers, supported him during two years of education in Germany, tramps barefoot into Austria, France, and Italy, and passage home. His vagabond education, which had made him a fair master of five languages, had backed up the ambition which, in his twenty-fourth year, brought him to San Francisco to teach languages, write for the *Golden Era*, work on a novel, and dance with Ada Clare. She found him as interesting as anyone she had known back at Pfaff's — except Walt Whitman.

Writing under the nom-de-plume of Alloquiz, Keeler served for two years, from 1864 to 1866, as columnist for the *Golden Era*, furnishing comment, gossip, and occasionally narrative for the weekly issues. His " Lucubrations " were expressed in a quiet, easy style with a genial facetiousness that kept them amusing if not impressive. The reader was soon aware that Alloquiz had been to Germany, for on every possible opportunity he disseminated the culture of the Rhineland.

Also he made the customary rounds of fairs, theaters, museums, and beer-gardens in San Francisco, writing them up with copious dashes of Western humor. After sleeping with a judge at his boarding-house, he wrote vulgar descriptions of Gargantuan snoring; he vividly described how he suffered under two hundred pounds of judicial bulk. When in a beer-cellar on the Barbary coast a fleshy siren singled him out and wailed: " Come rest on this bosom, my own stricken deer," he reconnoitered and found it large enough for several beside himself — in fact, for a small herd of deer.

He also wrote a number of short stories for the *Era*. Western readers have always called for horror yarns full of brutality and gruesomeness; Ambrose Bierce's tales followed a long line of blood-curdlers. Keeler wrote a fairly good one in which a surgeon discovered that the beautiful young lady he was about to dissect was not a cold-blooded corpse but a warm-blooded heroine. " The trance-dead raised herself slowly up, and gently sank into the open arms of Claudsley, as if she had long been his." In fantastic satire, a type of writing common in Western journalism, he took his readers to Bohemia in a dream. The men were all ink-bottles, with stopples terminating in Tyrolese hats, arms and legs colossal pens with holders, and faces dexterously contrived out of large pairs of scissors astride rolls of commercial note-paper used for noses. The long-waisted women wore blue paper stockings and waterfalls of curled proof-sheets, scented with vinegar. When the Bohemians held a dinner for him — at his own expense — he discovered that they were cannibals, living off each other. This type of sketch was always well liked on the frontier.

Keeler supplemented his *Era* earnings by teaching and lecturing. Of the former we know little except that, as a German Ph.D., he must have ranked high in the educational world; he once presented a learned paper to the teachers' institute advocating the founding of three schools in San Francisco which would give all their instruction in German, French, or Spanish, respectively. Like nearly everyone of literary pretensions in the America of his day he tried his tongue at lecturing — and succeeded passably well. His subjects were " Broken China," " Views Barefooted," and " Three Years as a Minstrel." Bret Harte wrote of one of his lectures : " The pleasant ripple of his narrative only changed when the quieter depths of pathos or sentiment demanded it." How much that sentence tells us of both Keeler and Harte!

Keeler's most cherished ambition, however, was to write the first good California novel. He wrote a novel, but it turned out to be neither good nor distinctively Californian. Strangely, this boy who had seen life, not as a writer looking for stories, but as an orphan thrown headlong into unconventional experiences, produced in *Gloverson and His Silent Partners* such a dull, orthodox book that it fell from the hands of the publishers with a thud that would have chilled any less enthusiastic heart than his.

For his dish Keeler mixed the oldest and most insipid of ingredients — a conventional hero and heroine for romance, a dastardly villain for trouble-making, a man-chasing old maid for comic relief, an early-dying philosophic student for pathos — all stirred up in a plot that did not jell. When done, there was nothing but the names of San Francisco streets and an oc-

casional glimpse of scenery to make the novel Western. He had
failed, as a number of others had failed, to catch the significance
of the Pacific frontier.

Colonel Lawrence was about to give up his editorship of the
Golden Era and retire to his boyhood home on Long Island,
where, with the twelve thousand dollars he had saved up, he intended to buy an old homestead and spend his remaining years
presiding over the S.P.C.A., entertaining friends, and enjoying his mellow meerschaum and cold tea with a spike in it. For
nearly six years he had been the genial host to the local writers
and distinguished visitors who had made the *Era* offices their
club and the Miner's Rest their rendezvous. Before his departure, however, Lawrence added one more interesting writer to
his staff. As a climax to his series of columnists, which had included a printer's devil, a New York wit, an Ohio poetess, and a
vagabond Ph.D., he needed a genuine miner. This he found
in Prentice Mulford, ex-sailor-cook-miner-pedagogue-politi-
cian, who was now the writer known throughout the state as
Diogenes of the Tuolumne.

During the five years that Prentice Mulford, wanderer from
Sag Harbor, had spent in the hills since the day he gave up
pocket mining, he had continued to look for a job for which he
was fitted. During two of those years he taught school at Jim-
town, having qualified himself for the position by spelling
" cat " and " rat " to the satisfaction of a friend who was chairman of the school-board. He soon found that keeping order
among sixty children of all ages, cooped up summer and winter
in a hot little church with a tin roof, was even more arduous
than swinging a pick. He obtained some relaxation by partak-
ing in practical jokes in the spirit of E Clampus Vitus, the burlesque lodge of the Mother Lode country. In this company he
learned to be a past master at the tall story and the thin-spun

MARK TWAIN AS A YOUNG MAN.

Courtesy of California State Library

JOAQUIN MILLER IN 1863,
When he was editing the Eugene City *Review*.
Courtesy of Miss Pherne Miller

yarn. Abandoning pedagogy, he succumbed to the copper fever and unsuccessfully prospected the Sierra from Sonora to Mono Lake; then, after a spell at digging post-holes, he got up a humorous lecture which he delivered in the camps near Sonora, taking up little but buttons in the collection plate; and finally he ran for the state assembly.

Mulford confessed after the campaign that he ran for office not for his country's good, but for his own good. But he so startled the convention by deliberately speaking nonsense instead of " making the eagle scream " that he won the nomination; to make up for it, he lost the election because, under the influence of liquor, he declared that he favored more and cheaper money, when his party was opposed to greenbacks. Perhaps the voters mistrusted the candidate who could write thus of the politician: " What a glorious land of liberty is this! See in the clear azure sky above us, floating a mere speck, the eagle, the bird of freedom! He poises himself for a swoop. He comes rushing down on quivering pinion. Nearer! Nearer! It is a turkey buzzard, who has scented a dead horse! "

It looked as if Mulford would have to fall back on writing in spite of himself. It was some time ago that the community drunk which started his literary career had been consummated. Along with the rest of the miners, he had celebrated the first fall rains with abandon. The morning after, as he sat beside the swollen stream, watching the sluice-boxes wash down the valley, he was moved to put his feelings on paper. His graphic description of the hangover, published in the Sonora *Union-Democrat* under the nom-de-plume of Dogberry, scored a success among his fellow debauchees. Many another sketch followed, and his writing became known in the other mining camps and in San Francisco. When Joe Lawrence, always on the look-out for new talents, wrote to ask if he would join the *Era*, he packed his suitcase and was in the city in no time. Lawrence gave him the welcome of a fellow Long Islander, lodged him in the Occidental Hotel, and told him to tell the public what he had seen of the " elephant."

Dogberry soon justified the confidence Lawrence had placed in him. His articles on his experiences appealed because they were both accurate and funny. Not many miners had literary ability, but Prentice Mulford in his own field showed that he could write as well as anyone on the coast. He wrote detailed sketches describing mining methods from panning to crevassing. He told of cooking in the mines, tracing the art from the pork-and-bean era, through the canned-oyster years when " canned oysters were as destructive as cannister shot, for they penetrated everywhere," to the advanced stage of saleratus bread and salt-pork mince pie. He gave his harrowing experiences with a literary cook who never washed the dishes; a combustible cook who broke everything in sight; an abstracted cook — " an unfeathered ostrich " — and a fussy cook who tried to make him chop hash on a flat board with a hatchet.

In addition to his autobiographical sketches, he wrote a series of " Compressed Novels," most of which were burlesques on mining life. Barney McBriar kept a private graveyard in which he buried recalcitrant school-teachers after blowing their heads off without warning; Peleg Cowcopper brought his Patent Integral Gold Separator to the mines and panned gold to keep it going; the Murdered Maid of the Continental Brigade died of seasickness as she rounded the Horn in a ship-load of girls imported as wives for Western miners. The last compressed novel was aimed at Mercer's celebrated venture in supplying damsels for the webfeet in Oregon, and it ended with Dogberry's only attempt at poetry:

> The retched maiden was dead.
> They wrapped her in a sail,

> While to her toes they tied some lead
> And chucked her to a shark.

With Ada Clare furnishing the sophisticated touch and Prentice Mulford the indigenous strain, Colonel Lawrence felt that he was leaving the *Era* in safe hands. Accordingly, in the spring of 1866, he left for home by way of Nicaragua, having piloted the most interesting of Western journals through its most illustrious days.

CHAPTER VI

VISITORS

WHEN Joaquin Miller came from the wilds to San Francisco in 1863 with plans to break into print, he discovered that the *Golden Era* office was the heart of the literary activity in the city. He was impressed by the luxuriousness of the *Era* rooms, "the most gaudily carpeted and most gorgeously furnished that I had then seen," the cordiality of editor Joe Lawrence, and most of all by the distinguished company that was associated with the journal. A decade later, when he had become famous himself, he looked through his notebooks and found that during his short stay in the city he had recorded seeing in Lawrence's office Adah Isaacs Menken, Orpheus C. Kerr, Prentice Mulford, Bret Harte, Mark Twain, Charles Warren Stoddard, Fitzhugh Ludlow, Artemus Ward, and Albert Bierstadt.

Miller's list of names reads like a roster of local writers and notable visitors to San Francisco in the early sixties and bears witness to the effectiveness of Colonel Lawrence's policy of persuading talented travelers to contribute to the *Era* during their visits to the coast. Particularly during the year 1863 did Lawrence bag some remarkable talent for his paper, making up in a way for lost opportunities. For had not Sir Richard Burton been allowed to *flâner* about the streets of San Francisco for nearly two weeks without being persuaded to lecture on " Meccah or El Medinah " or to write a note for the *Era* on his impressions of the West? After his arrival direct from Salt Lake City, big with a book on the Mormons, the illustrious translator of the *Arabian Nights* and the world's most accomplished traveler was permitted to sail through the Golden Gate with the impression that the most interesting sight in California was the miserable village of Benicia, home of Benicia Boy Heenan, world champion boxer. Likewise Theodore Winthrop, Connecticut novelist and essayist, remained silent in San Francisco before going north to write *The Canoe and the Saddle* about Oregon and Washington Territory. Even Joseph G. Baldwin, author of the famous *Flush Times of Alabama,* had failed to contribute to Western letters, although he not only visited California but settled down to finish his career in San Francisco and Nevada. Unfortunately the *Flush Times of California and Nevada* which he projected never materialized.

During a notable year Joaquin Miller and his wife, whose writing name was Minnie Myrtle, came down from Oregon; Mark Twain, the Washoe Giant, roared into town from Virginia City; Albert Bierstadt and Fitzhugh Ludlow, the period's best-known landscape painter and hasheesh-eater respectively, came across the plains and departed for the isthmus by steamer; Adah Isaacs Menken and her husband, Orpheus C. Kerr, kept the town by its ears for several months; Artemus Ward, accompanied by his clever agent, A. P. Hingston, lectured on the *Babes in the Woods* to full houses; and Ada Clare, Queen of Bohemia, heralded as the wittiest of American journalists, fluttered into the city planning literary and dramatic triumphs. To Lawrence's credit it may be said that he captured them all. His office was their headquarters, and the *Golden Era* their mouthpiece.

Joaquin Miller and Minnie Myrtle came to San Francisco on their honeymoon, but they hoped to earn enough writing sketches and poems to remain indefinitely. The nervous young man with yellow hair, blue eyes, and clean-shaven face was as diffident in the city as the tall girl with the dark eyes and unruly long hair whom he had brought down from Cape Blanco. They counted on romantic love and ambition, however, to make up for lack of funds and reputation.

A year before, " Minnie Myrtle " Dyer had been living with her aged father, a fisherman, near Port Orford, on the tree-fringed, rocky coast of southern Oregon. One of the few girls in the settlement, she had led a simple rustic childhood, finding diversion in such tomboy pursuits as ferrying travelers across the " little lisping river that ran between the ocean and the house." Restlessness came with adolescence, and her world was considerably enlarged one day when she discovered a copy of Lord Byron's poetry in a miner's cabin. After devouring " all the beautiful and naughty things ever written by the great bard," she began to dream of the coming of a brave, worldly-wise hero to take her away from her wilderness. While she waited she composed gushingly sentimental poems, which she sent to various newspapers in Oregon and even as far away as San Francisco, where they were published in the Poet's Corner under the nom-de-plume Minnie Myrtle.

By chance a poem describing the loneliness of the heroine as she watched the waves dashing high against jagged Cape Arago came to the attention of Joaquin Miller when he was helping carry the express in western Idaho. Sensing a kindred spirit, he wrote to the poetess. Flattered at receiving her first fan-mail, even though she could decipher the handwriting only in parts, she replied in unrestrained passages describing the wild country and confessing the yearnings of a turbulent but lonesome heart. The first exchange of letters took place shortly before Joaquin Miller left Idaho and became editor of the *Democrat Register*. While he was writing the subversive editorials mentioned in an earlier chapter, his letters to the Grace Darling of Cape Blanco grew more and more fervid. She became lyrical about the gloomy pines and the moaning cedars, the spotted fishes and the white lagoon; he replied in frenzied numbers, couched in eloquent hieroglyphics; finally she wrote that a delightful, dreamy trail wound over the mountains from Eugene to Port Orford and that if he would come to see her, she would ferry him over the river in her little boat.

What embryo poet and fellow worshipper of Byron could resist such an offer? Certainly not Joaquin Miller, who forthwith mounted his spotted courser (so he called his horse in his poems) and crossed the hills between the Willamette valley and the sea. Minnie was waiting for him with her boat. When he dismounted and swept the ground with his sombrero, she felt the magnitude of the situation, but could think of nothing more poetic to say than to invite him to get in, sit down, and make himself comfortable while she rowed him to her home.

Honeyed words soon followed, and with them a whirlwind romance. During his short visit, they lived in " an atmosphere of poetry," which Miller later described in ecstatic terms:

> He came to fall like a king of the forest
> Caught in the strong storm arms of the wrestler;
> Forgetting his songs, his crags and his mountains,
> And nearly his God in his wild deep passion.

He had arrived on Tuesday; on Sunday they were married. The only disturbing note at the wedding was the remark made by the bride's father to the effect that she might better have married a corpse. The lovers consoled themselves with the thought that fishermen are not supposed to appreciate poets.

The couple stopped in Eugene City long enough to sever connections with the local journal and then, in the spring of '63, proceeded to San Francisco on a coastal steamer. Their high hopes of success in San Francisco journalism were not to be realized, however. During the months they lived in their little house on Folsom near First, they gained neither great fame nor many friends. Although Miller gazed at many famous writers in the *Era* office, he was able to get acquainted only with such second-raters as Kendall and Densmore, who were finding it nearly as hard to get along as he. The honeymooners' bower acquired a faint and somewhat stale aroma of beer, drunk from tin cups in true Bohemian fashion, but the atmosphere, even at its best, suggested wistfulness rather than gaiety.

It is true that the *Golden Era* accepted and published contributions by both the golden-haired Miller (Cincinnatus, Agricola, or Professor Bones in print) and the raven-locked Minnie, but apparently Colonel Lawrence paid nothing for the material. Certainly the items that Miller submitted to the *Golden Era* deserved no pay. Lawrence, used as he was to hayseeds among his trochees, appeared downright scornful of the verse that Miller gave him; he admitted that " Oregon " was " the longest string of rhyme of the coast," but refused to publish it; he said that the poet's rhymes were as suggestively simple as a schoolboy's, and he recommended that their author cease wooing the muses and return to Oregon to grow " taters." Several of Miller's effusions appeared in the Correspondents' Column, accompanied by disparaging remarks, but only two of his poems, those on Vicksburg and Gettysburg, were accorded space in the professional columns of the paper. Judged by his *Era* material, Miller gave no indication of latent talent. It is possible that he did better work in " The Devil's Castle," a serial no longer extant which, according to his statement, appeared in the *Police Gazette* during the fall of '63. Finally, he wrote a

novel at the time which he failed to publish; he said that it put
to sleep an editor who tried to read it.

Though Minnie Myrtle's writing was more acceptable than
her husband's, it belonged to the sort of female journalism
which has no lasting interest for the reader. She wrote a good
number of sentimental short stories with such titles as " The
Stranger's Grave," " May Bell," and " Side by Side." Their
only interest lies in an occasional personal reference, such as her
naïve (or perhaps brazen) remark

> Breathes there a miner with soul so dead
> Who never to himself has said —
> This is my own, my native *Love?*

" There are few, if any, who have resisted the charms of the
dusky natives on the Pacific Coast." These were strange words
to come from the wife of an ex-miner who not only had taken
unto himself a dusky native but had fathered a semi-dusky
child. Less compromising were her hopeful lines:

> We will go ; we will leave the calm and the shore
> For others — and you, and I,
> We will see the world in its lights and shades
> Before it is time to die,
>   Dear Ned,
> Before it is time to die.

If one could feel pathos in doggerel, one would find it there,
for shortly after these lines were written not only were Joaquin
Miller and Minnie Myrtle forced to give up their ambitious
plans to make a place for themselves in San Francisco, but
their romance came to an end. The story of their separation as
told by the deserted bride was that Miller returned her to her
parents at Cape Blanco with the words: " A man never becomes
famous until he leaves his wife, or does something atrocious to
bring himself into notice; and besides, literary men never get

along well with their wives. Lord Byron separated from his wife, and some of my friends think I am a second Lord Byron. Farewell." And in no time he was off over the mountains, across the Willamette, and on into the wind-swept plains of eastern Oregon. He went back to the wilderness he loved, temporarily abandoning both wife and civilization with the parting gesture:

> Gay Frisco! To one who was reared in the mountains,
> Your beauties are dim and your pleasures are spare;
> Though maybe to those who are born in commotion,
> My forests were ever as irksome and bare;
> Yet a day with my mountains and billows and fountains,
> Were dearer to me than a century there.

Although Mark Twain had existed for only four months, having been Samuel Clemens for twenty-seven years but Mark Twain only since February 1863, he was by no means a stranger in San Francisco during his short visit to the bay city. As he strolled down Montgomery Street, he felt that he knew half of the people he passed; "it is just like being in Main street in Hannibal and meeting the old familiar faces," he wrote his mother. He felt grand — a man of importance; not since he had been a pilot on the Mississippi had he been so confident that he amounted to something. Many of the men who waved him a greeting were citizens of Washoe, in town for the moment; they recognized at once the slight figure and noble head with its mop of auburn hair, the keen gray eyes, the delicate hands and feet, the half-skipping, half-shambling gait. They pointed him out to their friends who knew him only by name. He was a man to watch. Yes, he was the chap who had caused a sensation with his scientific description of the petrified man thumbing his nose at posterity. He was the only man in the West who could sub for Dan de Quille for a winter and beat that inimitable humorist at his own game. "I fare like a prince wherever I go, be it on this side of the mountains or on the other," he crowed.

He and his friend " Unreliable " Rice were spending a well-earned vacation at the Lick House. They dined; they drank; they stayed out late. They went across the bay to the rustic village called Oakland; they saw the emu at the Willows and the cassowary at North Beach; they drove out to the Cliff House to watch the sea-lions and listen to the surf. As a matter of fact, they spent very little time at the Lick House — but enough to swear at the chambermaids who did everything wrong and the children who played in the halls of early mornings. The good-natured grumblings were later to appear in sketches for the *Territorial Enterprise* and the *Golden Era.*

Like all good times, the vacation soon ended and Mark Twain went back to work over the mountain. The summer would pass rapidly and then perhaps he would be looking for a new job, as Dan de Quille would be back to take over his column in September. A bad cold forced a lay-off, a trip to Lake Tahoe, a sojourn at Steamboat Springs to steam out, and the idea for an article on amusing ways to cure a cold. Late in August he was back in San Francisco reporting on prize fights and politics. These trips to the city were becoming more frequent — before Mark Twain left the West he figured he had made the Sierra crossing thirteen times, which qualified him as a commuter. During his August visit Joseph Lawrence approached him with the suggestion that he write some squibs for the *Golden Era.*

Colonel Lawrence chose a good moment to get Mark Twain to write for his journal. Not only did the close connection between the *Era* and the *Territorial Enterprise* make easy the borrowing of the humorist for the moment, but, now that Dan de Quille was returning, Mark Twain might be persuaded to remain in the city. At the same time Dan would continue his amusing column from Virginia City for the *Era.* It had already been heralded by his first report of his visit to the

States. In " Petrified, or the Stewed Chicken Monster," he warned his readers that months of home cooking had turned him into " a stewed chicken ghoul — a crab-apple sauce monster." There followed a characteristic de Quille fantasy with lurid pictures of a Washoe mine dug in a hill of chicken and gravy; of shafts cut through stuffing insecurely timbered with chicken bones; of a petrified giant discovered in a drift of cranberry sauce. No one could better Dan at that sort of orgy. A few days later he disembarked in San Francisco, and, after a round of drinks with Mark Twain, he went on up to Virginia City, where he announced that with his return the moral tone of the local column would be greatly improved. It was the first shot of a friendly and side-splitting war that was to be a tradition on the Comstock for years to come.

Lawrence's plans failed partially to materialize, for the *Territorial Enterprise* was not willing to give Mark Twain up and the humorist wanted another year to make his fortune in the silver town. He explained: " No paper in the United States can afford to pay me what my place on the ' Enterprise ' is worth. If I were not naturally a lazy, idle, good-for-nothing vagabond, I could make it pay me $20,000 a year." But during his visit to San Francisco he made arrangements with the *Era* to send in an occasional article; the evidence indicates that he also came to an agreement with the *Morning Call* to become their Washoe correspondent during the winter.

Most of Mark Twain's articles for the *Era* were burlesques of types of contemporary journalism. Robust, sometimes coarse, always expressive, they followed a formula old on the frontier and well suited to Mark Twain's love of epithet and his skill in *reductio ad absurdum*. For instance, fulsome society reviews that appeared in the local press after each important ball were a perfect set-up for travesty. After the Lick House Ball, the Pioneers' Ball, the Russian Ball, fair critics such as Occasia

Owen and Sally Sorrell tried to say something nice about every-one present. "Mrs. Hon. F. F. L— wore a dark pink silk beautifully and tastefully trimmed with black lace; the ar-rangement of her hair was faultless, and the ornament neat and *àpropos.* She was beautiful and captivating . . . the 'fairest of the fair.' Miss F—d was dressed in a plain sky blue silk. She danced as gracefully and seemed as charming as ever. Mrs. F. J—n looked exquisitely. Her dress was a light pink *moiré antique;* hair artistically arranged in puffs." Mark Twain could not pass such an opportunity. He duplicated the tone of the original, making up his own initials and dashes (which fre-quently contained personal hits), introducing absurd " foreign expressions," and describing weird hairdresses and gowns. Though the method grew tedious after a few paragraphs, an occasional neat phrase strikes the fancy even today; such are the " tasteful tarantula done in jet " and the " gorgeous bou-quet of real sage-brush imported from Washoe " which rested proudly on Mrs. J. B. W.'s bosom.

" How to Cure a Cold " burlesqued the many " home cures " which appeared in the journals. With his knack for invective when cursing a physical irritant, Mark told of following the ad-vice he received while nursing a running nose at Steamboat Springs. He tried warm salt water and " threw up my immor-tal soul "; he drank gin, molasses, and onions and got a breath like a buzzard; he resorted to the sheet-bath, the mustard plas-ter, and many another remedy. Finally whisky at the Lick House cured him. Mark liked this sketch well enough to retain it in his collected works.

A more amusing travesty, however, was " The Great Politi-cal Prize Fight," though he failed to reprint it, probably be-cause of its topical allusions. Here the pugilistic jargon of the day formed the point of departure. While San Francisco gave its enthusiastic though illegal support to the lengthy fights, such journals as the San Francisco *Police Gazette* described them with exuberant metaphor. "Dooney comes up fresh, but bleeding from hash trap and bugle. He strikes out for Chandler, whom he hits heavily on the kisser, but receives it good on the sconce in return." Mark Twain took a hit at both politics and fisticuffs, staging his fight between F. F. Low and Leland Stanford, a retiring Governor and a Governor-elect. He really let himself go in this article. " No sooner did Low realize that the side of his head was crushed in like a dent in a plug hat, than he ' went after ' Stanford in the most desperate manner. With one blow of his fist he mashed his nose so far into his face that a cavity was left in its place the size and shape of an ordinary soup-bowl. It is scarcely necessary to mention that in making room for so much nose, Gov. Stanford's eyes were crowded to such a degree as to cause them ' to bug out ' like a grasshopper's. . . . [Apparently Low got the better of the argument.] He dashed out with his right and stove Stanford's chin clear back even with his ears. Oh, what a horrible sight he was, gasping and reaching after his tobacco, which was away back among his underjaw teeth. . . . [He] sent one of his ponderous fists crashing through his opponent's ribs and in among his vitals, and instantly afterward he hauled out poor Stanford's left lung and smacked him in the face with it. If I ever saw an angry man in my life it was Leland Stanford. He fairly raved. He jumped at his old specialty, Gov. Low's head; he tore it loose from his body and knocked him down with it." So the fight continued for two and a half columns. It scored such a success with the San Franciscans that they named Mark Twain " the Washoe Giant."

One of these early sketches even made its way east and was published by the New York *Sunday Mercury.* " Those Blasted Children " was partly made up of the blasphemous curses hurled at the brats that ran down the halls in the Lick House;

it also contained Mark Twain's deadly remedies for the illnesses of children. At the time of his appearance in the East, Mark Twain was so pleased with this sketch that he planned to use it as the opening number in his first book. Later his Eastern friends decided that it was " scarcely refined in character," which was true. Nevertheless, not only were the travesties the Washoe Giant produced in 1863 good for many a belly-laugh in the West, but their author thoroughly enjoyed writing them. He was feeling his oats.

In the fall of '63 the San Francisco pageant was at its best. The minstrels sang the hit of the day, " Yes, I would the war were over," while men pledged each other at the bar with the cryptic " Thus we cross the Yuba." Special trains carried sports down the peninsula to picnics which turned out to be prize fights, while bulls and bears were fought at Mission San Jose on the Contra Costa shore. Two railroads were started, with the San Francisco and San Jose pushing south to the end of the bay and the Central Pacific puffing seven miles out of Sacramento on the first step of its long journey across the country. The hoax-loving San Franciscans got up an elaborate parade and funeral for the street-dog Lazarus with the same enthusiasm they had displayed for the pony express. Emperor Norton, a gold-seeker who had gone mad and imagined himself ruler of California and Mexico, was accepted as part of the pageant; his royal box was kept ready at the theater and his pronunciamentos were given favored location in the newspapers. Emma Hardinge was drawing huge crowds to her lectures on spiritualism, and Pepper's mechanical ghost at the Opera House was the talk of the town. The war had settled down to a matter of speeches and leading articles; editors turned invective on Thomas Carlyle and " perfidious Albion," accused of favoring the Southern cause, while Starr King led the campaign to raise millions for the Sanitary Fund. The postillion jacket and the hoop skirt, the latter but recently invented to hide the Empress Eugénie's pregnancy, were the latest importations from Paris; the Duke of Cariboo was the most fashionable visitor; and Julia Dean Hayne and Lotta Crabtree were the theatrical sensations of the moment. Then the Genial Showman came to town to add another blotch of color to the spectacle.

Although he was not yet thirty, Artemus Ward was the best-known humorist in the country at the time he spoke his piece in San Francisco. And to a modern reader, Ward (Charles Farrar Browne) was one of the few period humorists who not only deserved their popularity in their own day but still evoke a laugh today. A cub reporter from down East — a true Yankee, born in Maine in 1834 — he was inspired to become a humorist when he read Derby's *Phœnixiana*. The result was a series of letters to the Cleveland *Plain Dealer* from one Artemus Ward, a showman of wax figures and wild animals, who was approaching Cleveland with his exhibit. One of the few humorists ever to use the device of mis-spelling with real effect, he gave substance to his humor by injecting into it Yankee philosophy on social and political events.

The Artemus Ward letters were soon reprinted far and wide; within a year their editor had become the editor of *Vanity Fair*, and in 1862 *Artemus Ward: His Book* was the national rage. Most American schoolboys know that in the autumn of that dark year Abraham Lincoln opened a cabinet meeting by reading from Artemus Ward, after which he presented to his startled listeners the Emancipation Proclamation. When Artemus Ward discovered that he was even more successful as a lecturer than as a writer, he decided to see the West that had nourished John Phœnix and at the same time to obtain material for new books and lectures.

Artemus Ward was not only well known for his writings, but

ARTEMUS WARD AS A PUBLIC LECTURER.

A cartoon from *Vanity Fair* of 1862.

Courtesy of California State Library

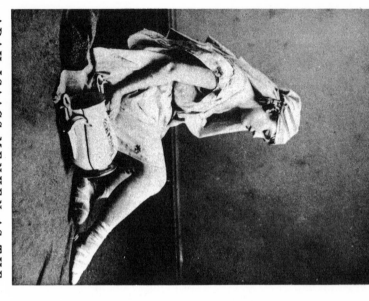

ADAH ISAACS MENKEN AS THE
FRENCH SPY.

Courtesy of California State Library

ADAH ISAACS MENKEN AS
MAZEPPA ON THE "WILD HORSE
OF TARTARY." A contemporary play-bill.

Courtesy of California State Library

his approach as a lecturer was advertised weeks before he sailed
into the Golden Gate. Almost a cliché even then was his reply
to manager Maguire's telegram: " What will you take for forty
nights in California? " with the answer: " Brandy and water."
The *Era* had for some time been reprinting his sketches, and
Webb, who had known him at Pfaff's, heralded the coming of his
fellow Bohemian in his column, assuring the public that " He
is on the wax, you see, not on the wane." Florence Fane wrote
that he was to lecture on " The Southern Cross " under the impression that it was a mulatto. On the other hand, rumor had
it that his subject would be " Robinson Crusoe, born of poor but
respectable parents," or " Brigham Young's Mother-in-Law;
Showing how many there are of her." Any title would do as
well as " Babes in the Wood," but the last turned out to be official.

A fortnight before Artemus Ward was due to arrive, his advance agent and manager, E. P. Hingston, took the town by
storm. It was this enterprising Englishman who had started
Ward on his career as " a moral lecturer," and one would have
to look far to find a more satisfactory impresario. His aggressive personality is still to be met in his account of his experiences
in the West, *The Genial Showman*, which presents an unex-
celled portrait of California in the sixties. He was ready to be
artist or Philistine with equal enthusiasm; on one hand he wrote
his poem " Pictures in Silverland," and on the other he speculated on the advertising value of plastering " Artemus Ward
will Speak his Piece " in great letters on the cliffs above the
Golden Gate.

He laid his plans in a whirlwind of activity. First he called
on the famous Maguire and so impressed the tough-minded
manager that the latter announced that he would close his theater the night Ward spoke at Platt's Hall. Then, told that
Starr King's support would be better than a large poster, he

interviewed the minister at once and came away with his consent
to sit on the platform during Ward's performance. With theater and church support in his pocket, he next tackled society.
He saw to it that Lillie Hitchcock, popular tomboy and pet of
the firemen, who had recently stolen the limelight by riding the
cow-catcher on an engine of the Napa Valley railroad, pledged
her energies to advertising Ward in her own ingenious way.
And last and most important he called on Colonel Lawrence of
the *Golden Era* and made arrangements for Ward's official connection with that journal during his visit.

Hingston's account of the interview gives a typical glimpse
of the *Era* editor and his methods. " The colonel chanced to
be at his desk, and received me very graciously. My mission
was soon executed. The assuring phrase of ' We'll put him
through ' was enough to satisfy me that the cause of Artemus
Ward would be quite safe in his hands. . . . ' You are stopping at the Occidental, are you not? ' he asked. I replied that I
was. ' Then,' said he, ' I'll drop in there late tonight, and take a
drink with you and we'll talk it over.' " Before the bar, the two
planned a campaign to put Ward across. Not only did Lawrence run many of the humorist's writings but, with Hingston,
he concocted an article, combining Ward, Shakespeare (with
the aid of Clarke's *Concordance*), and spiritualism, the current
interest of San Franciscans. The hodgepodge of puns that resulted had little literary value but served as effective advertising.

On the night of November 13th, Platt's Hall was filled to ca-
pacity with an eager audience that had paid $1,624 in gold to
hear Artemus Ward lecture. The crowd was made up of an odd
assortment. Hingston had presented his star in a lecture hall
because he had been told that " the better element " of the city
would not come to hear him in a theater. However, manager
Maguire had expressed the friendship of the theatrical profes-

sion by darkening his house in honor of the visitor. On the one hand there were pious citizens who anticipated moral enlightenment; on the other there were theater-goers who wanted Ward to outdo the end-man at the minstrel show. Also there were farmers and miners in flannel shirts who confidently expected to be amused with wax figures and a menagerie.

A very quiet-looking, faultlessly dressed young man with a prominent nose stepped out upon the bare platform. He was very tall and thin, with a touch of red in his hair and in his heavy, drooping mustache. His long slender hands and soft gentle voice were in keeping with his quiet and subtle technique as a lecturer, and the only suspicion of humor in his face was his mirthful eyes. His lecture was unprecedented; it was humor without any other purpose than to amuse. He didn't even tell what became of the babes in the wood. Instead, for nearly two hours he chatted with his audience, introducing quaint thought, whimsical fancies, bizarre notions, ludicrous anecdotes. Atrocious puns were followed by fits of abstraction, during which he appeared to be miles away. Then he would return to his audience and artlessly and unexpectedly come bang up with another side-splitting remark. He was a born showman; he played on his listeners as a musician plays upon an organ. Webb described his method by saying that it reminded him " of the vein of thought in which a clever man, two-thirds tight, indulges when he sits down with a friend or two to finish the business."

Remarkable as Artemus Ward was, he failed to satisfy some of his listeners because he did not give them what they expected. The next day several of the reviewers felt it necessary to apologize for his lack of moral purpose. San Franciscans were in the habit of expecting a lecture to be an institution to instruct or to elevate the ethical tone of the community. Moreover, Ward had dressed like a gentleman and should therefore have done something besides merely entertain. As Harte put it: " Had Arte-

mus appeared habited as a showman, surrounded by wax figures, even the most captious critic would have been satisfied."
Enough were delighted, however, to make it possible for him to
get a good house for a second lecture, delivered after making a
tour of the mining regions, during which he even sang songs and
hired a brass band to give the natives what they wanted.

Those who were the most deeply impressed were the writing
men of the city. Through both his lecture and his personal contact he stimulated them greatly. They realized that he was producing something indigenous, that, as Webb expressed it, he
was a walking " museum of American humor." Here was a true
home-born product that could be turned into an art. In a long
article for the *Era* Harte pointed out that Ward's strength lay
in " the humor of audacious exaggeration — of perfect lawlessness ; a humor that belongs to the country of boundless prairies,
limitless rivers, and stupendous cataracts." He hailed him as
the American humorist *par excellence*, finding in him " the es-
sence of that fun which overlies the surface of our national life,
which is met in the stage, rail-car, canal and flat boat, which
bursts out over camp-fires and around bar-room stoves." These
were significant words from a young writer whose humor had
too often reflected the books he read rather than the life he saw
around him. Within a few years Harte was to draw from the
raucous life of the mining camp a vitality which had been absent from his early work. Certainly Artemus Ward helped to
show him the right direction.

After Artemus toured the Sierra mines, he moved on over the
mountains to Virginia City, where he spent a fortnight in lecturing and going on sprees with the staff of the *Territorial Enterprise*. The stories of his riotous parties with Goodman, Dan
de Quille, and Mark Twain have been told so often that they
need not be repeated here. Artemus Ward met Mark Twain
just when the latter, after two years of journalism, was begin-

ning to thirst for a wider audience. The visiting humorist's personality, his enthusiasm, and his championing of American humor all made their impression on the Washoe Giant. When Artemus left for Austin and Salt Lake, he carried with him the promise that Mark Twain would send him some of his best articles for publication in the East — a promise that eventually brought valuable results. Also, Mark Twain watched the technique of a humorous lecturer who would be eclipsed in skill only by himself in a later day. Thus the Genial Showman, in his casual visit, left his mark upon Western literature.

One of the most celebrated of the Pfaffians was Fitzhugh Ludlow, author of *The Hasheesh Eater, being passages from the Life of a Pythagorean,* known in his day as the American De Quincey. His short career seemed designed to fit the pattern of the true Bohemian. The son of a Presbyterian minister, he had been seduced in the midst of a theological training by the pagan thrills of hasheesh-eating. By the time he was twenty-one he had shocked and fascinated the country with his baroque account of the sensations and sufferings following the taking of *Cannibis Indica.* The New York Bohemians welcomed him generously, and magazine editors treated him as a boy genius. Though he had produced nothing of consequence during the six years since *The Hasheesh Eater* had appeared, he was still a sensation when he came west in 1863. He and Albert Bierstadt, the noted landscape painter, crossed the plains by stagecoach, taking notes and sketching pictures to be used in a book dealing with the Mormons and the scenery of California and the Northwest.

If San Franciscans expected the hasheesh-eater to be blasé and corrupt, experienced to the point of being dissolute, they were in for a surprise. Instead they met a slight, boyish-looking chap, with quick, bright eyes, who eagerly saw and delighted

in everything about him. If they had read his book carefully,
they should have been prepared to find him sensitive and high-
strung; on the long coach trip he had ridden day and night at
the driver's elbow, not frightened, but too nervous, too keenly
stimulated by the new sights, the new experiences, the new sensations, to sleep — until exhaustion forced him to break his
journey. They should also have anticipated his bookishness.
They found that his retentive mind held a vast store of miscellaneous and recondite knowledge about geology, zoology, botany, history, mineralogy, and literature which he used liberally
in his conversation. He apparently considered himself a missionary for Darwin's *Origin of Species*, which had started its
revolution in modern thought only four years previously. Nor
was his information limited to orthodox fields, for he knew the
abracadabra of astrology, necromancy, and other black arts.
But if they expected any wickedness, they must have been disappointed when he asserted that the sight of two wives of one
Mormon living peacefully together made him blush to his tem-
ples.

In spite of his nervousness and pedantry, Ludlow was a
friendly chap, eager to give Western writers the benefit of his
experience, but in no wise patronizing. Mark Twain wrote
home that the young visitor had encouraged him to do something better than ephemeral journalism; and Charles Warren
Stoddard in his unpublished autobiography wrote gratefully
that Ludlow was the first visitor of note to commend his poetry.
But even better in the eyes of the San Franciscans than his help-
fulness was the fact that he was a good sport, quite able to take
their ragging. They were so amused to have the famous drug-
addict, the De Quincey of America, turn out to be an ingenuous
proselytor for the evolutionary theory that they held a mock
trial in which they accused him of heresy. Ludlow, dressed in
gray flannel breeches and dragoon boots, spectacles on nose and

Darwin under arm, testified in polysyllables to an amazed court and obtained a verdict of acquittal.

Ludlow became one of the *Golden Era* crowd professionally as well as socially, contributing a number of original articles to the weekly, just as his friend Albert Bierstadt designed a new masthead. In his articles Ludlow inveighed against frying steak in lard; he called the epicure a true spiritualist; he raved about " the tender, earnest eyes and lovely, pleading mouth " of La Menken; and he announced that " the candid visitor must regret that the grading of San Francisco seems to have been done by a Giant armed with a fish-slice and a coal-scoop under the influence of Delirium Tremens."

In his " Good-bye Article " of November 22nd, 1863, Ludlow distributed words of cheer to the local writers. As he had known Starr King in the East and had been his guest in San Francisco, he paid him a glowing tribute. Webb he advised to return to Pfaff's, as he feared that his ventures in the stock market had brought not one but a hundred vultures to fatten on his liver. Over Bret Harte's " M'Liss " he was very enthusiastic, commending its author for " beauty of style, unique depth, and sweetness of thought." He praised the poems of Charlie Stoddard, but advised him to drop the ridiculous pen-name Pip Pepperpod. And of Mark Twain he said: " He makes me laugh more than any Californian since poor Derby died. . . . He is a school by himself." He lingered over the medley of " California cleverness, Nevada naivete, and New York naughtiness " which he had noted in the literary gatherings in the *Era* office, but deplored the prevalence of talk about money-making, fearing that in the West property was not yet " stable enough for the safe erection of Art's and Literature's ornamental superstructure."

From San Francisco Ludlow went on horseback and river steamer to Oregon, where, by the Columbia River, he collapsed with a severe case of pneumonia. He returned to California only to bid farewell to his friends and sail out through the Golden Gate, New York bound, late in November 1863. During his fourth months' visit he influenced the isolated community of San Francisco writers in a subtle, pervasive way, entangling himself in the web and woof of Western literary tradition. He was a voice of encouragement from the outside world.

Whether you agree with the old-time actor Walter Leman, who called Adah Isaacs Menken " a rattle-brained, good-natured adventuress," or with Joaquin Miller, who thought she was the most soulful poetess he ever met, you must acknowledge that she created a new high in excitement among both theatergoers and literary men during her year in California. In the light of her influence, Menken cannot easily be labeled or put in a category. Her principal claim to fame lay in putting on the most successful strip act of her day, but she was certainly more than a burlesque dancer with literary pretensions. She held her audience by combining a breath-taking illusion of nudity, though she wore tights and a wispy loin-cloth, with the tricks of a bareback rider and the voice if not the talent of a good actress. Yet, although the press of her day ecstatically declared she was " the most perfectly developed woman in the world," her photographs reveal a form far from classical in proportions. Surely flesh-tights and daring equestrianism were not sufficiently novel to the San Francisco public to account for a tyro with crisp black curls, plump curves, and a pleasing voice changing the course of theatrical offerings in the city for a decade. Apparently Menken had her share of sex appeal; she also most evidently had personality; and, most important in understanding the romantic reaction of the Westerners, she had a past, a soul, and aspirations to be known as a poetess. Thus, to a great measure, she achieved her desire of making an even more lasting impression upon the writers than upon the playgoers.

Because no actress since Lola Montez had made such a stir in San Francisco, comparisons of the careers of the two are inevitable. Lola Montez had been the mistress of a monarch before she came west to dance her spider-dance and marry a miner. Adah Menken, on the other hand, was on her way up; San Francisco was near the crest of a slope which led to love affairs with Swinburne and Dumas and dipped abruptly into poetry and tragic death. Already Menken had taken three husbands, and her current mate, Robert H. Newell, was beginning to strain at the end of his matrimonial tether, yet she posed as a woman with a broken heart.

Perhaps most of her personal sorrow was pretense of the same nature as the literary pretense which made her claim that she had translated the *Iliad* before she was twelve and that convinced her that she had been born to write the great American novel. Histrionic to the core, she turned on ambitions and emotions with equal ease, perhaps deceiving herself even more than she deceived her public. Her habitual indulgence in hysterical emotions is seen in the pictures Miller gives of her throwing herself into the sand at the Cliff House, sobbing: " They are killing me at that old playhouse, and I had to come out here to cry or die "; or of her lying swathed in yellow silk on a tawny hearth-rug, head to the golden fire, pouring forth a tale of disappointed love. And when Harte wrote her into a character in " The Crusade of the Excelsior," he let her die by burning herself out with hysterics and excitements, and by using drugs to subdue them.

Her lack of restraint was largely responsible for the appeal of her poetry, marked by its frankness and emotional surge in a period of cold formality. At her best, she attained lyrical heights inaccessible to her restrained companions. No corset-stays of restricting prosody or conventional hesitation confine the lines of " Resurgam ":

Years and years the songless soul waited to drift out beyond the sea of pain where the shapeless life was wrecked.

The red mouth closed down the breath that was hard and fierce.

The mad pulse beat back the baffled life with a low sob.

And so the stark and naked soul unfolded its wing to the lonely dimness of Death.

A lonely, unknown Death.

A Death that left this dumb, living body its endless mark.

And left these golden billows of hair to drown the whiteness of my bosom.

Whitman, Byron, and the Song of Songs were combined and heated by that temperament to produce page after page of physical and spiritual exhibitionism, sometimes made poignant by the use of themes of pain and regret, frequently rendered interminable by the absence of the black-out. They appeal, as did her beautiful and audaciously draped figure, evoking passion for a moment and then fading into the languid, enervating satiety which Swinburne was to catch in his " Dolores," the ashes of the fire the poetess ignited in him for a brief hour.

Still under the spell of Menken's personality, chroniclers have assumed that she won the hearts of nearly every writing man on the coast, citing Miller, Stoddard, Harte, Webb, Mark Twain, and even Artemus Ward as her victims. Miller possibly succumbed to her lush approach, although his friendship with her may have been just another of his fictions; and Stoddard quite worshipped her with his girlish enthusiasm: " Every curve of her limbs was as appealing as a line in a Persian love song." His interest may have been stimulated by a quality in the actress noted by one reviewer, who said she displayed " an idealized duality of sex, uniting the more delicate and muscular compactness of the masculine frame with the willowy elasticity of the feminine in its finest type." Safely married, Bret Harte left no record in his contemporary journalism of being unduly attracted to Menken, and when he later portrayed her in a short story, he admitted that she was a fine figure in tights, but called her superficial, hysterical, and shameless and referred to her poetry as gush. Webb admired her performance in *Mazeppa* and used her as a subject for some of his best puns: she was a thing of beauty and a boy forever; she rode her horse with nothing on but eye-lashes and hempen-lashes; and her play rested upon a stable basis. Mark Twain, who met her in Virginia City, referred to her as a fellow " literary cuss," but no extolling review by his hand has been discovered. On the other hand, a few months later, when he was presumably writing the unsigned dramatic reviews for the *Call*, the paper carried an indictment of *Mazeppa* as a play. " Let a pure youth witness *Mazeppa* once, and he is pure no longer. . . . Strip the play of the obscene and as a theatrical display it is worse than a Chinese tragedy, wooden shoes, gongs, and all the rest." This was written, however, after Menken had departed and four other Mazeppas had taken her place, including a comedian bound to a fractious mule out at the Mission, and another who pranced across the minstrel stage lashed to a rocking-horse on casters.

For *Mazeppa* was a success only when Menken played the title role, and Menken was a success only in *Mazeppa*. Her repertoire also included *Dick Turpin, Jack Sheppard, The French Spy, Lola Montez*, and *The Three Fast Women*, in the last of which she sustained nine characters, sang five songs, and executed three dances, but she satisfied only in *Mazeppa*. In this melodrama, based loosely on Byron's poem, she could display her charms in the part of the noble Tartar boy, her passion in love scenes with the beautiful Olinska, and her bravado in the duel with the Count. In the climax, fearless and beautiful, she held her audience entranced as she was stripped and lashed helpless to the back of an " untamed steed," which dashed up a zigzag to the very top of the stage and finally disappeared in the sky-borders amidst thunderous applause. The combination of Byron, drama, circus thrill, and nakedness was perfect. Men did not soon forget it.

Menken was so pleased with her reception in the West that she thought for a while of making it her home. She would give up acting and devote herself entirely to literature, continuing her poetry and branching out into journalism and fiction. Each week the *Era* carried one of her free-verse poems, with titles such as " My Spirit Love," " Aspiration," " Working and Waiting," " Saved." In both form and mood they owed much to Walt Whitman, whom Menken had met and admired at Pfaff's Tavern. She not only followed him in writing free verse when free verse was heresy, but she dedicated herself to championing him wherever she went. She preached her gospel in San Francisco, writing a long article for the *Era* explaining Whitman's importance to America. She also confessed her own desire to be known to posterity as a maker of poetry, a hope which was encouraged by the reception of her work in the West and was modestly achieved when her poems were collected and issued in the year of her death in a little volume entitled *Infelicia*.

Menken's literary aspirations may have been partly responsible for her marrying Robert Henry Newell, then a well-known humorist with what appeared to be an assured future. After the election of Lincoln as the first Republican President, Newell started the Orpheus C. Kerr papers, basing his nom-de-plume on the many office-seekers who plagued the new administration. The war increased both the range and the popularity of his writing. Using the devices of Gargantuan exaggeration, gross misspelling, and willful irreverence for solemnity, he alternated humorous thrusts with sentimental lapses and became known as an important social satirist. When, early in her career, Menken was charged with bigamy, Newell befriended her, published some of her poems in his paper, the New York *Sunday Mercury*, and married her after her second husband, the well-known prize-fighter " Benicia Boy " Heenan, deserted her. He hoped that she would give up acting and that the two of them would become great writers together. He came with her to California.

Although he was welcomed by Colonel Lawrence and at once began printing the Orpheus C. Kerr papers in the *Era*, it was soon apparent that he was playing a very insignificant second fiddle to his stellar companion. Though the writers on the coast had prepared to hail Newell as an important addition to their brotherhood, they changed their tune soon after his arrival and offered him, at the best, sympathy ; at the worst, veiled contempt. For one thing, his appearance was against him ; short, homely, " foppish " in his dress and small pomaded mustache, he was colorless and somewhat of a nuisance. In addition the Westerners had little respect for a man who was less important than his wife, who was married to a woman who stripped her body and her soul for them daily. No, they were ready to publish his articles, to acknowledge his love of culture, to call him a gentleman, but they could not accept him as a " regular fellow."

A few months after Orpheus C. Kerr and Adah Isaacs Menken became members of the *Golden Era* group, their queerly assorted menage was augmented by the arrival of Ada Clare, known as the Queen of Bohemia, who, attracted by her friend's success, had come out to try her luck on the Gold Coast.

" Ada Clare," born Jane McElheny, had published ardent poems when she was nineteen, had gained a bizarre reputation by writing frankly on love and its pangs, and had gone to Paris to visit Bohemianism at its fountain-head in the Latin Quarter. There she continued to shock her public by writing home of the pleasures experienced by a twenty-one-year-old girl living

abroad as " a youth without guidance." She returned with an
illegitimate child and a burning desire to establish a Latin
Quarter in New York. Soon she was installed at Pfaff's as the
queen of the coterie, ravishing, literary, and a little sinful.
Whitman sang her praises and young William Dean Howells,
visiting in Manhattan, thought her Pfaff's greatest attraction.
When the Pfaffians were dispersed by the war, she sought new
fields to conquer.

Adah Isaacs Menken and Ada Clare had more in common
than the similarity of their first names. Both were of Southern
birth and of Southern sympathy during the war, both were in
their late twenties when they arrived in the West, and both had
defied convention sufficiently to be at odds with society. Menken's marriages had become a matter of public scandal, while
the unmarried Queen of Bohemia traveled with her boy as " Ada
Clare and Son." In no way ashamed of his presence, she went
out of her way to hint that he was the issue of a love affair with
Louis Moreau Gottschalk, noted as widely for his philandering
as for his ability as a pianist and composer. Finally, both were
ambidextrously creative; whereas Menken dabbled in literature
as a side-line to her acting, Ada Clare nourished a desire to be an
actress to supplement her fame as a writer.

Although, in keeping with their unconventionality, the
charmers both wore short hair, parted at the side, Adah was a
brunette with black, crisp curls, whereas Ada was a blonde, with
fluffy golden locks which in moments of excitement fell charmingly across her eyes. Those eyes were pansy blue and they
were frequently dimmed with a sadness appropriate to a trim
little person with a past. The tip-tilted nose that went with the
eyes made the fluttering pose her best attitude. Adah Menken,
on the other hand, often affected a manly bravado, going in for
riding astride, visiting the saloons, and bucking the tiger with

the boys, while at other times she fell back on deep emotional strain and disillusionment with the world.

A bizarre, histrionic pair they made, as Dan de Quille and Mark Twain discovered one Sunday afternoon in Virginia City during Menken's triumphant invasion of Washoe. The actress threw a party with Ada Clare and the two *Territorial Enterprise* writers as guests. It was more than a bid for publicity, for Menken wished to discuss her proposed novel, and Ada Clare was considering writing a play. In spite of the literary atmosphere the men became more and more bored. Dark, moody Adah and flaxen-haired vivacious Ada did their best to arouse shy Dan de Quille and diamond-in-the-rough Mark Twain. Perhaps they were over-conscious of the deserted husband, Orpheus C. Kerr, who was not invited, wandering up and down the hall and glancing in furtively while the creative ones discussed the future of literature. Eventually, under the stimulus of wine, the foursome shifted from art to music and raised a horrible din which ended with Mark Twain singing his favorite ditty: " There was an old horse and his name was Methusalem." This set Menken's dogs to yapping (de Quille, who described the party, said she had ten), and Mark Twain, in trying to reach one of them under the table, gave Menken a vigorous kick, breaking up the party. Thus ended a famous literary get-to-gether on the Comstock.

Before Ada Clare left San Francisco, she had turned against it, finding its winds " poisonous " and its atmosphere " malarious." Part of her disappointment was due to her failure to please Maguire's audience, when, after months of planning, she at last appeared in *Camille* on December 29th, 1864. She found that the Westerners did not approve of her as an actress, just as she had found that they did not think much of her as a columnist for the *Golden Era*.

Her debacle was not entirely her own fault. The *Era* had caused its public to expect too much from her; it had hailed her as " the fairest and most accomplished lady ever associated with American journalism." Yet there were many who shrugged a shoulder when they read: " We doubt not, that in San Francisco as in New York, the finest minds in the world of *belles lettres* will instinctively yield a chivalrous intellectual allegiance to a throne occupied by genius in its most delicate and charming presentiment." What was the *Golden Era*, erstwhile distributor of rough food to the virile miners, doing with a columnist who was " delicate," " charming," and " piquant "? Is that what imported Bohemianism, imported culture, imported cosmopolitanism were going to do for the frontier?

Ada Clare, as the *Era's* featured columnist, showed her piquancy by remarking that she had expected to find bears in the streets and " miners developing their gold and their babies in the same cradle." She showed her gentility by rebuking Mark Twain for writing " Those Blasted Children," and saying that he was " guilty of misunderstanding God's little people," and by finding the Hawaiians " so exquisitely refined that there is no sibilant in their mother tongue." She expressed her revolt against society by championing the character of Camille against the prudes, and she lent her hand to reform by speaking out in a review of *The Drunkard*, against corruption in high places. " As a whole, I esteem Edward Middleton's to be one of the severest *rolls* in the modern drama. I know of no one with sufficient of ardent spirit, or liquefaction of intellect and emotion to truthfully portray this character, but a certain California Senator at Washington."

Ella Sterling Cummins, in *The Story of the Files*, was not far wrong when she said Ada Clare was notable among *Era* journalists principally for writing: " But, as usual, I am wandering from the subject." Although she doubtless did her best for that

The Californian

"SURELY THERE IS A VEIN FOR THE SILVER AND A PLACE FOR GOLD WHERE THEY FIND IT"

VOL. 1.—NO. 1.   SAN FRANCISCO, MAY 28, 1864.   TERMS: {$5 A YEAR, BY MAIL, IN ADVANCE. {12 CENTS A MONTH, BY CARRIER.

CONTENTS:

NEIGHBORHOODS I HAVE MOVED FROM.

BY A HYPOCHONDRIAC.

A BAY WINDOW once settled the choice of a...

THE BALLAD OF THE EMEU.

O my, have you seen at the Willows so green—
So charming and rurally true—
A singular bird, with a manner absurd,
Which they call the Australian Emeu?
            Have you
            Ever seen this Australian Emeu?

THE COUNTESS DIANA.

[TRANSLATED FROM THE FRENCH OF HARDI MIRAND.]

I.

I HAD a godmother I a guardian—fain had made them...

BIRD'S-EYE VIEW OF SAN FRANCISCO AND BAY
IN 1868.

Courtesy of Society of California Pioneers

SAN FRANCISCO IN 1869.

Courtesy of California State Library

journal, her writing was symptomatic of a disease which was to bring on its decline. Years later, J. Macdonough Foard maintained that the women killed the *Era:* " Yes, they killed it — they literally killed it, with their namby-pamby school-girl trash." There was no doubt that the *Era* was beginning to lose its grip, and not the least of its errors was an attempt to become cosmopolitan by absorbing refinement and piquancy from the East. The visitors from New England and Manhattan were not unalloyed blessings. Ward, Ludlow, and Kerr, Menken and Ada Clare were stimulating, but they brought two dangerous germs with them: they encouraged writers like Bret Harte and Mark Twain to think of escaping to the East and Europe where as pilgrims from the frontier they would make a sensation; and they aided in the process of making Western letters more polite, more refined, and eventually more stereotyped.

CHAPTER VII

☼

POLITE LITERATURE AND GHOSTS

DURING the mid-sixties San Francisco celebrated the winning of the Civil War and mourned the assassination of Lincoln; it was shaken physically by the earthquake of '65 and financially by the panic on the Comstock; it built a stock exchange and inaugurated the Pacific Mail for trade with the Orient. And as the rails crept west from Omaha and climbed east from Sacramento, the end of the frontier came closer day by day.

San Francisco continued to grow in population and wealth in spite of temporary set-backs. When Nevada silver slumped in '64, stocks which had been selling for as high as two thousand dollars became worthless and the entire mining investment in Virginia City fell to an evaluation of only five millions. To balance the decline in mineral output, however, four generous, wet winters followed the pinching droughts of the early sixties, making a major wheat-producing area of the San Joaquin Valley. Merchandise exports swelled to fifteen millions in 1865, to seventeen millions in 1866. In the same year the Comstock Lode again took on life and moved towards a second bonanza. Realtors anticipated the completion of the railroad by selling property at boom prices to the greatest annual influx of newcomers that the city had ever seen.

In keeping with its physical expansion, San Francisco lived high in the sixties, displaying a sophistication that belied its youth and frontier vigor. Many of its most picturesque institutions had given way to metropolitan counterparts. Instead of open gambling around the monte-table or roulette wheel, which had been driven under cover, the new stock market and the fluctuations of Nevada silver provided means for bucking the tiger with bigger sums than had ever been stacked on the green felt. Although gaudy prostitution had been relegated to the back alleys, a fast set of " Washoe widows " kept the town lively. The volunteer fire-companies, with their gay uniforms and hand-drawn engines, crumbled beneath corruption and succumbed to the efficiency of a paid force and the dispatch of spirited horses. As if to compensate for the loss of the drill-teams, the people made much of street characters, encouraging the eccentricities and outlandish garbs of Professor Coombs — " Washington the Second " — the Great Unknown, the American Eagle, the Money King, and, of course, Emperor Norton. And, although the red flannel shirts of the miners were rarely seen, the fashion parade on Montgomery and Kearney streets daily displayed broadcloth and silk hats and dazzling gowns imported from Paris. The women made the most of the current fads; they adorned their heads with " waterfalls " and furnished their hoop skirts with " tilters."

In spite of the prevailing winds, San Franciscans continued to spend much of their time outdoors, driving out the Mission road to Tony Oakes's tavern or over the Pt. Lobos turnpike to the Cliff House in gaily painted barouches, broughams, and landaus, or dancing and drinking beer at the open-air gardens — North Beach with its beer-garden and menagerie, Russ Gardens with its Spanish fiesta, the Willows with its bear-pit and sea-lions, or Woodward's with its artificial lakes and pretentious copies of old masters. In the evening imported opera troupes as well as the local companies sang Verdi and Mozart, and the half-dozen theaters offered a range of fare from Kean in *Hamlet* to the tremendously popular *Arrah-na-Pogue*. Lovers of the curious could choose between going to hear Gottschalk lead a fourteen-piano rendition of the March from *Tannhäuser* or dropping in at the Hippotheatron to guess at the sex of Zoyara, billed as an equestrienne in spite of the fact that she was " the best husband in the world and the most excellent of fathers." Intellectual entertainment was to be had at the Mechanics Fair, with its agricultural and mining machinery and its huge statue of Lincoln, or at Platt's Hall, where one could hear lectures by Mark Twain, Prentice Mulford, J. Ross Browne, Seymour Colfax, and a host of other travelers and dignitaries. The religious fad of the moment was spiritualism, and table-rapping and ghosts were more discussed than any subject other than the war and the climate. Morality expressed itself in a city ordinance forbidding the breeding of animals within the public gaze and in the arresting of the proprietors of the Anatomical Museum, San Francisco's edition of Barnum's Museum, for " giving a dirty show."

The growing sophistication of Western society was mirrored in the *Californian*, the most ambitious journal to appear during the mid-sixties. Advertised as " The Best Journal on the Pacific Coast, and the Equal of any on the Continent," it attracted the most able writers of the metropolis during its short but expensive life. Its principal failings — that it confined itself too much to polite essays and satires and that it ignored local color almost entirely — were results of the temper of the period.

During their last days on the *Era*, Charles H. Webb and Bret Harte had shown the way the wind was blowing by joking in their columns about their plans for founding a new journal. " Inigo " Webb had suggested that it be called " Inigo's Christian Weekly Watchman " or " Bret's Hebdomadal Social Guardian " — later he added " The Ishmaelite " — and he also proposed that Harte write the clever things for it, Webb receive the credit, and Florence Fane (Frances F. Victor), furnish the money. When Webb made the assertion that Harte, as a married man, would be allowed to entertain only the homely feminine contributors, Harte charged Webb with melancholy but no depth, hinting that he was known to arrive drunk at the *Era* office and place his hat on the bust of Plato. As for the journal, Harte suggested that it be published entirely in French to give it tone. The joshing ended with the appearance, on May 28th, 1864, of the *Californian*, with C. H. Webb as owner and editor and Bret Harte as chief contributor.

Webb and Harte planned to make the *Californian* the best-written and best-printed journal that San Francisco had seen. The extent to which they succeeded and the cost of that success may be measured by the statements of two participants in the venture. Mark Twain noted in a letter written four months after the journal started: " I have been engaged to write for the new literary paper — the ' Californian ' — same pay I used to receive on the ' Golden Era ' — one article a week, fifty dollars a month. I quit the ' Era,' long ago. It wasn't high-toned enough. The ' Californian ' circulates among the highest class of the community, and it is the best weekly literary paper in the United States." And long after the journal died, Webb wrote in his memoirs, " The Californian nearly bankrupted me in an inconceivably short time."

Although Webb aimed to circulate his magazine chiefly among the urban population, he appealed for support from the miners in his motto for the paper. Blazoned across the masthead was a quotation from Job: " Surely there is a vein for the silver and a place for gold where they fine it." In keeping with its motto, the journal was presented in a form that did credit to the growing interest in good printing in the city. Its firm, white imperial sheet, its three wide columns of large, clean type, its sixteen pages in magazine format made it a great improvement over the *Era*, with its muddy paper, its eight narrow columns of small type, and its eight-page newspaper format. Issued every Saturday morning, at a subscription rate of five dollars a year, the *Californian* was distinctly a metropolitan literary journal, planning to be to San Francisco what the *Round Table* was to New York.

Though Webb relinquished financial control of the paper to a group of printers a few months after it was inaugurated, he edited it continuously for two years except for two short periods when he left it in Harte's hands while he was on vacation. In 1866 it was purchased by a local bookseller, J. P. Bogardus, who persuaded James P. Bowman to edit it. Under Bowman, who had both ability and experience in journalism, the magazine widened its interests somewhat; but, in spite of support from such writers as Prentice Mulford, Henry George, Ambrose Bierce, and Ralph Keeler, it died of financial strangulation in its fourth year of publication.

Although the *Californian* with able editors and cash for its contributors attracted the best talent in the city, it fell far short of its aim to carry only original material in its pages. As a matter of fact, the proportion of " selected " to locally written contributions was about three to one. The first issue was typical; its original material consisted of four articles and two poems, in addition to the usual departments of editorials and reviews of drama and music. For fiction, the editors resorted to a common practice of using translations from a foreign language, printing a tale from the French by Mario Uchard. The rest of the contents was garnered from other journals or the encyclopedia.

The offerings in fiction remained disappointing. The early issues continued to print translations from the French, but these were eventually displaced by the ever popular " sensation novels " of May Braddon and her like. Though the editor apologized for the fare, he offered no substitute: " All the characters move about in the dark from beginning to end, knocking their heads against each other without any motive, and doing the wickedest and strangest and most incomprehensible things for the attainment of no apparent or adequate end." Under the circumstances, poor local fiction would have been an improvement, but none was to be found in the *Californian;* neither Webb nor Harte nor Mark Twain deviated from his policy of presenting " sketches," and lesser writers were probably not considered. The only local color in the journal, other than the essays and satires, was found in incidental departments, such as " Casualties, Criminal, and Miscellaneous," which contained notes on the pickled Indian found in Salt Lake, descriptions of the stage journey to Virginia City, and succinct accounts of frontier shootings.

In the opening issues Webb presented his original material anonymously, hoping thereby to attain objectivity, a practice of dubious value pursued by a good many American magazines of the period. However, he soon gave in to public pressure and allowed his feature writers to sign their contributions. These writers were, in prose, Bret Harte and Mark Twain (Webb also continued his column entitled " Things " which had formerly appeared in the *Era*), and, in poetry, Charles Warren Stoddard, Bret Harte, Ina Coolbrith, W. A. Kendall, and Emilie Lawson. In addition there were many occasional contributors, such as Henry George and Ambrose Bierce, and the usual mess of small fry using nom-de-plumes: Theophilus Potsherd, Black Annan, Podgers, Trismegistus, Touchstone, Hagar, Ingle, and others.

The growing critical spirit of the west-coast writers was apparent in their contributions to the *Californian.* Webb, already on the *Era* a skeptic about " California values," continued to make unkind remarks about forty-niners, patriotism, and literacy. Bret Harte left the field he had touched in " M'liss " and some of his earlier short stories, and devoted himself entirely to informal essays and parodies in prose and verse, culminating in his condensed novels, which satirized the styles of the leading novelists of America and Europe. Mark Twain confined his writing to burlesques and humorous skits ranging from mock enigmas to bogus art reviews; he sent his first narrative, " The Jumping Frog," elsewhere for publication. Not only was the scorn for local color implicit in the selective policy of the *Californian*, but the editor openly attacked the cult of " the honest miner " and the pioneer, questioning " whether the individual who contributed a fund of impious slang to the national vocabulary was peculiarly estimable as a moral teacher." The gunman was ridiculed in a half-dozen satires, and even miners' place-names that were considered by some to be romantic, such as Shirt Tail Band, Whiskey Diggins, and Poker Flat, were condemned as vulgar — " outright offences against public decency."

These sophisticated journalists were trying to destroy the pioneer's confidence in the fundamental principles of the pioneer's credo. Not only did the critics suggest that California might not have the best climate and finest scenery in the world, but they went deeper still; they implicitly hinted that hard work did not always bring success and that virtuous living did not always bring a reward. The institution that suffered the first barrage was the time-honored Sunday-school story. The *Californian* published a series of sketches by Inigo, Bret, and Mark Twain ridiculing the moral lessons found therein and throwing doubt on the first law of moral economy. Heresy was in the air.

The reasons why Charles H. Webb referred in *John Paul's Book* to his three-year stay in California as a " comparative eternity " are not difficult to account for. Although he was full of energy, was an excellent wit, and easily made friends among the metropolitan writers, his critical attitude towards the self-conscious society he saw about him frequently made him enemies. In his column for the *Californian* he showed little respect for such sacred Western institutions as the climate, the hospitality, and the pioneer vigor. He not only made cutting remarks about the wind, unseasonal rains, and the earthquake, but he said that the " Eureka " beneath the bear in the state arms should be translated " whole animal or nothing," for the Californians never did things by halves. Their men were so strong that no one could jump so high or dive so deep or come up so dry as a Californian and their women were either barren altogether or else threw triplets without a moment's warning. Home-town boosters were not yet ready to take that kind of remark with a smile.

Then, during the campaign to raise funds for the Sanitary Commission, he was thoughtless enough to print the statement: " If we may not die ourselves in behalf of the national cause, let us smooth the pillows of those who do. In our willingness to sacrifice our wife's brother, as Artemus Ward says, let us not forget to see that he is decently buried when the sacrifice is complete." Artemus Ward might get away with his part of that quotation, but Webb, who had made other caustic remarks about stay-at-home Californians, was living in a society which easily took offense. None other than the fire-eater Calvin McDonald singled him out for attack in the *American Flag*, and though no well-informed person seriously doubted Webb's loyalty, he spent some uncomfortable moments. He came away with the feeling that it was not safe to walk down the street unless you clothed yourself with the star-spangled banner and slapped its folds in your neighbor's eyes.

Probably Webb's heavy losses in Mexican mining companies had something to do with his lack of enthusiasm for the West. Nor was he pleased with the reception accorded his drama, *Our Friend from Victoria,* produced at Wheatleigh's Eureka on August 15th, 1865. Although it attained the not unsuccessful run of ten days, he felt that it had been inadequately acted, accusing several members of the cast of being drunk during the performance.

That was only one side of the story, however. Webb had served San Francisco well as an excellent journalist, an able critic, and an enterprising editor, and his contributions under the name of Inigo for the *Era* and the *Californian* and of John Paul for the Sacramento *Union* gained him a deservedly wide audience. Although he left San Francisco in 1866, soon after retiring from the *Californian,* and spent the rest of his life in the East, where he wrote a number of volumes of parodies and verse, invented an adding machine and a cartridge-holder, and was eventually buried with his ancestors, he was, in spite of his protests, remembered principally as a Western Humorist with a capital *H*.

While Prentice Mulford was trying everything from digging post-holes to writing newspaper sketches in his attempt to find what he was " cut out for," while Charlie Stoddard was failing as an actor and poet and contemplating turning monk so that he might find peace and livelihood in a monastery, while long-haired " Comet Quirls " Kendall was scraping along on the niggardly returns from casual journalism, supplemented by " loans " from his friends, so that he might write the poetry that was in him, Bret Harte was continuing his education in writing and supporting his wife and two children without suf-

fering the financial pinch which cripples so many artists. His
late twenties were devoid of any visible emotional strain, of any
fears of economic failure. His salary from the Mint adequately
served his material needs; he was three times promoted until he
found twelve men working under him and was receiving an income of $270 a month. His sketches reveal that he did not neg-
lect his domestic duties, for he applied himself with good humor
to house-hunting, gardening, and playing with his boys. And
yet he found ample time and energy to keep up his writing, giving meticulous care to his manuscripts and showing steady improvement in his style. Though for the most part undistinguished, his many contributions to the *Californian* displayed a
craftsmanship superior to that of any other writer for the
journal.

Much of this writing was devoted to describing domestic and
urban life with the light touch of the literary essay, but the customary topics for the journalist-around-town also received his
attention. He wrote of the people he saw on the sidewalks and
street-cars, of beggars and lawyers and audiences at theaters.
Like Mark Twain he joked about the remedies friends offered
to cure a cold and described trips out to the Cliff House behind
fast trotters. He anticipated George Ade in his amusing Fable
of Beauty, the Beast, and the Perfect Gent, with its moral:
" This fable teaches us that we should endeavor to be a Beauty
and a Perfect Gent, rather than a Beast or an Ugly Old
Woman." And he liked nothing more than to end an article on
the opera with a purple passage *à la* Thackeray: " Question not
the theology of the Priestess, for the rippling curls of the lady
before thee are false, the diamond that glitters on the bosom of
yonder snob is paste. We are stuff as operas are made of, and
our little life is rounded by the fall of the green curtain."

In his reviews he occasionally expressed his attitude towards
contemporary writing. He lamented the " attenuated senti-

ment and moral pathos " of the cheap romances, and spoke mournfully but emphatically of the " gradual decay of short-story telling." Perhaps that phrase reflected his own discouragement with the *genre*. The policy of the *Californian* can hardly be blamed entirely for his almost complete lack of interest in narrative at the time. Rather one would suppose that for the moment he found no congenial subject for his pen. Only pre-gold-rush California interested him and he did some reading in books dealing with the period of Spanish occupation. The presence of the devil in the early California tales and the stories of ghosts of Drake's sailors haunting Western shores prompted a few sketches, which included " A Legend of Monte del Diablo " and " The Legend of Devil's Point." It is significant that the tone of these stories shifted gradually from straight narrative to satire and burlesque; they started with a graphic picture of Satan meeting Father José on Mount Diablo and impressing him with the panorama of history, and ended with an account of a less impressive devil being tricked by a broker, who snagged even His Satanic Majesty while fishing from the top of a San Francisco building, using Wildcat Mining Stock as bait.

Harte's occupation with satire also yielded non-historical sketches — squibs exploded under brokers, real-estate agents, and Western bad-men. The best of these was the mock history of Sylvester Jayhawk, who, like Barney McBriar, set out to fill a private graveyard with his victims. In this satire on the actual confessions of a gunman named Jenkins, Harte left his own quiet manner to indulge in typical Western humor; he had Jayhawk complain: " I had killed twenty-nine men up to the fall of 1860; I wanted to finish up the year with an even number. So I killed a man keerlessly and without forethought." And clearly in Mark Twain's field were the concluding remarks: " The loss of his upper lip in a prizefight on the banks of the Carson led to a frequent and cheerful exhibition of his front teeth, and produced an open and not unpleasant breadth of feature. Mr. Jayhawk, though he never married, left a large family to mourn his loss."

Harte's best writing for the *Californian* was found in his verse parodies, of which the most amusing was " To the Pliocene Skull," and in his *Condensed Novels*, prose parodies of the styles of thirteen contemporary novelists. Although they reveal that Harte was still too much concerned with how other people wrote, they were both skillful and amusing and not only justified their inclusion in Harte's first volume, but established him as one of the nation's best parodists. Not until Harte got most of the travesty out of his system, however, was he to write the short stories which were to bring him fame.

Mark Twain moved from Virginia City to San Francisco late in May 1864. Since his visit the year before, he had become increasingly well known to the California reading public through his correspondence for the San Francisco *Call* and his articles for the *Golden Era.* Those who had never heard of him before learned his name through the notoriety of his burlesque news story called variously " The Dutch Nick Massacre " and " The Empire City Hoax." This gory account of how P. Hopkins of Washoe clubbed six of his children to death, scalped his wife, and cut his throat from ear to ear because he had been foolish enough to invest in a notorious San Francisco stock issue thoroughly amused most of its readers and may perhaps have deceived a few who did not read it closely enough to see that it was aimed at the bay-city speculators. At least, the Westerner always liked to think that the next man was fooled, and the story that the item had been taken seriously to the embarrassment of the writer naturally took hold, until today books carry the statement that Mark Twain made himself so unpopular that he had to go into hiding till the storm blew over. Even the humorist dressed it up in his old age. Actually, the story was labeled a hoax from the beginning, its first printing in San Francisco, in the *Evening Bulletin*, carried the telltale admission: " I take it all back. Mark Twain."

Mark Twain had spent a very busy last winter in Virginia City. The next excitement after the Dutch Nick Massacre was Artemus Ward's convivial visit; this was followed by a meeting of the burlesque " Third House " in Carson City, when the humorist was elected Governor for the evening and was presented with a gold watch by his admirers; and this in turn by a strenuous campaign of selling and reselling a flour-sack to raise money for the Sanitary Commission. Throughout the winter he carried on a good-humored paper warfare with Dan de Quille, which reached its heights when Dan reported how Mark's nose looked after his boxing-match at Chauvel's gymnasium, and Mark told how he took care of Dan after the latter fell off his horse.

But in spite of his triumphs Mark Twain was getting restless on the sagebrush hill. The constant strain of horseplay, of practical jokes which were not always genially received, of burlesque feuds with other Virginia City journalists told on his temper. With gusto he had labeled Rice " The Unreliable " and yet retained him as a close friend; with many a guffaw he waged war with Dan de Quille, and yet he not only loved him but roomed with him in peace. Ultimately fingers were burned, however, and feelings riled in a tiff with Laird of the Virginia City *Union*. Tradition, furthered by Steve Gillis's love for tall tales, has established the story that Mark Twain took the stage-coach out of Virginia City because his quarrel with Laird passed the joking point. A minor fracas may have hurried the humorist on his way — although the story of a duel rests on

questionable evidence — but Mark Twain had exhausted the
opportunities of Virginia City and his time for departure had
arrived. Moreover, the flush days of the first Virginia City
bonanza were over; hardly had he shaken the alkali dust from
his boots before the crash came. A change for him was inevitable, and San Francisco was logically the next rung in his
ladder.

Soon after his arrival Mark Twain went to work for the San
Francisco *Morning Call*. The *Call*, which competed for the
morning field with the long-established, sedate *Alta California*,
was described by a contemporary as " a remarkably spirited and
chatty little journal, published at a very cheap rate, having a
large circulation, and being full of piquant paragraphs, bits of
scandal, sensational ' items,' and special scraps of news interesting to its numerous lady readers." A perusal of its files for 1864
reveals paragraphs no longer piquant, items no longer sensational, and none of Mark Twain's characteristic writings. Not
only was he denied the privilege of signing his articles, but
either his reports were reduced at the copy-desk to the standard
news style, or he learned to write them without leaving traces of
his individual manner. It is not surprising that he disliked intensely the daily routine of visiting police courts, running after
fires, and visiting each of the six theaters in his evening round.
Moreover, he could not adjust himself to the night work demanded of a reporter for a morning paper; in his search for a
lodging in which he could catch up on his sleep during the day,
he tried two hotels and five lodging-houses in four months. In
desperation he arranged with the *Call* to do only daylight assignments, with his pay cut from thirty-five to twenty-five dollars a week. Even under this regime he could not reconcile himself to the job. " It was fearful drudgery — soulless drudgery
— and almost destitute of interest. It was awful slavery for a

lazy man." At the end of a few months his employer took the initiative in breaking a relationship which was not satisfactory to either party.

While he was suffering from this uncongenial city reporting, Mark Twain was writing for the *Golden Era* and the *Californian* the sort of things he wanted to write. For the former he composed three articles telling of his joy at arriving in the city, his dislike for the proceedings of the police court, and his harrowing experiences in following the local custom of rising early for a ride to the Cliff House.

Possibly Mark Twain left the *Era* for the *Californian* at the suggestion of Bret Harte, whom he had met through George Barnes, editor of the *Call*. Harte has left a vivid picture of his first impression of the Comstock humorist. " His head was striking. He had the curly hair, the aquiline nose, and even the aquiline eye — an eye so eagle-like that a second lid would not have surprised me — of an unusual and dominant nature. His eyebrows were very thick and bushy. His dress was careless, and his general manner one of supreme indifference to surroundings and circumstances." Mark Twain, in turn, was pleased to find Harte quiet, well dressed, and very much interested in writing. Because he felt Harte was the most experienced craftsman he had met, he decided to learn all he could from him, submitting his articles for advice in revision. Harte taught him for the first time the value of form, the effectiveness of the well-chosen phrase. Years later Mark Twain acknowledged the debt he owed to Harte: " He trimmed and trained and schooled me patiently until he changed me from an awkward utterer of coarse grotesquenesses to a writer of paragraphs and chapters that have found a certain favor."

Whether Mark Twain imparted any of his enthusiasm and vitality to Harte is difficult to say. Certainly the association of the two best writers on the coast was a fortunate one. Each had developed far enough to be his own master and each was sufficiently avid for knowledge to learn from the other. At the time of their meeting they were both in their twenty-eighth year, although Mark Twain was nine months the senior. Their acquaintance remained largely a professional one, for they differed too much in temperament to become warm friends. Much about their relationship can be read from Mark Twain's remark: " Bret Harte was one of the pleasantest men I have ever known; he was also one of the unpleasantest men I have ever known."

Between October 1 and December 3, 1864, Mark Twain wrote ten weekly articles for the *Californian*, for which he received one hundred and twenty dollars. In them he practiced a system of drifting from the point which may have been suggested by Artemus Ward's lecturing methods. Thus, he presented a conundrum: " Why was Napoleon when he crossed the Alps like the Sanitary cheese at the Mechanics Fair? " but never got around to divulging the answer. He started out to describe the Fair and ended up by discussing a game he called Muggins. His story of a trip to the Cliff House drifted into praise of the view seen through the bottom of a glass from which the whisky was being drained; and his scientific account of a meteoric shower similarly rested upon observations made through a telescopic tumbler, in which had been placed a gill each of *eau de vie* and Veuve Cliquot, and elevated the whole to an angle of ninety degrees. In " Daniel in the Lion's Den — and Out Again " he said he was going to describe the stock exchange, but ended by making nonsense out of brokers' gibberish; and his opera review turned into a detailed appraisal of the work of the principal scene-shifter.

His rambling exaggeration was seen at its best in a sketch entitled " Love's Bakery," which started out poorly as an echo of John Phœnix's Eagle Bakery story, but picked up when he began to describe the sad disintegration of Aurelia's young man, a lover who passed away from his sweetheart by piecemeal, losing progressively his two arms, his two legs, his eyesight, and finally his scalp. " There was but one man scalped by the Owens River Indians last year. That man was Williamson Breckenridge Caruthers." His persistence in surviving in part raised the delicate question: was there enough of him left for Aurelia to marry? That was another conundrum that Mark Twain never answered.

In December Mark Twain made a trip to the Mother Lode country, where he spent three months at Jackass Hill and Angel's Camp. It is said that Steve Gillis, who had accompanied him from Washoe and was his roommate and fellow prankster throughout the fall, made the visit necessary by involving him in the consequences of one of his many bar-room fights. The story goes that after Steve nearly killed a bully who was beating up a man half his size, Mark Twain went bail for his friend, and the two skipped town until the victim recovered. Albert Bigelow Paine assumed that Clemens's troubles were further complicated by a feud with the city police, whom he had angered by attacking them for corruption in his letters to the *Territorial Enterprise*, but he does not seem to have started writing these letters until six months after the incident. The trip was probably the result of the coming to town of Jim Gillis, Steve's brother, an excellent talker, full of countless good yarns, who invited Mark and Steve to return with him to his cabin in the gold hills for a vacation. He offered many inducements that were hard to resist — Western hospitality, a chance at making a strike in pocket mining, and an opportunity to hear some of the tall stories that abounded in the region.

Mark Twain visited the southern mines not during their flush days but during their decline. The intense activity of the early fifties had passed completely, leaving behind it dying villages inhabited by handfuls of old-timers who panned only enough gold to keep alive while they dreamed of making a strike. In their spare time — of which there was a great deal — they developed hobbies and hoaxes. Jim Gillis, with his library and his interest in nature study, and Dick Stoker, " forty-six and gray as a rat," with his tales of his famous cat, Tom Quartz, were good examples of the men who lingered in the mines because they were happy there. They tried to teach Sam (as they always called him), how to pocket-mine, but his resistance was too much for them; they persuaded him to join in the operations of the " Jackass Sindikite of Mine Workers " and the proceedings of the Hospital for the Insane on Jackass Hill; they showed him a lunar rainbow at Vallecitos and took him along to help court the two pretty girls whom they called the Chapparal Quails.

While his companions were prospecting near Angel's Camp, Mark Twain spent most of his time loafing in a local saloon. A notebook he kept at the time reveals that he was hardly living in luxury. It contains terse comments on the rain, the hard beans, the bad coffee, and the four kinds of soup: Hell-fire, General Debility, Insanity, and Sudden Death. It also shows what Mark Twain was really doing while he loafed: he was listening to stories and jotting down notes for future reference. One was about a crazed man who asked after his wife, who had been dead for thirteen years; one told of a squatter whose house was borne off on the backs of some grunting hogs; and still another commented on a stranger who wagered an old-timer fifty dollars that he could beat him in a frog-jump, and won by filling the old-timer's frog with bird-shot. The last of these brief jottings developed into Mark Twain's first short story. He had found something more important than the plot for a famous yarn, however; he had absorbed the manner of telling that yarn, the manner of the frontier raconteur, which had been familiar to him all his life, but which seemed for the first time to have literary possibilities. As Ben Coon yarned before the fire at the hotel in Angel's Camp, Sam Clemens realized that he had at last found a value in being lazy. You had to be made that way to tell a good story!

When Mark Twain returned to town and wrote his next article for the *Californian,* he digressed from his avowed purpose of reviewing the exhibition at the California Art Union and told his readers about his experiences in the hills. He gave a life-sized portrait of ex-Corporal Ben Coon, the bald-headed man who had told him about the jumping frog and also about his " responsible old Webster-unabridged " which, as the most likely reading-material in Calaveras County, went sashaying around from camp to camp, but never seemed to satisfy anybody, really. After which Coon would " proceed cheerlessly to scout with his brush after the straggling hairs on the rear of his head and drum them to the front for inspection and roll-call, as was his usual custom before turning in for his regular after-noon nap."

The enthusiastic humorist said that if he had his way he would go back to Calaveras County, in spite of the rain, and argue the sewing-machine question again with the boys around Coon's bar-room stove. The camp was divided between those who supported Grover and Baker machines and those who thought the Florence would save civilization. They were not satisfied with citing the advertisements, but made up a good many arguments of their own. During a lull in the sewing-machine campaign they argued over the relative values to man-kind of different makes of safes. While they were busy with these momentous issues, another group over in the Bella Union Saloon at Jamestown was discussing the affairs of the Pound Package Jamestown Smoke Company, which was organized to import smoke in pound packages from the East, by water right up to the Wood's Creek landing. There were other old-timers doing the same thing in Tuttletown, in Jackson, in Dutch Flat, in Downieville, in Shasta City. The tall talk was even better than the yarn-spinning Mark Twain had heard in the cabins of river boats on the Mississippi.

Artemus Ward had suggested that he send him a sketch for his forthcoming book, and Mark Twain decided the frog story would make a good subject. While he was in the mood, he yarned it out in a most natural fashion; he could still hear Ben Coon telling it, but he added quite a few flourishes of his own. As Ward's letter had lain for three months in the Occidental Hotel while Mark Twain was in the hills, the story arrived in New York too late for the book, and Carleton, the publisher, turned it over to Henry Clapp, editor of the *Saturday Press*. When it appeared in the final issue of that expiring paper on November 18, 1865, it was copied widely and became the sensation of the moment, carrying its author's name to many who had never heard it before.

Mark Twain did not follow up " The Jumping Frog " with other short stories, but continued writing for the *Californian* the same sort of articles he had been writing for two years. His reference to " The Jumping Frog " as " a villainous backwoods sketch " indicates that even he was laboring under the false impression that polite literature was superior to indigenous tales, and certainly the *Californian* did nothing to discourage this attitude. He continued to write burlesques, including an account of the murder of Julius Cæsar, done in current journalese, a sketch about how the accompanist to a scriptural panorama played profane selections at sacred moments, and a verse parody called " My Ranch," which ended

> It hath a sow — *my* sow — whose love for grain
>   No swearing subject will dispute;
> Her swill is mine, and all my slops her gain,
>   And when she squeaks my heart with love is mute.

In the early fall of 1865 Mark Twain started writing a daily San Francisco letter for the Virginia City *Territorial Enterprise*. Though no complete file of that journal exists, it is possible to get a fairly good idea of the nature of these letters by reading the reports of them in the San Francisco press. Usually the most interesting articles were reprinted in full in one of the city papers, and more than once an item was repeated in the *Alta California*, the *Golden Era*, and the *Californian* before the week was out. The bulk of the writing was routine reporting of theater attractions, political speeches, arrivals. from Washoe, and the like. Mark Twain invented a new straw-man called Fitz-Smythe — possibly he had Evans of the *Alta* in mind — making fun of his poetry, ridiculing him for his grammatical mistakes, and joshing him about his horse, who was supposed to have succumbed under a diet of dry *Bulletins* and *Altas*. He made so much of Fitz-Smythe that the name was bandied about for years by west-coast journalists.

The most significant feature of the *Territorial Enterprise* correspondence, however, was the emergence of a moralistic strain in the humorist's writing. Though in retrospect there is no paradox in finding Mark Twain both a humorist and a pessimist, a blasphemer and a reformer, a vulgarian one moment and an idealist the next, his frontier audience was surprised and to some degree unconvinced when he essayed the roles of social censor and amateur philosopher. The Mark Twain they knew was rough and frequently crude in his humor. They were used to his saying when he had a bad cold: " If I had you in the range of my nose I would blow your brains out," to commenting on the " young bucks and heifers " in the panoramist's audience, who came because it gave them " a chance to taste one another's complexion in the dark," to picturing an old man in the act of " spitting on his shirt bosom and slurring it off with his hand." They were prepared for his hits at the clergymen who were candidates to succeed Bishop Kip at Grace Cathedral, at his suggestion that the modest salary of forty thousand dollars a year could be augmented on the side by a few deals in cotton, grain, or petroleum, and at his pretense that many candidates had accepted his offer of lodgings and the loan of shirts while in town. " The tradition [on the Mississippi] goes that three clergymen on a steamboat will ground her, four will sink her, and five and a gray mare added will blow her up. If I had a gray mare in my stable, I would leave this city before night."

But they were not prepared to see that Mark Twain, who declared himself a " sinner at large," a " brevet-Presbyterian," and a skeptic by nature, was in reality much concerned with the philosophy of religion, the problem of morals, and the personalities of ministers. Unlike Bret Harte, who had a marked dislike for the clergy, Mark Twain had already started a lifelong practice of making ministerial friends by getting acquainted with the Reverend Mr. Rising in Virginia City and the Reverend Mr. Wadsworth in San Francisco. Also they were surprised to find that beneath the burlesque of Sunday-school stories in " The Story of the Bad Little Boy " and " The Story of the Good Little Boy " lurked a defense of natural morality as opposed to conventional propriety.

Finally he came out in the open as a satirist and reformer, directing towards city corruption a stream of ridicule in articles on such subjects as " The Black Hole of San Francisco," " How They Take It," " Not a Suicide," and " What the Police are Doing." Thus he turned his irony on the police for letting a petty thief die in his cell after breaking his head for stealing some empty flour-sacks. " And why shouldn't they shove that half senseless wounded man into a cell without getting a doctor to examine and see how badly he was hurt . . . ? And why shouldn't the jailer let him alone . . . because he couldn't wake him — couldn't wake a man who was sleeping and with that calm serenity which is peculiar to men whose heads have been caved in with a club? "

As the San Franciscans began to realize that Mark Twain wanted to be something more than a journalistic humorist, they revised their estimate of him. A contemporary writer explained that he was " radically a rather grave man "; another journalist, after reading his Sandwich Island letters, dubbed him " The Moralist of the Main "; and Webb, in writing the preface to Mark Twain's first book, assured the public that the author was more of a social philosopher than a humorist. When the *Californian* published a letter pretending to be from Mark Twain, one of a series of bogus applications for the editorship, the humorist's interest in morals was chosen as the theme:

" What you want is Morality. You have run too much poetry; you have slathered — so to speak — you have slathered too many frivolous sentimental tales into your paper; too much wicked wit and too much demoralizing humor; too much harmful elevating literature. What the people are suffering for, is Morality. Turn them over to me. Give me room according to my strength. I can fetch them! . . .

Yours,

' Mark Twain '

Surnamed The Moral Phenomenon."

The *Californian* published incongruous apprentice work by several young San Francisco writers. In its pages Ina Coolbrith, whose mature work is marked by restraint, sang of tropical love in torrid verse; Ambrose Bierce, later an out-spoken opponent of feminism, wrote pleas for the emancipation of women; and Henry George, soon to speculate on economic determinism, inaugurated his writing career with sketches on the supernatural. Although Ina's erotic poems and Bierce's support of the new woman were probably the results of early enthusiasms, Henry George's interest in the spirit world was not so much prompted by faith in the occult as by a desire to capitalize on a fad of the moment. Having determined to utilize every resource at his disposal to attain success, he had turned to writing ghost stories as a likely source of revenue.

After five years of living from hand to mouth, with a wife and two children to support, the twenty-six-year-old printer had decided that a complete reorganization of his life was imperative. Investments in Comstock silver stock had proved even more disastrous than his two attempts to earn his fortune at mining in person; he found himself paying out money on assessments rather than cashing in on premiums. Nor had his work as a type-setter assured him a steady income. His combativeness and independent attitude had led inevitably to disagreements, followed by resignations or dismissals. Alternating between San Francisco and Sacramento, he subbed for regular printers, went into job-printing on his own with little success, and even resorted to selling clothes-wringers and attempting to market his invention of a new type of wagon brake. For a while he talked of starting a newspaper in Reese River, Nevada, or in La Paz, at the tip of Lower California. In the meantime the George family frequently was reduced to a diet of corn meal, milk, potatoes, and sturgeon. At one time George became so desperate that he stopped a stranger and asked him for five dollars. He said he would have used a gun if the stranger had not realized his plight and helped him.

After five years of such uncertainty, George pledged himself to a threefold regime: to adopt habits of regularity, punctuality, and purpose; to spend nothing unnecessarily and to avoid debt; and to utilize every resource at his disposal to earn more money and to further his career. Writing suggested itself as a means of augmenting his income and at the same time improving his habits of thought and expression. Enthusiastically he set to work during his spare moments. Just for practice he wrote an essay, " On the Profitable Employment of Time," which he sent home to his mother; when Lincoln was assassinated, he penned some fiery editorials, which were published in the *Alta;* and he tried his hand at writing literary sketches for the *Californian.* He even contemplated writing a novel.

In his three articles published in the *Californian,* Henry George treated the supernatural in a matter-of-fact style reminiscent of Defoe. He told the unusual in a quiet, pedestrian manner, unconcerned with imaginative description or charge of emotion. " The Boatswain's Story " dealt with a premonition that came to a sailor in Callao that there was something wrong at home in Scotland; months later he found that his father had murdered his mother on the night that he had received the psychic message on the other side of the globe. " Dust to Dust " was also based on experiences which took place during George's voyage on the *Shubrick.* A sailor's dying request that he be buried on land was thwarted by the Uruguayan quarantine officers, who refused to permit the corpse to be brought ashore. But the sailor's spirit was not to be denied. Twice the corpse rose to the surface in spite of its heavy lead weights, and eventually it followed the ship right into the river's mouth at Montevideo. The superstitious captain decided that there was nothing to do but defy regulations and bury the body on shore. The third story, " The Prayer of Kahonah," was based on a legend of an Indian who interviewed the Great Spirit and was granted immortality, only to give it up voluntarily because life became a burden to him.

Told adequately but hardly vividly, these stories were probably accepted by the *Californian,* not for their narrative quality, but because they dealt with the supernatural, a theme which was being featured by that journal because of the great interest of San Franciscans in spiritualism. Not only Henry George but almost every writer of the period was participating in the current debate about the existence of ghosts.

It was nearly two decades since modern spiritualism, inaugurated when the Fox sisters heard mysterious rappings in Rochester, New York, had become the rage in the United States and England. During the fifties converts to spiritualism numbered as high as two million, but recantations brought reaction and loss of adherents during the following decade. In California, however, the new religion had been received so enthusiastically that it continued to grow even during the Civil War period. Emma Harding in her history of spiritualism explains that her cult thrived on the Pacific slope for three reasons: the wonderful transparency of the atmosphere encouraged spiritual phenomena, the heavy charges of mineral magnetism from the gold deposits set up favorable currents, and the notably strong passions of the forty-niners tended to create " unusual magnetic emanations." On the other hand, skeptics have suggested that a strong taste for gambling and the disappointments of mining and frontier life were largely responsible for the popularity of such activities as phrenology and spiritualism. Not entirely unexpected, then, are the stories of the famous Spanish-Californian grandee, General Vallejo, delighting in the twanging of a spirit guitar, of James Marshall, discoverer of gold, putting all of his faith in spirit guidance, or of Peter O'Riley, co-discoverer of the Comstock, going insane after following the advice of a spirit to use all of his money in sinking a shaft in a barren hill near Genoa, Nevada.

While the rest of the nation was growing skeptical about ghosts, Emma Harding, one of the most prominent American spiritualists, came west to strike where the iron was hot. She aided her cause by combining patriotism and table-rapping, for not only had her spirits ordered her to California and protected her from Indians and brigands on her journey, but they told her to lecture throughout the state in support of the Union cause and the re-election of Lincoln, whom the spiritualists claimed as one of their members. But even Emma Harding's visit had not aroused as much interest or created as much excitement as did the activities of the mediums Ada Hoyt Foye and Laura Cuppy in the spring of 1866. Mrs. Foye, young, auburn-haired, and good-looking, filled her auditorium on Fourth Street each week when she demonstrated her ability as a "rapping and test medium" in a public seance. On the other hand, dark-haired, middle-aged, dumpy Mrs. Cuppy rested her appeal on a shrewd combination of spiritualism and social reform. She organized a society called the Friends of Progress and lectured to her followers on topics such as "Woman — her End — her Aim." She not only saw a connection between spiritualism and feminism, but rounded out her program by working passionately for the Fellowship of God, the Brotherhood of Man, and Eternal Progression of the Human Race.

While the curious thronged to the meetings, the opponents of the movement, led by the *Evening Bulletin,* attacked Foye and Cuppy, accusing them of being immoral and dangerous influences in the community. The charge of immorality was made specific by a Miles Grant, who published a pamphlet, *Spiritualism Unmasked,* in which he maintained that the cult went hand in hand with prostitution, and he offered to name threescore mediums who were carrying on illicit relations with their clients. His charges were interestingly borne out by Charles Warren Stoddard, who confessed in *A Troubled Heart* that he was almost won over at this time by a spiritualist whom he described as an "inspirational speaker" and who may have been Mrs. Cuppy. He looked upon her as one of the most exalted natures he had ever met until he discovered, much to his horror, that she "was a priestess among the modern pagans and an advocate of lascivious rites." He successfully repelled the advances of the

importunate medium, but his experience added to his complicated nervous problem.

The spiritualists were also accused of driving men insane.
The fate of converts was thus described in the *Era:* " Your hair
commences growing long, and your eyes assume a wild glare,
and you believe in nothing and everything at once, and you become a friend of progress, and talk of naught but ' influences,'
' influxes,' ' affinities,' and ' conditions '; and finally you kick
over the traces of reason and are borne howling along Montgomery Street in the arms of two able-bodied policemen on your
way to the Stockton Asylum." Within the space of a month
the *Bulletin* reported three cases of insanity arising from expo-
sure to spiritualism; one of the victims actually went berserk
while attending a Friends of Progress meeting and was taken
from there straight to the asylum.

It was inevitable that Mark Twain should investigate spiritualism, for he had more than the usual curiosity about bizarre
religions and psychic manifestations. As a matter of fact, he
devoted a whole series of articles to the subject. He started his
campaign by burlesqueing a story, then going the rounds
among the believers, that a servant girl had been thoroughly
mauled by a spirit. He marveled that the spirit left nine bloody
kittens on her pillow! A week later he told how he attended Ada
Foye's meeting and asked questions; the following week he reported his observations as a member of the committee that sat
on the stage and watched for tricks during a seance.

In his reports he neither scoffed nor believed, but he went so
far as to state that he found no more fanaticism among members of this " wild cat religion " than he had among more orthodox creeds. " I can remember when Methodist camp meetings
and Campbellite revivals used to stock the asylums with religious lunatics, and yet the public kept their temper and said
never a word." He told, also, of attending a seance in a private

house and there communicating with spirits by means of a spirit dial. After watching " a very intelligent person of a dead man " spell out an unintelligible two-page article on " Space," he was relieved to exchange some banter with one of his friends, the Smiths. The ghost of Smith, after capping Mark Twain's rhyme, departed for a bottle of whisky, leaving the dial needle agitated with his mirth. The humorist dropped the subject with the sage remark : " I'm not afraid of such pleasant corpses as these ever running me crazy. I find them better company than a good many live people."

The writer most influenced by the spiritualists of San Francisco, however, was not Charlie Stoddard, who was almost seduced by a medium, nor Mark Twain, who attended their meetings and joked of their experiences, nor May Wentworth, who wrote a long series of articles for the *Californian* on the history and beliefs of spiritualism, but Prentice Mulford, who not only became a convert to the creed but later in life advanced his own particular brand of occult philosophy. With his habits of speculation, his willingness to try any idea at least once, and his search for a way of life that would develop his self-confidence, he was ripe for revelation when the spiritualists stormed the town.

Soon after Lawrence brought him to San Francisco to write for the *Golden Era*, Mulford began to slip into his old unsocial ways. His few acquaintances found that the sandy-haired man, with twinkling brown eyes and ragged mustaches, was extraordinarily shy and retiring — was, in fact, preternaturally afraid of people. As soon as Lawrence left for the East — early in 1865 — Mulford moved from the Occidental Hotel to cheap lodgings, where he existed on what he called the " cheese-paring " order of life. After wandering from one cheap rooming-house to another, he moved across the bay to live for a while with James Bowman in the Hotel de France in Oakland. Eventually he bought an old whaleboat, rigged a sail, took his blankets and spirit lamp on board, and spent his days cruising, his nights sleeping, anchored in the most lonely parts of the bay. He had become the west-coast hermit.

He preferred to write with his pad on his knee, his left arm hooked over the tiller. Life afloat was very simple. All the clothing he wanted was a knitted one-piece suit, whose blue had been turned to gray by the elements. All the food he wanted was a little fruit, vegetables, bread, and occasionally a fish brought up from the bay. All the company he wanted — usually — was his own thoughts, as he speculated on where his " self " went when he slept or on whether mental activity was spiritual or material.

At odd intervals he turned up at various newspaper offices with contributions. Although his writing came to be in demand, he could not persuade himself that it was valuable; he would, therefore, accept a pittance in wages. Even then he took only enough money to keep him in grub, and left the balance in the editors' hands. So shy was he that, contributions in hand, he would often pace up and down before the *Golden Era* office until some acquaintance arrived in whose company he would find courage to enter.

In his columns for the *Era* and later the *Californian* Dogberry began to mix philosophy with his mining sketches and compressed novels. He championed the lazy life; he questioned material progress; he analyzed his many defeats. When Ada Foye and Laura Cuppy held their meetings, he attended frequently. He was present the night that Mark Twain served on the committee, and complimented him in his column in the *Era* for his good behavior. At first he treated the spiritualists with some levity, but soon it became apparent that he was becoming deeply interested in their activities. He began taking part in seances at private houses and reported to his readers that he had talked with the ghosts of John Wilkes Booth, Wawona, the Indian maiden, and many another. Mulford was not at all afraid of being called a crank, and his humor and sincerity saved him from ridicule. As he talked with the spirits, he became convinced that a new philosophy of living could be built up from his experiences.

He wrote a series of articles for the *Era* called " The Invisible in Our Midst " in which he expressed the germs of the ideas that he was to develop in his White Cross Library. But he was not as yet willing to proselyte for his ideas; his readers could take them or leave them as they pleased. " I am not particular that my readers should imagine that I am a sort of spiritual Barnum keeping a keen lookout for curiosities of this sort. Nearly all I have seen of this science has come into my path. I have been forced to see it. . . . I do not care to be regarded as a high priest and authority in these matters. . . . Catch your own ghost and convince yourselves that it is a reality or a humbug. True, the subject is very interesting to me. But it has slums and I desire not to wade through them."

A few years later, convinced that spirits were as real as mountains, he was to promulgate a doctrine of living that was to rival the teachings of Mary Baker Eddy for a day. He met his ghosts in San Francisco, where they abounded in the mid-sixties, but he waited till he became a hermit in a New Jersey swamp before he gave their message to the world.

CHAPTER VIII

A RASH OF POETRY

THE OFT-REPEATED generalization that frontiers are hostile to poetry is amply refuted in the records of the Pacific Coast. Devoted as the Westerners were to making money as fast as possible, they at the same time displayed a surprisingly strong urge to express themselves in rhyme and an equally violent taste for reading even the worst verse in print. After the morning of April 24, 1847, when young Edward C. Kemble's " Blowing up the Wind " appeared in the *California Star*, the " poets' corner " was accorded the place of honor on the front page of the local news-sheets. Throughout the following three decades the small rural weeklies as well as the large metropolitan dailies continued to print verses composed by aspiring amateurs, many of them grave, practical businessmen, sage financiers, fierce speculators, and plodding traders, never before suspected of poetry.

Like their fellows elsewhere, most of these amateur poets were highly imitative, echoing particularly the moods and strains of Byron, Poe, Hood, and Tom Moore. Moreover, they usually ignored the local scene, assuming that poetry should deal either with a vacuum or with some part of the world more definitely

established as poetic. Accompanying a few poems dealing with
mining life there were thousands lamenting lost loves, preach-
ing the better life, or even retelling the myths of Greece and
Rome. The only local subjects to be treated often were the scenery of the West and the homesickness of the pioneer. Scribblers
described the view of the Golden Gate, the canyons of the
Sierra, the majesty of the redwood trees, the climate, the flowers, and the birds. They also rhymed wistfully of seasons in
New England, farms in Pennsylvania, and friends in Missouri.

Not infrequently, however, an interesting poem dealing with
frontier conditions, described artlessly but effectively, would
appear in a local journal or would find its way into one of the
many ballad collections, such as Put's songsters. Typical of its
class was " The Emigrant's Dying Child," by Major G. W.
Patton, which was printed in the *Era* in 1853. It told a true
story of the hardships experienced by a family of emigrants in
crossing the plains. The mother was buried in the alkali flats
of the Humboldt sink and the father struggled over the mountains with his daughters, one a girl of six and the other a baby,
only to find the San Joaquin Valley flooded and no food to be obtained. Death was swift to follow the privations of the crossing.
The poem presented the lamentations of the little girl soon after
the baby died and not long before she perished in turn.

> Father! I'm hungered! give me bread;
>   Wrap close my shivering form!
> Cold blows the wind around my head,
>   And wildly beats the storm.
> Protect me from the angry sky;
>   I shrink beneath its wrath,
> And dread this torrent sweeping by,
>   Which intercepts our path.
> Father! These California skies,
>   You said, were bright and bland —

But where, tonight, my pillow lies, —
  Is this the golden land?
'Tis well my little sister sleeps,
  Or else she too would grieve;
But only see how still she keeps —
  She has not stirred since eve.
I'll kiss her, and perhaps she'll speak;
  She'll kiss me back I know;
Oh! father, only touch her cheek,
  'Tis cold as very snow.
Father! You do not shed a tear
  Yet little Jane has died: —
Oh! promise, when you leave me here,
  To lay me by her side.
And when you pass this torrent cold,
  We've come so far to see,
And you go on beyond, for gold,
  O think of Jane and me.

The principal handicap of the Western poet was that he was
too consciously literary. Thus side by side with the author of
" The Emigrant's Dying Child " as a representative writer of
the fifties we have Edward Pollock, whose lofty ambition was to
compose a national epic. Because of that aspiration and because he died in his thirty-fifth year without having achieved it,
he was held in veneration by later generations. Pollock was further endeared to his fellow frontiersmen by the fact that he was a
self-educated man. He had gone to work at the age of ten back
in Philadelphia, but during the long hours spent first in a cot-
ton-factory and later as a sign-painter's apprentice he had
kept up his reading. In his early youth he had begun publishing his verse in local journals. After coming to San Francisco
in 1852, he had continued earning his living as a sign-painter,
but in the evenings he studied law and eventually passed the bar
examinations. In addition, he found time to write; to the *Pio-*

neer he contributed poems in the manners of Coleridge and Poe, and he followed the latter in a number of short stories.

An article entitled " Thoughts toward a New Epic " set a high standard for his life work. Pollock announced that the tradition of Homer, Virgil, Tasso, and Milton was yet to flower in a great modern epic, of which the theme would be right against wrong; the source, the heart of man; and the place, America. He said that the maker of this epic must regard America as the most important of countries and, while adhering to the principle that art is of divine origin, receive no inspirations or impulses from sources beyond the sea. His essay ended in a peroration: " Beyond question, this is the country, where else could exist the bard of liberty and of change? Where else could a poet's mind rise and expand to the sublimity of such themes? The land should grow giants: and will; — or our history, our institutions, and our destiny are the changes of a distempered dream."

No notebook retains the details of Pollock's plans for his epic. His poems are perhaps a little better than those of his contemporaries, but they reveal no marked poetic talent. His " Falcon " is a ballad modeled on " The Ancient Mariner " in theme and style, in which a touch of weirdness fails to atone for lack of originality ; his " Chandos Picture " is a pale dilution of Poe with a bust of Shakespeare substituted for the raven ; and his " Legend of the Pacific Coast " is just another poem about the lost Atlantis. Moreover, such subjects as " Fragment: Different Effects of Natural Scenery on the Just and the Corrupt Mind," make one wonder how he would treat the epic of America. Pollock left an impression, however, for today many a Californian can quote the opening lines of his poem on " Evening ":

> The air is chill and the day grows late,
> And the clouds come in through the Golden Gate.

The first decade after the gold-rush produced a great many
journalistic poems, a number of song-books, and a few dramas
in blank verse, and made known such names as Pollock, Ridge,
Soulé, Rhodes, and Linen, but not until the second decade did
there flourish anything resembling a Western school of poetry.
In the mid-sixties, when Californians had grown more interested in belles-lettres, two rival San Francisco publishers
printed several important volumes of local poetry. Anton Roman and Hubert H. Bancroft turned out the books, while the
newspaper critics furthered their sale by making collections of
poems the subjects of journalistic wars. Frontier editors loved
nothing so much as a good burlesque literary feud, and when the
volumes began to appear, they backed their favorite poets with
humorous bombast. The most celebrated of these feuds, that
which accompanied the appearance of Harte's *Outcroppings,*
was but one of several.

The furore over *Outcroppings* was closely related to a literary war that had reached an armistice in Virginia City just before Harte's collection of California verse appeared. To understand the methods used by the Washoe journalists when they
turned their guns on San Francisco, one should know something
of customary military tactics on the Comstock. Thus Sam
Davis described the Daggett-Goodman feud:

" These were the flush days of the Comstock, and everything
was in the high tide of a rushing and riotous regime. Who
would suppose that with all the hurly-burly of money-making
there would have been much poetry or sentiment? But the ledge
maintained two verse-makers and rhyme-weavers of the highest
order. One was Joe Goodman and the other Rollin Daggett.
On all other propositions these two men were like brothers, but
when it came to poetry they were like two pugilists in the ring.
About once a week, a poem written by Daggett or Goodman
would appear in the *Territorial Enterprise,* and each effusion

drew forth its quantum of praise or criticism. Each of the bards had an army of followers, and the *Enterprise* office had its warring factions. Steve Gillis was a pronounced Daggett man, while Denis McCarthy was an unwavering partisan of Goodman.

" It was an amusing sight to see Steve, well filled with Joe Mallon's whiskey, delivering a barroom lecture on the excellence of Daggett's verse. ' This is the real stuff! ' he would shout, waving the *Enterprise* in the air. ' This has the true ring. Hear this, everybody,' and in a voice like a ton of coal rattling down the cellar stairs he would roll out the strong passages of Daggett's verse and point out their beauties to the admiring crowd.

" ' No use talking, boys, no one in this country can trot in double harness with this man. The pace is too rapid. Joe Goodman is no slouch of a writer, but he can't stay the distance with a speed like this.' Then the crowd would empty foaming tankards of beer to Daggett, the Comstock bard and the glory of the town. But a few evenings later the followers of the Goodman school of verse-making would gather around Denis McCarthy and listen spell-bound while he dilated on the beauties of Goodman's verse. Denis had a rich, melodious voice, and he would lean back and roll out the lines which had flowed from Goodman's pen. ' Talk about poetry! This is the only true music ever written on this ledge. Here's a line, gentlemen, which strikes the heart like a soft beam of moonlight falling from a cloud. I tell you, it's the divine fire from Olympus. Where is the man who says Daggett can write poetry? That man can't write mottoes for a first class candy factory! Haven't I seen him up there with a rhyming dictionary, with his head twisted to one side and his tongue trying to poke a hole through his cheek, squirming around on his chair and twisting his feet nine ways for Sunday trying to squeeze out a rhyme? '

" ' Did you ever see him tackle spenserian verse? No; it's too high for him. But Joe can sit there just as straight as if he were keeping books and roll the verses out just as cozy as I could write the Lord's Prayer, and telling good stories all the while. No mental effort whatever and every line full of first class euphony and alliteration as smooth as oil.' "

With such able backers, the rival poets ran a close race. For a while the lead was held by Goodman, who won a poet-of-the-day contest and received so many requests for verses that he nearly wore himself out wrestling with the muse. Then Daggett forged ahead with a stupendous ode, delivered to the colored population on the anniversary of the Emancipation Proclamation.

Daggett now felt so secure that he crowed over his rival: " Better acknowledge I'm the boss, Joe. You can't ignore the poetic judgment of the colored race. Old Piper had to reshingle the opera-house roof after the crowd quit applauding my work."

" My poetry has been loosening those shingles for years, Daggett," was Joe's laconic reply.

Daggett's triumph was short-lived, for when the *Enterprise* boys held a poetry-writing contest against time, Goodman finished a half-column in twenty minutes while Daggett was producing a few lines. The latter's revenge came when the poem was published anonymously and a reviewer stamped the unfathered thing to pieces: " A weak imitation of Wordsworth," said the critic, " diluted through a brain enfeebled with the fumes of contraband opium and moonshine whiskey."

Of course Daggett made much of the review and Goodman accused him of writing it, but the feud had reached a stalemate. The boys looked elsewhere for sport. They found it when *Outcroppings*, edited by Bret Harte and published by Anton Roman, appeared without including poems by either Daggett or

Goodman. This slim first collection of California verse, issued for the Christmas trade of 1865, was limited to some forty poems, the work of only nineteen poets. Although it opened with verses by the hallowed Pollock, although it gave the second place of honor to Lyman R. Goodman, Joe's younger brother who had died of mountain-fever at twenty-four, the old-timers of established reputation were omitted from its pages. Where was Joe Goodman's celebrated ode to Lincoln? Where was Frank Soulé's " Labor," John Swett's " In the Mines," Caxton's " The Enrobing of Liberty," Colonel Baker's " To a Wave "? Why was John R. Ridge represented by one of his least effective stanzas when everyone knew that Yellow Bird was one of the best poets in the West?

The he-men among Pacific Coast poets were outraged to find that the meager collection was made up chiefly of poems by city-bred Bohemians, slight effeminate fellows who had never toted a gun, newcomers who had not yet got used to the atmosphere. This weak-winged writing covey included such triflers as " Inigo " Webb, a New York importation who had lost all his money playing mining stocks and was about to take his sore head back where he came from, young " Pip Pepperpod " Stoddard, who was so much like a girl that he blushed when the fellows told dirty stories in his company, and dark-haired, wild-eyed " Comet Quirls " Kendall, who divided his time between writing passionate and somewhat indecent poetry to the girls and mooning by the hour in the Cobweb Saloon down by Meiggs's wharf. Here was a good subject for a real fight, one that they could all enjoy.

Harte said he was caught by surprise when his first venture in editing raised such a rumpus. Publisher Roman had handed him a sheaf of clippings that had been lying in his shop and had told him to select the ones he considered the best. When it became known that he was preparing an anthology, many other contributions poured in. Carefully he eliminated the obvious plagiarisms, the pieces containing acrostics of patent medicines, and " certain veiled libels and indecencies such as mark the ' first ' publications on blank walls and fences of the average youth." After choosing from the remaining verses the ones which he felt to be most promising, he prepared his volume almost as if he wanted trouble; he refrained from including any of his own poems; he supplied a preface in which he apologized for the poor quality of local poetry; and he wrote a patronizing review to appear anonymously in the *Californian*. In this review he implied that the West had not yet produced any first-rate poets and suggested that *Outcroppings* was premature.

With such a send-off, there was sure to be fun. The *News Letter's* account of the excitement was perhaps the most amusing of the journalistic notices. " Mr. Frank Bret Harte's long-promised and much talked of book of the California poets has at last arrived in the city. Within two hours after it was known to be in town, a mob of poets, consisting of 1100 persons of various ages and colors, and of both sexes, besieged Roman's bookstore, all eager to ascertain whether they had been immortalized by Harte. . . . On Tuesday the book arrived in San Francisco; on Thursday the news had been circulated throughout the State, and the ' country poets ' were in a state of fearful excitement. Yesterday it was rumored that a delegation of three or four hundred of these were coming down on the Sacramento boat, in a ' fine phrensy,' and swearing dire vengeance on Harte. That gentleman, by the advice of his friends, immediately repaired to the Station House, to be locked up for protection."

While Ward's Furnishing Store capitalized on the excitement by issuing an advertising pamphlet entitled *Outcroppings No. 2*, by A Rum-Un and Co., the *Evening Bulletin* made a specialty of reprinting the vitriolic reviews from the hinterlands

— from Shasta City, from Grass Valley, from Los Angeles, and particularly from Washoe. The writers in Washoe, partly in earnest and partly in fun, went after the volume with hammer, tongs, and blank cartridges. The editor of the Gold Hill *Daily News* called the poetry " purp-stuff " and its editor " a lop-eared Eastern apprentice." Other Comstock reviews referred to the poetry as " hogwash ladled from the slop-bucket," " flop-doodle mixture," " feeble collection of drivel," and " quantity of slumgullion that would average about 33⅓ cents a ton," and they said the editor " has strayed away from his parents and guardians while he was too fresh. He will not keep without a little salt."

The attacks that gained the most attention, however, were those that appeared in the Virginia City *Territorial Enterprise* and the Sacramento *Union*. In the former, Joe Goodman devoted nearly five columns to destroying the vile publication. The supporters of *Outcroppings* said Goodman had gone too far; they accused him of losing his temper and of implying that Harte was a hypocrite and a liar, and they pounced on him for using figures of speech based upon obstetrics, a subject " not commonly canvassed in public." The row was rapidly turning into a fight between Virginia City and San Francisco. A most amusing salvo was fired by the *Californian* in reply to Goodman; it took the form of a review of an imaginary volume, *Tailings: Rejections of California Verse*, supposedly filled with Comstock verse. To Goodman, hailed as " Bold chieftain with vitreous eye, Old Stallion of the land of Storey," was ascribed an obstetrical poem entitled " Sunrise on Mt. Davidson ":

> Lo! Where the orient hills are tipped with snow,
> The pregnant morn slow waddles o'er the plain,
> Big with the coming day; the shameless child
> Of Erebus and Nox, wrought in the slow
> And sure gestation of the rolling hours.

Methinks I see the swaddling clothes of mist
Roll down the bosky glens, and standing here
Notebook in hand, I really seem to be
Accoucher of the universe.

The Sacramento *Union* reviewer's charge against *Outcrop-pings* was that it contained little poetry treating with local sub-jects. But when he suggested that someone should write an epic dealing with the Gold-Hunting Crusade, the *Californian* of-fered the following as a sample of the heroic treatment of West-ern life:

And through the valleys rose between
The pleasant hiss of the succulent bean,
And the jay bird's thrilling song was stopped,
When the luscious flap-jack softly flopped.

No one in the San Francisco camp was willing to take a Western epic seriously; the days of the gold-rush were not yet far enough in the past to be heroic. One writer gibed that such an opus might well begin with the escape of the members of Stevenson's Regiment from the sheriff in New York and end with the mock justice dealt out by the first vigilante committee; another pro-posed that the great poem be written in the style of the *Argo-nautæ*, with Sam Brannan for Jason, Michael Reese for The-seus, and the editor of the *Union* for Orpheus.

Though the newspaper battle over *Outcroppings* ended in a draw, the San Francisco poets won in the end, for the first an-thology of their poetry, which might easily have collected dust in the book-stores, sold out in a short time. The controversy had aroused so much interest in local verse that a bigger, more inclu-sive collection was in order.

Sam Brannan might not be a Jason, although he had aban-doned his Mormon followers for gold-hunting as readily as Jason had left Medea for Glauce, but he was quite willing to play the more congenial role of San Francisco's Crœsus. He felt that he was a public-minded citizen: while making a fortune in real-estate and mining speculation, he had benefited the city by founding its first newspaper and leading its first vigilante movement. Nettled by remarks such as that in the *Californian* review, he now proposed to encourage the arts by giving financial backing to a genuine collection of Western poetry.

When the *Californian* writers heard that Brannan was to sponsor an ambitious literary venture, they hooted; what that gold-lined Philistine knew about art and literature, especially poetry, was hardly worth knowing. Probably several of them had heard the story about his interview with Gottschalk, the famous pianist, and had repeated it as illustrative of Brannan's lack of culture. When the musician was admitted into his presence, Brannan remained slouched in his office chair, amorously caressing the big toe of his bare foot with the index finger and thumb of his right hand. " Gottschalk! Gottschalk! " he drawled, without letting go of his big toe, " I know that name. Ain't you one of them opera singers? What do you sing, bass or tenor? " Gottschalk left Brannan and California firmly convinced that both were hopelessly barbarous.

The new volume, to be called *The Poetry of the Pacific*, was sure of support from the poets, however. Its avowed purpose was to answer " the vexed question of who are the California poets, or whether we have any poets, by giving everyone a fair chance to show up his Pegasus, and trot him through the course in open day." The book was to be published by Hubert H. Bancroft, eager to emulate Roman, and it was to be edited by May Wentworth, who had many friends and no enemies. As a columnist for the *Era*, a composer of an occasional lyric, and the author of three volumes of stories for juveniles, she had some reputation as a writer; and as a woman editor, she would be treated with gallantry by members of the hostile camps.

When *The Poetry of the Pacific* appeared in 1866, a few months after *Outcroppings*, it was at once clear that no poet had been slighted. Its pudgy form held nearly one hundred and fifty poems, the work of more than seventy-five poets. The only writer of local repute not represented was Bret Harte, and his poems were omitted probably at his request. The tolerant editor had explained in the preface that if any one were slighted, it was not through intentional neglect. But sensing that quantity hardly made up for lack of quality in her volume, she asked indulgence from the reader: " It must be remembered that California is still an infant state, a Hercules in the cradle. The toiling gold-seekers have had but little time or encouragement to cultivate *belles-lettres*, and to the future we look to develop the rich mines of intellect as well as those of gold and silver." *The Poetry of the Pacific* started no new war among the journalists; there was nothing to fight about since everyone except the aloof Harte was included. Although it failed to receive a bombardment such as had been given *Outcroppings*, its financial solvency was assured, for Sam Brannan gave it liberal support, although he probably never got around to reading the poems.

As the most inclusive volume of early California poetry, *The Poetry of the Pacific* offers a fair cross-section of the verse of the Pacific Coast frontier. Mediocre in quality and repetitious in theme, the collection illustrates above everything else the failure of the Westerners to use the local scene as the subject of their poetry. The few exceptions to this generalization, such as John Swett's " In the Mines " and Anna M. Fitch's " The Song of the Flume," stand out as the most interesting items in the anthology.

The poem most representative of the frontier, however, dealt not so much with mining life as with labor in general.

Frank Soulé, forty-niner, newspaper editor, and principal com-
piler of *The Annals of San Francisco*, wrote this poem, entitled
" Labor," and recited it on many occasions before San Francisco audiences. With its text, " Despise not Labor," the didactic poem sang the praise of hard work, the compelling necessity of the frontier, while as a corollary, it derided the soft
life of cultured and effete civilizations. With such lines as " The
trowel is as worthy as the pen," " The sceptre is less royal than
the hoe," " There is no deed of honest labor born that is not
Godlike," and " The miner's cradle claims from men of sense
more honor than the youngling Bonaparte's," it made a virtue
of necessity. In other passages it turned scorn upon the pre-
tenses of the man of leisure:

> Let fops and fools the sons of toil deride,
> On false pretensions brainless dunces live;
> Let carpet heroes strut with parlor pride,
> Supreme in all that indolence can give,
> Be not like them, and pray envy not
> These fancy tom-tit burlesques of mankind,
> The witless snobs in idleness who rot,
> Hermaphrodite 'twixt vanity and mind. . . .
> There's more true honor in one tan-browned hand,
> Rough with the honest work of busy men,
> Than all the soft-skinned punies of the land,
> The nice white-kiddery of upper ten.
> Blow bright the forge — the sturdy anvil ring,
> It sings the anthem of king labor's courts,
> And sweeter sounds the clattering hammers bring,
> Than half a thousand thumped pianofortes.

Soulé thus presented the attitude of the frontiersman, who ridiculed the fruits of culture so long as they were beyond his
reach.

The poetry most esteemed by the frontier public was that
which served a practical purpose. Such was the official poetry,

written to be recited before meetings of the Pioneer Society, conventions of fraternal groups, Fourth of July celebrations, and countless other civic gatherings, for which official poets were as indispensable as official orators. The normal output was augmented during the Civil War by the verses written extolling patriotism, attacking Southerners, and hailing Union victories. Also there were many elegies for fallen soldiers and for hero martyrs like Colonel Baker, Starr King, and, above all, Abraham Lincoln. They ranged from tributes in doggerel like the one lampooned by Mark Twain because its monotonous refrain, " Gone, gone, forever," contained too much " Gone " and not enough " forever," to moving poems like Harte's tributes to Starr King and Joe Goodman's ode prompted by Lincoln's assassination, a fierce lament which ended with the prophecy:

> And in the lapse of countless ages, Fame
> Shall one by one forget each cherished name;
> But thine shall live through time, until there be
> No soul on earth that glories to be free!

In San Francisco the favorite poets-of-the-day were Bret Harte, Frank Soulé, James F. Bowman, and William H. Rhodes. Among these Harte could always be depended on to write good verse, but he dreaded reciting his poems before an audience. Soulé was looked upon as the veteran of rhetoric in orations or poems; Bowman had the greatest stock of classical allusions and was sure to lend dignity, erudition, and fire to any patriotic gathering; while William H. Rhodes (Caxton) was the favorite among the fraternal groups and Irish societies of the city. On St. Patrick's Day he rose to forensic heights in his plea for Irish independence:

> Strike! till the Unicorn shall lose its crown!
> Strike! till the Eagle tears the Lion down!

Strike! till proud Albion bows her haughty head!
Strike! for the living and the martyred dead!
Strike! till fair freedom on the world shall smile
For God! for Truth! and for the Emerald Isle!

Although many of these poems ring hollow today, they did not sound so pretentious at the time of their writing. In the eighteen-sixties a public not yet satiated with radio speeches or blazoned headlines was easily moved by declamatory poems. Caxton's " The Enrobing of Liberty," Soulé's " Labor," and Goodman's " Abraham Lincoln " evoked a hearty co-operation from listeners who were in the habit of cheering orators with ingenuous enthusiasm. The frontiersman not only approved of forensics, but he joined readily in the expression of group emotion, obtaining from it a strengthening of his prejudices and hopes.

Another type of poetry, bulking large in *The Poetry of the Pacific* as well as in the journals of the period, can best be described as domestic. In a city in which the men greatly outnumbered the women, in which family life frequently was reduced to its minimum by residence in hotels, in which divorce was common and prostitution flagrant, sentimental poems on home and children were even more in demand than they were elsewhere in the Victorian age. Little verses on subjects such as " Purified," " Waiting for the Rain," " No Baby in the House," " The Empty Stocking," and " Theo — Aged Fifteen " were produced without number. Many of them were written by a score of women versifiers, scattered all the way from San Francisco to Salt Lake City, whose names became familiar to the metropolitan readers.

Perhaps the most prolific of these song-birds were Sarah Carmichael, known as the Sappho of Salt Lake City, and Anne Fitzgerald, who sang sweetly and preached earnestly in her verse. When these poets ran out of subjects, they wrote poems

INA COOLBRITH IN THE SIXTIES.

Courtesy of California State Library

CHARLES WARREN STODDARD IN HIS
EARLY TWENTIES.

Courtesy of Mr. Finlay Cook

to each other. Anne Fitzgerald added to the cultural ferment by encouraging her younger sister to compose; and, as a result, the readers of the *Era* were weighed down under lengthy odes by Marcella A. Fitzgerald. Clara Clyde was so successful with domestic lyrics such as her " No Baby in the House " that she published a volume which attained a nation-wide circulation. The serious and rather stodgy May Wentworth and the pert and light-hearted Alice Kingsbury wrote many verses in addition to their journalism and books for children. But more coy than Alice Kingsbury was Carrie Carlton, also called Topsy-Turvy, whose real name was Elizabeth Chamberlain Wright. In her collection of verse entitled *Wayside Flowers* she thanked a friend prettily for presenting her with a glass of ice-cream. After issuing a volume of children's stories called *Inglenook* and a dainty, playfully ironic handbook on letter-writing addressed to bachelors, she died in her thirty-second year and was buried beneath a tombstone inscribed " Topsy-Turvy — Called Home."

In addition to writing sentimentally of hearth-fire and babies, the women poets championed the many social reforms and panaceas that flourished in California during the sixties. The perfect society to come out of the West was the theme of many a grandiose poem such as Fanny G. McDougal's " The Genius of American Liberty " and Mrs. S. M. Clarke's " Is It Come? It Is Come." The most extreme and certainly the most eccentric of these crusaders was Eliza Pittsinger, who tried to make up for her weak lyrical fire by glowing warmly on social themes. Because she claimed supernatural aid in writing her poetry, the journalists nicknamed her " The Prophetess." Not only had she been visited in a dream by a being of transcendent beauty, possibly one of the Muses, but on Telegraph Hill in broad daylight she had conversed with a purple-clad spirit who, after playing divinely on a golden harp, had given the instrument to Eliza to be used in furthering her causes. With this extraordinary aid, she applied herself enthusiastically to the support of spiritualism, feminism, and the single standard, while she declared war on rum, vice, and Roman Catholicism. The quality of her frenzy can be seen in a couplet from " Kissing the Pope's Toe ":

> The toe of the Pope! let it molder away,
> Let it sink in oblivion, vanish, decay!

Three of the women represented in *The Poetry of the Pacific*, however, showed more than mediocre ability in handling verse. Emilie Lawson, one of the principal contributors to the *Californian*, wrote love lyrics that were both effective in imagery and genuine in emotion. Also clever as a satirist, she was commended by Oliver Wendell Holmes for her " Arkansaw Jackson Regarding the Medical College of the Pacific." Soon after the demise of the *Californian*, she abandoned poetry; in order to support a sick husband, she took up medicine and found no time for the unremunerative pursuit of writing verse. Frances Fuller Victor, who had written for the *Era* as Florence Fane, sent poems down from Oregon. In her verses she showed her increasing interest in the Northwest, and her " Sunset at the Mouth of the Columbia " made a good companion-piece to Pollock's poem on the Golden Gate.

The third and most promising of the triumvirate was Ina Coolbrith. When *The Poetry of the Pacific* was issued, she was already known on the coast as a consistently able poetess. She was a regular contributor to the *Californian*, for which she wrote under the nom-de-plumes of Ina and Meg Merrilies. As she spent six hours a day earning her living by teaching " the English branches " in a school of languages conducted by Professor J. Mibielle and an equal amount of time keeping house for her parents, she must have been hard pressed to find energy for her poetry and journalism. She also managed to be a good friend to Bret Harte and Mark Twain, who are said to have been rivals for her smiles. One story even credits Mark Twain with calling his rival a dirty name in the heat of the contest, but the charge can hardly be taken seriously, for Harte, as a married man, was in no position to defend himself against fighting words.

Ina's poetry during this period revealed a strong personal emotion not often glimpsed in her later and better-known work. " Fragment from an Unfinished Poem " recalled in lush sensuousness the days of her disillusionment in Los Angeles.

> Oh, balm, and dew, and fragrance of those nights
> Of Southern splendor 'neath a Southern sky!
> The soft star closes to the golden days
> I dreamed away, in that far, tropic clime,
> Wherein Love's blossom budded, bloomed and died!

Again, in " Unrest " she told of a tragic love which had left a slowly healing wound.

> I cannot sleep! For mourning memory opes
> Her dream domains, and sorrow roams the bowers,
> Searching, amid the withered leaves and flowers
> That strew these ruined footpaths, for the hopes
> That perished with them — perished utterly! . . .
> Through all my life have pain and passion wove
> Their subtle net-work; by the grave of Love
> I've knelt, and shed no tear.

In " A Mother's Grief " she mourned the loss of an infant child, suggesting that possibly she had borne an heir to Robert Carsley and that its death had been yet another blow that she had suffered during the dark days of her marriage.

Already, however, she was looking to the flowers and hills for conventional subjects for her poems. With time she was to grow more and more reticent about using intimate experiences and expressing strong emotion in her lyrics. The rigidly shut door on the closet of memory unfortunately cut off the freedom of expression necessary to the creation of deeply felt poetry. Those who search for the real Ina Coolbrith will find glimpses of her only in her earliest San Francisco writings.

Only one poet besides Ina Coolbrith among those represented in *The Poets of the Pacific* dared to write truly erotic lyrics. This was W. S. Kendall, long-haired, six-foot " Comet Quirls " from Petaluma, who had left school-teaching in that small village to follow a literary career in the metropolis. Barely able to keep himself alive on the proceeds from odd jobs for the San Francisco press, he put most of his energy into writing warm lyrics on how women affected him, poems such as " The Lips of the Girls " and " Near to Thee." Beside the monotonous restraint of most frontier love poetry, his verses seem almost torrid.

> Oh were my soul as high as Jove,
>   My limbs, like Samson's, lithe and strong,
> And were my heart as full of fire
>   As an unprinted passing song,
> Still heart and soul to thee would bow
> As rapturously then as now.
>
> Nearer and nearer I would lean
>   Toward thine eyes of changeful hue,
> To catch the import of the thoughts
>   That flash their melting centers through;
> And back in flame would shoot from mine
> An answer written out of rhyme.
>
> And nearer yet, and nearer yet,
>   However pure, and good, and bright,
> Unto thy presence I would cling
>   In honeymoons of full delight!
> And in the waning ashen year
> Thy snowy breast should be my bier.

He wrote of voluptuous maidens, whose lips were ripe for crushing kisses and whose bodies were eager for strained embraces. He sang of bare breasts and warm limbs. It is probable that the frontier public allowed him to express his emotions in print only because they considered him irresponsible; they felt that his lyrics lacked the ennobling quality that was expected of poetry, that his themes were wrongfully confined to selfish enjoyment of the senses. Before many years had passed, Kendall's long-suffering friends were to conclude that his genius was not great enough to compensate for his eroticism and improvidence.

In addition to the two anthologies of California verse, a number of volumes of collected poetry by California poets were issued during the sixties. Some of these appeared in the East, some were published by Roman or Bancroft but printed on Eastern presses, and a few were adequately turned out by San Francisco printers such as Bosqui, and Towne & Bacon. Some of them, financed by subscriptions, were issued for Christmas trade, in pretentious form with illustrations by local artists. There were also the customary freakish collections, books in which the writers furthered their pet ideas or tried to perpetuate their names. Such were *Glimpses of Spirit-Land* by Samuel H. Lloyd, who delivered in pedestrian verse his peculiar brand of theology, and *Pleasant Hours in an Eventful Life* by " Professor " W. Frank Stewart, who was given to lecturing on novel scientific theories, including the idea that Western earthquakes were caused by electrical disturbances in the air, and that as soon as the transcontinental railroad was completed it would form a conductor to carry them East.

Among the volumes were also a few memorial collections, the most important of which was John R. Ridge's *Poems*, published by his widow. In addition to some mildly pleasing but entirely conventional personal lyrics and a number of poems written for formal occasions, the collection included " A Cherokee Love Song," which smacked faintly of the Indian, and " The Humboldt Desert," which was based upon Western experiences. In the latter Ridge vividly pictured some of the horrors faced by the emigrants in crossing the ghastly alkali flats of Nevada.

Finally, the rash of poetry of the mid-sixties included first volumes by James Linen, Bret Harte, Charles W. Stoddard, and Edward Rowland Sill. *The Poetical and Prose Writings* of James Linen is dull even to the antiquarian. Only in a day when verses such as " I Feel I'm Growing Auld, Gude Wife," and " I Canna Leave My Minnie " were popular with amateurs who recited in plush parlors was the emigrant from Edinburgh a man of some importance.

Bret Harte's *The Lost Galleon, and Other Tales*, published in 1867, was his second book, following his *Condensed Novels and Other Sketches* by only a few months. The book of poems, printed in San Francisco by Towne & Bacon, was much better turned out than the volume of prose that had been done in New York. *The Lost Galleon* was well received by the critics, who had apparently forgotten the war over *Outcroppings*. Including the best of the poems which Harte had written for the *Era*, the *Californian*, and the *Evening Bulletin*, the bulk of its contents consisted of war poems and parodies already well known to local readers. Though it offered little that was new, its appearance helped to establish Harte as the leading writer of the Pacific slope.

The appearance in 1867 of the collected poems of Charles Warren Stoddard in his twenty-fourth year marked the climax of its author's short career as the boy prodigy among San Francisco writers. Since the day six years before when Starr King had dropped in to see him in C. Beach's book-store and had given him words of encouragement, Pip Pepperpod had devoted himself to writing verse, feeling that his development as a poet was more important than anything else. True, he had attended college at Brayton Hall in Oakland for a few months. There he was happy at first, finding pleasure in reading the *Anabasis*, Virgil, Tennyson, and George Herbert; but presently things began to go badly. The routine work he could not do, the set assignments he could not meet. Even English classes proved impossible; he could write passable sonnets, but a prose theme, on a definite subject, in a prescribed manner, due a certain hour of a certain day — it was impossible. His instructor remarked that he might become a poet, but he would never be a student. Daydreaming ended in consternation when examination time came at the end of the year. Charlie felt that his mental depression was as deep as the sorrows of Werther. Again he collapsed — another nervous breakdown — so his short college career ended in escape to Hawaii, where one of his sisters had married a wealthy planter.

When he returned to San Francisco, he began writing for the *Californian* and Bret Harte took him in hand. The latter suggested that he collect his poems in a book. Stoddard had been contemplating such a step for some time, for praise of his poems had long been coming to him from great writers when he had solicited autographs and advice. Seven years earlier he had shown the first symptoms of tuft-hunting, a practice he never outgrew. His large album had grown fat with autographs from everybody from Charles Darwin to Adah Isaacs Menken. To supplement his collection, Stoddard had a dozen of his poems struck off on proof sheets and sent them far and wide for criticism. George Eliot wrote that she was pleased to find him planting and watering a little garden away off in San Francisco; Longfellow detected in addition to beauty " a certain flavor of the soil " in the verses; and Emerson wrote that he was much touched by the poems. Whitman suggested that he look to the hard, pungent, gritty, worldly experiences and qualities in American life for subjects. Less encouraging were John Stuart Mill, who advised the boy that no poetry but the very best was worth publishing, and Oliver Wendell Holmes, who warned him to think well before relinquishing any useful occupation to write poetry.

Keeping the kindest of these remarks in his mind, Stoddard felt that a real career was ahead of him. The collection of his poems was to be the most pretentious volume yet issued by a California press; it had been illustrated by a popular artist, William Keith, and was to be handsomely printed by Bosqui on the finest paper to be obtained. The subscription list had been made up of " nearly every well-known name in the Professional, Political, Religious and Social Circles of California." Everything had been done to make the work of San Francisco's boy poet a signal success: Bret Harte had selected and edited the poems with his usual meticulous care, and all of Charlie's friends had seen to it that pledges were signed to buy on publication. But Stoddard became so nervous while the book was in the press that Harte and Roman suggested that he go to Yosemite till it came out; thus the poet himself was the last to see the new work.

The book aroused almost as much comment as had *Outcroppings*. When Stoddard came down from the mountains to glimpse his offspring, he found himself the center of a storm of words, a lengthy storm, lasting two or three months, and a voluminous one, as is shown by the four scrapbooks of reviews in one Stoddard collection. His friend Bowman wrote for the *Californian*, in most fulsome language, an eloquent eulogy which assured the readers that a Western poetic movement was here inaugurated; in turn the *Dramatic Chronicle* attacked Bowman and accused the young poet of being a pompous blockhead with an " owlish air of ponderous and all-embracing wisdom," and insisted that his verse was consummately bad. It was rather fun, this being the center of the stage, until Stoddard discovered that Bowman had written the attack as well as the first article, just to keep the battle of words at a high pitch. Sympathetic editors came to his defense; those with a satiric turn of mind quoted his own lines against him. Soon it was clear that the war over Stoddard's poetry was just another battle for the amusement of the public.

Meanwhile the Eastern critics, who were confused by no mock warfare, were even more unkind: the reviewer in the *Nation* called the poems " imitation spasms," while Stedman wrote: " It is very clear that Mr. Stoddard would have written differently had there been no Tennyson; still, there are melodious echoes." Their strictures undoubtedly touched a vital spot, for the poems, though often felicitous in phrase, were original chiefly in a preciosity that soon tired the reader. The figure in " A Fancy " was typical:

> Perhaps the Sun is an egg of gold
> In a nest of Cloud, and Night must be
> A fidgety hen — for, look! she has rolled
> Out of the nest the egg of gold,
> And spilled the yolk in the sea.

The volume was clearly intended to lie on the drawing-room table so that members of the family and guests could while away the time reading light verse according to their mood from sections entitled " Idyllic and Legendary," " Of the Heart," " Of Fancy and Imagination," " Of Aspiration and Desire," and " Of Meditation."

The over-sensitive Stoddard grew despondent as he read the reviews. He told himself that the critics who were most encouraging were not judging his work sanely — some were his friends, who were interested in him as a precocious infant; others were simply using him as an excuse for a warfare of words in which they could enjoy the exercise of their wit. The truth of the matter was, he concluded, that he had rushed into print prematurely and that his poetry was highly imitative, without a spark of real genius. He did not stop to consider that most juvenile verse is subject to the same criticism, and that further experience might bring better lines. Instead, he decided that his poetry was worthless and that he could never become a good poet.

In the depression that followed, Stoddard became more than ever aware of painful struggles within him: a conflict between creative enthusiasm which lashed him to work, and an over-powering lethargy, which made even the slightest schedule of living almost a physical impossibility to follow; and a clash between the moments of pagan love of life, and the harrowing sense of damnation, instilled during the two years he had spent with his grandparents, for sins incomprehensible.

Then too, as he had grown older, Stoddard had come to realize that there was a fundamental maladjustment in his nature, an epicene turn to his friendships which made him too dependent on his male companions. Sympathetic acquaintances explained his nature by saying: " He has a woman's soul in all its strange and endless changeableness." He in turn asked why the world made no greater effort to understand the girlish boy, and consigned the bitter moments of his anguish to his many diaries. With marriage out of the question, he would always be the prey of unsatisfactory and frequently unsocial friendships. How was he to escape from the unrest inherent in a body that craved comfort, bound him in lethargy, or drove him onward towards forbidden pleasures?

His temporary haven was religion, but not the faith of his parents. In the year that he gave up poetry he became an ardent convert to Roman Catholicism. The beauty of its ritual, the mysticism of its creed, the consolation of its confessional,

all appealed to him intensely. It answered for him, as nothing
before had done, the question which was with him constantly:
" What shall I do to be saved? " When he was baptised, he
felt that all of his problems were solved. " I laid my heart in
absolute surrender. From the steps of that altar I seemed
to rise a new being. I had shattered the chrysalis and the wings
of my soul expanded in the everlasting light that radiates from
the Throne of Grace." If he could not find a place in lay society, he would become a monk.

The Hermitage and Other Poems by Edward Rowland Sill,
issued in 1868 by Henry Holt of New York and H. H. Bancroft of San Francisco, was the first work of a poet hitherto
unnoticed on the Pacific slope. Its reflective lyrics revealed a
character as sensitive and restless as Stoddard and decidedly
more analytical. Its long title poem told the story of a disillusioned young man who had turned his back on the " old,
foolish, wicked world " to live as a hermit on the slopes of Mount
Tamalpais, overlooking San Francisco Bay. Here, like a true
Wordsworthian, he communed with nature, finding rocks and
trees more noble than crowds and cities.

> But I am tired of what we call our lives;
> Tired of the endless humming in the hives, —
> Sick of the bitter honey that we eat,
> And sick of cursing all the shallow cheat.

Though the story in the poem was fictional, the thoughts expressed by the main character were the thoughts of the poet
himself; and though love cured the hermit of his temporary
misanthropy, no such easy solution was at hand for Edward
Rowland Sill. That tall, slender, chestnut-haired youth suffered from an incurable disease; he was an idealist in search of
a world which did not exist. Like Oliver Alden of Santayana's

Last Puritan, his demands from life were too rigorous to be satisfied; and like Arthur Hugh Clough, his nature demanded a faith which his skepticism put beyond reach. His credo was based on the Puritan tenet: " I know that Duty is the one end [of life] "; and his frustration was summed up in his lament: " I wish I had more faith in *men,* as well as in God."

Sill was a New Englander, steeped in the culture of a passing order. The descendant of a long line of Connecticut ministers and physicians, he had been raised in an intellectual atmosphere. He found Yale too monastic and objected to students debating such futile questions as " Is Language of Divine or Human Origin? " Though he was both a diligent reader and an accomplished writer, he was rusticated for neglecting his duties; and though he thought more about religious subjects than most of his fellows, he was one of the three nonconformists in his class who refused to join the church in the revival of 1858. When he graduated in his twenty-first year, he felt that he was not yet ready to take up a lifelong profession. Deciding to gain experience in the West, he sailed round the Horn and arrived in San Francisco in January 1862.

During the next five years Sill experimented with life, trying to find an answer to his question: " What was I born to do? " He worked for a while in the post office in Sacramento; he spent several months on a ranch in the Coast Range, riding fifty miles a day herding cattle; he lived for more than a year at Folsom, near the mines, where he weighed out gold dust for " Pikes, fools, fools, fools, and other fools." In his spare time he studied law and medicine to discipline his mind, but decided he did not care to be a lawyer or a physician. He even considered becoming an actor, but never quite got around to applying for a job. Gradually he realized that one of two professions was to claim him in the end; he would be a minister, if he could find a faith that suited him, or, failing that, he would be a school-teacher. He eventually became a school-teacher.

Sill's letters reveal that many aspects of California life were distasteful to him. He protested that he found no culture, no thought, no art; he suffered from " the terrible isolation " and pronounced the people money-mad. He called himself a pilgrim and stranger in heathendom, but took consolation in the thought that in a heathen country " one's only companions are Shakespeare, Shelley and Mill and Browning and Spencer and the others." In addition to his reading, he found twin pleasures in contemplating nature and in creating poetry; as his Western sojourn lengthened far beyond expectation, he came to love the brown hills and rugged mountains of California and wrote nature lyrics which for the moment remained in his notebooks. Nearly always these slight and somewhat conventional poems were a mixture of imagery and analysis; speculation permeated his verse as well as his letters home.

In his twenty-sixth year he returned to the East and took up divinity studies at Harvard. But the society for which he had been homesick so long did not satisfy him; he gave up his training for the ministry, mourned that even the springs of poetry had ceased to flow, and found himself most unreasonably longing for the West.

> Ah, give me back the clime I know,
> Where all the year geraniums blow,
> And hyacinth buds bloom white for snow.

And in 1870 he returned to Oakland, where he taught in the high school for several years and then joined the English faculty at the University of California.

Though Sill wrote most of his early poetry in California, he made no contact with Western writers and journals during his first sojourn on the coast. *The Hermitage* received little attention from the San Francisco critics, for no one was interested either in sponsoring or in attacking the small book of verse. When Sill returned to the West, he contributed to the *Overland Monthly* and in time won some recognition as a nature poet, but his retiring temperament kept him from appearing large in the public eye. Thus *The Hermitage* was the only collection of Sill's poems to be published during his lifetime; it was an important, though neglected, item in the rash of poetry that came out of California in the sixties.

CHAPTER IX

THE TOWN CRIER

No writer connected with the Far-Western frontier has given rise to more bizarre stories and conflicting theories than Ambrose Gwinnett (" Almighty God ") Bierce, known to posterity as Bitter Bierce. Was he a social-minded editor who set about reform with a trenchant pen backed by a six-shooter, or merely a selfish misanthrope who gained sadistic pleasure in breaking butterflies on the wheel? Was he a soft-hearted sentimentalist who mocked at a world which hurt him too much, an idealist who turned bitter because he could not find the perfection he craved, or a wit who was spoiled by early adulation and adopted the satiric pose as his most effective role? Were his many idiosyncrasies, such as his refusal to eat spinach, his loathing of dogs, and his fondness for skulls as desk ornaments, simply acts in a show which culminated dramatically in one of the best-staged disappearances of modern times? Or was he a strange, powerful genius whose talent fell on fallow ground because he was unfortunately born into a society that would not stomach satiric medicine?

Though critics are even today by no means agreed on the intrinsic value of Ambrose Bierce's literary output, they unite in recognizing him as one of the first American writers to portray war realistically and one of the few satirists who refused to sell out during the Gilded Age. His war fiction and his satire both show the love of the macabre and the malicious and biting wit which were the foremost characteristics of his misanthropy. This misanthropy was so pronounced that many theories have been advanced to explain it. Some hold that it was the result of physical distress caused either by a head wound received in the Civil War or by the incessant discomfort of chronic asthma, contracted by sleeping on a gravestone in Laurel Cemetery. Others maintain that his marital troubles made him cynical. Most popular is the theory that the inadequacies of frontier society aroused him to attack, and that the refusal of that society to allow criticism turned him bitter. This frustration school of critics would have us believe that, just as Mark Twain was diverted from a great career because the frontier would accept nothing but humor from his pen, so Bierce was thwarted and angered by the materialism, the optimism, the conventionality of a pioneer society. A careful examination of Bierce's earliest writing, that done shortly after he reached the Pacific Coast, should help to determine the correct answer.

Ambrose Bierce was twenty-four years old when he arrived in San Francisco late in 1866. His frame of mind was that of perhaps the majority of young men who came west; he didn't know what he was to become, but he was certain that he did not like the opportunities for a livelihood that presented themselves in the country of his childhood. The war had liberated him from the farm in Indiana; and having decided that his parents were " unwashed savages," he was determined not to return to carry the load of the ninth child of an indigent farmer. He did not intend to repeat his early tasks of farming, working in a saloon, or making bricks, nor did he desire to emulate the sister who had become a missionary or the brother who had taken a job as a strong man in a circus.

AMBROSE BIERCE AS A YOUNG MAN.

Courtesy of Society of California Pioneers

JOHN PHŒNIX'S PROPOSAL
FOR IMPROVING UNIFORMS.
A section from Derby's notebook illustrat-
ing the use of his patent ring to be sewed to
the trousers of infantrymen.

Courtesy of Mr. George R. Stewart

THE POLITICAL PRIZE RING.
This cartoon, drawn by Edward Jump for *Puck*, was undoubtedly suggested by Mark Twain's "The Great Prize Fight," in which he described
the contest between Low and Stanford in pugilistic terms. All of the
figures at the ring-side are well known California politicians. Jump's
contest of 1865 is between the Long Hairs and the Short Hairs.

Courtesy of the Bancroft Library

Nineteen-year-old Ambrose Bierce had welcomed the opportunity to fight for the Union. He enrolled as a private in Company C, Ninth Indiana Infantry, and saw active service throughout the war, rising to the rank of first lieutenant of topographical engineers in 1862. He fought in West Virginia, along the Mississippi, and in Georgia. He took part in the battles of Shiloh, Murfreesboro, Nashville, Chickamauga, and Franklin, was once captured by the enemy and escaped, was wounded severely at Kenesaw Mountain, and was cited several times for bravery.

Like his companions, Bierce saw many horrible things during the war — the sickening spat of lead against flesh, the brain protruding in bosses from the chipped skull, the shriveled remains of soldiers cremated in a burning wood, etched pictures not easily to be erased from his mind. The impingement of horror on beauty he tried to escape by making cynical remarks. He said he had hired out as an assassin for his country; he announced he had found humanity frothing mad — cursed with illusions; he tried to pretend that nothing mattered. Pain came to have a strange pleasure for him, the pleasure one gets in picking at a scab or teasing a sore tooth.

There is, however, no reason to assume that Bierce was still suffering from his war experiences when he reached San Francisco. Since the days of Chickamauga and Pickett's Hill he had spent several months collecting the iniquitous cotton tax in Alabama; he had made a pleasure trip to Panama from New Orleans and had confided to his notebook no fierce comments on human nature; and he had thoroughly enjoyed accompanying his former commander, General W. B. Hazen, on a military survey through the Black Hills of the Dakotas, past the frontier forts of Wyoming, and into the spectacular country of the Shoshone Falls and the Yellowstone. He had drawn sketches in his notebooks of buffalo heads, Indian inscriptions, and hill contours, and had often remarked on the beauties of nature, but he had indulged in no minor misanthropy during those days of '66.

Having been brevetted major for distinguished service during the war, Bierce expected to find a satisfactory commission awaiting him in the West. When it turned out to be only a second lieutenancy, he was insulted and refused to have anything more to do with an army career. Soon he obtained a position with the United States Treasury Department in San Francisco and was working there when he began to write for the newspapers.

Nor did Bierce leave any impression of bitterness among the friends he quickly made in the city. The slender, golden-haired young man with his blue-gray eyes and baby-pink complexion was a favorite with the employees of the Subtreasury and the Mint, and, a little later, a good companion to the writers on the *Californian* and the *Overland Monthly*. He probably did not meet Mark Twain, for the latter left the West about the time Bierce arrived, but he was on the best of terms with Harte and a close friend of Ina Coolbrith and Charlie Stoddard. His letters to the latter indicate both enthusiasm for life and an engaging playfulness; the only hint of his official position as social castigator is found in the flippant remark: " Tell anybody anything that is not complimentary, and attribute the same to me." He probably meant it no more seriously than his statement in print about a Mr. Fennell, whom he called Flannel to annoy: " I intend, merely as a matter of duty, to chew up Mr. Flannel and spit him against a stone wall the first time I catch him coming out of Dr. Zeille's steam bath house."

Bierce's earliest journalism in San Francisco did not appear in the satirical *News Letter*, where he first gained his reputation as a wit and misanthropist. In fact, he did not become the Town Crier until the fall of 1868, after he had been in the

West for two years. During this period he printed a few poems and articles in the *Californian*, items of special interest in following Bierce's development because they contain very few of the later characteristics of the satirist. Further, they suggest that possibly " Bitter Bierce " became bitter chiefly because he inherited and furthered the Town Crier tradition on the *News Letter*.

The poems show that Bierce was writing under the influence of Poe. One, entitled " Basilica," hinted at a deep-lying corruption in nature. While the poet was feeling in the sands of the seashore for a beautiful gem, he was horrified to discover that he had grasped a hideous basilisk:

> With ivory throat of pallid white,
> And snaky folds concealed from sight . . .
> With jeweled teeth, alas! and breath
> Whose touch to passion ministreth.

" A Mystery " was a reflective lyric describing life as a moment between memory and illusion.

> Wouldst thou know, O mortal, the secret of Pain?
> 'Tis the payment in blood for each wish we obtain.

In addition to these poems, the *Californian* carried some prose sketches which may be assigned to Bierce. " Concerning Tickets," an undistinguished satire on women's activity in selling tickets for benefits, was signed by A. Gwinnett. More worthy of consideration was the series of four articles signed A. G. B. on the subject of " Female Suffrage." In logical and compelling prose the writer asked that the feminists be accorded a sympathetic reception. He excused the fanaticism of the suffragettes on the ground that fanaticism was " essentially progressive, and progress was truth." He deplored the absence of opportunity for women to be educated, and assured the public that, if allowed to vote, women would make politics decent

and respectable. The only sentence in which the reader de-
tects the typical Biercean flavor is one in which women are
excused for having but few interests. " Her babies and her
visitors are about her only society; and though the former are
usually a source of delight and the latter of annoyance, neither
are particularly well-calculated to give her broad views or mental culture."

The Ambrose Bierce of later days would have scorned both
the grammar and the attitude of these articles. Shortly, he
was to lead an attack on the feminists, and, as time went on, he
was to earn the name of woman-hater. Furthermore, he was
to become a poet-baiter, ridiculing writers whose versification
was no more amateurish and diction no more fulsome than that
of which he had been guilty. That he shifted his ground so
quickly was probably the result of becoming the Town Crier
on the most satiric journal in a city at the moment delighting
in satire. The policies and prejudices of the Town Crier were
to a very large extent created by the *News Letter* and the environment in which it was printed. A word about that environment will aid in explaining the emergence of Bitter Bierce.

Bierce joined the staff of the *News Letter* at a time when
satire was increasing in San Francisco journalism. An adolescent sophistication grew with the mid-sixties, a critical attitude
which was adopted even by those writers who were least satiric
by nature. The trend of the times was seen in the substitution
of the polite literature and social satire of the *Californian* for
the comparatively naïve fiction and poetry of the *Era*. Local-
color stories gave way to articles ridiculing the efforts of the
local poets, joking about the climate, and satirizing the old-
timers, who, in Harte's words, were " blanked fools who landed
here when the water came up to Montgomery Street." Fast
nearing the end of its frontier youth, the Western metropolis

was trying to appear grown up by imitating the tone of older cities. This stage of development would have to be lived through before Western writers, achieving maturity, could gain perspective on the frontier social experiment and see in it good material for fiction, economic theory, and history.

Hardly a journalist in San Francisco resisted the movement towards satire. Mild-mannered Charlie Stoddard and lovesick W. A. Kendall tried painfully to adapt their verse to the satirical purpose of the short-lived *Puck*. Good-humored, philosophic Prentice Mulford stooped to the invective of personal journalism, attacking the *Bulletin* in an editorial opening with the line: " Hear the corrupt and ulcerated tongue which with its stench renders almost impassable the mouth of Market Street." Versatile Jimmy Bowman, who had written learned articles on " The Age of Alfred " and " The Anglo-Saxon Writers " for the *Hesperian* and sentimental lyrics entitled " Homesick " and " At the Ball " for the *Californian*, became overnight the stinging scorpion among Montgomery Street editors.

It has already been observed that the prevailing mood in the journalism of Mark Twain gradually shifted during the mid-sixties from good-natured burlesques to satirical attacks upon both man and his institutions. His letters from the Sandwich Islands continued to sound the note of the satiric moralist which had been detected by his readers even before he sailed on the *Ajax* on March 1, 1866, bound for Honolulu to write travel letters for the Sacramento *Union*. In his Hawaiian correspondence, his first sustained writing, he experimented in a field which he was to make famous in *The Innocents Abroad;* but, more important, his journalism showed clear development in three lines. His humor raised itself from the low level of jokes about seasickness, curio-snatching, and equestrian adventures to the rich dialogue with his companion and inner voice, Mr. Brown, a practical-minded Mephistopheles, whose debates with Mark Twain foreshadowed those between Huck and Tom. His descriptive work moved towards forceful, modeled prose in such passages as his picture of the crater of Kilauea. And his satire grew more purposeful and devastating, particularly in his asides about missionaries and politicians in the islands.

His attacks on minister Harris, a renegade American from New Hampshire who made a dismal spectacle of himself in Hawaiian politics, and his gibes at Bishop Staley as a bishop made " out of very inferior material " continued in the tradition of the Virginia City school of personal journalism. More socially philosophic in tone, however, were such touches as his summing up of the gift of the missionary to the heathen: " The missionaries braved a thousand privations to come and make them permanently miserable by telling them how beautiful and how blissful a place heaven is, and how nearly impossible it is to get there."

Good satire, also, was his arraignment of the legislators of Honolulu, typical, as he pointed out, of legislators throughout the world. " Few men of first class ability can afford to let their affairs go to ruin while they fool away their time in Legislatures. . . . But your chattering, one-horse village lawyer likes it, and your solemn ass from the cow countries, who don't know the Constitution from the Lord's Prayer, enjoys it, and these you will always find in the Assembly; the one gabble, gabble, gabbling threadbare platitudes and ' give-me-liberty-or-give-me-death ' buncombe from morning to night, and the other asleep, with his slab-soled brogans set up like a couple of gravestones on the top of his desk."

In the mid-sixties Bret Harte also followed the popular trend, turning from local fiction and polite essays to satires in verse and prose. The bulk of his writing during the interim between the time he left the *Californian* and the day he started the *Overland Monthly* was done for the *News Letter*. Never a thoroughgoing satirist at heart, Harte's *News Letter* contributions were light-spirited burlesques. In verse he mocked the exaggerated stories about stagecoach-drivers, telling a tall one about a driver who brought his coach in safely after losing all four wheels. Again, he twitted the boosters of California's climate in " California Madrigal." Two of the stanzas read:

> Oh, mark how the spring in its beauty is near!
> How the fences and tules once more reappear!
> How soft lies the mud on the banks of yon slough
> By the hole in the levee the waters broke through! . . .
>
> Then fly with me, love, ere the summer's begun,
> And the mercury mounts to one hundred and one;
> Ere the grass now so green shall be withered and sear,
> In the spring that obtains but one month of the year.

In prose he specialized in take-offs on the meetings of the California Academy of Natural Science, which also served as the subject for one of his most amusing poems, first called " Proceedings of the Academy of Natural Sciences at Smith's Crossing, Tuolumne Country," later known as " The Society upon the Stanislaus." In addition, he parodied the Western newspaper correspondents who sent home letters from Europe telling how far it fell below California standards; he ridiculed the advertisements of local spas, gravely listing the composition of the healing waters as silex (broken soda-water bottles), phosphorus (poisoned gopher), and iron (mule shoes) and adding: " The patients who most profit by the water are those of enfeebled intellect." He printed a passage of a translation from Homer by a Californian who could read no Greek, citing it as " only another evidence of the self-sustaining power and originality of the true Californian." And he pictured St. Patrick's day among the Irish in Slumgullion Center, Calaveras

County, telling how they extolled liberty just after beating up a Negro and cleaning out several Chinamen. Michael O'Shaughnessy twisted the lion's tail vigorously and taunted a local Englishman with the challenge: "Go back to your cowardly masters. Tell them Calaveras County rejects their bribes — despises their filthy lucre." After the speech, transparencies announced the Fenian slogan: "Ireland for the Irish, America for the Naturalized, and H-ll for the Niggers and Chinese."

Western journalism with its blunt boldness furnished an excellent medium for a satirist like Bierce. The policy of resorting to invective and personal attack in editorial columns had been pursued with so much license that it had more than once led to gun-play; it had brought death to Edward Gilbert on the dueling ground and martyrdom to James King of William in front of the *Bulletin* office. Many frontier editors went armed to back up their convictions or their blackmail; when the Concealed Weapons Ordinance was passed in 1875, a city editor applied for a license to carry a gun on the grounds that "the position which the journal with which I am connected has assumed in the present political campaign, and the character of the aspirants for office, render it necessary for me to provide myself with a weapon of defence." And in that same year the son of San Francisco's Mayor shot and killed Charles De Young, editor of the *Chronicle*, for printing derogatory statements about his father.

The popularity of satire in the San Francisco press gave life to a number of journals, many of them weeklies, which specialized in picturesque invective. From the *Bulletin* of the fifties, which set out to clean up municipal corruption — and incidentally the firm of Adams & Company — to the *Wasp* of the eighties, which attacked a thousand abuses and made a thousand enemies, the local journals mixed in politics, furthered their own interests, and indulged in outspoken attack under the protection of a code which assumed that if a victim didn't like it he could shoot it out with the editor. In fact, many of these short-lived publications, like the *Mazeppa*, were nothing but blackmail journals. In 1866 the Sacramento " informer " of the latter scandal sheet was publicly horsewhipped by a woman who had been traduced in its columns.

Milder in their methods were the journals that lived on their advertising and used satire merely as a medium for filling their columns and keeping themselves in the public talk. *Puck*, which ran from 1864 to 1866, appears to have been an advertising sheet for the questionable Pacific Museum of Anatomy; its literary activity embraced dull puns, " stingers " directed at the local press under the titles of the " Blanket " (the *Alta*) and the " Morning Scream " (the *Call*), and some Hogarthian drawings by Edward Jump. The *Dramatic Chronicle*, started by the De Young brothers during this period, was a daily theater program distributed free throughout the city and financed by the advertisements it carried. The limited amount of reading-material was almost entirely satirical; and, as the De Young boys combined energy and irreverence and did not hesitate to play the dangerous game of personal attack, the sheet soon became notorious. Not long after its inception, the brothers altered it into a daily newspaper, the San Francisco *Chronicle*, which has survived as a leading metropolitan daily. Similar to the *Dramatic Chronicle* was *Figaro*, a four-page theater program carrying editorials, jokes, theater and sporting gossip, and satirical quips at local men and institutions. Edited by Tremenhere Lanyon Johns, a Cornishman who had once held a position in the British Admiralty, it flourished for ten years on its theatrical information and spicy reading. A typical paragraph read: " The *Alta* had rabies badly on Monday. Yesterday one of the *Call* pack was similarly afflicted. . . . If the *Alta* and *Call* proprietors would muzzle their mad dog editors, they would do the public a service. If they don't, *Figaro* will feel it a duty to strew strychnined cigars in the passages leading to the editorial rooms, and thus abate the nuisance."

The most successful and widely circulating of the satirical journals and the one which introduced Ambrose Bierce to the San Francisco public was the *San Francisco News Letter and Commercial Advertiser*, official organ of the Aerial Steam Navigation Company. It was founded in 1856 by Frederick Marriott, an Englishman whose love for fighting journalism was equaled only by his interest in aviation. He had for years been experimenting with flying machines and in 1842, before he left London, had applied for a patent for a steam-driven plane. Failing to gain recognition and backing in England, he had come to California during the gold-rush and had turned to journalism to obtain financial support for his hobby. His *News Letter* first appeared as a single sheet of thin blue paper folded once. Two pages were for advertisements, news, and an occasional lithograph; a third was left free for correspondence; and the fourth was reserved for the address. Like similar news letters used by the Westerners in the days when postage overland to the east coast was five dollars an ounce, the sheet served as a booster leaflet, a memento for the recipient, and a convenient light-weight form of stationery. Marriott's sheet, however, not only survived the era of the printed news letter, but expanded into a sixteen-page weekly journal, the most profitable advertising organ in the city, and eventually brought in enough funds to raise the Flying Aviator, a twenty-eight-foot model steam-driven airship which its owner launched before an enthusiastic crowd in 1869. After entertaining the visitors to the Mechanics Fair for a season, the model burned and was never rebuilt.

Marriott early found that the best kind of reading-material

to leaven the sizable lump of advertising was satire, and he succeeded so well in making his journal the bad boy of San Francisco newspapers that it was banned as immoral by the University of Michigan. An emphasis on the macabre went hand in hand with irreverence for all institutions, particularly religious ones. The customary department devoted to births, marriages, and deaths was headed: " The Cradle, the Altar, and the Tomb "; the feature page was written by the Town Crier, who was allowed to say almost anything he pleased; and the journal made a special policy of exposing medical quacks. Under a skull and cross-bones and the caption: " Gentlemen, you call yourselves doctors. Have you a diploma? " Marriott weekly printed a list of doctors whom he suspected of practicing illegally. Sometimes he added titles after the names, such as " late hospital steward," " colored barber," " cobbler," " bartender," or " jail-bird."

The extent to which San Franciscans allowed their journalists to go is illustrated by the openness with which Marriott expressed his Southern sentiments during the Civil War. All during the conflict he specialized in satires and burlesques on Northern generals, local patriots, and particularly Abraham Lincoln. No ridicule was too outspoken to heap on the President's head. The *News Letter* survived the war undisturbed, but when the news of Lincoln's assassination reached San Francisco, the hysterical populace broke into the Copperhead's plant, wrecked his press, and scattered his type upon the street. The *Bulletin* expressed the general feeling when it published the rhyme:

> Little Fred Marriott, Fly quickly! Tarry not,
>   Picking up News Letter pi!
> Stay not sucking your thumb,
> Lest a worst thing should come,
>   And a noose let a Briton hang high!

The San Franciscans, however, could not long be angry with the venerable Marriott, whose fresh pink cheeks, limpid eyes, and silky white hair made him look more like a seraph than a devil. They continued to quaff the mental dram he prepared for them, though it might be killing them by inches. And when, in December 1868, Marriott announced that he had obtained a new Town Crier for the *News Letter*, a promising young writer named Ambrose Bierce, they were prepared for a weekly message expressed with the outspokenness of a Rabelais, the irreverence of a Heine, and the misanthropy of a Swift.

It was soon evident that Bierce would give his readers what they wanted. He was well fitted to improve on the technique of his predecessors. Having watched the flies crawl on battered skulls in the war, he was ready to be flippant about death in a manner to satisfy even the San Franciscans, who had long made a specialty of the macabre. Even the less sensational daily papers of the city at times went in for the combination of irony and horror that was the specialty of the *News Letter*. The *Bulletin*, for example, carried the following editorial on the discovery of a baby's corpse in an ash-can: " It seems impossible for a man to dig potatoes in a garden, or excavate a post hole in a front yard, without turning up some little innocent thing that has been dumped there without either coffin or shroud. Yesterday the body of a baby was found lying at one of the wharves, in a tin-can. When it comes to canning babies, putting them up, so to speak, ' for exportation,' as though they were oysters, shrimps, green turtle, or jellies, it becomes time to speak and remonstrate."

It was much in this vein that Bierce commented weekly on the violent accidents, homicides, suicides, and attempts at mayhem that were reported in the daily press. " The Italians continue their cheerful national recreation of stabbing one another," he wrote. " On Monday evening one was found badly gashed in the stomach, going about his business with his entrails thrown over his arm." The Town Crier never missed an opportunity to be ironical about an execution. " A man in Vermont was recently hanged by the neck until he was dead, dead, dead, and for the trifling offence of stealing another's shirt. He had previously removed the head that the garment might not be soiled with hair oil." At this early date Bierce was already specializing in suicides. (He later became an ardent defender of the reasonableness of taking one's own life, and many believe he took his own.) Among methods he recommended white arsenic: " Ratsbane is winning golden opinions upon all sides, as a perfectly safe and efficacious specific for life's fitful fever." But he warned against interfering with its workings and so clouding ethical problems. " One day last week a woman at the Brooklyn Hotel attempted to refute some imputations against her character by passing through an ordeal of arsenic. She was speedily pumped dry by a meddling medico, and her chastity is still a bone of contention."

Among other devices for causing shock and expressing irreverence Bierce developed his paragraphs of general and local jottings, gaining his effects by terse comments on events, placed in startling juxtaposition. The following composite paragraph illustrates the method. " Woman fell in the sewer. Sweets to the sweet. — Two men fell, each in his respective fit. — Man hanged himself in a barn. — 63 persons went to heaven in July. — 187 couples married in July. The nights have been uncomfortably warm. — Successful abortion. Woman died. — Several babies staved off. — Mr. Bancroft is about to build a new sty on Market Street. — French priest has abandoned the errors of the Romish for those of the Protestant Church. — Olympic muscle men elected performing and executive apes. — The weekly rape is of a milder nature. Money will settle it this time. — An insurance company was robbed. Tit for tat. —

Assorted incendiarism. — Miscellaneous grand larceny. — Young ruffians insult school girls. School girls like it. — Frightful atrocities of Chinese. Theft and murder of a hen. — Pioneer's going East. Our credit is ruined."

Bierce rarely missed an opportunity to ridicule ministers, to jibe at churches, or to mock at religion. In posing as a Satanic atheist he may merely have been continuing a *News Letter* policy, an affectation common among California journals and writers, or he may have been entirely sincere in his violent attacks on evangelical religion. It is true that he had revolted against the camp meetings of his childhood, and it is said that his first writings in San Francisco were atheistic tracts; probably he fell in whole-heartedly with the *News Letter's* policy of ribbing churches and churchmen. Thus he defended Judas Iscariot at the expense of the other apostles; he implied that St. Paul was a hypocrite, and he defined religion as "the church member's ticket entitling him to a reserved seat in the dress circle of heaven, commanding a good view of the pit." Of the Methodist Book Concern, then in financial difficulties, he wrote: "This mammoth conversion machine will never be decently managed until the elect are all turned out, and it passes into the hands of secular thieves who have sense enough to cover up their rascalities with something more opaque than the cloak of religion." And he joyfully bade farewell to all departing ministers, sending them on their ways with cheerful messages, such as: "Goodby, Doctor [Cox]; may God grant thee a safe — and speedy journey to that blessed clime where the *News Letter* ceases from troubling and the parsons are at rest."

He was so proud of one of the prayers he wrote that he reprinted it in his first book. "O, Lord, who for the purposes of this supplication we will assume to have created the heavens and the earth before man created Thee; and who, let us say,

art from everlasting to everlasting; we beseech Thee to turn
Thy attention this way and behold a set of the most abandoned
scalawags Thou hast ever had the pleasure of setting eyes on."
After a number of worldly requests, he ended: " But in consideration of the fact that Thou sentest Thy only-begotten
Son among us, and afforded us the felicity of murdering him,
we would respectfully suggest the propriety of taking into
heaven such of us as pay our church dues, and giving us an
eternity of exalted laziness and absolutely inconceivable fun.
We ask this in the name of Thy Son whom we strung up as
above stated. Amen."

The unchristian behavior of some Christians was one of his
favorite themes, which he used to inveigh against the persecution of the Chinese by those who preached brotherly love. On
several occasions children stoned the yellow men on San Francisco streets. After one such episode Bierce wrote: " On last
Sunday afternoon a Chinaman passing guilelessly along Du-
pont Street was assailed with a tempest of bricks and stones
from the steps of the First Congregational Church. At the completion of this devotional exercise the Sunday-scholars retired
within the hallowed portals of the sanctuary, to hear about
Christ Jesus, and Him crucified." Perhaps it was such attacks
on helpless Orientals that made Bierce deplore the existence of
boys. " The fact that boys are allowed to exist at all is evidence
of a remarkable Christian forbearance among men — were it not
for a mawkish humanitarianism, coupled with imperfect diges-
tive powers, we should devour our young, as Nature intended."

Bierce, however, did not confine his genial comments to suicides and religion. Thoroughly enjoying the license granted
the Town Crier, he sent his shafts in all directions. He opposed
the reformers who asked for an eight-hour day; he ridiculed organized sports of all types; he bluntly called the public schools
a failure. One day he mocked the Caucasian Society; the next

he warned the people that no woman could be trusted with a secret. He added the advice: "There is positively no betting on the discreet reticence of any woman whose silence you have not secured with a meat ax."

When the news leaked out that a shipload of Chinese prostitutes had arrived in the harbor, he announced that the Oriental harlots were met by a delegation of first citizens, housed in apartments at the Occidental Hotel, and shown the town by the Mayor and the Board of Supervisors. A few days later he defended a candidate for the Board of Education accused of consorting with a prostitute by putting forth the unique plea that the accused would necessarily reform if elected, for " no respectable harlot who cares for her reputation would continue her acquaintance with a man who had been elected to the Board of Education." And he never missed an occasion to twit the pioneers and California boosters, even going so far as to express boundless relief when news arrived that Bierstadt's famous painting of Yosemite had been destroyed by fire. He said the only thing that could make him happier would be to hear that some daring spirit had blown up the infernal valley itself with giant powder.

Only rarely did Bierce turn his consummate wit on the human comedy in any large or impersonal sense. Occasionally he indulged in such ordinary misanthropic remarks as: " It is usual to call a grossly sensual man a hog. It would be more correct to call a grossly sensual hog a man." More novel was his reason for admiring John Allen, a famous criminal of his day. " His fame as the wickedest man in New York places him beyond the reach of calumny. . . . Unknown, unhonored, and unhung, he drags out the miserable and purposeless existence of a church member." But in his satire for the *News Letter*, Bierce demonstrated the weakness he showed throughout his career: he delighted in blasting a local poetaster, in ridiculing a fad, in

THE *PIONEER*.

First monthly magazine devoted to
literary purposes in the West.

Courtesy of California State Library

THE *HESPERIAN*.

Founded by women to appeal to
the feminine public.

Courtesy of the Bancroft Library

*HUTCHINGS'
CALIFORNIA MAGAZINE*

Founded to advertise the scenery
and material offerings of the Pacific Coast.

Courtesy of the Bancroft Library

THE *OVERLAND
MONTHLY*.

The cover design includes the
famous bear snarling at the on-
coming train.

Courtesy of California State Library

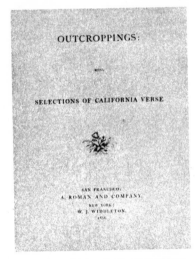

TITLE PAGES OF THREE BOOKS OF POETRY
PUBLISHED IN SAN FRANCISCO
IN THE SIXTIES.

Outcroppings, edited by Bret Harte, started a critics' war, as did Stoddard's first volume of poems. *The Lost Galleon* was Harte's second book but his first collection of verse.

Courtesy of California State Library

mouthing large a petty prejudice, but rarely did he strike sparks from the flinty mass of life's incongruities.

Apparently no one objected very much to Bierce's satire. The treatment that was accorded the *News Letter* was also accorded its Town Crier. That journal boasted of being " at once the enemy and the friend of everybody "; the public enjoyed the blasphemies and sallies of Marriott's writers and took everything good-humoredly. There are no records of libel suits, gun-play, or even hot words in connection with Bierce's four years of apprentice writing.

That Bierce enjoyed the role of Town Crier is evident; that he wrote in the savage spirit of a misanthrope or with the burning ardor of a reformer is seriously to be questioned. A special brand of frontier license suited his talent; his continuation of the role of devil's advocate in later life followed logically from his early success and did not in itself indicate unnatural spleen. More than war wounds, more than asthma contracted in graveyards, more than bitterness engendered by domestic strife, more than disillusionment with an imperfect world, frontier journalism, through its unusual freedom, created the satirist who was later to be hailed as its anathema.

CHAPTER X

THE *OVERLAND MONTHLY*

THE DESIGNS on the covers of the *Pioneer Magazine* and the *Overland Monthly* strikingly illustrate the change in the West during the fifties and sixties. The exultant emigrants on the cover of Ewer's *Pioneer* looked westward towards the Pacific, confident that they had arrived at the promised land; fourteen years later the grizzly bear on the front of Harte's *Overland Monthly* stood with his feet planted on iron rails, his snarling muzzle turned towards the approaching locomotive. The men who edited and wrote the *Overland Monthly* realized that they were nearing the end of San Francisco's frontier days; their grizzly symbolized the last stand for independence on the part of a pioneer society.

Between the *Pioneer*, the earliest of San Franciscan monthlies, and the *Overland*, the last before the arrival of the railroad, two other monthly magazines were published in the West. The cover design of the first pictured a miner's cabin beside a stream in the Sierra Nevada, and that of the second presented three Western maidens in classic draperies reaching for the Golden Apple of Literature, while the ominous Dragon of Ignorance menaced but did not frighten them away. The miner's cabin suggested the policy of *Hutchings's Illustrated California Magazine*, founded in 1856 by J. M. Hutchings, who felt that the *Pioneer* had been too literary and that the West needed a magazine with fewer essays on the epic and more articles on the glories of California. This enterprising Englishman, who wrote the *Miner's Ten Commandments* mentioned earlier, was one of the first Californians to realize that the scenery of the Sierra might in time reap more profits than its gold. Accordingly, he spent two years and six thousand dollars preparing to issue a magazine devoted to advertising the sights of the West, particularly Yosemite Valley. He published his magazine for five years, successfully enough to earn the price of a suit of clothes, and ably enough to attract later generations to the files of his journal, wherein may be found many a striking lithograph by Nagle or Nahl and many an article on such unusual subjects as Snowshoe Thompson's carrying the mail across the Sierra on skis or the introduction of Bactrian camels to the American desert.

When Hutchings, forced by ill health to retire to Yosemite, where he became a tavern-keeper and traditional greeter, sold his periodical to Lawrence and Brooks of the *Golden Era*, *Hutchings's Illustrated California Magazine* was merged with the *California Mountaineer* and, under the title of the *California Magazine and Mountaineer*, presented for the next two or three years a monthly collection of *Era* materials to the smaller towns of the hinterland.

The *Hesperian*, the journal which carried the aspiring maidens on the cover, was openly a woman's magazine during most of its existence. Founded in 1858 by Mesdames Schulz and Day, it promised to beckon its readers " from the cares and anxieties of business and adventure to the pleasant walks of taste and imagination "; its stellar offering was a monthly colored frontispiece picturing the latest styles in Parisian gowns and hats. In its mission of inculcating lessons of morality, purity, and wisdom, it suffered many vicissitudes, flourishing for a year or two under the energetic editorship of Mrs. Day, languishing under that of Mrs. Schenck, and reviving for a moment under the Strongs, who changed its title to the *Pacific Monthly* and broadened its offerings to appeal to the men. Its death in 1864 was a very quiet affair. Resting as heavily upon " selected " sketches of the more polite type as had *Hutchings's* on puffing literature, it nevertheless printed many an article and poem by such local perennials as James Bowman, J. S. Hittell, and John R. Ridge. Its contents varied from sublime thoughts upon Milton to the best methods of making muffins and embroidering flannel skirts. Perhaps the greatest of its virtues was the series of pioneer reminiscences by Thomas O. Larkin, Jacob T. Reese, Peter Lassen, and others.

The *Overland Monthly* was more than a successor to these early monthlies; it attempted to accomplish feats considered impossible in the publishing circles of the West, and for a while it succeeded. In a day when many American magazines were able to make expenses only by pirating a good deal of their material from English and continental journals, the *Overland Monthly* proposed to print nothing but original material in its columns and to pay cash for every contribution. Throughout the seven and a half years of its life the *Overland* maintained this policy: never did it " borrow " poems and stories from uncopyrighted sources, and though its payments were not large, never did it fail to pay for what it printed. Its ink-blotted account-books reveal that the editors ordinarily paid fifteen dollars for poems and from twenty-four to thirty dollars for articles and stories, and that at times they raised their remuneration for special contributions, giving a hundred dollars each for Bret Harte's later stories, " Tennessee's Partner," " The Idyl of Red Gulch," " Brown of Calaveras," and the " Iliad of

Sandy Bar," and five hundred dollars to Joaquin Miller for his serial poem, " The Isles of the Amazon." Moreover, the magazine actually made money during the early years of its history.

Though it was Bret Harte who made the *Overland Monthly* famous, he was not responsible for the founding of the magazine. In fact, he joined the venture with considerable reluctance. The enthusiasm and business ability which made the magazine possible were supplied by Anton Roman, a local bookseller and publisher, who never wrote anything more ambitious than a prospectus. Roman had come west in 1850 to mine gold and had had fair luck in washing dust from the sand of Scott's Bar in Shasta County. He invested one hundred ounces of gold dust in books, peddled them with success in the northern mines, in time went east to buy up a large consignment of volumes, and in 1859 set up his store in San Francisco. Enthusiastic about Western literature, the sociable bookseller soon knew most of the writers on the coast and by the mid-sixties was publishing an occasional volume of their works. He issued both Harte's *Outcroppings* and Stoddard's *Poems;* he published J. S. Hittell's *Resources of California* and John Franklin Swift's *Going to Jericho;* and he sponsored the coy letter-writer of Carrie Carlton, the home-made fairy tales from the Gold Land by May Wentworth, and the indifferent novels of Laura Preston.

With so many manuscripts coming into his office, Roman felt he could make a success of a monthly magazine written entirely by local talent. The *Overland Monthly* was, of course, to be devoted first to the Development of the Country and only incidentally to the encouragement of the arts. Roman felt that all conditions favored a healthy support from both advertisers and readers: the city was very prosperous; the farming country near the seaboard was attracting a large immigration; the transcontinental railroad to be completed within the year would bring both settlers and new money; and the Pacific Mail was about to inaugurate trade with the Orient that promised to push the economic frontier beyond the Pacific. While Harte hesitated to accept the editorship, Roman discussed his project with local merchants, obtained advance advertising contracts of nine hundred dollars, and assured himself of a circulation of three thousand copies with the first issue. To clinch the argument, he showed Harte a map of the two hemispheres, with San Francisco holding the central position on the Pacific. With the Union Pacific workmen pushing the rails west towards the Sierra and the P.M.S.S. *Colorado* sailing for Hong Kong, who could fail to see that the future of the West was unlimited? Finally, when Harte insisted that he would have difficulty finding enough local writers to fill a first-rate magazine, Roman pledged himself to obtain at least half of the contributions and to employ two competent journalists, Noah Brooks of the *Alta* and W. C. Bartlett of the *Bulletin*, as the editor's assistants.

In arranging for the services of Brooks and Bartlett, Roman was looking out for his own interests as well as those of Harte. Though he felt sure that the latter was the most competent writer in the city and wished to make him editor to give distinction to the magazine, he feared that Harte might lose sight of the promotional function of the journal. As he put it, " My only objection at that time to Mr. Harte was that he would be likely to lean too much to the purely literary articles, while what I was then aiming at was a magazine that would help the material development of the coast." Experience proved that he was correct in suspecting his editor's booster instincts. Before Harte had been long at his job, he disturbed the good citizens of San Francisco by refusing to ignore the earthquake of 1868, by printing an article by Henry George prophesying that the railroad would bring poverty as well as prosperity to the coast, and by featuring an iconoclastic article about San Francisco written by J. W. Watkins, who had had good training as the

Town Crier on the *News Letter* and did not hesitate to arraign the city for failing to live up to its possibilities. He asserted that the famed El Dorado was badly built, that it was not progressive, that the climate was only fair, that the populace was provincial, that capital earned less than in the East, and that the city led only in insanity and suicide rates. Noah Brooks, who thought that " The Luck of Roaring Camp " might be injudicious and affect immigration unfavorably, must have despaired when he read Watkins's article.

Paradoxically, it was the practical-minded Anton Roman who suggested the writing of " The Luck of Roaring Camp " and thus introduced into the equation the non-material, literary element that made the *Overland* one of the greatest magazines of its day. In his prospectus Roman had stated one purpose of the journal to be a study of Western manners and civilization. An Argonaut himself, he prized the romance of an era that Harte had long scorned as crass and uninteresting. Roman took his editor with him on a trip to the Santa Cruz hills, where by dint of example and argument he changed the Harte who had been satirizing the old-timers into the Harte who was ready to idealize the gold-rush in romantic fiction.

Harte's shift was symptomatic of the new attitude, the culminating attitude among Western writers. Near the end of its frontier days, the West, having passed from naïveté to satire, reached the stage in which its early days became romantic. With the passing of two decades had come the perspective necessary for the setting up of a heroic tradition. Significantly, Bret Harte's *The Luck of Roaring Camp and Other Sketches*, Mark Twain's *Roughing It*, and Joaquin Miller's *Songs of the Sierras* all appeared within three years of the completion of the railroad.

From its birth, the *Overland Monthly* had been at the mercy of the railroad. Made possible by the boom preceding the completion of the track, it declined during the years of the depression that followed. The railroad, which had taken many copies of the *Overland* to the East, took Harte also just after he had given the magazine a reputation. After Harte's departure the editors worked under the handicap of anticlimax. W. C. Bartlett did his best for seven months; Benjamin Avery of the *Bulletin* staff was just getting the magazine back on its feet when he was appointed American Minister to China; two Englishmen connected with H. H. Bancroft's historical plant, T. A. Harcourt and Walt Fisher, piloted the journal during its dying days after most of the best local writers had gone east. In 1876 the depression that came with the railroad culminated in the closing of the Bank of California, the drowning of W. C. Ralston, and panic. During the hard days that followed, the *Overland Monthly* ceased publication.

Though Bret Harte planned to have a story ready for the first issue of the *Overland Monthly*, his dilatory habits, coupled with his meticulous care in writing, postponed the appearance of " The Luck of Roaring Camp " until the second number. The remaining seven stories that he wrote for the *Overland* followed at uneven intervals during the two and a half years that he was editor of the journal. " The Luck of Roaring Camp," " The Outcasts of Poker Flat," and " Tennessee's Partner," the best stories he was ever to write and the ones responsible for his reputation to this day, were the first, second, and fourth stories that he printed in the *Overland*. By the time he left the magazine, the quality of his writing had dropped to the level of " Mr. Thompson's Prodigal " and " The Iliad of Sandy Bar."

" The Luck of Roaring Camp " mixed humor and pathos in a story telling of an illegitimate child, borne by the camp prostitute, who regenerated a rough mining community. Not even the reforming of a gold camp nor the heroic death of a drunkard mollified the shocked sensibilities of the polite reading class, represented in advance by a lady proof-reader, whose principal interest in life was her Bible class. She arraigned " The Luck " on three charges: she objected to the introduction of a prostitute, even one doomed to a painful death; she was shocked at the mention of obstetrics; and she was determined that the *Overland* should not sully its pages with such an improper expression as " The d—d little cuss." Anton Roman, who was no slave to the genteel tradition, concluded that the public would be more touched than shocked and ordered the story to be printed. It was an immediate success — the sensation of the day. It created a new world of fiction, a world which was made up of ramshackle mining camps in which hearts of gold beat beneath rough exteriors, in which characters expressed themselves picturesquely in the jargon of the card-table, and in which sinners and sometimes saints were almost certain to make the renunciations expected of them by all good Victorians.

Harte's stories for the *Overland* continued in the formula set by " The Luck." A gambler gave up his life in an attempt to save his companions from starvation, and a prostitute starved to death that a young virgin might live. Another prostitute shamed her virtuous sisters by her faithful attendance on a helpless, paralyzed lover. A ne'er-do-well tried to save his partner at the court of Judge Lynch by offering his hoard of gold dust; when he failed, he gave his pal a decent burial and soon followed him to a world where partners are never separated. A prostitute in Red Gulch gave up her son that he might receive an honorable education, and a school-teacher gave up the drunkard whom she had reformed so that she could educate the prostitute's son. Jack Hamlin, the gambler, almost ran away with the wife of Brown of Calaveras, but his better instinct won out at the last moment and he went on his way singing.

The deaths of Kentuck and the Duchess and Tennessee's

partner were planned to bring tears to the eyes of a generation that wept over the deaths of Little Nell and Camille. That they did so was borne out by many testimonials: Anton Roman finished " The Luck " with a lump in his throat, and Ralph Keeler read " The Outcasts " to passengers on an Eastern train and found them mopping their tears when he finished. When Charlie Stoddard told Harte by way of compliment that a reader of one of his stories had wept over an incident, Harte replied: " Well, he had a right to. I wept when I wrote it."

But Bret Harte's tales were not merely successful tear-jerkers in a sentimental era; they succeeded in turning the gold-rush days into what he called " an era replete with a certain heroic Greek poetry." Roaring Camp, Poker Flat, Sandy Bar, Wingdam, and Red Gulch were mythical towns inhabited by a society grown in two decades almost as romantic and unusual as Camelot or Bagdad. With unforgettable characters like Colonel Starbottle, John Oakhurst, Jack Hamlin, and York and Scott, with situations in which what was said was only less forceful than what was implied, Harte created the land of a million Westerns, a land in which gun-play was chronic, vigilante committees met before breakfast, and death was as common as a rich strike in the diggings. The picture was not painted, however, with a complete disregard for facts; Harte merely concentrated the irregularities of early California life, developed the possibilities in such character types as the Southern orator and the gentleman gambler, and adapted the perennially successful romantic formulas to the Western scene. In addition he displayed a skill in constructing short stories hardly surpassed since his day. His discovery of the California scene did much to further the local-color movement throughout the nation.

Because Bret Harte knew that he had done a good job in his short stories, he was annoyed that his greatest fame came from " The Heathen Chinee," a dialect poem which he had hardly considered worthy to be published in the *Overland* when he wrote it. To his mind, it was just one of a score of satirical and humorous verses that he turned out in his spare time, a simple story, which he titled "Plain Language from Truthful James," of a Chinaman who outwitted two gamblers in a round of euchre. The Easterners enjoyed it because it presented the boastful pioneer being beaten at his own game by the Oriental whom he despised; but the line the Westerners remembered was "We are ruined by Chinese cheap labor," written in satire but quoted in earnest when demagogues cried: "The Chinese must go." Such a misuse of his writing must have been more than a joke to Harte, who had long resented the Westerner's mistreatment of aliens.

As well as contributing short stories and poems to the *Overland* Harte wrote a number of book reviews, two factual articles, and a monthly editorial department called "Etc." In his reviews, as in his editorial policy, he raised the magazine above the provincial level, never hesitating to give sound critical analyses of local books as well as of more famous publications. As editor he refused to accept material that he considered second-rate, once remarking to an ardent female applicant: "I will not trouble you to leave the manuscript; I am not publishing a Sunday-school paper." Doubtless his editorial policy caused him to refuse many an inadequate manuscript from local writers who had found little difficulty in placing their wares in the less critical dailies and weeklies of the city.

The life of an editor is hardly an enviable one, and when that editor has risen rapidly from type-setter to dictator, he may anticipate a reasonable amount of jealousy. Harte's position was made even more irritating to his fellows by the fact that he had not for years depended upon his journalism for his living; with his income from the Mint, he had escaped entirely the dull routine and penny-pinching faced by many of those who contributed to his magazine. Nor was he without enemies among the local writers. That the *Outcroppings* feud still smoldered was shown when Joe Goodman resorted to anonymity and the intercession of a friend to get a poem into the *Overland*. He doubtless did Harte an injustice in assuming that he would refuse to publish it if he knew who had written it, but Goodman's action shows the distrust which many of the old-timers had for Harte.

To be liked even by those whose manuscripts he refuses, an editor must be genial, enthusiastic, and hospitable. Harte was so aloof as to annoy his closest friends; he was rarely enthusiastic about either his own or other authors' writings; and he had at his disposal few of the many means a successful editor uses for entertaining his writers. A sociable wife might have helped him, but Mrs. Harte showed no interest in his editorial work and, according to his secretary, was more likely to force him to leave his office to help with her shopping than to invite a contributor to dinner. Entertainment would have been difficult at any rate, for the couple isolated themselves by living across the bay in San Rafael. Furthermore, Harte's display in dress and his reputation for snobbishness did not help him. And finally rumors, not without basis, accused him of borrowing money and failing to return it — a charge made doubly grievous when the injured men remembered that he was one of the most affluent writers in the city. After his success with " The Luck " he became so petty in cutting old acquaintances and so undependable about paying his debts that he earned a reputation which remains unsavory to this day.

Under the circumstances an estrangement between Harte and California society, which he had never much loved, was inevitable. From the estrangement, coupled with his accusation that California was cold and ungrateful, critics have since evolved the theory that Harte was unappreciated in the West, a theory they use to substantiate their more sweeping contention that many sensitive writers were thwarted by frontier conditions. The evidence, however, does not bear out either Harte or the critics. For example, the charge that the California public failed to appreciate " The Luck of Roaring Camp " is satisfactorily refuted by the facts that the contemporary local reviews showed that the story was well received and that the success of Roman in making money during the first year of the publication of the *Overland* was largely due to the local popularity of " The Luck of Roaring Camp " and " The Outcasts of Poker Flat." That a proof-reader should have attempted to bowdlerize the tale is a picturesque but hardly significant incident, which might as well have happened in Boston; and that a single proof-reader has little to do with determining the fundamental policies of a magazine, Harte and Roman promptly demonstrated.

The truth is that the San Franciscans not only appreciated Harte's writing but made strenuous efforts to hold him in the West. When he bought the *Overland* from Anton Roman, John H. Carmany generously met Harte's threefold demand for a salary of two hundred dollars a month, " exceptional editorial assistance," and adequate remuneration for all non-editorial writing. Instead of paying Harte the rate received by other contributors to the journal Carmany quadrupled the normal figure for his short stories. When, in 1870, Harte was offered the unheard-of sum of ten thousand dollars a year to come east and write for the *Atlantic Monthly*, Carmany desperately attempted to retain him, offering him five thousand dollars a year, one hundred dollars for each poem and story, and a quarter interest in the magazine. At the same time the regents of the University of California offered him an appointment as Professor of Recent Literature and Curator of the Library and Museum, with minimum duties, at a salary of three hundred dollars a month. But Harte's departure was not to be put off. Certain laws of economic and social change, far stronger than salary considerations, pointed his way east. The railroad took him to the Atlantic Coast on February 2, 1871.

Once more, in 1875, when the *Overland* was dying, Carmany tried to persuade Harte to return to the land which had given him his fame. Though Harte had already slipped badly in national reputation, he was unwilling to consider the frantic appeal. He replied: " I can make here, by my pen, with less drudgery, with more security, honor and respect thrice as much as I could make in California at the head of the *Overland* — taking the peak as the estimate. As far as I can see the tastes, habits, and ideas of you people have not changed since you and I were forced to part company, because I could better myself here. . . . I do not see how I could make the *Overland* ' Sanctum ' the literary Mecca of the West, after the Prophet had been so decidedly renounced by his disciples. I think that even a California community would see the ridiculousness of my returning to a magazine that had, under the thin disguise of literary criticism, abused me at *the expense of its own literary record*." He ended with remarks about the " shameless ingratitude " and the " blundering malice " of Californians and their magazine and concluded that their mistake as well as his decision was " irretrievable." The break between Harte and his West was complete.

In the glorious days of its youth, Frank Brett Harte, Charles Warren Stoddard, and Ina Coolbrith, known as the Golden Gate Trinity, looked upon the *Overland Monthly* as their literary child. They owned the three keys to the *Overland* office on the Plaza, and when they gathered in that office, talk was genial and wit sparkled playfully. Occasionally an outsider like Clarence King was allowed to join in the favorite game of making limericks, laughing with the trio over the one about a certain young girl from Yreka or the one about " The Luck of Roaring Camp ":

> And they added in language emphatic
> That his wit was not really quite Attic;
> And a verdict was had
> That his style it was *bad*,
> And his characters all — well — erratic.

Often on an afternoon Ina and Charlie and Frank, who was never known as Bret by these friends, would walk up Russian Hill to Ina's lodgings to spend a quiet few hours drinking tea and being lazy. The tall slender girl with the large dark eyes, smooth olive complexion, and handsome eyebrows that looked so much like those of her Uncle Joseph — the Mormon prophet whom no one knew to be her uncle — had about her an air of maturity that gave her friends great confidence in her judgment. She felt almost motherly about Charlie Stoddard, who, with his blue eyes and curly brown hair, seemed to her as beautiful and decidedly as impractical as Shelley. She anticipated his moods, warmly returned his friendliness, and put up with what she called his " moonstruck vacuity." While her friends talked about prose poems and cannibals, she idly compared Frank's deep rich tones with Charlie's mellow voice. Frank, she decided, was a little more manly, more distinguished. In spite of his pock-marks she felt him ideally handsome. Doubtless the drooping mustaches and the streak of silver in his hair made up for the loss of the pink and white complexion which had once earned him the embarrassing nickname of Fanny. She liked to persuade him to come home with her from the office for an occasional supper. As he helped shell peas and set the table, he seemed more at ease and more natural than he ever did behind the editor's desk or, for that matter, at home with his wife. She encouraged him to talk about his ambitions or about his two boys; Anna Griswold Harte, whom Ina described coolly as talented and witty, but not beautiful, was seldom a topic of conversation.

It was pleasant for Ina to think of Charlie and Frank as her brothers. There was no thought of anything else: Charlie was obviously not the marrying kind, and Frank had his wife and boys. Yet — if she were ever to take another husband, he would be a man like Harte — or Mark Twain, whom she also found talented and handsome. But no, too much was to be said for confining her relations to the sisterly sort.

During the *Overland* days Ina was happier than she had ever been before or would ever be again. The future looked promising. Perhaps she would be able to publish a volume of her poetry, receive her share of national recognition, and even travel east where the great poets lived. It was commonly acknowledged that her poetry was the best that was appearing in the *Overland*. Though she piped but one silvery note, a wistful one in which unhappiness was temporarily submerged in pleasure over flowers, birds, and the wind, she knew that her tone was true and her touch was sure. Hidden in poems with such titles as "Loneliness," "Longing," and "When the Grass shall Cover Me " were glimpses of a passionate nature not unlike that of Emily Brontë.

> And I could kiss, with longing wild,
>   Earth's dear brown bosom, loved so much,
> A grass-blade fanned across my hand
>   Would thrill me like a lover's touch.

Surely, now that her companions were gaining recognition on Parnassus, she would taste a small morsel of glory.

Both Ina and Frank were convinced that Charlie had at last found himself and was about to arrive. Together with his many other friends, they had doubted whether his poetry would ever amount to much. They had suffered through the period when

CLARENCE KING AT HIS FAVORITE HOBBY
OF MOUNTAIN CLIMBING.

Courtesy of Mr. Francis P. Farquhar

JOHN MUIR AT THE AGE OF TWENTY-THREE.
From William F. Badés *Life and Letters of John Muir.*
Courtesy of Houghton Mifflin Company

he talked of becoming a sheep-herder near Los Angeles and had laughed with him when he described the sheep " circling about him and staring him out of countenance with their blank eyes like smoked buttons of mother-of-pearl." They may have felt some hope when he joined a dramatic company as the juvenile lead, but they soon realized what a mistake he had made when he deserted the show in Sacramento, unable to put up with the routine assignments of an actor in stock. Doubtless they were pleased when he announced that he had found spiritual consolation in the Roman Catholic Church, but they hardly took him seriously when he talked of going into a monastery.

He assuredly had talent as a writer; would he ever learn to use it? How about prose? Could he find a subject that would suit his precious, over-sensuous style? His first effort for the *Overland* produced a meringue-coated article entitled " A Debutante's Dream," after which Henry George took him aside and told him that if he couldn't write simply he shouldn't write at all. But what could you do with a chap who would thus describe a breakfast dish of codfish and potatoes: " This frugal repast was to consist of three baked potatoes so mealy that they burst like cottonballs at the bottom of a yellow sea of creamed codfish breaking upon the shores of two poached eggs "?

And then Charlie Stoddard discovered that he would rather be a South Sea Islander sitting naked in the sun before his grass hut than the Pope of Rome — and he also discovered that readers liked the South Sea idyls which he wrote during " emotional spasms " that made him feel as if he were treading on air. After " Chumming with a Savage " was printed in the *Overland*, Harte told Stoddard: " Now you have struck it. Keep on this vein and presently you will have enough to fill a volume and you can call it South Sea Bubbles! " Immoderately pleased with his success, the new-born pagan sold a dozen of his prose poems to the *Overland* and in addition placed two in the *Atlantic* and one in *Lippincott's*. In 1873 he collected the essays into a volume entitled *South-Sea Idyls*.

Stoddard first visited the Sandwich Islands, now known as the Hawaiian Islands, in 1864, just after suffering a nervous breakdown while attending college in Oakland. His pretty sister Sara, who had married a Hawaiian planter named Parker Makee, invited him to come to Rose Ranch to rest and forget his troubles. The tranquil, indolent months which followed soothed his body and quieted his nerves; as he sunned himself on the beach, made friends with the indulgent and friendly natives, and lunched on mangoes and bananas, he decided that, though his skin was white, he was inwardly purple-blooded, supple-limbed, and invisibly tatooed after the manner of the dark pagans about him. After his return to San Francisco and failure at acting, he once more retreated to the islands. During this stay he visited the leper colony on Molokai under the guidance of Catholic ministrants and there met Father Damien, whom he later brought to the attention of Robert Louis Stevenson and through Stevenson to a million readers.

In 1870, after his first Hawaiian sketches had appeared in the *Overland*, Stoddard decided to go to Tahiti, try to find work there, and write of his experiences. When he reached the island paradise which his beloved Melville had described in *Omoo*, he found that there was no way for an outsider to support himself. He speedily came to grief in Papeete and, hungry, naked, and unvisited, suffered the torments of a perfumed purgatory. When his small sum of money ran out, he worked a few days for his board, and then he slipped out into the native villages, where he enjoyed hospitality in grass huts under tropical trees, and watched " the flying fish baptize themselves by immersion in space, leaping into the air like momentary inches of chain-lightning." Returning to Papeete, he slept in a hencoop and tried to allay the distress of an empty stomach with copious draughts of water. Eventually the respectable citizens of Papeete persuaded him to return to San Francisco C. O. D.

In writing of the tranquil islands which he loved, Stoddard made little attempt to keep to the truth. His sensuous descriptions, his bizarre metaphors, and his mustang humor were as far removed from ordinary existence as the threads of plot upon which he strung his artificial beads. The emphasis in this unusual picture of island life is not on the customary brown maidens with firm breasts, lithe limbs, and generous impulses, but on the strong-backed youths, human porpoises who drive their canoes through the mists of the storm and share their joys and sorrows with the prodigal from California. Kana-ana welcomes Stoddard to a native Hawaiian village, where he adopts him as his brother; later, when Stoddard returns to San Francisco, he sends for his friend, only to suffer with him when the boy discovers that a tobacco-store Indian is the only idol in the city and that the city dwellers are shocked when he swims in the nude. When Kana-ana at last returns to Hawaii, he is too restless to be happy. Lonesome for his white companions, he attempts to paddle a canoe across the great ocean to the Golden Gate and in so doing loses his life.

Joe of Lahaina, a charming rascal of a servant, shows his audacity by whistling his master out of chapel and " borrowing " his money to buy a fine suit; that master later finds him among the lepers of Molokai, his features deformed, but his song unchanged. In " Tahiti " Stoddard goes in search of a phantom waterfall, meets a deformed creature, tabooed by his fellows, and visits the fete at Papeete in company with the grotesque cripple, whom, in some inexplicable way, he makes attractive to the reader. In " The South-Sea Show " he tells a fanciful story of taking a brace of South Sea babes and a tatooed boy on a lecture tour in New England, and of the sad

end of the boy, who, after nearly killing himself by experimenting with *eau de Cologne* and kerosene as beverages, finishes
the job by succumbing to the idea that a pious spinster is
praying him to death. The latter story was all that came of
Stoddard's plan to lecture throughout the country with living
examples of South Sea Islanders.

The charm of Stoddard's *South-Sea Idyls* resulted partly
from his skill in adapting his poetic talents to sonorous prose,
pleasing when not overdone, and partly from his unforced acceptance of pagan life. His indolent nature was suited to the
way of the Tahitian, and pangs of conscience bothered him
very little in southern waters. His attitude was very different
from that of Mark Twain, who had not a drop of pagan blood
in his veins. In his " Sandwich Island Letters " Mark Twain
indicated that he considered the natives lascivious in their
dances and corrupt in their morals; Stoddard found them only
frank and natural. Mark Twain often found it impossible to
be comfortable in Hawaii because he was irritated by the dirt
and the insects; Stoddard could lie down with the natives under a grass roof, watch the roaches drop upon the matting,
muse on the resemblance of the centipedes to toy trains, tuck
his head under his *kapa*, and go to sleep without a shudder.
Just as he drifted off, he would think how curious it was that
he, an ardent Catholic neophyte, was almost ready to forget
God in the tropics.

Shortly after the *Overland* started, Charlie Stoddard received a letter and a thin volume of poems from a small town
on the dry plateau of eastern Oregon. From Canyon City
C. H. Miller wrote that he was sending his *Joaquin et al* to
Stoddard because he knew that the latter was a true poet and
would see to it that his volume of poems received adequate attention in the *Overland*. Miller further confided that he was

at the parting of the ways: if his hopes of being named to the Supreme Court of Oregon came true, he would invite the poets of San Francisco to come up to see him; if he failed to obtain the appointment, he would pull up stakes, drop down to the bay city for a visit, and then press on to Europe and perhaps round the world. Whatever happened, he was done with eastern Oregon, which he had found was no place for a poet. " Good fellows here but ignorant as asses, while our ladies . . . have about as much sentiment as a cow eating swill," he added.

As Miller had long ago proved his resourcefulness, he would probably land on his feet whichever way he jumped. His versatility had been evident during the six years that had elapsed since his failure to make a living in San Francisco writing for the *Golden Era.* He had moved into a sparsely settled district, had made himself known and respected by leading a punitive expedition against the Indians, without regular legal training had been admitted to the bar, and had eventually been named to a judgeship in Canyon City. " Without learning I was trying to administer the law, and without knowing how to read, I was trying to write a book," he boasted. Old-timers maintained that he accomplished the former with one law-book and two six-shooters, and his wife said he achieved the second with a rhyming dictionary and the Bible. Both failed properly to evaluate Miller's two trump cards, audacity and imagination.

Miller had kept his poetic iron in the fire by printing a pamphlet in 1868 called *Specimens,* in which he warned his friends that, though rhyming in his vicinity was considered a form of insanity, he expected to follow these specimens with a good output of ore. *Specimens* contained only two poems: the first, " Loua Ellah," was a sort of " Sohrab and Rustum " of the Rogue River Indians; while the second, " Shadows," was made up of autobiography and stray opinions.

The ore began to come to light in *Joaquin et al,* issued in

Portland in 1869, again presumably at the poet's expense. This was a book of some hundred pages, containing a number of poems that Miller later used in his *Songs of the Sierras.* The curious title was composed of a legal term tacked on to the name of the most important poem, a long, loosely knit romance based upon the legend of Joaquin Murieta. During the fourteen years since John Rollin Ridge had written his account of the fabulous Joaquin, the story of the Mexican bandit had taken many forms; but not even the dramatist who used the tale as the basis for an anti-Catholic diatribe had stretched it as far as Miller had. In his poem Joaquin and his Rosita had become the sole descendants of Montezuma. After the Mexican War, during which the Americans had driven them from their ancestral castle on the shores of Lake Texcoco, they attempted to avenge their race by attacking the gringos in California. When they saw their cause was lost, Rosita leaped into the flames of a fire she had built to worship the Sun God, and Joaquin fled to Mexico to fight Maximilian. Wounded in battle, he died trying to choke a priest who affronted his pagan faith by making the sign of the cross over his bleeding body. So proud was Cincinnatus Hiner Miller of this poem and so devoted to its hero, Joaquin, that soon after the publication of *Joaquin et al* he adopted Joaquin Miller as his nom-de-plume.

Hoping to get a good review in the *Overland,* Miller sent copies of his book to both Harte and Stoddard, together with letters asking for sympathetic criticism. Less friendly than Stoddard, Harte replied with what Miller called " a savage little letter," returning two poems contributed to the *Overland* and suggesting that the Oregon poet accept a bit of sound advice rather than subject his volume to a public review in the monthly. Disturbed perhaps by such exaggerated figures as that of Diana's maid hanging her mistress's garments on the ridge of the Sierra after washing them in liquid moonlight, he suggested that Joaquin check his " theatrical tendency " and " feverish exaltation " and cultivate a measure of restraint. But as Miller still insisted on a review, Harte commented on the book in his department " Etc.," remarking that he found in the poet, in spite of crudities and dubious taste, a true poetic instinct, evidenced by felicity of diction and dramatic vigor. He added that Miller was given to pawing and curvetting, " and at such times his neck is generally clothed with thunder, and the glory of his nostrils is terrible."

In 1870 fate — or more probably his own legal inadequacies — thrust Miller into a poetic career, for he was not named to the Supreme Court of Oregon. In a letter to his brother he attributed his failure to receive the appointment to " the tricks and treachery of one-horse politicians." Possibly the talk attending his separation from Minnie Myrtle affected his chances adversely. After a brief estrangement following their return from San Francisco in 1863, Minnie had rejoined her husband in Canyon City, where she had produced three children but no more poems. Their union had never been satisfactory, and, as Joaquin grew increasingly restless, she charged him with pettiness, infidelity, and a mania for imitating Byron even in his domestic relations. When he finally decided to leave Oregon, Joaquin said farewell to Minnie Myrtle, expressing his passion in a poem titled " Myrrh," which was printed in an Oregon paper:

> I clutch'd my hands, I turned my head
> In my endeavour and was dumb.
> And when I should have said Farewell,
> I only murmured, " this is hell! "

When Charlie Stoddard met him at the dock in San Francisco, he found the Oregon poet in the best of spirits. Dressed in a sombrero, a long linen duster, and moccasins, he immediately announced that he was ready to visit the poets. Stoddard took him to a restaurant on the Plaza, where Miller stood at the counter and ordered a glass of water and a toothpick, and then they went up to the *Overland* office. There Miller met Harte, whom he declared the " cleanest man he had ever met," both a genius and a gentleman. Just what Harte thought of Miller has not been recorded, but the *Overland* printed none of his poems while Harte was editor. When they went to see Ina, Joaquin whispered to Charlie, " divinely tall and most divinely fair " and at once assumed that Ina and his new friend were engaged. After installing Joaquin in a lodging-house on one of San Francisco's hills, Charlie said farewell, for he was off to Tahiti. Joaquin would have joined him if he had not been so determined to make his pilgrimage to Europe. He contented himself by writing Charlie that he envied him " beside some nut brown beauty where even the traditional fig leaf is a nuisance."

He also confided to Stoddard that the month he spent in San Francisco was the happiest of his life. He was free — free from routine law duties, free from hostages to fortune. He was about to go to England to visit the homes of his beloved Shakespeare and Byron, to write poems for publication in London, to show the Britishers what a frontiersman was like. Ina Coolbrith enthusiastically talked with him about his plans for conquering Europe and accompanied him over to Sausalito to gather laurel for a wreath for him to place on Byron's tomb. They had their portraits taken, too, and Joaquin gave one of his to Ina and sent one to Charlie, inscribing on each the cryptic message: " 1870:1875? "

At the end of the month Joaquin departed for New York. He had made arrangements with the *Bulletin* to publish his travel letters if the editor could decipher his handwriting. And, although the men on the *Overland* had given him little encouragement, he knew that if he could gain a reputation abroad, he could name terms at home. That he was correct is shown by the fact that, two years later, after Harte had departed, the *Overland* paid Miller five hundred dollars for the " Isles of the Amazons," hoping that the Oregon poet who had made a sensation in London would revive the ebbing fortunes of the Western magazine. Joaquin Miller had taken his leap and had landed firmly on his feet.

Harte had expected most of the material for the *Overland Monthly* to come from a half-dozen journalists of the city — Noah Brooks of the *Alta*, B. P. Avery, W. C. Bartlett, George B. Merrill, and Samuel Williams of the *Bulletin*, William V. Wells and Henry George of the *Times*. These newspapermen, whose services had been secured by Roman, supported the editor as consistently as the *Overland's* owner had promised they would; but, much to Harte's surprise, many other local writers and scholars also got behind the venture. They even overwhelmed him with more factual articles than he could use. The church was represented by the Reverend A. W. Loomis, who wrote a series of essays on the Chinese in California, and by William Ingraham Kip, the Episcopal bishop, who turned out essays on various lay subjects. From the newly founded university came learned treatises by President Gilman and many of his faculty, including Martin Kellogg and John LeConte.

Independent scientists, discovering that they had a reliable journal at their disposal, sent in papers: California maritime problems were presented authoritatively by Captain G. M. Scammon of the U. S. Revenue Service; results of his intensive study of Pacific Coast Indians were offered by Stephen Powers, an ambitious young ethnologist; field trips in Mexico were described by the noted ornithologist A. J. Grayson; valuable and interesting mountain sketches came in from Josiah D. Whitney and Clarence King of the California Geological Survey. Specialists as far away as Massachusetts and even England contributed an occasional article; from Cambridge Louis Agassiz sent " The Natural History of the Animal Kingdom," from Washington came an article by General W. T. Sherman, on his participation in the San Francisco vigilante movement of 1856, and from London " Our Norse Forefathers " by Charles Kingsley. And then there were always such old reliables as J. Ross Browne, traveler and mining expert; James Bowman, who could write equally well on Anglo-Saxon poetry and modern art; and J. S. Hittell, perennial statistician and expositor of everything from phrenology to the history of morals.

But though Harte and his successors might be overstocked with factual material, they were hard pressed to find poetry and fiction that met their demand. As a whole the poetry they used in the *Overland* was rather commonplace — orthodox, quiet, typical of the domestic verse popular throughout the country at this period. Stoddard, who still wrote an occasional poem, Coolbrith, and Harte himself were the poets most often represented in the journal. Then, after Joaquin Miller's success in England, the *Overland* featured his work, printing eighteen short poems in addition to the serialized " Isles of the Amazons." Edward Rowland Sill, now back on the west coast teaching in the University of California, turned out a few poems of real merit; W. S. Kendall scribbled verses somewhat subdued in their eroticism; Benjamin P. Avery and Frances F. Victor offered a nature lyric now and then; and a few new poets, such as the capable Emma Frances Dawson and the ebullient Daniel O'Connell, made sporadic appearances. In general, however, the poetry department of the *Overland* was not one of its stronger features.

In the field of the short story Harte had less difficulty finding adequate material. That was due, in an oblique way, to himself, for his " Luck of Roaring Camp " made a handful of

Westerners recognize the value of narrative dealing with the California scene. Soon stories came trickling into the *Overland* office with such titles as " The Spectre Bull of Salinas," " Our Brother from California," and " Bold Dick Donahue." The local scene was used effectively in " The Diamond Maker of Sacramento " and a half-dozen similar tales by Noah Brooks, who later wrote popular books about his boyhood in Kansas; and there are many glimpses of pioneer life in Josephine Clifford's sketches based on her life in Arizona as the wife of an army officer stationed among the Navajos. Stimulated by the California setting, Emma Frances Dawson proved to be a good craftsman in the short story as well as in poetry. Mrs. Victor widened the field to include Oregon and Washington, and Prentice Mulford used his mining experiences on the Mother Lode as a source for many stories and autobiographical sketches. Nevada was the setting for " Big Jack Small," one of the most effective stories the early West produced and certainly the best of the promising, though scant, work turned out by J. W. Gally, Comstock miner and journalist. Gally's laconic simplicity and realistic attitude were illustrated by his answer to the question why he wrote fiction: " First, applause; second, glory; third, grub." His handful of sketches have long awaited a modern reprinting.

Finally, Ambrose Bierce published his first short story in the Western monthly. Interesting principally because of its use of local setting and its testimony that Bierce, in this early period, was already dedicated to the horror story, " The Haunted Valley," with its roots in the macabre and its branches shrouded in mystery, tells why an insane man decided to frighten a miner to death and how he went about doing it.

With the exception of Stoddard's unsatisfactory " Hearts of Oak," the *Overland* carried no serial novels, probably because, as elsewhere in America, the novel matured more slowly than other forms of writing and no frontier novel of any importance had yet been produced. Clearly not up to the high editorial standards maintained by Harte and Avery were thrillers such as Densmore's sensational novels, sentimental trash like Laura Preston's *In Bonds* and Ianthe's *Greek Slave*, or even serious though futile efforts like Ralph Keeler's *Gloverson and His Silent Partner*. No more acceptable was *Zanita, a Novel of the Sierra*, by Therese Yelverton, Countess of Avonmore, who came west to capitalize on the notoriety resulting from her lawsuit against her titled Irish husband, who had tried to disprove their marriage. Born of her experiences in Yosemite Valley, where she got lost and met a bear, the silly romance with its special chapter on kissing and its lush description of the beautiful corpse of the heroine floating on Mirror Lake was not of sufficient worth to interest the *Overland* readers.

During the first year of the *Overland* John Franklin Swift was writing *Robert Greathouse*, a novel which contained a fairly skillful portrayal of San Francisco and Virginia City society during the first Comstock boom; but as politician Swift's purpose was, at least in part, to attack his enemies through a *roman à clef*, he apparently felt that it would not meet the editor's policies and that it would be useless to submit it to the *Overland*. Unfortunately, *Braxton's Bar*, by Rollin M. Daggett, once editor of the *Era*, was not written until after the death of the *Overland*. Though marred by cheap fictional situations, it was the best novel to be produced by a forty-niner.

It is impossible to comment in detail on the many lesser writers for the *Overland*, though one would enjoy lingering over that entertaining raconteur Cremony and his tall tales about his Patagonian wife and his experiences among the Apaches. William V. Wells, too, is an interesting figure. San Franciscans knew him as an enthusiastic adventurer who had sailed the seas, explored the tropics, and assisted in the running of an empire, though today he lives in the less romantic role of able biographer of his grandfather, Samuel Adams. While Wells was writing his accounts for the *Overland* of his experiences in Mexico as an aide at Maximilian's court, he was struggling to keep afloat as a journalist. Not much later he had reached the end of his career in the state hospital for the insane.

But let the student interested in San Francisco's literary frontier go to the files of the buff-covered *Overland Monthly* to meet many a picturesque ghost for himself. There he will find the remains of the best that Western journalism was to produce. In no later journal printed on the Pacific slope — not even in the revived *Overland* of the second series — will he discover the true pulse of a pioneer society.

CHAPTER XI

PRACTICAL LITERATURE

Of the four main streams of Western journalism — humorous sketches, poems, local stories, and factual articles — the last was the most constant and the greatest in volume. From the *Pioneer*, with its articles on "The Odic Force" and "The Equality of the Sexes," to the *Overland Monthly*, with its essays on "Art Beginnings in the Pacific" and "A Plea for Female Conventualism," the San Francisco magazines were filled with discussion articles, travel descriptions, scientific treatises, and historical summaries. Even full-length books dealing with practical subjects or weighty discussions were popular, whether imported or written in the West. When W. C. Bartlett, in a lecture delivered at the University of California in 1875, surveyed the literature which had appeared in California during the quarter-century following the gold-rush, he pointed out that the interests of Western writers had been more practical than æsthetic. Among the hundred and fifty books of native authorship that he enumerated, those that could be classified as belles-lettres were decidedly in the minority. Treatises on mineral resources outnumbered volumes of humor, accounts of travel were more numerous than collections of poetry, and historical tracts were more plentiful than short stories.

The range of subjects in the expository field was surprisingly wide. San Franciscans might be expected to read J. Ross Browne's statistics on the natural resources of the state, or Theodore Hittell's account of James Capen Adams, bear-fighter and trapper; but one would hardly anticipate interest in J. S. Hittell's *A Plea for Pantheism*, A. W. Loomis's *Confucius and the Chinese Classics*, or the Reverend W. A. Scott's novelized sermons, including *Daniel*, addressed to young men, *Esther*, aimed at the young women, and *Moses and the Pentateuch*, designed to refute Bishop Colenso.

One need not look far for the reasons for this emphasis on practical literature. The forty-niners were members of a generation which held, whether in Boston or San Francisco, that a good, serious, informative tract was of more importance than a mere novel or a decorative volume of poems. Moreover, the factual article served a special purpose in Western journalism; it was prized by editors for much the same reason that the humorous sketch was valued. To fill a column with jokes, discussions, or factual summaries, was easier than to give a detailed, accurate news-story. News from the outside world was limited to brief dispatches, and local reporting had hardly begun to develop into a profession. Just as Mark Twain would dismiss a murder with a couple of inches and sit down and fill up a column with a fancy sketch, so Kemble would devote a column in the *Alta* to foreign and local news and a half-page to an account of the plants indigenous to Australia. Moreover, articles were not hard to get, for almost any San Franciscan considered himself qualified to write an authoritative essay on almost any subject. When miners became supreme court justices, and sea-captains ministers of the gospel, why should not a lawyer write history, a journalist become a specialist in mineralogy, or an actor an authority on entomology?

One subject upon which everyone could write with some authority was the scenery of California, and the literature dealing with it ranged from the homely letters written by emigrants to their " folks back east " to the ridiculous boasting of the state's first crop of real-estate promoters. Hidden in the mass of indiscriminate writings about the wonders of the west coast, genuinely a paradise to the eyes of those who had crossed the alkali plains, there were a few essays and books written by nature-lovers with some gift of expression. Several of these dealt with the sunny glades, the vineyards, the redwoods, and the trout-streams of the Coast Range, which lay at San Francisco's door. Benjamin P. Avery, for a while editor of the *Overland,* wrote a volume of quiet poems and sketches about his camping trips into the country; Edward Rowland Sill based many a sensitive lyric and thoughtful essay upon his walks in the Berkeley hills and on the Marin Peninsula; and William C. Bartlett expressed the warm, playful spirit of a genuine nature-lover in his volume of *Overland* articles entitled *A Breeze from the Woods.* A follower of Wordsworth in his mingling of description and reflection but not in his lively humor, he caught from the Napa and St. Helena country the charm that was to captivate Robert Louis Stevenson a generation later when he became the Silverado Squatter. And in expressing his disapproval of man's encroachment upon nature, Bartlett said mildly a few things that Robinson Jeffers was to cry bitterly in a later day.

However, it was the Sierra Nevada with its rugged peaks and glacier lakes that stimulated the best nature writing to come out of the West, for during the sixties the granite range captured the imaginations of its two greatest eulogists, Clarence King and John Muir. Clarence King was a geological Micawber, a scientist who always expected an adventure round the corner, a wit whose sprightliness hid one of the greatest talents of his generation, an amateur mountain-climber who was a little mad. Though he never attained the degree of success which friends like Henry Adams and John Hay expected from him, he left his mark both as a scientist and a writer. His single volume, *Mountaineering in the Sierra Nevada,* is probably the most exciting book ever written about mountain-climbing.

In the Sheffield Scientific School at Yale, King had, without any great effort, proved himself an able student, an imaginative writer, and a good athlete. Only twenty when he graduated, he felt that he had time for adventure before settling into a profession. A trek across the country with a college chum offered a good substitute for the traditional European *Wanderjahr.* After traveling by railroad to the end of track at St. Joseph, Missouri, the youths set out on horseback to follow the emigrant trail across the Rockies. In Virginia City, Nevada, they lost all their money and luggage in a hotel fire, but by working a few weeks in a quartz-mill, they earned enough to take them over the mountain. On the river boat plying between Sacramento and San Francisco, they met William H. Brewer of the California State Geological Survey, who was glad to find two Yale men to add to his exploring party. Clarence King so enjoyed the work he did during the summers of '63 and '64 climbing and surveying the Sierra Nevada and Mount Shasta that he decided to make geology his profession. By the time he was thirty, he had persuaded Congress to put him in charge of the Fortieth Parallel Survey, and soon afterwards he was made the first director of the United States Geological Survey. Twenty years of distinguished work were followed by ten years of broken health, and in 1901 America lost one of its most versatile geniuses.

King's intimates frequently expressed regret that he did not use his writing talent to a greater extent. John Hay said that when he listened to King's talk around the camp-fire, he realized that much good literature was going to waste: " There were scores of short stories full of color and life, sketches of thrilling adventure, not less than half a dozen complete novels, boldly planned and brilliantly wrought out, — all ready for the type or the pen; which now — an infinite pity! — are only of the stuff that dreams are made of." But, with the exception of the spurt of literary activity which produced his mountaineering sketches, King never found time to write what was in him. As the first of these sketches appeared in the *Overland Monthly*, it is possible that they were written at the suggestion of Bret Harte, whom King met during one of his short visits to San Francisco. The next seven, however, were printed in the *Atlantic Monthly. Mountaineering in the Sierra Nevada*, composed of these articles plus a few additional chapters, came out in 1872.

This entertaining book is composed of accounts of daring climbs in the region of Mount Whitney, of descriptions of the Yosemite during summer and winter storms, and of incidents dealing with peculiar types of emigrants whom King met in the mountains. The narrative episodes, such as " Kaweah's Run," belong to the Harte school and are more impressive for their bold imagination than for their fidelity to fact. Their most memorable paragraphs contain vignettes such as the description of a typical Pike woman. " The mother was a bony sister, in the yellow, shrunken, of sharp visage, in which were prominent two cold eyes and a positively poisonous mouth; her hair, the color of faded hay, tangled in a jungle around her head. She rocked jerkily to and fro, removing at intervals a clay pipe from her mouth in order to pucker her thin lips up to one side, and spit with precision upon a certain spot in the fire, which she seemed resolved to prevent from attaining beyond a certain faint glow."

But when King starts scaling mountains, he really slips the fetters from his imagination. Those who have lived through the suspense of accompanying him along the Kings-Kern divide and up the shale of the western ridge will find the present Sierra trail a dull affair. Skeptics have suggested that King's dangers lay principally in his own mind, and perhaps there is some justice in their suspicion. However, King always took the most difficult route up a cliff or down a glacier. Not that he sought out the perilous step, but his temperament led him in that direction by instinct. He was an amateur, not a scientific climber, and he delighted in thrills. Moreover, as a pioneer he had no trails nor maps to help him; he was the first white man to scale many of the highest peaks of the Sierra Nevada.

King's style of mountain-climbing can be judged from his account of descending Mount Tyndall with his friend Cotter: " The rock was so steep that we descended in a sitting posture, clinging with our hands and heels. I heard Cotter say, ' I think I must take off these moccasins and try it barefooted, for I don't believe I can make it.' These words were instantly followed by a startled cry, and I looked round to see him slide quickly toward me, struggling and clutching at the smooth granite. As he slid by I made a grab for him with my right hand, catching him by the shirt, and, throwing myself as far in the other direction as I could, seized with my left hand a little pine tuft, which held us. I asked Cotter to edge along a little to the left where he could get a brace with his feet and relieve me of his weight, which he cautiously did. I then threw a couple of turns with the lasso round the roots of the pine bush, and we were safe, though hardly more than twenty feet from the brink. The pressure of curiosity to get a look over that edge was so strong within me, that I lengthened out sufficient lasso to reach the end, and slid slowly to the edge, where, leaning over, I looked down, getting a full view of the wall for miles. Directly beneath, a sheer cliff of three or four hundred feet stretched down to a pile of débris which rose to unequal heights along its face, reaching the very crest not more than two hundred feet south of us. From that point to the bottom of the cañon, broken rocks, ridges rising through vast sweeps of débris, tufts of pine and frozen bodies of ice, covered the farther slope."

Clarence King and John Muir shared an unlimited enthusiasm for the Yosemite Valley, but they disagreed violently as to the manner of its origin. In the battle, King was a lieutenant implicitly following his leader, Josiah D. Whitney, who, in his state-authorized *Geology of California* and *Yosemite Guidebook*, asserted that the box-like valley had undoubtedly been created by some great prehistoric cataclysm. Much to the annoyance of the members of the California Geological Survey, an amateur geologist name John Muir, a thirty-year-old Scot whom King and Whitney at first contemptuously referred to as " that shepherd," refused to accept the cataclysmic theory and insisted that the valley was caused by glacial erosion. The stubborn young amateur not only resisted the attacks of the professional geologists, but eventually won the battle, proving beyond a doubt that his theory was correct.

It is not surprising that at first Whitney and King refused to take Muir seriously, for when he entered Yosemite in 1868, the naturalist had neither geological training nor scientific reputation. A penniless wanderer, he had hiked into the valley, where he supported himself by breaking mustangs, running a river ferry, herding sheep, and operating J. M. Hutchings's sawmill. Because he kept his eyes open to read the nature he loved so well, after six years in the valley he knew it much better than anyone else.

The wiry young man with auburn hair, full beard, and electric blue eyes had one trait that outweighed all other elements in his nature, the trait of persistence. That persistence was in part a heritage from his Scottish Covenanter ancestors, in part a product of his rigorous upbringing. In a school in Dunbar, where the use of the rod was more common than kind words, he had memorized the New Testament from St. Matthew to Revelation. When his father migrated to a farm in the lake district of Wisconsin, the eleven-year-old boy learned to do a man's work, driving oxen, splitting rails, hoeing corn, and even chiseling a well through sixty feet of sandstone, single-handed. The hardships he experienced as a boy may have stunted his growth, but they did not break his spirit. Once, after nearly drowning in a lake near his home, he rowed out to deep water and dived time after time from his boat, shouting to the water: " Take that! And that! " When his father refused to let him read at night, he invented a clock which awoke him at one in the morning by tipping his bed on end, putting him on his feet, and doing everything to arouse him except to throw cold water in his face. He could then read for five hours before plowing started.

Twenty-two-year-old John Muir left the farm for Madison, hoping to establish himself as an inventor. His ingenious mechanical contraptions, among which were several strange clocks and thermometers as well as a device for guillotining gophers, brought him considerable attention at the state fair and an opportunity to attend the University of Wisconsin. He thought for a while of becoming a physician, but was diverted by a love for botany, which started him on the first of his many long tramps. He left the university, planning once more to make a living through his mechanical skill, and he might have spent his life as a machine-shop foreman had he not injured an eye while at work. A few weeks of blindness convinced him that he should abandon his own inventions to study those of God. After his recovery he tramped a thousand miles from Louisville, Kentucky, to the Gulf of Mexico with copies of the Bible, Milton, and Burns in his knapsack, with the address " John Muir, Earth-planet, Universe " on his notebook, and with a singing joy in his heart. Then, after a near-fatal siege of fever in Florida, he took the boat for the isthmus and California. Immediately upon disembarking in San Francisco, he startled a citizen by asking the direction to the " wild part of the state," boarded the Oakland ferry as directed, and by evening had made a good start on his walk to the Yosemite.

Muir spent the following six years doing the things he loved to do. He slept in the open, he climbed cliffs, he collected specimens for his botanical notebooks. He had no ambitions that required more money than he could earn at odd jobs and he was not much interested in the outside world, although he occasionally sent for books on botany and geology. As he gained a reputation for knowledge of the valley, he found that noted visitors made a special point of getting acquainted with him. Joseph LeConte insisted on his companionship during his geological trips; Henry Edwards sought his aid for his entomological collection; and Albert Kellogg consulted him about the botany of the region. After Therese Yelverton, Countess of Avonmore, spent a summer in the valley, she made him the hero of her novel *Zanita.* Ralph Waldo Emerson crawled on hands and knees up the narrow runway to Muir's hang-rest, attached to the end of Hutchings's sawmill, so that he could compare notes on man and nature with the young philosopher. But Muir felt that his idol from Concord had been too long exposed to civilization when he failed to persuade him to camp out under the redwoods.

While Muir eagerly expounded his theory of glacial erosion to visitors to the mountains, the world outside began to discuss his personality and show interest in his scientific ideas. Eventually there was nothing for him but to pack up his notebooks and go down to the Golden Gate, a geological formation which he considered of interest only " as a mouthpiece for a portion of my ice," and write up his findings. The New York *Tribune*, *Scribner's*, and other Eastern magazines carried a number of his articles, but the bulk of his writing appeared in the *Overland Monthly*. In fact, he became one of the leading contributors to that journal, writing for it articles supporting his geological conclusions, essays lauding the beauty of the Sierra Nevada, and accounts of his long hikes into the country near Kings River and Mount Whitney. His style was marked by a flair for unusual metaphors and an intensity which at its worst produced the overflorid, at its best the phrase that glowed. In John Muir's work, man and style were indistinguishable. " There is at least a punky spark in my heart and it may blaze in this autumn gold, fanned by the King. Some of my grandfathers must have been born on a muirland for there is heather in me, and tinctures of bog juices, that send me to Cassiope, and oozing through all my veins impel me unhaltingly through endless glacier meadows, seemingly the deeper and danker the better."

Man has never had a better opportunity of watching a society evolve overnight than on the Western frontier during the two decades following the gold-rush. With rapid change removing the blinders set up by habit, did there follow a clearness of vision ordinarily denied to a comparatively static world? Did man learn anything of significance from the phenomenon?

The answer presented by the evidence is as a whole disappointing. Most of the writers of the period were living so fast that they had little time to speculate on what they saw. And when they did draw conclusions, they usually disagreed with one another. One might easily assume for purposes of generalization that the philosophy expressed in J. S. Hittell's *Short History of Culture* was typical of the frontier mind. Hittell was a materialist who asserted boldly that art and science were of value only as handmaids of the kitchen and workshop, and that such men as James Watt had accomplished more good for humanity than a score of poets like Robert Burns.

As representative of the period as Hittell, however, was Josiah Royce, born in a Western mining camp, who more than once asserted that his social ideas were the direct reflection of frontier life. Royce's first published essay, which appeared in the *Overland Monthly* in 1875, was a plea for poetry as man's greatest spiritual food; and his first book came to idealistic conclusions after examining man's experience in governing himself during the decade following the American occupation of California. After studying the actions of a score of vigilante committees, he could still write: " I have learned, as I have toiled for a while over the sources, to see in these days a process of divinely moral significance." Though they were both spokesmen of the frontier, Josiah Royce championed an idealism which J. S. Hittell scorned.

In the field of economic theory we look for more positive results. If economists such as Loria are right in stating that " colonial settlement is for economic science what the mountain is for geology, bringing to light primitive stratifications," the Far-Western colonial experiment, in providing the most concentrated cross-section to be found in history, should have been very suggestive to an intelligent observer. When we prospect for such observations, our lead dives directly into the rich vein of Henry George's *Progress and Poverty*. Henry George arrived at his theories by observing the special conditions governing ownership of land on the frontier give way to the normal procedure of the rest of the country.

Since the time Henry George had stopped a stranger to ask him for five dollars, he had advanced slowly in the newspaper profession. Though he had tried to hold his combativeness in check, he was constantly changing employers as the result of disagreements. Between 1866 and 1871 he worked on five different newspapers, and that he spent the four following years on the San Francisco *Post* was probably the result of the fact that he was part owner of that journal. His determination to make a fortune was likewise slow of achievement; he had arrived too late to make a strike in the diggings, and he had lost every cent he had invested in mining stocks.

Henry George had a good share of the crusader in his nature and, like all crusaders, was an easy victim to a fixed idea. It is, therefore, a clear error to call him a reflective liberal. At the same time that he was working on his liberal theories in economics, he was expressing most illiberal ideas in other fields; in one editorial he justified lynching, and in another he advocated exclusion of the Chinese on the grounds that they were " utter heathens, treacherous, sensual, cowardly, and cruel." Again, he followed the method of the crusader rather than that of the dispassionate scientist in evolving his economic theory; he often stated that the truth reached him in moments of ecstasy. One such moment occurred when a man in Oakland told him that land could be had for a thousand dollars an acre. " Like a flash it came upon me that there was the reason for advancing poverty with advancing wealth. With the growth of population, land grows in value, and the men who work it must pay for the privilege." Then: " Once, in daylight, and in a city street, there came to me a thought, a vision, a call — give it what name you please. But every nerve quivered. And there and then I made a vow." Such is the nature of prophets, and such was the nature that made it possible for an unschooled frontier newspaperman to set about rewriting the science of political economy.

George had come to California in a day when each miner was allowed to stake a claim as large, but only as large, as he could work with his own hands; when the " land squatter," fighting the big Mexican land grants, was contending that every agriculturist was entitled to a living from the soil, but to no more soil than he could till. When George arrived, he had believed that he was coming to a land of opportunity for the common man. But as the West developed, he noticed a drop in wages, an increase in poverty, and a progressive drift of property into the hands of the privileged few.

As the transcontinental railroad approached completion, Henry George pondered on the meaning of progress. While the last rails were being laid, he raised a discordant voice among the myriad of enthusiasts by suggesting that the new era would benefit not all the people but only a few — that " increase in population and in wealth past a certain point means simply an approximation to the conditions of older countries — the Eastern States and Europe." When the railroad failed to produce the boom everyone had anticipated, he set to work to discover the basic causes that made poverty accompany progress. He suspected the traditional attitude towards landownership. Did not the evidence show that land pre-emption for speculative purposes was at the root of industrial troubles in the West?

The hard times that followed the arrival of the railroad were disheartening even to the most ardent real-estate promoter. In '68 and '69 anticipation of an inpouring of emigrants and wealth, coupled with four bumper years in the San Joaquin Valley, had brought drunken land speculation. Then the newcomers failed to arrive, a formerly beneficent nature stopped supplying rain for the farmers, and the richest Californians found themselves land-poor. A new bonanza on the Comstock should have improved conditions, but it actually made matters worse by encouraging the speculative mood of a gambling-mad public, eager to invest even in salted diamond mines. Stocks rose to a thousand dollars and then dropped to forty cents. A few men on the inside made fortunes, but the man on the street lost as he had never lost before. Ralston's failure, followed by the closing of the Bank of California, brought on a panic. By the mid-seventies San Francisco was experiencing riots among the unemployed, and Denis Kearney was leading a mob with cries of " Hang the capitalists! " Even the resurrection of the old vigilante committee failed to convince the populace that all was well in California. The railroad was now called " the Octopus " and blamed for all misfortunes.

During this period of social unrest Henry George's crusading spirit grew ever stronger. He throve on causes. The blue-eyed man with the large head and the short body — he had to stand on a board in order to work at the compositor's case — came to be known throughout the city as a champion of liberal ideas, a debater and a fighter for what he thought was right. Horrified at the poverty he saw in New York City when John Nugent of the *Herald* sent him east in '68 to oppose the Associated Press, he returned with the determination that San Francisco should not follow in its course. Were slums and crushing poverty inevitable accompaniments of growth? Did progress invariably mean the driving of a wedge between those who have and those who want? Such had always been the case, he concluded, but he believed that by using his observations of the development of the frontier, he could evolve a theory that would put an end to such injustices.

When Henry George wrote " What the Railroad Will Bring Us " for the fourth number of the *Overland Monthly*, he had read no Mill or Ricardo, nor had he any intention of advancing

a new economic theory. He was merely setting down those observations and reflections which had convinced him that poverty
was increasing in California. Only a few years before he came
west, an ounce of gold — $16 — was looked on as the normal
day's wage for the miner and, perforce, the normal day's wage
for the city worker. When he arrived in 1858, wages had
dropped somewhat, but were still above those in the East. During the sixties they had sunk from $5 a day to $2.50. He had
always been told that capital gained in earning power with
a lowering of wages, but he noted in California that interest
rates, the return on capital, depreciated with wages. He had
seen the earning power of invested money drop from 24 per
cent to 8 per cent as the Western frontier came to take on
the characteristics of older societies.

Concomitant with these movements, the natural resources
of the new land, which he considered to be the property of the
common man, became increasingly inaccessible and were plainly
drifting into the hands of a plutocracy. Thus the day of individual placer claims had been followed by the day of company
mining, when men no longer worked for themselves, but for
great financiers; laborers who had once taken their earnings
directly from the gold gravel now obtained their wage by par-
boiling themselves two thousand feet underground. Similarly,
the emigrant farmer could no longer get a share of the public
domain. With an entire state to plow and plant, he now found
it difficult to obtain land at a price which made it possible for
him to till it. Litigations over the inadequately defined Spanish land grants had transferred much of the property of the
state into the hands of lawyers and speculators who held it
from use in anticipation of large profits in the future. George
wrote indignantly: " On uncultivated tracts of land in the
new State of California may be seen the blackened chimneys
of homes from which settlers have been driven . . . and great

stretches of land which might be populous are desolate." Men starved while the land, their heritage by God-given rights, lay idle.

The more that Henry George thought of the paradox displayed when progress and poverty went hand in hand, the more he felt the trouble lay in restricting the use of land, the ultimate source of all wealth. The solution lay in returning the land to the people. No revolution was necessary, however, to accomplish this revolutionary step; it could be done merely by taxing the land to its rental value. And during the process of thus eliminating the greatest source of speculation in the economic system, his scheme of taxation would provide ample revenue to run the government. This panacea for man's woes was called the single-tax.

Henry George first outlined his theory in a pamphlet entitled *Our Land and Land Policy, National and State,* which he published in March 1871. Using the magnitude of the railroad grants for a text, he forecast the pre-emption of even the poorest free land by 1890; pointed out that in the older countries the number of landowners was constantly diminishing, a movement that showed the drift of property into the hands of the wealthy minority; and then asked the Western public whether the right to nature's bounty was not a right that should be protected. He reasoned that the earning power of all wealth was made up of three parts: wages, interest, and rent; and that when rent took too large a portion of the total, wages and interest fell, and the laborer and the capitalist suffered. He proposed as a remedy for industrial depressions and maldistribution of wealth, both of which he considered results of land speculation, the inauguration of a tax equal to the rental value of land.

Though his pamphlet gained few readers and even fewer supporters, Henry George's faith in his idea was unshaken.

He decided that his next steps would be to read all the important books on political economy and, if necessary, rewrite the science to conform to his conclusions. The facts that he had never attended high school or college and that he was unversed in the methods of research and scientific speculation daunted him not at all. He felt that he had the advantage of not being blinded by books. In a lecture at the University of California he asserted that " for the study of political economy you need no special knowledge, no extensive library, no costly laboratory." On that occasion he offended many a professor by remarking: " A monkey with a microscope, a mule packing a library, are fit emblems of the men who pass through the whole educational machinery, and come out but learned fools." A resourceful pioneer who used his brains ought to be able to see truths that were hidden from the specialized scholar. And Henry George was a true frontiersman, a jack-of-all-trades, who was willing to try anything.

He soon discovered that two such scholars, John Stuart Mill and David Ricardo, had come to false conclusions because they lived in a comparatively static society. Habituated by custom to accept the *status quo*, they had confused the science of political economy by starting from false premises. As for Malthus, George went after him as if he were flaying the devil. After referring to him as " the reverend gentleman " with " the most ridiculous incapacity for logical thought," George attempted to destroy his theories by using logic, by citing evidence, by ridiculing his ideas, and by appealing to God.

When he started *Progress and Poverty*, George had intended to write only an article, but by the time he had settled with Mill, Ricardo, and Malthus and added his own ideas, he had a five-hundred-page book. In the first half he disposed of most of the theories of contemporary economics, accepting only Ricardo's law of rent, and had redefined wages, capital, and interest, and the laws that govern them. In the latter half of the book he proposed his theory of the single-tax, anticipated the objections to it, and attempted to answer them. By the time he reached the end of the book, he had grown lyrically apostolic and appended an essay on " The Problem of Individual Life." When, with a flourish, he laid down his pen in 1879, he dedicated the rest of his life to spreading the gospel of the single-tax.

That gospel has not to this day been given a trial. During the reform era early in the present century it appeared that George's remedy might be tested in some individual communities such as Cleveland, but today the chances that a city or state will experiment with the single-tax are small indeed.

In less direct ways, however, George was more influential than he might ever have dreamed. No book coming out in his generation did more to undermine the acceptance of *laissez-faire* economics than did *Progress and Poverty*, and the twentieth-century proponents of a planned, socially directed economy acknowledge a heavy debt to " the prophet from San Francisco." To that point Sidney Webb has stated that " the event which, more than any other, stimulated the revival of socialism in Great Britain was the publication of an American book, Henry George's *Progress and Poverty*." Moreover, in his detailed argument George not only anticipated many later theories, such as Turner's analysis of the effect of the frontier on American civilization, but he was the first American economist to attempt a careful examination of the causes of depressions and their relations to the growing inequality of distribution of wealth in the nation. Most important, George was surprisingly successful in achieving his avowed aim of making " the dismal science of political economy " intelligible to the average man. With the frontiersman's belief that special knowledge should be made available to all and with the veteran editor's skill in handling imaginative, rhetorical prose, he wrote a book which was not only clearly expressed but entertaining. *Progress and Poverty* ultimately gained a circulation of over two million copies; no modern best-seller even in fiction has approached such a number of sales.

Progress and Poverty was more evidently a product of the frontier than any other book written west of the Rockies. The theories it propounded evolved from observations of an infant civilization. The affrontery which made it possible was a product of the frontiersman's irreverence and versatility, and the language which caused it to be read from San Francisco to Moscow was that of a frontier editor who was not afraid to speak out in eloquent terms and measured periods.

In a cow pasture on the south side of Market Street, far out between Third and Fourth in a region opened up by the pre-railroad boom, the Bancroft Building was erected in 1869 to house the largest bookselling and publishing business west of Chicago. The huge brick structure, with its five stories topped by a gargoyle-studded cornice, contained the firm's retail department on the first floor, its stock of stationery and musical instruments on the second, and its latest model printing presses and binderies on the third and fourth. The entire top story, like Doctor Johnson's attic, was occupied by " the workshop," a library and writing-room in which Hubert Howe Bancroft was using business methods to create literature on an unprecedented scale. This was Bancroft's history-factory, the home of the Bancroft system. To the bookseller turned historian, the presses and binderies, the lithographing and engraving units, the wholesale and retail departments, and the two hundred employees on the lower levels were but ramifications and useful aids to the ninth and most recently created department of the business, called Literary Industries.

There on the fifth floor the Literary Industries employed

HENRY GEORGE IN 1865.

Courtesy of California State Library

HUBERT HOWE BANCROFT.
Courtesy of California State Library

some twenty men who, scattered at small tables, busily copied notes, indexed material, translated documents, or proof-read copy. Among them were five directing assistants, scholars who had flourished under the system and could be trusted to know their assigned fields well enough to prepare rough-draft notes for the final work. These picked men, who labored from eight till twelve and from one to six every day but Sunday, had learned to turn out the maximum number of words during the week. Mr. Bancroft found them dependable in every way, except that they suffered somewhat from insomnia. Two of them slept in the cubicles at the end of the library, while the other three dwelt in lodgings near by.

In addition to whole-hearted enthusiasm for the Bancroft project, these assistants had three things in common: good education, ill health, and liberal religious views. There was but one American among them, the librarian Henry L. Oak, a native of Maine and graduate of Dartmouth, who had taught in both high school and college and who had given up pedagogy to devote his patience and energy to creative work. His able right-hand man, known as William Nemos, was a Finnish nobleman who had been educated in a gymnasium in Stockholm and by a tutor at Upsala, had been smuggled into Russia and had lived for years in India, and had failed to make a fortune digging for gold in Australia. This wanderer with the assumed name was an accomplished linguist; when he turned up in San Francisco, Bancroft heard of him and offered him a steady income in return for his indispensable talent. Lesser men were Albert Goldschmidt, a German who spoke a half-dozen languages and specialized in Old Dutch; Walt M. Fisher, the son of an Irish clergyman, who had studied in Queen's College at Belfast, had browsed in Paris and in the British Museum, and had come west to get ideas which he hoped to translate into literature; and T. Arundel-Harcourt (or so he was called), a brilliant but erratic scion of British nobility who had gone to school in Germany, had adventured in India, and was in California looking for excitement. Twenty-three years old, he was the youngest of the group, while Goldschmidt, the eldest, was thirty-five.

The fortunate visitor allowed to enter " the workshop," one of the most curious exhibits of the Far-Western frontier, was sure to be impressed by the ordered activity which he saw under the skylights. Lining the four walls were shelves which held some twenty thousand books, pamphlets, and manuscripts. Ancient vellum, parchment covers, and improvised slip-cases enclosed transcriptions of the records in California mission archives, rare accounts of early voyages to Central America, and Spanish documents from such collections as the Biblioteca Imperial de Méjico, recently collected for the ill-fated Maximilian, now serving as grist for the history-mill. At one end of the room stood a case invented by librarian Oak, in which an index of the materials in the thousands of volumes was patiently being accumulated. Strung upon another device were hundreds of paper bags, each containing many sheets of summaries and quotations, digested material to be used in time by Mr. Bancroft. In the center of the workshop stood a breast-high revolving table, upon which were spread out many volumes, manuscripts, and sheaves of notes; beside it was a tall desk at which one could write standing up. The pieces of furniture were so arranged that the writer could turn the table to bring any desired material within his reach. This was the focal spot of the workshop, the point from which the finished product issued forth.

Behind the desk stood Mr. Bancroft, a tall, broad-shouldered man, already slightly stooped from his labor, who made a commanding figure with his wavy iron-gray hair, full beard, and mustache, his thin face and large, expressive eyes, sparkling with enough energy and self-assurance for two men. Naturally rather genial, he could be stern and exacting on occasion; a glutton for labor, he had no patience with lazy or inefficient help. At thirty-seven years of age he had given up the active headship of his business to write a series of elaborate and exhaustive works on the political and natural history, antiquities, geography, climate, resources, inhabitants, and productions of the western half of the North American Continent. He did not intend to stint in energy or money (he was to devote at least a half-million of his earnings to the enterprise), and he was determined to get the work done before he died.

The lack of a formal education did not dampen Bancroft's confidence in his ability to write history any more than it did Henry George's to revolutionize political economy; the fact that he had had but a few years of schooling back in Ohio bothered the self-made businessman not a whit. " Where are your college men? " he asked. " Few of them, indeed, put in an appearance among those who move the world or conduct the great affairs of life." Lack of an education had certainly not prevented him from being successful in everything he had tried to date. Coming to California in '52, he had dug at Rich Bar just long enough to secure means to buy a small stock of books, with which he had established himself in business in Crescent City. In three years spent in that unpromising community, he had made enough money to open a good sized book and stationery store in San Francisco. During the Civil War, he had done so well by buying his merchandise with greenbacks and selling it for gold that he found himself one of the most successful merchants in the West. By the time he was thirty-five, he was wealthy. He then decided that there was time enough in life to accomplish something more lasting and more important than selling and publishing books. He would do some writing himself. He would create something substantial, not merely contribute an article or two to the newly founded *Overland Monthly*. He need only apply to literature the energy and ability which had worked so well in business, and books by Bancroft would roll from his presses.

Of course, when he started he did not intend to write thirty-nine volumes of history; he assumed that Gargantuan task by a series of steps. In '59, while considering the publication of a San Francisco directory and fact-book, he had gathered together all the books in his store dealing with California. He was surprised to find that though he had more than seventy-five volumes he had by no means exhausted the field. A little browsing in other local book-stores soon doubled the number, and by the time he visited Europe in 1862, the collecting mania had taken a strong hold on him. He set out to buy everything he could find dealing with the western half of the North American Continent, from the Isthmus of Darien to Bering Strait. As he traveled, he ransacked the stock of book-dealers in England, France, Germany, and Spain. Still unsatisfied, he sent out representatives to buy up entire libraries and collections such as Andrade's Biblioteca Mejicana, E. G. Squier's library of Central American source-materials, and José Fernando Ramirez's manuscripts and books dealing with the Jesuit missions. Bancroft declared his ravenous appetite for books increased by what it fed on. " Books! Books! I revelled in books. After buying and selling, after ministering to others all my life, I would now enjoy them; I would bathe my mind in them till saturated with the better part of their contents." He announced in his own inimitable Latin phraseology that during this period of his development he changed from a bibliopolist into a bibliophile.

In 1869, ten years after he began collecting, Bancroft felt that it was time to start producing. He now possessed some sixteen thousand volumes and could leave to his agents the task of adding to the collection. The next problem was to decide what to write. The idea of using his materials to compile directories and handbooks had long since given way to plans for a series of encyclopedias and these in turn to a project for making a detailed record of early voyages and explorations on the Pacific Coast. But the more Bancroft fingered his many documents and contemplated the virgin territory at his disposal, the more he realized that he would be satisfied with nothing short of a complete and detailed history of the whole field. And yet how could such a task be accomplished? How could one man even read through all of the original sources, much less make notes on them and build them into a massive history? If it could be done, system alone would accomplish it. He would hire capable assistants, pay them to read all of the items in his library, and train them to extract important passages, summarize others, and index the material in an efficient catalogue. Then, as the director and creator, he would go through the thoroughly digested material and fit the parts together. With good luck and plenty of funds, the great work might be accomplished in this manner.

While his staff was busy collecting notes, he would start the project by working out the earliest part of the history. That part proved, much to his annoyance, to be a study of the aboriginal inhabitants of the western slope. He would rather have started with the coming of the Spanish *conquistadores*, but he realized that something must first be done with the aborigines. " Wherever I touched the continent with my Spaniards they were there, a dusky, disgusting subject. . . . I would gladly have avoided them. . . . My tastes in the matter, however, did not dispose of the subject. The savages were there, and there was no help for me; I must write them up to get rid of them." *The Native Races* was written to get rid of them.

When Bancroft started to write *The Native Races*, he

thought that he could condense all the material on hand into two volumes. But as he worked, he realized that he would not be able adequately to describe all the natives of the vast territory in the allotted space, much less discuss thoroughly their mythologies, their languages, and their origins. Powerless, he saw the two volumes grow to five before he was done. Nor was he able to do all the important work himself, as he had planned. He estimated that if he relied solely on his own labors, *The Native Races* alone would take him a quarter to half a century, and then when would he reach the more important sections of his history? There was nothing for it but to utilize his capable assistants to the fullest possible extent. Each was assigned to a special field and contributed " rough notes " for his perusal. He altered them occasionally in wording, expanded some, contracted others, and signed his name to the whole. When the work was completed, his assistants calculated that they had written 3,730 pages of the 4,000 that made up the five volumes, but Bancroft felt that he had done much more than write 270. After all, the work was largely a network of quotations from source-material and it was he who had conceived the synthesis and given it form. And if the history was actually to be composed by business methods, it would be well to establish early the principle of economic and efficient use of labor.

When *The Native Races* was completed, in 1874, Bancroft next turned his business ability to the distribution of the work. He felt that the success of his history as a whole would depend upon the manner in which the first unit was launched. Printed with the best type and engravings the Bancroft Company could buy, published through arrangements by a reputable Eastern firm, D. Appleton & Company, *The Native Races* needed only good reviews to make it a success. He would see to it personally that the reviews were satisfactory.

His campaign was shrewd, direct, and efficient. First before the volumes were issued, he submitted sheets of proof to local writers whom he felt he could trust, obtained their enthusiastic consideration, and printed their letters in a circular which soon " reached sixteen pages of flattering testimonials." He next arranged to have a long laudatory review appear in the *Overland Monthly*, a courtesy not difficult to obtain, as Bret Harte had departed for Boston, and the magazine was being edited by two of Bancroft's assistants, Fisher and Harcourt. With the circular of testimonials in his pocket and a hundred author's copies of *The Native Races* in his trunk, he then invaded the East, arriving in New England just in time for an important congress of academicians and savants. Prepared for indifference and rebuffs, he was not surprised when at first he was coldly received. His persistence and enthusiasm were too much even for the Bostonians, however, and when he returned to San Francisco after his triumphal tour, he brought with him praise from all sorts of famous men, ranging from James Russell Lowell to Wendell Phillips. Moreover, he had been able to engineer favorable and lengthy reviews in the leading periodicals, in the *Atlantic Monthly*, the *North American Review*, the *Nation*, and others. He had also arranged to publish his work in London and in Paris and had obtained many eulogies from abroad to add to his brochure. In the future all he would have to do to ensure good reviews for the thirty-four additional volumes of history as they appeared would be to submit these appraisals to the critical journals. Who would dare to disagree with Francis Parkman, with Clarence King, with T. S. Higginson? The launching of *The Native Races* was a great success. Bancroft wrote that " never probably was a book so generally and so favorably reviewed by the best journals in Europe and America. Never was an author more suddenly or more thoroughly brought to the attention of learned and literary men everywhere."

The Bancroft method had justified itself. The gold-miner metamorphosed into the historian had demonstrated the desirability of applying commercial methods and division of labor to historical and scientific research. The practical man of business had triumphed over "the purely garret philosopher or student." The task of condensing fifty thousand volumes into thirty-nine no longer appeared insurmountable. It was now possible for one man, using business methods, to deal adequately with three million square miles of territory, one twelfth of the world's surface, two thousand times as great an area as that covered by Herodotus. Though it would take the old-fashioned scholar, working eight hours a day, four hundred years to go through Bancroft's collection by himself, a corps of trained readers could draw the pith from the material in only twenty years. The two thousand authorities on Central America could all be consulted under the Bancroft system; the ten thousand books and manuscripts dealing with Mexico could be examined meticulously by five men working for ten years extracting and systematizing the references. Other assistants could, at the same time, be working on Utah, on Alaska, on Spanish California, on the Northwest. In twenty to thirty years self-abnegation, a liberal outlay of money, and a well-balanced mind could accomplish the task of centuries by utilizing the four processes of the system: collecting, collating, eviscerating, and re-creating. The last process especially stirred Bancroft's imagination. "It was my ambition to do for this western earth's end what Homer did for Greece, with these differences: Homer dealt in myths, I should deal in facts: Homer's were the writings of poetical genius, mine of plodding prose." If his health remained good, he would be able to complete the work — and then let the end come. "Let me die like Plato, at my table, pen in hand, and be buried among the scenes of my labors."

Hubert Howe Bancroft was, as a matter of fact, to outlive the completion of his labors by some thirty years. In 1890 the last of the thirty-nine octavo volumes of *Bancroft's Works* appeared, the " assistants " were dismissed, and shortly thereafter the valuable library was sold to the University of California. The work had proceeded according to schedule and Bancroft was satisfied.

The sixteen years devoted to the completion of the *History* after *The Native Races* appeared came after frontier conditions had ceased to exist, when the West was no longer isolated. For the sake of completeness, it is well, however, to sketch the rest of the details in the picture of Bancroft and his literary activities.

The method used in the later volumes was essentially that of *The Native Races*, though in the history of California and the adjacent states he made a notable addition with respect to his sources: the recording of the testimony of early settlers. Never a man to do things half-heartedly, he set about obtaining statements from every pioneer of importance living in the West. He also borrowed or copied every journal or sheaf of letters that might contain information in his field. After he hired a charming bogus general named Cerutti, with whom lying was a fine art, to worm his way into the confidence of the leading Spanish-Californians, the memoirs and papers of Vallejo, Castro, Alvarado, Bandini, Pio Pico, and many lesser fry were added to the library. Consul Larkin donated his papers, General Sutter spent three days dictating his reminiscences, and Judge Hayes turned over a collection of clippings and notebooks made during a lifetime spent in southern California. Bancroft or his representatives journeyed into Arizona and Utah, into Oregon, Montana, and Wyoming. Emissaries gleaned the grain from the archives of countries from Panama to Alaska and consulted everyone from the embittered Frémont to the head of the Mormon Church. The most valuable part of the Bancroft collection came to be hundreds of memoirs dictated by men who had seen the West grow, men whose stories would never have been told had not Bancroft obtained them.

Of the early assistants, Oak and Nemos continued diligently with their work, held by their enthusiasm for the great history. Among the many others who were added to the staff from time to time, two were outstanding in their contributions. Thomas Savage, born of New England parents in Havana, served for twenty-one years as United States consul to Cuba before he drifted into Central America, where he worked in Panama, Guatemala, and San Salvador. In 1873 ill health brought him to San Francisco; within three months he was a member of Bancroft's staff. An excellent linguist, he became the library authority on Mexico and Central America. Then, in 1878, Frances Fuller Victor, now a widow, moved down from Oregon to join the corps of workers. The former Florence Fane of the *Golden Era* was the only one of the Bancroft assistants to come into the workshop with a literary reputation. She had already published two books dealing with Oregon history: *The River of the West* had built social history around the biography of Joe Meek, the mountain man, and *All over Oregon and Washington* gave a travel view of a large territory. Mrs. Victor was to supply the " rough notes " for the several volumes of Bancroft's history dealing with the Northwest as well as much of the text pertaining to California. A devoted worker until the history was completed, she revolted in 1893 by exhibiting several volumes of *Bancroft's History* at the Chicago World's Fair with her name as author on the title page.

With the volumes rolling from the press sometimes at the rate of three a year, Bancroft, also busy with trips and negotiations, found himself hard pressed to inspect, much less supply every word in the final draft. Perhaps unconsciously he came to trust more and more to his assistants. His " re-creating " sometimes reduced itself to crossing out all the " verys," adding classical allusions and Carlylesque phrases, and making derogatory remarks about earlier historians such as Irving and Prescott. He thus described his method of writing: " The work of my assistants besides saving me an immense amount of drudgery and manual labor, left my mind always fresh, and open to receive and retain the subject as a whole. I could institute comparisons and indulge in generalizations more freely, and I believe more effectually, than with my mind overwhelmed by a mass of detail."

Bancroft also gave some of his attention to the proper distribution of the volumes of history. They were printed on the best paper with the cleanest type, they were issued by the Bancroft Company, now in a position to act as publisher, and they were sold by the subscription plan under the able generalship of Nathan J. Stone. As the California legislature had approved the work, all the schools and libraries in the state bought sets. Pioneers who had contributed memoirs, merchants who were indebted to the Bancroft Company, and a great number of boosters also bought the books, although they probably never read them. Scholars throughout the world purchased them for their merits. Though many buyers, who had failed to read their contracts carefully, grumbled as the volumes kept appearing year after year, the public as a whole was pleased to find that the history of the West was so prodigious. The historian, unable to disregard his business instincts, made money on his venture. Let it be said, however, that even if he had faced the loss of his fortune, he would probably have continued with his work; as Ella Sterling Cummins put it, he " was morbid on the subject of histories."

Because the ethics of the businessman differs from those of the scholar, Bancroft was severely criticized for many of his policies. He always defended himself with the incontrovertible argument that if he had not followed business ethics, the history would never have been written. The most serious charge against him was that he had been " a purloiner of other people's brains." His answer was that his assistants knew when they joined his project that they were being hired for clerical work, not authorship; that they could have written nothing without the use of the library he had collected; and that, although they wrote many pages of his works, the central conceptions and synthesizing force came from him. The fact remains, however, that Bancroft actually wrote no more than one tenth of the work published under his name, and that Oak wrote an aggregate of seven volumes, Nemos five, Mrs. Victor three, and Savage three. As a return for their labors they received a fair living wage and acknowledgment for clerical and scholarly assistance in Bancroft's autobiography, *Literary Industries*, volume thirty-nine of the *History*. The arrangement was succinctly described by Bancroft when he said that Oak, who was paid two hundred dollars a month and room, produced history at a cheaper cost per page than any of his other assistants. Having furnished the tools, provided the raw materials, and paid the workmen, Bancroft felt no qualms in assuring the world that he was the sole author of *Bancroft's Works*.

Other charges of unethical practice made against Bancroft appear to have little basis in truth. Though he obtained aid from countless pioneers, he adhered remarkably well to an objective attitude, avoiding the temptation to flatter those who had furnished him with material. Charges that he borrowed manuscripts and never returned them are not borne out by evidence. That he seemed prejudiced in favor of the Mormons and Indians was probably the result of his attempt to be fair to groups usually misrepresented. He applied business methods to getting reviews, even going so far as to pay for space devoted to lauding his books, but he was only doing openly what many a racketeer in the writing field does covertly in the modern publishing game. He had no intention of damaging the prestige of his history by allowing it to be reviewed carelessly or unsympathetically. Finally, in selling his books he appears to have used no methods that are not standard in current business practice.

Bancroft's project was indeed an extraordinary one, hardly to be accomplished by ordinary methods. Because he had money and enthusiasm, he was able to bring into his library almost every book dealing with his vast subject as well as to make transcriptions of documents he could not buy. Through his business acumen he obtained the pioneer sagas of hundreds of men of action who would otherwise have died silent. With his perseverance and gift for organization, he was able to sift and classify his material — a marvelous accomplishment when one remembers that he started his project only ten years after the gold-rush and finished his work in thirty years without the aid of modern filing devices, the typewriter, the dictaphone, or the photostatic camera. He caught the history of a civilization before that civilization disappeared, leaving to scholars who followed an indispensable library of source-materials and thirty-nine volumes of intelligently arranged facts. Though the volumes of his history are naturally unequal in scholarship and in style, they have to date maintained their pre-eminence as the basic authority on the half continent with which they deal. One would not go far wrong in asserting that Hubert Howe Bancroft, the frontier bookseller who turned historian, accomplished the greatest feat of historiography since Thucydides.

FROM GOLD GULCH TO PARNASSUS

THE EARLY Californians were in some things more closely bound
to Europe than they were to the states beyond the Rockies. A
large percentage of them were foreign-born, and by sea London
was almost as near as New York; but quite as important as
these obvious reasons is the fact that even those emigrants who
came in from the east coast and the Middle West had their
cultural roots in England, Greece, and Palestine. The Pike
County farmer, the German shopkeeper, the Welsh miner, the
New York merchant knew more about Shakespeare than about
Emerson, were more interested in Milton than in Poe. They
read the poems of Byron and the novels of Dickens; they respected the law of the Romans and the philosophy of the Greeks;
and, above all, through their familiarity with the Bible, they
cherished Palestine as the birthplace of Adam and the native
land of Jesus. Accordingly, they dreamed that some day they
might visit Europe and the Holy Land. Few, of course, were
able to realize that ambition, but that most Westerners held it
accounts not only for the warm reception accorded the travel
letters of journalists sent abroad to report the Old Countries for
them, but for the very fact that travel letters were produced in

such large numbers. The Foreign Correspondent received generous space in San Francisco journals.

For some time these frontier reporters had been changing the traditional tune sung by American tourists, altering the song from one of cloying melodiousness to a faster one in which exaggeration made for humor and occasional dissonance gave variation and relief. One reviewer of Mark Twain's *The Innocents Abroad* described the change thus: "The dear, old book of travel, with its conscientious desire to instruct, its guide-book directness, its dreadful distances, and more dreadful dates; its feeble moralizing, its poetical quotations from Moore, Byron, and Rogers; its one or two thrilling personal adventures, and its reminiscence of at least one noted foreign character, is a thing of the past. . . . The modern tourists are plundered only by guides; they stand and deliver only backsheesh; they are devoured only by fleas." The members of this new school of travel-book writers were more inclined to use brick-bats on stained-glass windows than to shed tears over shrines and relics.

A pioneer of this school was J. Ross Browne, whose *Yusef* appeared sixteen years before *The Innocents Abroad*. Though Browne was an Irishman from Dublin and did not come to America until he was a boy of eleven, he wasted no time in acquiring many of the traits typical of the frontiersmen, especially those of restlessness and resourcefulness. Before he reached California in '49, he had worked on Ohio River flat-boats and Atlantic whalers; he had even been marooned in Zanzibar. After capitalizing on his knowledge of shorthand to make ten thousand dollars reporting the California Constitutional Convention, he used the money to finance a year of adventures on the shores of the Mediterranean, where he wrote the chapters and sketched the drawings for *Yusef*, and for diversion played " Old Zip Coon " on his flute to the amusement and delight of his Arabian friends. Though he always looked on California as headquarters, he wandered over the face of the globe, corresponding for numerous journals and sustaining his persistent jocularity in a half-dozen travel books covering territories from Iceland and Norway to Nevada and Arizona. Traveling was his delight; sketching and music, his hobbies; writing and lecturing, his avocations; and observing, his source of revenue. By substituting curiosity, industry, and resourcefulness for formal training, he made himself an authority on internal revenue, Indian affairs, and mining engineering and published several valuable statistical works in those fields. After a short experience as United States Minister to China, he spent his last years near Oakland in a house which typified his personality; Pagoda Hill was described as " a quaint mixture of Chinese, Indian, Moorish, Gothic, Italian and Russian architecture, painted cream and brown outside, and within charmingly irregular, sunny and roomy."

In his books of travel as well as in his lectures, Browne was a humorist and somewhat of a social critic; his exaggerated stories were likely to be followed by strictures on the short-comings of Old World culture — strictures which showed his essentially materialistic philosophy. " The smallest steam boat that paddles its way up the Hudson is greater than the greatest monument of antiquity, and does more to promote the civilization and happiness of mankind." Naturally he was a firm believer in the future of democratic America. The two greatest virtues of his work were the wealth of detail he used and the fact that he knew and fairly well understood the countries and peoples he described, for Browne was the type of traveler who, not content with a see-Europe-in-thirty-days tour, settled down to live with the natives here and there for indefinite periods of time. And the customs and characters of those natives he told about with a salty humor peculiarly his own.

Another member of the iconoclastic school of foreign cor-

respondents was John Franklin Swift, who was writing his observations of the Holy Land for the *Bulletin* at the same time
Mark Twain was reporting for the *Alta.* Swift, like Mark
Twain, was from Missouri; he was, in fact, from Pike County,
which furnished the name for the type of humor represented
by the work of both men. Trained as a blacksmith, Swift had
driven a mule team to California in '52, but once there, he
transferred his energies to the law. Suddenly he decided that
he had slaved long enough and accordingly he deserted his
law office to spend five years in Europe, absorbing the culture
he had missed in much the same spirit in which he had pounded
out horseshoes, cracked his whip over the mules, and plowed
his way through Blackstone. He wrote the *Bulletin* letters for
pleasure, and, in response to a wager, collected them into a
book which was issued by Roman in 1868 under the title of
Going to Jericho. In his writing Swift, like other Western
humorists, approached Europe boisterously, dealing out the tall
tale and ridiculing traditional objects of veneration. Though
less given to outbursts of indignation than Mark Twain, the
ex-blacksmith and mule-skinner could be nearly as humorous
at times as the erstwhile river pilot. After getting the travel
bug out of his system, Swift returned to San Francisco, wrote
his satirical novel, *Robert Greathouse,* and then settled down
to an orthodox career of law and politics.

The most important of these skeptical travelers was, of
course, Mark Twain. Because of that insatiable appetite for
European correspondence which Californians had developed,
Mark Twain found himself a heathen among the ministers who
went on " The *Quaker City* Pleasure Excursion to Europe and
the Holy Land " during the summer of 1867. The owners of
the *Alta California* knew that the Washoe Giant would describe Paris, Constantinople, and Jerusalem as vividly, as
frankly, and as amusingly as he had described the Sandwich

Islands. They were sure that his letters from such lands of interest would be a financial asset to their journal. Without hesitation they therefore advanced him twelve hundred dollars for his expenses on the tour; and by the time he returned home, they had gladly paid him an additional one thousand dollars for the weekly reports.

Thus it was that the Wild Humorist of the Pacific slope, sent by the members of the youngest frontier to describe for them the remnants of the most ancient peoples, was treading the stones which had once been touched by Jesus, standing in awe before the Sphinx, and pondering over the foot of dust which was supposed to cover the bones of Adam. The former silver-miner was sauntering through the corridors of Versailles and the Vatican, breaking quarantine to visit the Acropolis by moonlight, and acting as chairman of a committee paying its respects in person to the Czar of Russia.

The readers of Mark Twain's letters to the *Alta California* were with him to a man from the time he sighted Gibraltar, look-ing like a gob on the end of a shingle, until he said good-by to " our friends the Bermudans " on the voyage home. At his side they were visiting the spots they had read and dreamed about since childhood, worshipping where worship was due, but never forgetting their own independence. For Mark Twain was no effusively sentimental pilgrim; he was seeing the Old World with the eyes of a frontiersman who refuses to bow down to tradition and was ever mindful of the advantages of being brought up in a progressive democracy. His Western readers liked him because he affirmed their faiths, agreed with their prejudices, and shared their ignorances.

For example, Mark Twain was almost proud of his lack of background in art; where could he have learned to appreciate a Raphael in Hannibal or Virginia City? " We do not know much about art and cannot easily work up ourselves into ecstasies about it," he explained. He declared without shame that copies of the Old Masters looked better to him than the originals, that the white marble figures above the graves in Genoa's Campo Santo appealed to him more than " the damaged and dingy statuary " of the Louvre, and that " The Last Supper," which may once have been a great picture, was now no longer a pleasure to the eye. He distrusted the people who talked glibly about " line," " composition," and " expression," and he refused to join them in their indiscriminate praise of the Old Masters, objecting that Leonardo and his like wasted too much paint on martyrs as well as toadying in a most servile manner to " those damned Medici."

Similarly, he made no attempt at hiding the gaps in his knowledge of literary history. He doubtless was joking when he dismissed Petrarch's love for Laura as " a waste of raw material," but he was genuinely indignant that sentimental tears should be shed over Abélard, a cold-hearted villain and a base seducer for whom castration was none too drastic a punishment. Again, in social judgments Mark Twain expressed the attitude of the frontier equalitarian; he was constantly disturbed by the poverty of street beggars, the low wages of European workmen, and the presence of hovels at the feet of great cathedrals.

He gave his readers a good measure of the irreverence they expected from a frontier humorist, adding to the customary approach his own doubts and censures concerning man's religious behavior. In his frequent condemnation of Roman Catholic practices he displayed the usual attitude of American Protestants traveling in Europe. He pronounced Italy " a land which has groped in the midnight of priestly superstition for sixteen hundred years "; and he made sport of the sacred relics that were displayed to him, the hundreds of pieces of the true Cross, the many segments from the crown of thorns, the nails from the Crucifixion that would more than have filled a keg. But he did not limit his ridicule to the Catholics; the Protestant ministers on the *Quaker City* excursion came in for their share. Even on the voyage over, he criticized them for asking God to give them favorable winds when most of the traffic was moving in the opposite direction, and by the time he had made a few land trips with them he had classified the party into pilgrims and sinners, placing himself very decidedly among the sinners. During their fatiguing ride into the Holy Land, he became furious with the pilgrims for their unchristian act of driving their poor horses to exhaustion in order to reach Damascus before the Sabbath. And by the time the party had returned to New York he was so fed up with ministers that he referred in print to the pleasure excursion as " a funeral excursion without a corpse."

The Innocents Abroad is still widely read today after seventy years, whereas *Yusef* and *Going to Jericho* have long since ceased to circulate except among a few scholars. That the one should have lived while the others so early died is hardly the result of the subject-matter, for all three writers indulged in a common type of humor and all three grew indignant over the same institutions and lyrical over the same scenes, though Browne reported places in more detail, Swift gave clearer topographical pictures, and Mark Twain introduced more discussions and anecdotes. *The Innocents Abroad* has survived for two reasons: Mark Twain's frontier humor was more amusing than that of his fellows; and, of greater importance, he was more truly the spokesman of his generation and his civilization than were they.

Mark Twain spoke the language of the frontier humorist at its best. When it came to an exaggerated description studded with homespun epithets, who could beat him? " They say that the long-nosed, lanky, dyspeptic-looking body-snatchers, with the indescribable hats on, and a long curl dangling down in

front of each ear, are the old, familiar, self-righteous Pharisees
we read of in the Scriptures. Verily, they look it." Who knew
better how to point out an incongruity than the former river
pilot who described the famous Arno as " a great historical
creek with four feet in the channel and some scows floating
around "? And what Western raconteur could dish up his anecdotes more liberally and with a stronger personal flavor than
Mark Twain when he talked about his horses, Jericho and
Balbeek, or his attempts to find soap in a soapless land, or his
tortures with French billiard-tables, Italian barbers, and Turk-
ish baths? Also he could get more fun out of being vulgar than
could his fellow writers; witness his descriptions of the camel-
dung frescoes of Syria, the statue of the apostle without enough
nose to blow, the Queen of Sheba whose feet were not clean and
who smelled like a camel, and the Russian name that never came
out of his mouth without fetching a snag with it.

Along with that humor went the pioneer's comments on the
life, old in history but new and stirring to him, which he saw
for the first time. Mark Twain was a child of the frontier who
had come to walk in the land of his fathers. As such, he represented all those Americans who, forced to draw their culture
from books, had only dreamed of seeing that about which they
read. There in the Old World he was the spokesman of their
entire generation, of their unique civilization. Feeling as they
would have felt, he expressed the awe, the admiration, the indignation, the disgust they would have expressed. As they
would have done, he despaired when reality was not in accord
with ideals, rejoiced when it was. Above all he was honest: he
told only what he saw and gave tribute only to that which he
believed truly worthy of tribute.

The traveler returned to San Francisco in the spring of 1868
to ask the owners of the *Alta* to release their copyright that an
Eastern publisher might bring out the *Quaker City* letters in

book form as *The Innocents Abroad*. The release having been cheerfully given, he set about revising the series for book publication. The homecoming, as it turned out, was Mark Twain's farewell to the west coast. When he left for the East in June, he never returned.

Mark Twain had probably received all the Far-Western frontier could give him. During the seven years of his sojourn he had adopted the writing profession, he had been encouraged to laugh naturally and criticize indignantly, and he had discovered that he had great talent as a lecturer. Already the Western scene had been used in his first book, *The Jumping Frog and Other Sketches*; a San Francisco journal and a Western public had made *The Innocents Abroad* possible; and *Roughing It*, the next book to be written, was to be devoted entirely to the humorist's experiences in Nevada, California, and the Sandwich Islands. San Francisco had given Mark Twain the most valuable aid that could be offered to a writer during his apprentice days: it had provided financial support and an appreciative audience long enough for him to gain sufficient repute to stand on his own legs.

On the night of February 7, 1872, San Franciscans filled the Mercantile Library Hall to hear Joaquin Miller, the Western poet who had become the talk of London since the publication of his *Songs of the Sierras*. News reports and literary gossip had led them to anticipate strange things of the new sensation among poets; they fully expected him to be garbed in miner's boots, a red shirt, and sombrero and to come on the stage with an Indian war-whoop. He was said to have made his reputation in London by acting like a trapper or mountain man in the parlors of Mayfair.

A slight young man dressed in conventional business suit stepped on the platform. His eyes were blue-violet and very expressive; his sunny golden hair grew low down over his shoulders; and his mustache and whiskers, which were lighter and glossier than his hair, partly concealed a sensitive mouth. When he started speaking, his voice was thin and low, but as he gained confidence, his tone grew full. He emitted no war-whoop; he made no boast; he simply stated, in a quiet, almost diffident manner, that by some good fortune which he could not entirely understand, he had been received into the English home, the inside of which was as warm as the outside was cold. He now proposed to tell his friends in San Francisco something of his experiences.

Miller soon forgot his stage-fright when he began talking about taking tea at Westminster Abbey with Dean Stanley. " Here I met Tennyson, Carlyle, Père Hyacinthe, and Doré! . . . It was whispered that the Queen might drop in to tea some day when I was there. . . . Her Majesty never wears hoops, waterfalls or false hair, and she deserves an immortal crown for that alone. . . . I trust that you will excuse me from saying no more of the literary gentlemen of London than truth and propriety admit. . . . At the pre-Raphaelite gather-ings I met Dante G. Rossetti and his brother, Arthur Help, George McDonald, and Madox Brown. We generally had a Duke or two. . . . I have forgotten their names, but it is of no importance." There followed glowing memories of Jean Ingelow, of Robert Browning, of William Morris, and, most of all, of Swinburne, the poet of liberty whom Watts-Dunton was keeping out of mischief. " Swinburne said to me that if the world dealt unkindly with him he would come to America, and bury himself in the solitude of the forests."

It was evident that Joaquin Miller had indeed reached the very heart of London literary society. The few in the audience who had known him before he went abroad, Ina Coolbrith, Charlie Stoddard, and one or two others, marveled at the change they saw in him. A little over a year ago — in August 1870, to be exact — he had boarded the train for New York, equipped with a second-class ticket, a laurel wreath to place on Byron's tomb, and an agreement with the *Bulletin* to publish any of his letters that the editor cared to use. He had been without reputation as a writer even on the Pacific Coast, and he had set out with barely enough money to keep him alive in a garret for six months. He had known no one in London, and his only means of making acquaintances was his poetry. What his San Francisco friends had seen of the latter had not impressed them; it was energetic but hardly polished enough to win a ready audience. And yet he did have that which might enable him to go a long way: a resourceful, aggressive, and persistent temperament.

Surely no one had ever trod the sacred paths of his ancestors or set out to visit the shrines of the poets with more spontaneous enthusiasm than Childe Miller. He was hardly off the boat at Glasgow before he started for Ayrshire to visit the Burns country, and a few days later he lingered so long in Melrose Abbey thinking of Scott that he was locked in and was forced to spend the night " among the tombstones and fallen arches." His next stop was Nottingham; when some unimaginative train companions asked him what he would possibly find of interest there, he counted off the attractions on his fingers: " Cardinal Wolsey, Lord Byron, Kirke White, Miss Piggot, Mary Chaworth, Bailey (' Festus '), Dr. Livingstone, and finally and for luck, Cœur de Lion and Robin Hood. All have dwelt at Nottingham and left footprints there; and I shall go to see them." The greatest thrills of all came when he reached the land sacred to his hero, Lord Byron. Late in the afternoon at Newstead Abbey he told the gardener: " Boatswain's tomb, the oak the poet planted, and the tree where he cut his name. That is all today." The next day he hung the laurel wreath from Sauselito over

Byron's grave in Hucknall Church. England might neglect its great son, but Far-Western America would always hallow his memory. To make the pilgrim's happiness complete, he met Mary Chaworth's grandchildren and was invited to stay in their home.

When he reached London, he was at first afraid that he would be swallowed up. Its narrow streets, its old buildings, and its millions of people made him feel lonelier than he had been when he lived on the side of Mount Shasta with the Indians. He could always find companionship, however, by visiting the spots associated with his beloved writers. During his first month in the city he lodged in a half-dozen cellars and attics, following the shadow of Bayard Taylor to Mile's End, of Browning to Dulwich, of Tom Hood to Hemingford, of Abraham Cowley to a house at the back of Westminster Abbey. There, where he could hear the bells and commune with the poets buried near by, he decided to spend the winter.

He realized that, with his money running short, he must act at once if he were to achieve his great ambition and see a book of his poems issued in London. Manuscript under arm, he visited publisher after publisher, hoping that one might encourage him. He saved John Murray, son of the great John Murray, Byron's friend, for last. Murray took the manuscript, flipped the leaves, glanced at some poems, and then lifted his long finger. " Aye, now don't you know poetry won't do? Poetry won't do, don't you know? " A moment later Joaquin was in the street, shaking his fist with tears in his eyes. He refused to give up. He would fling his poems at the heads of those stolid Britishers even if he had to publish them at his own expense. He pawned his watch, took most of what remained of his resources, and paid a printer to set up a hundred copies of a small book entitled *Pacific Poems.* A number of these he distributed among his newly made English acquaintances, hoping thereby to gain some literary reputation. Under ordinary circumstances such a move would have borne no fruit, but an unusual chain of events led to surprising results from the scheme.

Shortly after his arrival in London, Joaquin had called on Tom Hood the younger, editor of *Fun*. He had been told that all one had to do to receive a welcome from Hood was to be an American, and he found the information was true. The black-bearded editor not only welcomed him warmly but took him to his house, offered to read his poems, and promised letters of introduction to London's literary great. The first letter took Miller to Frederick Locker-Lampson, who waved his monocle in the air while he admitted that there was nothing he loved more than an eccentric character and declared that, though he had met several Americans who were fools, he had never met one who was truly vicious.

Locker-Lampson in turn furnished Miller with a letter to Jean Ingelow, who at once invited him to dinner. He turned up in cowhide boots and a sealskin great-coat, which he kept on during dinner because he was wearing nothing but a shirt beneath it. The guests, including Edmund Gosse, Lady Franklin, and Mrs. Hawthorne, widow of the American author, were at first taken aback by the savage in sealskin, but then they decided to enjoy a real American frontiersman while they had the chance. Discovering that his unusual garb had publicity value, Miller set about making a virtue of a necessity. Later, when his boots, his sombrero, and his red shirt became his regular costume, he explained them by saying: " It helps sell the poems, you know, and it tickles the duchesses."

It seems to have been Locker-Lampson who introduced Miller to the Pre-Raphaelites — the Rossettis, Algernon Swinburne, William Morris, Ford Madox Brown, and their friends. His eager manner, his tales of exploits among the Indians, his love for poetry, and his outlandish costumes brought him immediate popularity with the group of poets and painters, who now had an eccentric frontiersman to add to their collection of monkeys, wombats, and exotic women — another Munchausen to match the bragging of their talkative friend Charles Augustus Howell. William Michael Rossetti, the spokesman of the group, hailed him as " a lover of beasts and birds, who finds them kin to him; a snake has its claim of blood relationship."

As soon as *Pacific Poems* was printed, Miller hastened with copies to his newly found friends. In the Rossetti circle an Irish poet named Armstrong and a second Irishman whose name is unknown were apparently the first to come to the conclusion that Miller's poems, if properly launched with encouraging reviews, would interest the English public. It would not do, however, to release them as a private printing job, unsponsored by a publishing house. Moreover, it would be a good idea to brush them up a bit before sending them out; they were rather shaggy, even for products of the wilds. Miller at first objected to making any changes in his verses, but the two Irishmen persuaded him to let them take the poems home, revise them without consulting each other, and then bring him the results. When they returned with the edited poems, Miller exclaimed: " I rather disbelieved what you two boys said about the meter of my poems, and so I put you both to the same test, and curiously enough your revisings of the same passage came out just the same; there must be something to your criticism, and I have decided to revise my book on the lines suggested by both of you."

A month later, *Songs of the Sierras* was ready for the press. During the interim Miller had been able to write an additional long narrative poem, which, with the contents of the thin little *Pacific Poems* and odds and ends from earlier volumes and newspaper work, made up a sizable volume. The well-known house of Longmans had in the meantime been persuaded to publish the book. William Michael Rossetti, who had for some time been championing Whitman's poetry in England, seized the opportunity to introduce another American genius, rough, outspoken, but genuine, and gave Miller's poems just the proper send-off with a lengthy review in the *Academy* for June 15th, 1871. " This is a truly remarkable book," he wrote. " To glance through its pages is to observe a number of picturesque things picturesquely put, expressed in a vivid flowing form and melodious words, and indicating strange, outlandish, and romantic experiences. . . . Excitement and ambition may be called the twin geniuses of Mr. Miller's poetical character. . . . Every now and then there is a sort of titanic and intrinsically poetical utterance in it which reminds one of Marlowe. . . . He is a poet, an admirable poet. . . . America may be proud of him."

As other critics fell in behind the enthusiastic Rossetti, *Songs of the Sierras* became the book for Londoners to talk about. Miller's poems, with their galloping meters and unconventional rhymes, their bold eroticism and melodramatic stories, their bizarre settings in Californian mountains, Arizona deserts, and Nicaraguan jungles, and their glimpses of wild beasts ranging from mustangs to ring-tailed monkeys, offered a real departure from customary poetry. Even the many crudities of Miller's diction and versification, as well as his mis-spellings and his bad grammar, which would never have been excused in an Englishman, were cited as just one more proof of their genuine frontier origin. The leading journalists vied with each other in acclaiming the discovery. Here was " a true and original singer," a " God-moulded poet-mind," whose verses revealed a " beauty as imperishable as the peaks of the mountains or the melodies of the sea." He was " the most remarkable narrative poet that America has yet produced," and at the same time " an Epicurean and a Broad Churchman." On the whole Joaquin Miller received an amount of attention and a degree of praise un-precedented in transatlantic criticism. The chorus of praise was almost unanimous, although occasionally a facetious tone might be heard and at least once a truly dissonant note was struck: " In heaven's name, let him not spoil a good mountain-eer on the chance that he will become a great poet."

Joaquin's first reaction to his success was to seize the oppor-tunity it afforded to meet the English writers he had long ad-mired. He dashed off a note to Locker-Lampson: " I should now like to see Mr. Browning and also go in to hear a debate in Parliament. Do you have any time or disposition to go with me to either or both places sometime next week? " There is no evidence that Miller heard the debate, but he left full notes describing a breakfast at which he and Browning were the honored guests. The two poets matched puns and discussed poetry. When Miller asked Browning's permission to use the meter of " How They Carried the Good News from Ghent to Aix " in his " Kit Carson's Ride," Browning smiled broadly and replied that there was no reason why they shouldn't both borrow from Virgil.

There followed breakfasts, luncheons, dinners, invitations to the White Friars Club, to the Savage Club, even a visitor's card to the Athenæum — a hundred opportunities to meet dis-tinguished company, with now and then a baronet or a duchess thrown in for good measure. Miller was in every way equal to the occasion; his adoration of his hosts, his naïveté, and his bizarre manners made him a welcome guest. The crowning event was a night-long Pre-Raphaelite dinner during which Dante Gabriel Rossetti, who had become his latest idol, delivered a glowing speech on the love of the beautiful. As he made his way home in the gray of dawn, Miller went the whole way in dedicating himself to beauty: " Study it every day, when you walk, when you ride, when you sit by the roadside — the flight of the bird gracefully drooping, curving through the air; the shape and tint of a single autumn leaf; the sweet curled moon in the heavens; the still, far stars; the presence of a proud, pure woman, the lifted face — the lovely lifted face as she looks into space for God."

Joaquin had hardly begun to enjoy his triumph, however, when he received news from America that his sister had died and that one of his brothers was very ill. He at once decided to go home. Just three months after *Songs of the Sierras* was published, he sailed from Southampton, reaching Washington, D.C., shortly before his brother's death. Home to Oregon he went to console his parents, and incidentally to face the bitter remarks of Minnie Myrtle, who had been telling reporters that while Joaquin was being feted in London she and her children were living on crusts and water. To add to his distress, he realized after reading a few American journals that his countrymen were more skeptical of his genius than were the English.

When he reached San Francisco, Miller found many old-timers indignant; once more the frontier had been misrepresented, this time by a scribbler who pictured the West as a place where it was romantic to steal a horse, live with a squaw, and fight as a renegade. The resourceful poet found that he had to be quick with his answers. When he was accused of " borrowing " a horse, he denied the charge and added that it was only a mule. When asked point-blank whether he had ever been in Nicaragua, he countered: " Was Milton ever in Hell? " When " Kit Carson's Ride " was reprinted on the coast, Edward F. Beale, who had scouted with Carson, savagely charged that Miller not only had shown hopeless ignorance of Western fauna and flora, customs and characters, but had so maligned Carson's character that he ought to be lynched. In the next printing Miller altered the poem so that Carson no longer abandoned the Indian maiden who had saved his life.

As Miller lingered on in San Francisco during the spring of 1872, after that first lecture when he showed he was willing to tone down his act for the home-town public, he realized that a prophet was wasted on Pacific shores, even though the *Overland Monthly* offered him liberal sums for his poems and the general public listened courteously as he boasted of contact with the literary great. He resolved that after he had disposed of some domestic matters, the most important of which was to find a home for his half-breed daughter, Cali-Shasta, whom he had brought down from the Indian Reservation, he would go back to London, where a frontier poet was truly appreciated.

With the successes of Mark Twain and Joaquin Miller before them, the other writers who had created literature in San Francisco during the sixties grew restless. Their eyes turned eastward; their hopes focused on Europe. Mark Twain had shown that the traveling correspondent could reap a golden harvest while enjoying the culture of the Old World. Joaquin Miller had demonstrated that the English appreciated the literature of the frontier more than the native Americans; the British had shown that they would welcome rugged individualists not genteel enough for the folks at home. With the old order gone, with depression gripping the West, with trains leaving daily for New York, just seven days away, why should they remain in San Francisco? Now that the frontier was dead, they would see the lands of Moses, of Cæsar, of Shakespeare. They would visit Parnassus and, perhaps, receive a measure of acclaim for themselves.

One by one they said good-by. Early in 1871 the Overland Express carried Bret Harte across the continent to Boston, where he was to pass seven discouraging years before becoming a European pilgrim and exile. In the autumn of that same year Prentice Mulford packed his meager belongings and boarded the day-coach for New York and London. Six months later Ambrose Bierce listened to the rhythm of the rails as his train sped across the plains. He was on his way to England, where he hoped to gain fame as a modern Juvenal. In the fall of that year, 1872, Joaquin Miller returned to London, where he expected to continue his conquest of Mayfair. Finally, in the summer of 1873 Charles Warren Stoddard curled up in a Pullman which was taking him swiftly to the land of poets and the center of Catholic Christendom. No more eloquent testimony to the passing of the West could be found than the departure of these five young writers. The oldest, Prentice Mulford, was not yet forty, and the youngest, Charlie Stoddard, was but twenty-eight. San Francisco's importance as a regional literary capital ended when the railroad arrived.

Prentice Mulford found himself in Europe as a result of one of his rare aggressive acts. Having concluded that he was wasting his time floating in a whaleboat on San Francisco Bay, he conceived the idea that he would like to go to England " to advance by writing and talking the good and glory of California." One morning he walked into the office of William C. Ralston, San Francisco's most ardent promoter, overcame his preternatural shyness long enough to outline his scheme, and asked for a subsidy. Three minutes later he was in the street clutching five twenty-dollar gold pieces. Within a few days Ralston had persuaded his wealthy friends to invest an additional four hundred dollars in Mulford, the *Bulletin* had agreed to publish his travel letters, and the Diogenes of the Tuolumne was on his way to sell California to England and to describe England to the Californians.

A few months later California Anglophiles were complaining that Mulford was reporting only the darker side of British life. He seemed particularly wrought up by the conditions of the poor, and the sight of royalty merely made him a better republican. Moreover, he failed to wax enthusiastic over the shrines which all Americans loved. He called the British Museum " an intellectual charnel house," the famous dead buried in Westminster Abbey reminded him of " dried rats in glass cases," and he could not appreciate the animals in the Regent Park Zoo because he was so depressed by the looks of the populace. " Here was congregated the pink of England's overworked, badly fed, and badly aired manhood, shuffling in gait, bent in form, dead in complexion, twisted, gnarled, strained, and cramped through over-exhaustion."

The predominantly gray tone of Mulford's picture of England was partly due to his attempt to live on ten shillings a week. He found himself hard pressed adequately to supplement the five hundred dollars with which he started. Having no skill as a showman and no entry into fashionable society, he lectured to small gatherings in Wesleyan chapels and library reception-rooms, making a charge of sixpence which netted him neither good publicity nor adequate income. Too poor to mingle with celebrities and fine ladies, he was forced to seek companionship from navvies and charwomen. Then too, his determination to advertise California in all regions which might supply emigrants took him to many towns that were more squalid than picturesque, particularly the grimy regions of the black country. He just about concluded that once again he had failed in an undertaking. He was barely able to feed himself, and he could see no indication that he was achieving the gigantic task he had set himself: " to operate on the United Kingdom like an immense oratorial blister, and draw from it two or three millions of industrious, sturdy emigrants." He wrote to Mark Twain: " Perhaps I have mistaken my vocation. Certainly, if I was back with my rocker on the Tuolumne, I'd make it rattle livelier than ever I did before." But he decided to stick on awhile longer. He occasionally met people who appreciated his quiet wit and peculiar philosophy, and, when everything else failed, he could always find a spot of happiness by persuading some housewife to let him " camp out " in her kitchen.

Ambrose Bierce, who fed Mulford tea and crumpets when he reached Bath, was one of those who disapproved of his fellow Californian's views on British institutions, going so far as to call him a " growler by constitution " because of them. Bierce was delighted with England. He called London a paradise and he described Stratford and Kenilworth in poetic language, without a touch of his usual irony. Bath brought him close to his beloved eighteenth century, and as he frequented the haunts of Pope and Fielding and Smollett, he imagined he was back in the day when a satirist was more than a macabre jester. In this delightful country, with congenial companions around him, he might help to create literature instead of wasting his talents in castigating the Barbarians. He confided to Stoddard: " My object in coming was to loaf and see something of the country — as Walt Whitman put it, when the paralysis had, as yet, invaded only his brain, ' to loaf and invite my soul.' " If he could establish himself here, he would have no inclination to return to America. As soon as he could learn to write stories with the proper local coloring, he would see what he could do.

In the meantime, however, Bierce had bread and butter to earn. Just before leaving San Francisco he had married a pretty girl by the name of Mollie Day ; as a matter of fact, his trip to England was a honeymoon gift from his affluent father-in-law. If he wished to remain abroad, however, he would have to find some use for his journalistic talent. Like Artemus Ward and Joaquin Miller, he called on Tom Hood, who at once agreed to use some of Bierce's squibs in *Fun*. Bierce also sold sketches fairly regularly to Mortimer's *Figaro*, as well as disposing of an occasional item to ephemeral humorous sheets like the *Bat* and the *Cuckoo*. Though he hoped in time to branch out in new lines, for the present his English journalism differed little from the work he had done on the *News Letter* in San Francisco; he merely changed his pen-name from the Town Crier to Dod Grile.

One journalistic adventure attending Bierce's English days has probably been given more importance than it deserves. This was the routing of Henri Rochefort, the famous — or infamous — critic of the Second Empire, who threatened to follow the Empress Eugénie to England after the death of Napoleon III in hopes of continuing her misery even in exile. Bierce may have looked forward to a protracted battle of wits when, at the request of the Empress, he wrote the first issue of a journal entitled the *Lantern,* which existed solely to prevent Rochefort printing his famous *La Lanterne* on English soil. The second number had barely appeared, however, when the Frenchman called off the quarrel, and what might have been an exciting war, with a frontier satirist avenging injured royalty, turned out to be nothing but shadow-boxing.

Though Bierce, as a matter of fact, never did break away from routine journalism in England, he had the pleasure of seeing three collections of his Town Crier and Dod Grile sketches appear in London book-jackets. *Nuggets and Dust* and *The Fiend's Delight* were small booklets, possibly intended for the railway stalls; *Cobwebs from an Empty Skull* was more pretentious and its contents were as good as its title. In these books Bierce boasted of a long-standing collaboration with his scholarly friend Satan, who had helped him in producing such macabre tales as the one about the girl who killed her mother so that her lover might have a skull to play with, the one about the wife who used a shotgun to cure her husband of sleepwalking, and the one about the woman who wisely squeezed the bump of benevolence off her small son's head.

During his four years in England, Bierce's asthma, which bothered him greatly in London, forced him to spend much of his time in the provinces, particularly in Bristol, Bath, and Leamington. Because he made them so seldom, his trips up to London were holiday affairs that usually culminated in a celebration in which his Fleet Street friends — Tom Hood, Henry Sampson, George Augustus Sala, James Mortimer, Captain Mayne Reid, W. S. Gilbert, and a few others — matched wits and " shed the blood of the grape " long into the night. One of their favorite amusements was coining epitaphs in anticipation of the passing of their enemies; the evening that Bierce enjoyed most was that during which they concentrated their venom on John Camden Hotten, a London publisher who had pirated many American books and had failed to pay the royalties he had promised for *Nuggets and Dust*. Bierce's simple:

Hotten
Rotten
Forgotten

illustrated his knack for announcing the deaths of the damned living; it was excelled only by his:

HERE LIES FRANK PIXLEY
AS USUAL

which appeared in black borders at a much later date.

John Camden Hotten received attention from Mark Twain also when the latter came to London in August 1872. Mark was out for blood because Hotten not only had pirated a number of his American writings but, more infuriating to the humorist, had attributed spurious and inferior jokes to his pen. The avenging journalist started his campaign by writing an article for a London daily ridiculing the pirate by calling him John Camden Hottentot, but he had no sooner finished his diatribe than he found that his anger had oozed out of him. The truth of the matter was that the English atmosphere seemed to take away all his spleen. English hospitality was extracting his sting just as it had done with Bierce. Here he had crossed the ocean with the intention of getting material for a book which would do for England what *The Innocents Abroad* had done for Italy and the Holy Land — a book which would give praise where praise was due, but which at the same time would display the skeptical attitude and would be seasoned with ridicule and exaggeration. He even made pages of notes to that end — but he never used them. The English defeated him with kindness and converted him with praise. The Washoe Giant had become the Mayfair Lion.

In Samuel Clemens's notebook, satire gave way to rapture and ecstasy. Never before had he been made over as he was that autumn in London. He received more invitations than he could accept; he was mentioned in *Punch* and welcomed by *The Times;* he was even asked by Charles Reade to collaborate on a novel. Whereas Boston had welcomed him coolly, not yet sure what to make of the diamond in the rough, London had received him as another Artemus Ward, a kinsman of Abraham Lincoln. He wrote home that he had come to make observations for a book, but had given them up for dinners and speeches. The country was so beautiful that he could now believe in fairyland. He even went so far as to make the unpatriotic confession: " I would a great deal rather live here if I could get the rest of you over."

Mark Twain was no longer a roving bachelor, however; he had a wife and child waiting for him in Connecticut. Reluctantly he left England in November, planning to return as soon as possible with his family. That short stay in London had brought about a curious shift in his outlook. He not only gave up the idea of writing a humorous book about England; he spent the winter collaborating with Charles Dudley Warner on *The Gilded Age*, his first book satirizing America.

In the following May, Mark Twain was back in England, this time with Livy and his small daughter in tow. His second reception was even warmer than the first. To his rooms at the Langham came Robert Browning, Turgeniev, Sir John Millais, and Sir Charles Dilke. He had luncheon with Charles Kingsley, tea with Lewis Carroll, dinner with Herbert Spencer. The smoking-room of his hotel became a rendezvous of London writers where almost every afternoon a visitor would be sure to find a few old cronies like Charles Reade, Wilkie Collins, and Lord Houghton swapping yarns with the best story-teller the West had produced.

But while Mark was being lionized, Livy was growing homesick. Forced to sit through dinners with ladies who snubbed each other she was often uncomfortable when her husband was thoroughly enjoying himself. Then, always frail, she became ill on hotel fare. Mark Twain hoped that a summer in Scotland would put her back in good health, but only the timely aid of a capable doctor kept him from losing her in Edinburgh. In the autumn she returned to London just long enough for her husband to keep his promise to deliver six lectures under the management of George Dolby, who was willing to gamble that he could star Mark Twain in England as effectively as he had featured Dickens in America. He proved he was right when the humorist filled the largest lecture hall in the city every night for a week with his talks on " Our Fellow Savages of the Sandwich Islands," and the public clamored for more. In order to meet the demand, Mark Twain took Livy and Suzy back to America and returned alone on the next boat.

The lecturer had hardly installed himself again in the Langham Hotel when Charlie Stoddard from San Francisco dropped in to say hello. Ostensibly, Pip Pepperpod had come to London to supervise the publication of an English edition of his *South-Sea Idyls*, but actually he had a more compelling purpose; like the others he was making his pilgrimage to Europe. He was paying his way by writing travel letters for the San Francisco *Chronicle*, and he was looking forward eagerly to joining his old companions who were living in England, Ambrose Bierce, Prentice Mulford, Joaquin Miller, and now Mark Twain. Whether Mark felt that it was his duty to look after the helpless or whether he craved company that would remind him of the good old times, he at once hired Charlie to be his " secretary." The latter's duties were to make a huge scrapbook of clippings dealing with the case of the Tichborne Claimant and to keep Mark Twain company when the humorist returned from his lectures so excited that he couldn't sleep. Frequently George Dolby came with him, and the two started in telling off-color stories to tease Stoddard, who had a strong dislike for pornography. He usually protected himself by going to sleep long before the night owls had finished their yarns.

Both lecturer and secretary enjoyed Christmas at a country home near Salisbury, but immediately after the holidays Mark Twain sailed for America, having completed a most successful lecture season. Charlie Stoddard moved in with Prentice Mulford, who was then living near the British Museum in a lodging-house which Joaquin Miller had discovered and which had become a sort of headquarters for the San Francisco pilgrims. The heart of 11 Museum Street was the basement, which " stood knee deep in eddies of waste paper and resignation "; in it were the kitchen, where Mulford fried his chops, and " the crypt," where the loquacious landlady hung the pictures of all her deceased friends and relatives. In addition to an exiled Polish Count, the establishment had a Little Marchioness in its midst, a dark-eyed, dark-haired little flirt named Josie Allen, who worked at a milliner's shop, lived upstairs, and flitted in and out of the crypt at any time of day or night. Though the roomers were on their guard against her " fellow-come-follow-me " look and staunchly maintained that they could not believe a word she said, they all adored her.

Joaquin Miller was given credit for discovering Josie. The story goes that when he found her selling flowers on the street, he brought her home to 11 Museum Street, scrubbed her up, and liked the result so much that he talked of adopting her — a questionable procedure, as she was eighteen and very lively. Then the poet had gone off to Rome on one of his vagabonding spasms, leaving Josie to be looked after by Prentice or perhaps by Charlie when he arrived. To the latter he wrote a long explanation of Josie's place in the picture: " I am glad you like Miss Allen. She is an angel and I expect you to treat her with all the deference and propriety that you would a wife of a friend. . , . She is a little thing that I am trying to bring up to the light of the sun and I hope not altogether for selfish purposes. I need not tell you she has been unfortunate; hence, as a Christian knight you will treat her the more gently."

At the same time that Joaquin was bringing Josie up to the light of the sun, he was engaged in more elite social activities. For some time before he left England he had been leading a double life, at night dwelling modestly at 11 Museum Street, during the day cutting a figure in titled society. He had done so well that when Mark Twain returned to England for his second visit he was surprised to find that Joaquin was engaged to marry the daughter of a baronet. Her name was Iza Hardy, the daughter of Sir Thomas Hardy. According to Mark, she was " about twenty-six, good looking, goodhearted, affectionate, frank, honest, cordial, unassuming, educated, intelligent . . . thoroughly English, and very much in love with Joaquin." Sir Thomas he declared to be " a delightful specimen of the right and true Englishman," married to a lady novelist of some ability who liked nothing more than entertaining American writers. Joaquin had confided to his friends that one of his ambitions was to marry a young, charming, and wealthy English girl of good family, and apparently he came very near doing it. Just why the marriage was never performed will probably remain forever a mystery. It may have been that Joaquin's unconventional life at 11 Museum Street had something to do with it, or perhaps he wore his boots and sombrero into the drawing-room once too often for his titled friends.

For it was during this period that Miller earned his reputation for startling the English with stunts and outlandish behavior. Hostesses never knew what to expect from him. He might attempt to swallow a fish whole; he was known to smoke two cigars at a time; he was likely to emit a few war-whoops on entering the drawing-room; and he delighted in pouring rose petals over the head of the prettiest girl in the company. Naturally other Americans were not above suggesting that Miller was no credit to his country. Thus, one fellow pilgrim (from the East) criticized the poet for wearing flashy rings and a heavy gold watch-chain and for placing his three diamond studs in his shirt bosom so close together that they could all be seen even when worn with a high-buttoned waistcoat. Furthermore, he objected to the frontiersman's unembarrassed use of the toothpick in the most distinguished company.

But most annoying to his compatriot were Miller's familiarities with the young ladies — his habit of playing them absurd and fulsome compliments, his practice of kissing their hands on every occasion, his trick of brushing their foreheads with his fingers. " Among men he says little and drops none of the pearls of poetry and sentiment that he is apt to spue out fully in the society of the softer sex. He told Mrs. Brooks that ' Tennyson was a dear old peanut.' He said that little Gretchen Brooks was pretty enough to set in a ring. After he had been in the house of Mrs. Brooks three minutes on his first visit, he crawled across the library floor on his hands and knees to bite Marjory Brooks on the leg."

A few of his English acquaintances were disgusted by Miller's behavior; this minority sized him up as either a fool or a charlatan, and cultivated him only to laugh behind his back. Their attitude was well expressed by Augustus Hare, frequently a guest at Lord Houghton's breakfasts when the Sierra poet was present: " Joaquin Miller would have been thought insufferably vulgar if he had not been a notoriety." On the other hand, there is no doubt that the Oregonian had a number of sincere friends, among whom were Lord Houghton and Anthony Trollope, who especially prized his skill as a horseman. And for the most part the British liked this frontiersman. The English and Miller made a rare combination: they enjoyed eccentricity, and he enjoyed being eccentric. As Julian Hawthorne, who was responsible for a number of good stories about Miller, put it, " Americans . . . were curiosities, and if they didn't eat peas with their knives and spit on the carpet, they were welcome. . . . If one played the picturesque barbarian, booted, spurred, red-flannel shirted, and sombreroed, he would become, like Scott's Fitz-James, the centre of the glittering ring and the louder he yawped, the more the great ladies stroked him."

But if at this time Miller enjoyed a showman's triumph, he was finding his second visit to Parnassus an anticlimax as far as his literary reception was concerned. To start with, when he arrived in London in the fall of 1872 with the manuscript of *The Songs of the Sun-lands* in his suitcase, he discovered not only that his Pre-Raphaelite friends were too busy to help him revise it but that the Rossettis actually hesitated to let him dedicate it to them. The devout Christina was particularly troubled over some poems dealing with Christ called " Olive Leaves," which she described as " implying a sort of religious, or at least personal, enthusiasm, mixed up with a good deal that had more relation to a sense of the picturesque than of the devotional." Dante Gabriel also paused, but finding no good reason to refuse the dedication, he finally accepted. The successor to *Songs of the Sierras* appeared in the spring of 1873.

The enthusiasm of the critics had almost entirely disappeared. Some stated mildly that Miller had repeated himself, but had added nothing new. Others were even more discouraging. The *Saturday Review* published a long essay trying to dissuade the poet from writing further, at least for the present. This critic went on to assert that Miller's genius had narrow limits, that his style showed no signs of improvement, and that he was one of the " Egotistical Poets " of whom England had tired. To clinch the matter, he declared that Miller's Biblical poems had a maudlin turn and his " Sea to Sea " bore about the same relation to poetry as a railroad did to music. The *Academy* grumbled that his bold gifts had rather run to seed, while his faults of imitation and incompleteness had been confirmed. The *Temple Bar* stated frankly that Mr. Miller's coming to England to publish his poems was a mistake and that the reviewers had found him out. The inevitable had happened. Having overpraised Miller's first book, the critics were now attempting to save face by attacking his second. Unfortunately the American poet had played into their hands by turning out a volume that was more imitative than his first and had nothing new to offer. The public had already discovered that his poetry was unreadable.

He was more fortunate, however, in his *My Life among the Modocs*, which was published in England in the same year, 1873. This autobiographical novel, his first extensive excursion into prose, was a highly romanticized account of his early life among the Indians on the side of Mount Shasta. The book was timed to take advantage of the momentary interest in the Modoc

Indians, who, entrenched in the northern California lava beds, were making a desperate stand against Federal troops sent to place them on a reservation. Though Miller knew little about the Modocs, having lived only with the near-by Pitt River tribe, he did not let a hundred miles or so interfere with his opportunity to capitalize on the excitement. *My Life among the Modocs* was better written than any of Miller's later prose works, but how much praise is due him is an open question; the poet himself testified on several occasions that Prentice Mulford rewrote the book before it was published.

My Life among the Modocs did much to renew Miller's popularity, it brought him " a pot of money," and it may have exerted much-needed pressure on the United States Indian Bureau, soon to be further chastised by Helen Hunt Jackson in her *Ramona*. It elicited a number of favorable reviews in London, but it also started a feud with the *Athenæum*, which called it a monstrously dull volume written by a man who was a scoundrel by his own admission. Miller wrote to the reviewer, that he wished " to tell him to his teeth that he was a liar, a coward, and a cur." There was no gun-play, but the journal, after publishing the offended author's communication, consigned him to oblivion.

Some time after the publication of the two volumes, Miller set out for Italy. What prompted his departure is unknown. Perhaps he had quarreled with Miss Hardy; perhaps his life was complicated by too many Josies and Marjories; perhaps he was disappointed at the reception accorded *Songs from the Sunland*; perhaps he was just restless. Whatever the reason for his leaving England, by the Christmas season of 1873 he was leading a romantic life in Rome, having delegated the domestic duty of looking after Josie in London to Prentice Mulford and Charlie Stoddard. The latter, however, with his customary objection to domesticity, refused to assume any responsibility for

CHARLES WARREN STODDARD IN MONK'S ROBES.
Reproduced from an oil painting by Jo Strong.
Courtesy of California State Library

JOAQUIN MILLER
AFTER HIS SUCCESS
IN LONDON.

Reproduced from a painting by
James Everett Stuart.
Courtesy of California State Library

JOAQUIN MILLER IN LONDON.

Cartoonist James Swinnerton pictures Joaquin at a Bohemian dinner
with Queen Victoria, the Prince of Wales, and Gladstone. The cartoon
appeared in the San Francisco *Bulletin*, December 13, 1916.
Courtesy of California State Library

the young lady and soon departed in order to worship at Shakespeare's grave. After he had struck up an acquaintance with the caretaker of Anne Hathaway's cottage and had found that he would actually be allowed to sleep in Anne Hathaway's bed, he settled down in Stratford-on-Avon for several weeks. In March he started towards Italy to join Joaquin, eventually arriving in Rome without his coat, his pocket-book, his luggage, or his ticket, all of which he had lost *en route*.

In Italy the paths of the two irresponsible wanderers grow indistinct and confused. Joaquin disappears into a nebulous melodrama from which he occasionally emerges walking in the Piazza de Espagna, an Italian cloak added to his customary disguise, or riding along the Pincio in a pink-upholstered carriage beside a mysterious pink Countess who was said to serve him pink tea in a pink boudoir and whose jealous but ineffectual husband was rumored to have challenged him to a duel and received " a biff in the solar plexus " for reply. No more distinct is the vision of Charlie Stoddard breaking his arm while riding horseback on the Campagna. He was now moving in the innermost circles of Catholicism, striking up acquaintances with bishops and cardinals and twice paying his respects to the Pope, but for some reason the enthusiastic convert to Catholicism decided while in Rome not to become a monk. After Rome, the pilgrims drift even farther away, vaguely in the direction of the Holy Land. When last seen they were intent on becoming *hadjis*, each in his own distinctive, desultory way.

Back in London at 11 Museum Street, Prentice devoted himself to looking after Josie, who was in reality quite able to look after herself. It was a little difficult for a forty-year-old bachelor to keep track of as coquettish a young lady as Josie without being affected by the process. And when Josie not only mended his clothes but surprised him one night with a snack of mutton chops and buns toasted over the open coals, Prentice felt his years of shyness slip from him. When they were married, all the inhabitants of the establishment, from the landlady to the Polish Count, joined in the wedding feast. The combination of a honeymoon and springtime in Paris made Prentice turn lyrical in his *Bulletin* letters, much to the surprise of his readers. He even announced his plans for the future in his column : now that he was married, he would start all over again ; he would cease giving sixpenny lectures to unappreciative Englishmen and return to his birthplace, Sag Harbor, Long Island, where he would start a newspaper. When he sailed for New York in July 1874, he was only nine dollars richer than when he had arrived in England two years before ; on the other hand, he had Josie for a wife and he still had at least a score of years in which to make a success of things.

A year after Mulford departed, Ambrose Bierce grudgingly relinquished his plans to establish himself in England for the rest of his life. Though his income from journals like *Figaro* and *Fun* was meager enough, he might have stuck it out had not his wife become homesick and returned with their two sons to San Francisco. When she wrote that she was about to give birth to another child, he realized that he would have to join her at once or break with her for good. He chose to do the former, even though he hated to return to San Francisco. With Mark Twain, Bret Harte, and the rest of the old guard dispersed, he would find little in California to compensate for the loss of the companionship of men like Tom Hood and Lord Houghton or the congeniality of dinners in London and tea in Bath. Moreover, he knew that he would always feel that the cup of fame was withdrawn from his lips just as he was at last to drink from it.

For the rest of his life Bierce was to be a pronounced Anglophile, looking back upon his English experiences as an oasis in an otherwise drab career, championing a theory of intellectual and social aristocracy he had learned abroad. His reaction was, of course, one-sided; ignoring British liberalism, he came home a Tory of the most reactionary breed. He demanded dress clothes for formal functions, he writhed at a split infinitive, and he groaned at the quality of representatives elected to Congress by the unintelligent masses. Correct deportment, " pure " English, and distrust of democracy came to be the criteria by which he judged all issues. He meant every word when he wrote: " For nearly all that is good in our American civilization we are indebted to England; the errors and mischiefs are of our own creation. In learning and letters, in art and science of government, America is but a faint and stammering echo of England. The English are undoubtedly our intellectual superiors."

Bret Harte did not reach England until the rest of the pilgrims had gone, but, although he was the last to arrive, he was the one to appreciate his English welcome the most deeply. The seven years that had passed since he left San Francisco in triumph had been far from happy ones. In 1871 his progress across the country had been the news event of the day, and literary Boston had welcomed him as the nation's most promising young author. In 1878 he found himself heavily in debt, broken in body and in spirit, and unable to write stories even if he could have sold them. His sudden popularity had been his downfall; he had found it impossible to live up to his reputation, trying vainly to capture the public fancy again as he had with " The Luck of Roaring Camp " and " The Heathen Chinee." His year with the *Atlantic Monthly* had proved unsatisfactory both to himself and to the magazine. His large salary had merely tempted him to live beyond his income, confident that his writing would provide a steadily increasing source of wealth. Then, pressed for cash, he tried his luck in fields which usually paid better than the short story, failing in turn at lecturing, at writing novels, and at composing plays. As the wheel of fortune carried him down and down, he heard a fickle public call him a snob, a swindler, and a drunkard. When he grew desperate, his friends obtained for him a minor consular post in Crefeld, Germany, and he left America forever.

Though they included such routine tasks as ascertaining the cost of manufacturing hat-bands, his duties at the consulate were not heavy and he found many opportunities to visit England, where he was received with as much warmth as if he had never suffered an eclipse in America. One of the highest honors that the English could pay an author was accorded him in 1880 when he was invited to respond to the toast to " Literature " at the annual dinner of the Royal Academy before a group of distinguished guests that included the Prince of Wales and the cream of England's artists and writers. Gradually he regained his confidence in himself. Friends like James Anthony Froude, Lord Houghton, the Duchess of St. Albans, and the Van de Veldes made him feel so much at home that he postponed bringing his family to England so long that he never did get around to sending for them. When his consular service was terminated by a change of administration in Washington, he settled down in England for his remaining years, content to live on the crumbs from hack writing as long as he could warm himself at the English hearth.

CHAPTER XIII

EPILOGUE

Up to the coming of the railroad San Francisco held an undisputed economic monopoly over the entire Pacific Coast: it was the port through which entered practically all the shipping from the Orient and from the Atlantic seaboard; it had much the largest population and the greatest wealth of any city in the West; and it contained the most important mercantile houses, banks, hotels, and theaters. It is hardly too great an exaggeration to say that San Francisco was the west coast. Then the railroad came, and with it the realization that not only San Francisco but hundreds of towns in the West would have direct communication with the East. The monopoly of trade by sea had been broken. And to make the situation darker, the importance of the city's excellent port received another blow: the Suez Canal, opened the year of the completion of the railroad, put an immediate end to San Francisco's dream of handling the bulk of Europe's trade with the Orient. The following year, the first year of the " Terrible Seventies," San Francisco felt in full force the depression which was not to hit the rest of the United States for three more years. Her golden era of commerce was past — and with it, just as decisively, her golden era of literature was past. Her men of letters took early trains to the East, and none came to replace them. Not until the turn of the century, when Frank Norris and Jack London appeared on the scene, was San Francisco to see another school of promising writers flourish in its midst.

Already beginning to talk of the period when Bret Harte and Mark Twain walked down Montgomery Street as " those good old days," a group of journalists and artists founded the Bohemian Club in 1872, unmindful of the fact that the desire to organize appears only after true Bohemianism has died. The club was hard pressed to find illustrious names for its roster, for surprisingly few of the writers of the golden fifties and silver sixties were left in the city. Some of them, like Avery and Swift and Daggett, had gone to the Orient as United States ministers, while others, like Webb and Harte and Mark Twain, had moved to the East to further their careers. Among the European pilgrims only Bierce had returned, and he had come back reluctantly. As he looked around a city nearly empty of talent, he announced: " It is my intention to purify journalism in this town by instructing such writers as it is worth while to instruct, and assassinating those that it is not."

Death had not been waiting for Bierce's pen, however, to reap its toll. The old-timers among California journalists were fast disappearing. In 1867 Yellow Bird had died of softening of the brain; his friend Old Block followed him to the Grass Valley cemetery in 1874. In the following year J. Ross Browne's funeral cortege set out from Pagoda Hill, in the next, Caxton ceased combining law and poetry, and in another three years John C. Cremony had told his last tall tale and succumbed to eating toadstools. Finally James F. Bowman's death from cancer of the stomach marked the end of the terrible decade. " Little Jimmy Bowman," with his wizened face, his sparkling black eyes, his Absalom-like ebon locks, and his legs which reminded one of Quilp, would no longer lecture on Anglo-Saxon poetry, write interminable serials on a wager, or worry his friends with his drinking. During his life he had produced every kind of literature that the frontier knew and had experienced all of the vicissitudes of its writers except success.

Even self-destruction added its macabre emphasis to the depression that followed the passing of the frontier. Tremenhere L. Johns, known as an inveterate jester and the editor of *Figaro*, took an overdose of laudanum so that he might no longer suffer from stomach ulcers. W. A. Kendall, the " Comet Quirls " who had written love poems for the *Golden Era* and a score of other local journals, committed suicide by taking poison. Failing to make enough money to live on, he had had to depend, during the last years of his life, on small " loans " to keep him in food — and liquor. Likewise he had failed to make a name for himself as a writer, a fact which caused him to rail against those who had succeeded, especially Bret Harte, whom he called a well-bred villain who had played dirty mischief with the public morals. And finally, like John Evereldown, he was cursed by his inability to forget the women; he left a note which contained a long explanation of why he was dying for love and ended with the terse postscript: " I have stated immediate cause of my death, hoping it will obviate the necessity of cutting me up."

Bierce, in writing the epitaph of another suicide, the T. Arundel-Harcourt who had worked on Bancroft's *Native Races* and had helped to edit the *Overland Monthly*, mixed with his own brand of bitterness something of the mood which settled into the hearts of the journalists doomed to remain in San Francisco in the seventies after their friends had gone on to Parnassus:

Thus my friend —
Still conjugating with each failing sense
The verb " to die " in every mood and tense
Pursued his awful humor to the end.
When like a stormy dawn the crimson broke
From his white lips he smiled and mutely bled,
And, having meanly lived, is grandly dead.

There was a moment during the days of the exodus that Ina Coolbrith hoped she might go with the others to Europe. A book of her poems was in the offing, and there would be no great difficulty in arranging to publish her travel letters. But still another disappointment was awaiting the poetess who had had a martyr for a father and a scoundrel for a husband. Her widowed sister, falling ill, needed a home for herself and her two small children. Six months after she arrived from Los Angeles, she died, and Ina found herself with two orphans to rear. How could she leave now, particularly as her mother, who was also dependent on her, was rapidly failing in health? To add to her problems, Joaquin Miller had deposited his Indian daughter, Cali-Shasta, on her doorstep before returning to London, and, as there was no one else to take care of the girl, Ina had assumed the task. It was ridiculous for her to think any more of going to Europe. Instead she went to work behind the desk in the Oakland Public Library, kept herself and her family of four alive and cheerful on her salary of eighty dollars a month augmented by any odd sums that Miller might send her, and still managed to write poetry. Her friends did not forget her; at one time the artists of the Bohemian Club auctioned some of their paintings at a benefit and turned a thousand dollars over to her to help pay the landlord and the grocer.

For thirty years Ina served as a librarian, first for the Oakland Library and later for the Bohemian Club. She brought up her nephew and niece; she cared for Cali-Shasta until the latter was married; and she interested herself in many of the children who came to the library, including a ragged urchin named Jack London. She even saw a volume of her poems issue from the press. But she did not go to Europe. As the years passed by in San Francisco, she heard of the triumphs and failures of her friends, her companions in the halcyon days of the *Californian* and the *Overland Monthly.* Sometimes they wrote to her; sometimes they came to see her. One by one, as the turn of the century approached, they dropped their parts in the drama.

The first to go was dear old Prentice Mulford. Word came in 1891 that he was found one bright May morning lying in a small boat on Sheepshead Bay, Long Island, wrapped in his blankets, his banjo by his side. No one knew how he had died, for it was several days since he had set out with provisions and spirit lamp on his voyage from New York City to Sag Harbor. His followers made a mystery of his death, just as they did of the strange jumble of words found on his writing-pad, which they maintained had been dictated from the spirit world. His unusual death was no more extraordinary than the career he had led since returning from England. First he and Josie had separated. It was rumored that the issue which disrupted their union was his refusal to let his pretty wife continue posing in the nude for commercial artists, a practice which he discovered when he received a picture of her naked figure in a package of cheap cigarettes.

Then he had become a hermit in a New Jersey swamp, where he had emulated Thoreau in both economy and reflection. He had emerged from his retreat with the conviction that he had thought out a philosophy that would make people healthy, happy, and efficient. With his few remaining dollars he had begun to publish the five-cent tracts of the White Cross Library, in which he set forth in a disarmingly serious manner his doctrine containing approximately equal amounts of spiritualism, mental healing, and common sense. Interrupting the didactic stream just once, he had included in the White Cross series his vivid and amusing account of frontier experiences entitled *Prentice Mulford's Story*. His little pamphlets had made their way so well that by the time of his death many considered him an important leader in the occult sciences. Ina felt that after all his failures Prentice Mulford had found his niche in life, albeit a strange one.

Six years later Ina knew with all of the rest of the nation that Henry George was dead. After the success of *Progress and Poverty*, he had become a front-page newspaper figure, a social reformer whose spectacular career was followed in every town in America. Forcefully and continuously he had preached his single-tax doctrine from the Pacific to the Atlantic and had even carried his gospel to Ireland. On a reform ticket he had nearly beaten Theodore Roosevelt in a campaign for the mayorship of New York City. In 1897 the prophet of San Francisco had been persuaded, against the advice of his physician, to champion his theories at the New York polls a second time. In the midst of the heated contest he died. The newspapers said that his funeral was the most impressive tribute the people had paid to a leader since the passing of Lincoln.

In 1902 word sped across the Atlantic from London that Bret Harte had succumbed to cancer of the throat. After his ordeal of the seventies, those last twenty years in England had treated him kindly. Though he had shown something of his former magic touch in a half-dozen stories, he had for the most part resigned himself to being an efficient and regular hack writer; "I grind out the old tunes on the old organ and gather up the coppers," he wrote to his wife and children, who had remained in America and were receiving a large share of the coppers. He continued to set most of his stories in a California society that had long since disappeared, and, as his memory be-

gan to play him tricks, he put woods beside the Carquinez
Straits and spoke of crimson poppies growing near the Golden
Gate. But while the slim, dapper, white-haired gentleman was
listening to his cronies of the Royal Yacht Club, a new generation of Californians was growing up, a generation that looked
upon Bret Harte as the most romantic figure in a romantic era.
Already the Bret Harte country had become one of the show-
places of the state.

Ina suffered her hardest blow when she heard in 1909 that
Charlie Stoddard had died in Monterey. She had seen him frequently since his return to the coast a few years before, fat and
bald, but still personally charming. As of old, he had been full
of enthusiasms, but just as restless as ever — only he had
learned to take his idiosyncrasies more as a matter of course.
How characteristic was a comment in his diary: " How awfully
glad I shall be to get out of this and to long for it with tears,
afterwards! " Equally self-revealing was the fact that, because
he could not make up his mind, his autobiographical novel,
For the Pleasure of His Company, appeared with two conflicting endings, published unabashedly in the same book.

Stoddard had never made any more compromises with the
ogre Routine than were absolutely necessary; when he had realized that he could not live on the meager proceeds from his
travel books and memoirs, he had resigned himself to the " terrible ordeal " of lecturing three times a week, first at Notre
Dame University and then at the Catholic University in Washington. He retained enough independence, however, to refuse
a position in the library at the University of California, saying
that if he had to choose between going to work each day at eight
o'clock and starving, he would prefer to starve. He was happiest when swathed in a silk dressing-gown, lounging in one of his
several " dens," with the little Florentine lamp burning peanut
oil beside his bed. He liked to be surrounded by his relics — a

pearl-inlaid chest from India, some bones of a saint under a Buddhist rosary next to a sheet of bark from the Fiji Islands, old swords from Japan, figurines from Grecian tombs, naked statuettes, an old slipper which had belonged to William Dean Howells, and a hundred other knick-knacks. In one mood he could fondle a miniature outrigger canoe while he dreamed of reincarnation as a South Sea Islander, while in another he could brood by the hour over the oil painting of himself in monk's garb, staring at a skull. His temperament had changed little since Ina met him as the boy poet of San Francisco.

When Mark Twain died in 1910, the world paid him such a tribute that it seemed to Ina hardly possible she had once known him as the rough young journalist who had pretended to be a rival with Harte for her hand. Of all her friends, he had gone the furthest; people no longer referred to him as an amusing frontier humorist, but as one of the great American authors. His books had been many, but as she looked back it seemed as if the early ones like *The Innocents Abroad*, *Roughing It*, *Tom Sawyer*, and *Huckleberry Finn*, books that dealt with his boyhood in Missouri and his life on the frontier, were the best. They were written before he had lost a fortune, a wife, and two daughters; now men said that he played billiards late into the night because he could not sleep and that he had more than once declared he hated " the damned human race," himself most of all. Perhaps she wondered why the restless author had crossed the Atlantic at least twenty times but had never come back to San Francisco. It was surely not because he had forgotten the West, for not long ago he had written a friend in Nevada: " Those were the old days! those old ones! They will come no more. Youth will come no more. They were so full to the brim with the wine of life; there have been no others like them. Would you like to have me come out there and cry? " And now she knew that he would never come back.

Joaquin Miller had played his part up to his last breath, drawn one February morning in 1913. When Europe had tired of him, he had returned to America and for a while had posed as a wild Western poet in a log cabin situated in a park in Washington, D.C. When the real-estate boom of the late eighties brought new life to the West, he came back to California and bought one hundred acres on the hills above Oakland, where he planted thousands of trees, built three small houses, and erected monuments to Frémont, Moses, and Browning, as well as a funeral pyre for himself. His assumption that the Californians one generation removed from the frontier days would cherish a poet who had worked in the diggings and fought the Indians proved to be thoroughly justified.

On "The Hights" he continued to produce abundantly, turning out novels, poems, plays, and even a history; he rewrote his autobiography in several versions; and he discarded the role of a frontier Byron for that of a Pacific Coast Moses, beginning his poems with such lines as " I cry aloud from my mountain top, as a seer." Joaquin invited other poets to come and stay with him as long as they pleased; he showed curious visitors how to throw the tomahawk; and he entertained club-women by producing rain from a cloudless sky, relying on a mixture of nonsense and profanity, which he called an Indian chant, to confound his audience, and on a sprinkler, which he had installed on the roof of his cabin, to create the shower. Ina had never greatly minded his spoofing, knowing how much he enjoyed it, and she was glad to hear that he had kept his jug of corn whisky handy under his bed to the very last.

That same year Ambrose Bierce made the most dramatic exit achieved by any member of the group. A long life of journalism in San Francisco and Washington had not broken his spirit nor exhausted the gall from his pen. Though he had wasted much of his strength on unimportant issues, he had exerted a much-needed influence in his crusade for high standards in literature and he had written some excellent short stories. In private life he had suffered more than his share of disappointments and tragedies. He had separated from his beautiful wife, he had lost his two sons by tragic deaths, and he had broken with his favorite pupils, George Sterling and Jack London, when they had taken up socialism. But at seventy his body was straight, his silver-white head was high, and his blue eyes were clear. Once more he visited the Civil War battlefields, the scenes of his fighting and the settings for many of his stories, and then he walked across the Mexican border at Laredo, Texas, never to return. The manner of his death, if ever fully ascertained, will add little to the record; the fact remains that by disappearing into Chihuahua he realized most literally the ambition of every frontiersman, to die with his boots on.

By the beginning of the World War they were all gone except Ina. As the last of the giants — and, from 1915 until her death in 1928, as the recognized poet laureate of the State of California — she took her place as the matriarch of a group of local enthusiasts called the California Literary Society, which met with due seriousness and earnestness of purpose every third Sunday in her flat. That purpose was frequently enunciated at the meetings by Ella Sterling Cummins Mighels, the perpetual secretary of the organization: " Why do we have this society? We have it, my good friends, so we can pass on to the next generation the memory of our writers. We have it so that the old traditions and customs of California may not die out and be forgotten. We must not forget the *pioneers*." Then, as though she were repeating the litany, she would add: " What can we do for California authors? " And the answer came in unison: " We can buy their books."

The members included, of course, Ella Sterling Cummins,

now Mrs. Mighels, who, in her *Story of the Files*, had preserved much information about San Francisco's literary frontier which would otherwise have been destroyed by the earthquake and fire of 1906 or lost in the passing of time; Henry Oak's widow, who would never forgive Mr. Bancroft; Zoeth Skinner Eldridge, author of a history of San Francisco; George Wharton James, who gained both profit and pleasure by keeping pioneer memories alive; and perhaps a dozen others of literary connections or ambitions. Then there were the visitors: a high-school poet, a local essayist, or even a writer as promising as George Sterling; and during the year of the 1915 Exposition, Edwin Markham, out from New York, dropped in occasionally, and, most thrilling of all, Bret Harte's grandson came to two or three meetings. But no matter who was there, it was Ina who dominated the gathering. It was to Ina that they all turned when Sidney's *Defence of Poesie* was read, Pollock's ode on the Golden Gate declaimed, or an original poem recited by its author. Her brief comment — or silence — was the cue for the round of buzzing comments to follow.

Such were the meetings of the California Literary Society for which this group of twenty or more people, most of them more than fifty years of age, trudged up the hill to Ina's apartment, situated high up on Broadway. Pausing a moment to catch their breaths and to look down over the city on to the bay, blue and wind-swept in the afternoon sun, they turned and entered the house. As they went up the stairs to the drawing-room on the second floor, the gentlemen tugged the waistcoats of their best dark suits into place and glanced at their polished shoes to be sure no dust had settled on them, and the ladies gave a final tilt to their hats and caught up the locks blown astray by the breezes. One looked his best when one went to Ina's soirées.

At the top of the stairs the ladies disappeared into a bedroom, while the gentlemen hung their hats and coats on a rack in the hall. And then — no matter how early one arrived, Ina was already seated in her big chair flanked by two windows, the north light from which left her person in shadow, elusively pontifical. Over her head she wore a lace mantilla, which hung at the sides in loose folds, and her heavy body was covered by a thick woolen gown, not unlike a sumptuous white bathrobe, generously figured with large lavender flowers. Her cheeks, which once had been plump, sagged a bit, and her generous mouth seemed pinched by the vertical wrinkles on her upper lip. But she shook hands firmly and looked her guests in the eye. A woman with a grip so strong and a pair of eyes that flashed so vitally was not old, no matter what her years. She made no speeches and read no poetry; her occasional remarks were but a few quick words thrown off as an aside to those nearest her chair. But once in a while she would turn to a youthful initiate sitting beside her throne and begin to chat:

" I was remembering yesterday what handsome men lived in San Francisco in the old days. It was hard to tell whether Frank Harte or Charlie Stoddard was the better-looking, and Joaquin Miller was quite striking with his curly brown hair. Mark Twain had an interesting face, but he was not as handsome as he was later. What a glorious time I used to have matching limericks with Frank — that's what we always called Bret Harte — or joshing with Mark Twain, who was just a lanky red-headed journalist when he was working for the *Call*! I was going to write a book about the early days, but all my notes and letters were burned in the fire. Maybe it is best that the secrets die with me; we were never afraid of life in those days, you know. Now, there was that time when . . ."

BIBLIOGRAPHY

THE SOURCE-MATERIAL for this study lies in the files of early California newspapers and magazines, particularly the *Golden Era,* the *Californian,* the *News Letter,* and the *Overland Monthly;* in collections of rare books, letters, and manuscripts owned by libraries and private individuals; and in a considerable body of published letters, autobiographies, and biographies dealing with Western writers. Among biographies I have received most help from *Bret Harte: Argonaut and Exile* by George R. Stewart, *Ambrose Bierce: a Biography* by Carey McWilliams, and *The Life of Henry George* by Henry George, Jr. I have also drawn on Albert Bigelow Paine's *Mark Twain: a Biography* and Bernard De Voto's *Mark Twain's America* for many ideas in directing my research on Mark Twain. In dealing with the minor characters I have found Ella Sterling Cummins's *Story of the Files* a constant source of both fact and suggestion. Another invaluable aid was the index of California newspapers and magazines in the State Library at Sacramento.

The principal collections examined during my research were those of the California Section of the State Library, Sacramento; the Bancroft Library, Berkeley; the University of California Library, Berkeley; the Huntington Library, San Marino; the San Francisco Public Library; the Los Angeles Public Library; the Harte and Miller collections made by the late Willard A. Morse of Santa Monica; the Coolbrith and Stoddard papers in the hands of Mr. Finlay Cooke of San

Francisco; and the Stoddard diaries owned by Mr. Edwin Grabhorn of San Francisco. To the librarians and owners of these collections, as well as to the numerous others who have responded generously to requests for information or for permission to examine material in their possession, I wish to express my thanks.

Among the many who have aided me in writing the book, I am particularly indebted to Miss Imogene Bishop, who has helped in every detail of the work, and to Mr. George R. Stewart, Mr. George Ezra Dane, Mr. Bernard De Voto, and Mr. Fulmer Mood, who have read the manuscript and have made suggestions for revision. To Mr. Mood I am also indebted for aid in establishing the facts concerning Ina Coolbrith's parentage and marriage. Miss Caroline Wenzel of the State Library has been of great help in obtaining illustrations.

I wish also to make acknowledgment with thanks to the following companies and individuals for permission to quote from copyrighted material not elsewhere acknowledged: to Harper & Brothers for several passages from *Mark Twain: a Biography* by Albert Bigelow Paine and from *Mark Twain's Letters* edited by Albert Bigelow Paine; to Houghton Mifflin Company for quotations from *Edward Rowland Sill* by William Belmont Parker, from *The Life and Letters of John Muir* by William F. Badé, from *Bret Harte: Argonaut and Exile* by George R. Stewart, Jr., and from *Shapes that Pass* by Julian Hawthorne; to The Beacon Press, Inc., for quotations from *Thomas Starr King: Patriot and Preacher* by Charles W. Wendte; to G. P. Putnam's Sons for a quotation from *Talks in a Library with Lawrence Hutton* edited by I. Moore; to Frank M. McCaffrey, Seattle, for quotations from *Joaquin Miller's California Diary* edited by John S. Richards; to The Book Club of California for a quotation from Ina Coolbrith's introduction to *The Hea-*

then Chinee; to the San Francisco *Examiner* for quotations from an article entitled " Virginia City " by Sam P. Davis which appeared on January 22, 1893; to Paul Bancroft for quotations from *Literary Industries* by Hubert H. Bancroft; and to Mrs. Marie M. George for quotations from *The Life of Henry George* by Henry George, Jr. I also wish to thank the Henry E. Huntington Library for permission to consult and quote from letters by Ambrose Bierce, Joaquin Miller, and Mark Twain.

Following is a list of the more important books consulted, together with the symbols used in referring to them in the notes and references:

Alta	*Alta California.* San Francisco daily newspaper.
Ba	Bancroft, Hubert Howe: *Bancroft's Works.* San Francisco, 1874–90.
Badé	Badé, William F.: *The Life and Letters of John Muir.* Boston and New York, 1924.
BaE	Bancroft, Hubert Howe: " Early California Literature." *Bancroft's Works,* Vol. 38, pp. 591 ff.
BaL	Bancroft, Hubert Howe: *Literary Industries.* (Vol. 39 of *Bancroft's Works.*) San Francisco, 1890.
BaS	Bancroft Scraps. " California Authors " scrapbook in Bancroft Library, Berkeley, California.
BrC	Browne, J. Ross: *Crusoe's Island, with Sketches of Adventure in California and Washoe.* New York, 1864.
Bul	*San Francisco Evening Bulletin.* San Francisco daily newspaper.
C	*The Californian.* Weekly journal. San Francisco, 1864–8.
Call	*San Francisco Morning Call.* San Francisco daily newspaper.
Ch	*San Francisco Chronicle.* San Francisco daily newspaper.

Cl — Clappe, Louise Amelia Knapp (Smith) : *California in 1851–1852: the letters of Dame Shirley.* Introduction and notes by Carl I. Wheat. 2 vols. San Francisco, 1933.

CleA — Clemens, Samuel L.: *Mark Twain's Autobiography.* With an Introduction by A. B. Paine. 2 vols. New York, 1924.

CleI — Clemens, Samuel L. (Mark Twain): *The Innocents Abroad.* New York, 1869. References in the notes are to Macmillan's one-volume edition, 1929.

CleL — Clemens, Samuel L.: *Mark Twain's Letters.* Edited by A. B. Paine. 2 vols. New York, 1917.

CleN — Clemens, Samuel L.: *Mark Twain's Notebook.* Edited by A. B. Paine. New York, 1935.

CleR — Clemens, Samuel L.: *Roughing It.* New York, 1871.

CleW — Clemens, Samuel L.: *The Washoe Giant in San Francisco.* Edited by Franklin Walker. San Francisco, 1938.

Cu — Cummins (Mighels), Ella Sterling: *The Story of the Files.* San Francisco, 1893.

DAB — *Dictionary of American Biography.* Edited by Allen Johnson. New York, 1928.

DagS — John Daggett's Scrapbook. In California State Library, Sacramento.

Dav — Davis, Sam P.: *The History of Nevada.* 2 vols. Reno, Nevada, 1913.

Debo — Debo, Angie: "John Rollin Ridge." *Southwest Review,* Vol. 17, pp. 59–71.

DeC — Delano, Alonzo: *Pen-Knife Sketches; or Chips of the Old Block.* Edited with a foreword by G. Ezra Dane. San Francisco, 1934.

DeL — Delano, Alonzo: *Life in the Plains and among the Diggings.* Auburn and Buffalo, 1854.

DeLive — Delano, Alonzo: *A Live Woman in the Mines.* New York, 1857.

DeO — Delano, Alonzo: *Old Block's Sketch Book.* Sacramento, 1856.

DeS — Delano, Alonzo: *A Sojourn with Royalty.* Edited by

G. Ezra Dane, with a foreword by Edmund G. Kenyon. San Francisco, 1936.

Dev De Voto, Bernard: *Mark Twain's America*. Boston, 1932.

DP Derby, George Horatio: *Phœnixiana*. Edited by John Kendrick Bangs. New York, 1903.

DrCh *San Francisco Dramatic Chronicle*. San Francisco daily newspaper.

DS Derby, George Horatio: *The Squibob Papers*. New York, 1865.

DT Derby, George Horatio: *The Topographical Reports of George Horatio Derby*. Edited by Francis P. Farquhar. San Francisco, 1933.

Era *The Golden Era*. Weekly journal. San Francisco, 1852–93.

Ex *San Francisco Examiner*. San Francisco daily newspaper.

Fish Fisher, Walt M.: *The Californians*. San Francisco, 1876.

GeG George, Henry, Jr.: *The Life of Henry George*. 2 vols. New York, 1911.

GeP George, Henry: *Progress and Poverty*. New York, 1880.

Good Goodwin, C. C.: *As I Remember Them*. Salt Lake, 1915.

Gra Graham, Howard Jay: " When the Bay Bridge was a Joke." Series of articles in the San Francisco *News*, August 27–September 15, 1934.

GrH Graham, J. B.: *Handset Reminiscences*. Salt Lake, 1915.

HaL Harte, Bret: *The Letters of Bret Harte*. Edited by Geoffrey Bret Harte. Boston and New York, 1926.

HaW Harte, Bret: *Collected Works* (Riverside edition). Boston and New York, 1902.

Hi Hittell, John Shertzer: *History of the City of San Francisco*. San Francisco, 1878.

Hing Hingston, Edward P.: *The Genial Showman* (Artemus Ward). New York, 1870.

HiT   Hittell, Theodore H.: *History of California*. San Francisco, 1897.

How   *Sketches of the Sixties*. Items from the *Californian* by Bret Harte and Mark Twain. Edited by J. Howell. San Francisco, 1926.

King   King, Clarence: *Mountaineering in the Sierra Nevada*. Edited with a preface by Francis P. Farquhar. New York, 1935.

Ll   Lloyd, Benjamin E.: *Lights and Shades in San Francisco*. San Francisco, 1876.

LyS   Lyman, George: *The Saga of the Comstock Lode*. New York, 1934.

McWB   McWilliams, Carey: *Ambrose Bierce: a Biography*. New York, 1929.

MiD   Miller, Joaquin: *Joaquin Miller's California Diary* (1855–7). Edited by John S. Richards. Seattle, 1936.

MiM   Miller, Joaquin: *Memorie and Rime*. New York, 1884.

MiW   Millard, Bailey: " When They Were Twenty-one." *The Bookman*, May 1913.

Mu   Mulford, Prentice: *Prentice Mulford's Story*. New York, 1889.

MuS   Mulford, Prentice: *California Sketches*. Edited with an introduction by Franklin Walker. San Francisco, 1935.

Ne   Neville, Amelia Ransome: *The Fantastic City*. Boston and New York, 1932.

NL   *San Francisco News Letter and Commercial Advertiser*. Weekly journal. San Francisco, 1856.

OM   *Overland Monthly*. San Francisco, 1868–75.

OM (n. s.) *Overland Monthly*, new series. San Francisco, 1883+

PaM   Paine, Albert Bigelow: *Mark Twain, a Biography*. New York, 1912.

Parry   Parry, Albert: *Garrets and Pretenders; a History of Bohemianism in America*. New York, 1933.

ParS   Parker, William Belmont: *Edward Rowland Sill.*
        Boston, 1915.
PeM   Peterson, Martin Severin: *Joaquin Miller: Literary*
        Frontiersman. Palo Alto, 1937.
Pi   *The Pioneer: or, California Monthly Magazine.* San
        Francisco, 1854–5.
PP   *Poetry of the Pacific.* Edited by May Wentworth.
        San Francisco, 1867.
RicM   Richards, John S.: " Bibliographical Materials for a
        Literary History of Joaquin Miller." Master's
        thesis in manuscript. University of California Li-
        brary.
RiM   Ridge, John R. (Yellow Bird): *The Life and Adven-*
        tures of Joaquin Murieta. San Francisco, 1854.
RiP   Ridge, John R.: *Poems.* San Francisco, 1868.
Ro   Royce, Josiah: *California.* Boston, 1881.
RoB   Rock, Francis J.: *J. Ross Browne.* Washington,
        D.C., 1929.
RoT   Rourke, Constance M.: *Troupers of the Gold-Coast.*
        New York, 1928.
SGN   Soulé, Frank; Gihon, John H.; and Nisbet, James:
        The Annals of San Francisco. New York, 1855.
StC   Stoddard, Charles Warren: " Confessions of a Re-
        formed Poet." Manuscript autobiography owned
        by Mr. Finlay Cooke, San Francisco.
StE   Stoddard, Charles Warren: *Exits and Entrances.*
        Boston, 1903.
SteBH   Stewart, George R., Jr.: *A Bibliography of the Writ-*
        ings of Bret Harte in the Magazines and Newspa-
        pers in California, 1857–1871. Berkeley, Califor-
        nia, 1933.
SteH   Stewart, George R., Jr.: *Bret Harte: Argonaut and*
        Exile. Boston and New York, 1931.
SteJ   Stewart, George R., Jr.: *John Phœnix, Esq.: the*
        Veritable Squibob. New York, 1937.
StI   Stoddard, Charles Warren: *In the Footprints of the*
        Padres. San Francisco, 1902.

StP   Stoddard, Charles Warren: *For the Pleasure of His Company*. San Francisco, 1903.

StT   Stoddard, Charles Warren: *A Troubled Heart*. Notre Dame, Indiana, 1885.

WagM   Wagner, Harr: *Joaquin Miller and His Other Self*. San Francisco, 1929.

WaM   Walker, Franklin: " Diogenes of the Tuolumne " (Prentice Mulford). *Westways*, June 1935.

WaP   Walker, Franklin: " Pip Pepperpod Grows Up " (C. W. Stoddard). *Westways*, August 1935.

Webb   Webb, Charles H.: *John Paul's Book*. New York, 1874.

Wendte   Wendte, Charles W.: *Thomas Starr King: Patriot and Preacher*. Boston, 1921.

WrC   Wright, Wm. (Dan de Quille): *History of the Comstock Lode*. Virginia City, Nevada, 1889.

NOTES AND REFERENCES

To AVOID annoying the reader with footnotes or index figures in the text, I have segregated my notes and have located them by reference to page and key words. I also refer to items in the bibliography of chief sources by using the symbols there assigned to them. In referring to books not listed in the bibliography I have followed the practice of giving the date and place of publication only when the work is rare or the edition of some special importance. At the beginning of the section on each chapter, I list the general authorities. I give additional references (1) for direct quotations not located explicitly in the text, (2) upon doubtful and controversial points, (3) for material not contained in the general authorities.

CHAPTER I

A PRECOCIOUS FRONTIER

General authorities: Hi; Ba; HiT; Ne; Era; Turner, F. J.: *The Frontier in American History;* Paxson, F. L.: *The Last American Frontier;* Caughey, J. W.: *The History of the Pacific Coast.*

Page 3. Completion of the Central Pacific Railroad. Era, May 1, 8, 15, 1869; OM, May 1869, June 1869; Sabin, E. L.: *Building the Pacific Railway.*

5. "The Pacific Railroad, Uncle Sam's Waistband." Caughey, op. cit., p. 389.

14. Fifty printers in San Francisco. Information obtained from H. R. Wagner, who is making a study of the history of printing in San Francisco during its early days.

CHAPTER II

THE FIFTIES

General authorities: Hi; SGN; Ne; Yo; Ba; Cu; files of the *Pacific,* Era, Pi.

Page 17. The one book of importance. Perhaps one should add Palou's life of Serra, written in San Francisco *circa* 1785.

22. Picturesque names. See Weigle, C. F.: "California's Pioneer Newspapers," *The California State Employee,* July 1937, for an interesting account of early journalism.

24. "Our circulation . . ." Era, April 3, 1853.

24. Letters carved out of quartz. Era, April 10, 1853.

24. The hold-up of Daggett. Era, April 17, 1853.

25. Ferdinand C. Ewer. Era, November 11, 1863; Ch, October 24, 1831; Preface to Cl, Vol. 2; Wagner, Henry R.: "The Life of Ferdinand C. Ewer," *California Historical Society Quarterly,* December 1934 and March 1935.

27. Benjamin Parke Avery. DAB; Alta, December 2, 1875; Ch, March 13, 1881.

27. Joseph Shertzer Hittell. DAB; BaE; BaL.

27. James M. Hutchings. DagS; Sacramento *Press,* November 5, 1902; Call, August 11, 1895; YZ; Badé.

28. Rollin M. Daggett. DagS; Ch, October 31, 1897, November 13, 1901; Era, April 22, 1860; Good; Ex, January 22, 1893; PaM; Sam Davis, *Nevada;* Dev.

29. Hubert H. Bancroft. DAB; BaL; Bas.

29. J. Ross Browne. DAB; BaL; BaS; RoB.

29. Stephen Massett. StI; RoT; Bul, May 15, 1897; Gra.

30. Louise Amelia Knapp Smith Clappe (Dame Shirley). StI; Pi; Cl. Best biographical account is in Carl Wheat's introduction to Cl. See also letter from Mrs. Lawrence, published in T. C. Russell's introduction to his edition of *The Shirley Letters,* San Francisco, 1922.

31. "I am bound, Molly . . ." All quotations from Shirley's letters are taken from the files of the *Pioneer.*

35. Alonzo Delano (Old Block). DeC; DeS; DeL; DeO; DeLive; Ch, October 24, 1897. Best biographical account is in George Ezra Dane's introduction to DeC.

36. "Californians! . . ." DeL, p. 349.

37. "He is famous . . ." DeC, Preface, p. xvii.

38. Nahl, Charles. See Dane's introduction to DeC.

40. George Horatio Derby (John Phœnix). P; DP; SteJ; DT; DS; BaS; Gra; DeC; DeS; C, May 28, 1864, September 24, 1864; Ch, October 24, 1897. Derby notebook in San Diego Public Library. Files of San Diego *Herald.*

43. Squibob. DP, p. 298.

44. "We held . . ." DP, p. 144.

45. John Rollin Ridge (Yellow Bird). Preface to RiP; Debo; GeG (Vol. 1, p. 110); BaS; RiM; Alta, May 27, 1861; Alta, October 8, 1867; *Shasta Courier,* May 20, 1871; Call, November 6, 1893; Era, October 13, 1867; Ch, October 24, 1897; OM (n. s.), Vol. 44, p. 128; *Westways,* November 1938.

45. The treaty of New Echota. For accounts of the Ridge faction among the Cherokees, see Eaton, R. C.: *John Ross and the Cherokee Indians;* DAB on Major Ridge; and Parker, T. V.: *The Cherokee Indians.*

46. Major Ridge's visit to Cornwall. For interesting accounts of this visit and John Ridge's marriage, see Starr, E. C.: *A History of Cornwall, Connecticut;* and Mabbott, T. O., and Pleadwell, F. L.: *The Life and Works of Edward Coote Pinkney.*

47. "She simply said . . ." Starr, op. cit.

48. "an article . . ." Debo, p. 62.

48. "there is a . . ." Debo, p. 63.

49. The ascertainable facts about Joaquin Murieta. Materia[l] this complicated subject may be found in DAB; Ba (*California,* Vo[l.] *California Pastoral*); HiT; RiM; Bell, Horace: *Reminiscences o[f] Ranger,* 1881; and F. Farquhar's preface to the Grabhorn printing the *Police Gazette* version of the life of Murieta, San Francisco, 1932.

50. "dozens of heads . . ." See *Report of Committee on Mil[i]tary Affairs,* California State Legislature Papers, Session of 185[3] Doc. 49.

51. "would have to be killed . . ." Call, November 6, 1893.

51. "swore a most solemn oath . . ." Cl, p. 76.

52. For a discussion of the varying editions of Ridge's *Murieta,* see Farquhar, F., op. cit.; and Walker, F.: "Ridge's Life of Murieta," *California Historical Society Quarterly,* Vol. 16, p. 256.

53. Police Gazette edition. This was in reality a pirated edition of Ridge's biography. See San Jose *Tribune,* December 27, 1861.

53. Anti-Catholic play on Murieta. *Joaquin Murieta de Castillo,* by Charles E. B. Howe, San Francisco, 1858.

CHAPTER III

APPRENTICE DAYS

General authorities: BaE; Cu; Hi.

Page 55. Francis Brett Harte. Harte was christened Francis Brett Harte; he started writing under the name of Bret and eventually adopted the writing name, Bret Harte.

55. Date of Miller's birth. The date is a matter of much dispute, being placed at various times from 1835 to 1841. The evidence in MiD is so compelling that I have accepted the date September 8, 1837, established in Mr. Richards's introduction.

56. "With what anguish . . ." San Francisco *Wasp,* November 3, 1883. Quoted in McWB.

57. Josephine D. Smith Carsley (Ina Donna Coolbrith). DAB; OM (n. s.), Vol. 87, p. 229; *National Magazine,* Vol. 26, p. 315; memoir by Charles Phillips in Coolbrith's *Wings of Sunset; California Historical Society Quarterly,* Vol. 13, pp. 335, 348, 354; *Grizzly Bear,* June 1915; Coolbrith's introduction to the Nash edition of *The Heathen Chinee,* San Francisco, 1934; *Lantern* (San Francisco), Vol. 3, p. 227; Call, April 21, 1892; *Sunset,* Vol. 9, p. 217; Coolbrith papers in the

. . . e, San Francisco, and personal memories of

on 　　　　　　　　　urther detail on Miss Coolbrith's birth and

. 7, 　　　　　　　　n " Aurora Esmeralda " (Ella Sterling Cum-

a　　　　　　　　all dated March 12, 1928, in Huntington Li-

of　　　　　　　　y Stella Haverland in *Pacific Bindery Talk,*
　　　　　　　　　Robert H. Davis in New York *Sun,* March 6,

　　　　　　　　　mith. Werner, M. R.: *Brigham Young;* Smith,
　　　　　　　　aphical Sketch of Joseph Smith; files of the *Mil-*
　　　　f.

　　　　ted her whole time . . ." Smith, op. cit., p. 203.

　　　　leg of Pharaoh's daughter . . ." Werner, op. cit.,

　　　　ophronia, second daughter of Don Carlos . . ." Smith,
　　　5.

Any man who will teach . . ." Linn, W. A.: *The Story*
mons, New York, 1902, p. 277.

James P. Beckwourth. DAB; *Life and Adventures of James*
ourth, New York, 1856.

. " At the close of day . . ." Beckwourth, op. cit., p. 428.

61. " a dark-faced man . . ." *National Magazine,* June 1907.

62. " The more they drank . . ." Footnote in Cl to eighth Shirley letter.

63. Ina Coolbrith's marriage and divorce. For marriage, see Los Angeles County Marriage Certificates, Vol. 1, pp. 22–3. For divorce, see Los Angeles County District Court, Case 853, Josephine D. Carsley vs. Robert B. Carsley, filed December 10, 1861; granted December 30, 1861. Further information on Carsley can be found in Carsley vs. Lindsay, *Supreme Court of California Reports,* Vol. 14, p. 390; Newmark, Harris: *Sixty Years in Southern California,* p. 187; and files of Los Angeles *Star,* 1859–61.

63. " already obtained almost . . ." Los Angeles *Star,* December 21, 1861.

63. " Were I to write . . ." OM (n. s.), Vol. 87, p. 229.

63. Pickett wounds Carsley. See Los Angeles *Star,* October 19, 1861.

64. The nom-de-plume Ina. In the Haynes collection in the Bancroft Library (R 12) there is a clipping of a poem by " Ina " indexed under the name of Mrs. Carsley. Josephine Carsley's mother, Agnes Coolbrith Pickett, consistently referred to her daughter as " Ina " in her testimony to the court.

64. Bret Harte. For biographical material on Harte I have relied constantly on SteH. In addition, see HaL; BaE; Dags: OM (n. s.), Vol. 40, p. 301; *Century,* Vol. 36, p. 447; Ex, January 24, 1926; Bul, January 6, 1860; Era; OM; HaW; C.

65. " insisted on working around . . ." SteH, p. 47. Harte's account of his experiences in the mines, written late in life, is found in " How I Went to the Mines," HaW.

66. Jim Gillis. See Gillis, William: *Gold Rush Days with Mark Twain* for an exaggerated account of this visit. Jim Gillis maintained that Harte snubbed him when he later called in San Francisco to collect the debt.

66. " hard, ugly, unwashed . . ." Harte wrote his comments on the unheroic fifties in his editorial department " Etc." in OM, July 1868.

67. " Oh, the blessed . . ." From " Jessie," Era, October 11, 1857.

67. " A child's shoe! . . ." From " Up the Coast," Era, November 1, 1857.

67. " Ah! well did the cynical Walpole . . ." From Harte's diary, quoted in SteH, p. 68.

68. " He was willing to do anything . . ." OM (n. s.), Vol. 40, p. 301.

68. " A mechanical curiosity . . ." etc. Era, January 27, 1861.

69. " Indiscriminate Massacre . . ." The *Northern Californian* (Arcata), February 29, 1860.

70. Prentice Mulford. The best account of Mulford is found in his autobiography, Mu. See also MuS, WaM; Ch, July 21, 1895; *Union-Democrat* (Sonora), June 6, 1891; White Cross Library #64 (New York, 1891); *History of Tuolumne County,* San Francisco, 1882; *Sacramento Union,* September 6, 1882; OM, September 1872; Upham: *Scenes from El Dorado,* 1878; *National Magazine,* Vol. 22, pp. 94–104. Sheaf of clippings on Mulford in California State Library, Sacramento. Many autobiographical articles in OM and C. Appears as Diogenes in StP.

73. Charles Warren Stoddard. Stc; StE; StI; StT; and StP contain a wealth of autobiographical material on Stoddard and his contemporaries. Also BaS; *U. C. Magazine,* Vol. 2, p. 276; Ch, January 11, 1902; MiW; OM (n. s.), Vol. 49, p. 374, Vol. 51, p. 135, Vol. 53, p. 527; files of Era, and C, and OM. Diaries in University of California Library, Mills College Library, and Grabhorn collection. See also Stoddard's articles in *Lippincott's, Atlantic Monthly,* and *National Magazine.* Letters in Huntington Library and Finlay Cooke collection.

75. " the blackness of darkness . . ." StI, p. 13. *A Troubled Heart,* which tells of Stoddard's conversion to Catholicism, was issued by the Notre Dame press. The autobiography is doubtless colored by the purpose of the book.

75. " I was threatened . . ." StI, p. 40.

77. " Charlie Stoddard, did you write . . ." StC gives in detail the early experiences of Stoddard in writing poetry.

78. Henry George. Biographical material on George based principally on GeG and autobiographical references in GeP. See also *Century,* Vol. 35, p. 549; GrH; Hart, Jerome A.: *In Our Second Century;* StC.

78. George's phrenological examination. Given in detail in GeG.

78. Stoddard's spelling. Stoddard, George, and Miller were all wretched spellers; George learned later to spell, but Stoddard and Miller never did.

79. " to drink Red Eye . . ." GeG, Vol. 1, p. 49.

79. " California is sadly . . ." GeG, Vol. 1, p. 90.

80. " Desires money . . ." GeG, Vol. 1, p. 53.

81. " I have not changed . . ." GeG, Vol. 1, p. 84.

82. " If Washoe only equals . . ." GeG, Vol. 1, p. 102.

82. Joaquin Miller. There is no adequate biography of Miller; even DAB contains several errors. WagM tells many colorful stories and PeM, though carefully done in parts, is neither thorough nor free from errors. I have relied heavily on MiM, MiD, and RicM for my account of Miller's early experiences in California. Miller's extensive and conflicting autobiographies are found in his magazine articles, in the three versions of *My Life among the Modocs,* and in the preface to the Bear edition of his poems, in MiM, and in many footnotes to his poems. See also letters in Huntington Library; files of Era and OM; Cu; StE; OM (n. s.), Vol. 87, p. 54; *The Frontier,* May 1931; ibid., March 1932; Ch, January 20, 1873; Call, June 9, 1909; *Bookman,* Vol. 51, p. 553; BaS; OM, Vol. 8, p. 165; *Lippincott's,* Vol. 38, p. 106; Bul, September 25, 1872; OM (n. s.), Vol. 43, p. 11. There is an excellent bibliography of material dealing with Miller in the Oakland Public Library. I have found the Miller collection of the late Willard F. Morse of Santa Monica very useful.

82. Miller's nom-de-plume. To avoid confusion, I have referred to the poet as Joaquin Miller from the beginning, although he did not adopt that name until after the publication of his book of poems *Joaquin et al* in 1869.

83. " In truth, I never had been . . ." Quoted in WagM, p. 7.

84. " I was alone . . ." *Life among the Modocs,* Hartford, Connecticut, 1874, p. 10.

85. " When the Modocs rose up one night . . ." *Joaquin Miller's Poems* (Bear edition), San Francisco, 1917, Vol. 1, p. 76.

86. Papers in the Shasta County Court House. These are published in Wells, H. L.: *History of Siskiyou County,* pp. 119 ff. See also Ch, January 20, 1873.

86. Miller's diary. Quotations from the diary are made from MiD. The diary gives every evidence of authenticity and apparently was not altered in Miller's later years.

CHAPTER IV

WASHOE SILVER AND THE CIVIL WAR

General authorities: Hi; Ba; Ne; files of Era.

Page 90. Census figures, 1863. Era, October 4, 1863.

90. Washoe. General references: BrC; Good; PaM; WrC; CleR; LyS; Dev; GrH; WrC; Dav.

90. " Let us be off! . . ." BrC, p. 320. Browne's account of his visit to Washoe, illustrated with his pencil sketches, shows Browne at his best.

91. " Gold coins jingle . . ." WrC, p. 49.

92. " a mud-hole . . ." etc. BrC, pp. 364, 405.

92. Mark Twain's hopes of a castle in San Francisco. CleR, Vol. 1, pp. 276 ff.

93. Staff of the *Territorial Enterprise.* See CleR ; CleW ; Good : PaM ; LyS ; Dev ; Dav ; GrH ; Ex, January 22, 1893.

94. " In youth . . ." Dav, p. 472.

94. " He had been living . . ." Ex, January 22, 1893.

94. Mark Twain. PaM ; CleR ; CleW ; LyS ; Dev. Benson, which appeared after this study was completed, contains an excellent survey of this period.

97. Dan de Quille's " quaints." CleW ; Cu ; files of Era ; files of the *California Magazine and Mountaineer.*

97. First use of Mark Twain. February 2, 1863 (PaM, Vol. 1, p. 222).

97. Civil War in California. General references : Ba ; Hi ; HiT ; Kennedy, Elijah R. : *The Contest for California in 1861;* Ellison, Joseph : *California and the Nation (1850–1869).*

98. " an influx of males . . ." Era, April 20, 1863.

99. " the auger holes of heaven . . ." Kennedy, op. cit., p. 145.

99. " Baptized anew . . ." Cu, p. 89.

99. Edward Dickinson Baker. DAB ; Kennedy, op. cit.

100. " surpassed any in Demosthenes . . ." Hi, p. 327.

101. " We are a city . . ." Hi, p. 328.

101. A young man. This was Bret Harte. See SteH, p. 104.

101. Thomas Starr King. Wendte ; Simonds, W. D. : *Starr King in California;* SteH ; StC ; Kennedy, op. cit. ; Good ; *Pacific Monthly,* Vol. 11, p. 504 ; OM (n. s.), Vol. 28, p. 583 ; Ex, June 19, 1887.

101. " You will be fascinated . . ." Wendte, p. 72.

102. " stretched out on its desolate hills . . ." Wendte, p. 110.

103. " There are only two kinds . . ." Wendte, p. 196.

103. " His cause is pollution . . ." Wendte, p. 198.

104. " The rebellion . . ." Simonds, op. cit., p. 60.

104. " Starr King made a tour . . ." Quoted in Buckbee, E. B. : *Saga of Old Tuolumne,* p. 254.

104. Anecdote on King's visit to Oregon. Good, pp. 114 ff.

106. " Relieving Guard." Bul, March 8, 1864.

106. Harte's Civil War activities. See SteH ; files of Era, Bul, C.

106. Jessie Benton Frémont. SteH; Frémont, Jessie B.: *Souvenirs of my Time;* Nevins, Allen: *Frémont.*

106. " a she-Merrimac . . ." Wendte, p. 190.

108. Celebration of July 4th, 1863. See Era, October 5, 1863; SteH, pp. 115–16.

108. " Far better the tempest . . ." Era, October 5, 1863.

108. " In exaltation . . ." from " Semmes," Era, January 11, 1860.

109. Sacramento *Union.* See Cu for a discussion of the Sacramento *Union* and its part in the war.

110. Calvin B. McDonald. Cu; DagS; files of the *Daily American Flag,* San Francisco.

110. " The man who dares stand up . . . " San Francisco *Sunday Gossip,* November 29, 1863.

111. Rowena Granice Steele. Era, May 24, 1863.

111. Acrostic poem. " Invocation to Patriotism," Era, February 1, 1863.

111. Ridge's Civil War activities. *Shasta Courier,* May 20, 1871; Bul, October 7, 1867; OM (n. s.), Vol. 44, p. 128; Grass Valley *Morning Union,* October 28, 1934.

111. " the re-election of Lincoln by all possible means . . ." *Reports of the Rebellion,* Series I, Vol. L, Pt. II, pp. 935–41. Secret agents notified Federal authorities: " John R. Ridge, at present of Nevada City, was a trading agent of the order, and is now an officer in the Nevada district."

112. " a traitor to God . . ." Ellison, op. cit., p. 193.

112. Joaquin Miller's Civil War journalism. RicM contains a photostatic copy of Miller's valedictory editorial in Eugene City explaining his Civil War activities.

112. " The drafting of troops . . ." Eugene City *Review,* February 14, 1863.

112. " a species of pious swindling . . ." Quoted in Eugene City *Review,* February 14, 1863.

113. " Only a private . . ." Eugene City *Review,* November 1, 1862.

114. John C. Cremony. Cremony, John C.: *Life among the Apaches,* San Francisco, 1868. *Reports of the Rebellion,* Series I, Vol. L, various entries. Autobiographical articles by Cremony in OM. For more detail on Cremony, see Walker, Franklin: " Bohemian No. 1: John C. Cremony," *Westways,* September 1937.

115. Henry George. As a supporter of Juárez, GeG.

CHAPTER V

THE GOLDEN ERA

General authorities: Cu and files of Era, particularly from 1863 to 1867.

Page 117. William H. Rhodes. San Francisco *Argonaut,* February 9, 1911; DagS; BaS; Era, May 15, 1869; *Caxton's Book,* edited by D. O'Connell, San Francisco, 1876.

118. "O sacred spirit . . ." DagS, Vol. I, p. 56.

118. *The Mormon Prophet.* See *California Historical Society Quarterly,* Vol. 10, p. 266, in notes on De Young diary.

118. Elbert Gerry Paige. Era, December 11, 1859, April 2, 1865; E. G. Paide in Cu, p. 17; Ch, October 24, 1897.

119. Rollin M. Daggett. See notes for p. 28. Daggett's nom-de-plumes on the *Era* were Blunderbus, Korn Kob, and Old Zeke. After several years on the Comstock, Daggett went to Congress and later served as United States Minister to Hawaii. His novel *Braxton's Bar* is to some degree autobiographical.

119. Joseph E. Lawrence. SteE; SteH; Call, September 4, 1892; Alta, July 16, 1878; DagS; StC; Hing; Upham, Samuel C.: *Scenes from "El Dorado."*

120. "Many times the *Era* . . ." Era, December 16, 1860.

121. "The first stanza . . ." Era, August 30, 1863.

121. "The humming bird . . ." Era, May 10, 1863.

123. "In summer when the sun . . ." Era, May 10, 1863.

124. Mark Twain's sensational novel. Described in detail in CleR, Vol. 2, pp. 76 ff.

126. "One of the pioneers . . ." Era, September 6, 1863.

126. "Mr. Marshall . . ." Era, December 6, 1862.

126. "Died, suddenly . . ." Era, July 5, 1863.

127. Harte's work on the *Era.* Harte was intermittently on the staff of the *Era* from April 1860 to the end of 1863. For bibliography, see SteBH.

127. "nothing but a poor hanger-on . . ." DagS.

128. "its ragged senility . . ." Era, March 22, 1863.

130. Densmore on Harte. DagS.

130. Another friend. Noah Brooks in *Century,* Vol. 36, pp. 447 ff.

130. Harte's taciturnity at San Rafael. See letter from J. H.

Wilkins in Stewart notes on Bret Harte, deposited in University of California Library.

132. " of making taverns . . ." Parry, p. 7.

133. Charles Henry Webb. DAB; SteH; DagS; New York *Times,* May 25, 1905; notes collected by G. R. Stewart for article in DAB; Webb.

133. The Pfaffians. Parry gives a detailed account of Pfaff's gatherings. Also see Era, February 28, 1864.

136. Phelps, Janette H. (Hagar). Cu, p. 26.

136. Alice M. J. Kingsbury (Cooley). (Hop o' my Thumb). Cu, pp. 29, 386; BaS. See also her *Secrets Told,* San Francisco, 1879, for coy sketches on marital problems.

136. Mary (Richardson) Newman Doliver (May Wentworth). BaS; Ch, April 17, 1881; Alta, January 13, 1867.

137. Frances Fuller Victor (Florence Fane). Cu; BaL; W. A. Morris in *Oregon Historical Society Quarterly,* Vol. 4, pp. 429 ff.; for her writings, see Victor, F. F.: *The New Penelope and Other Sketches; Poems,* San Francisco, 1900; and volumes of Ba on California and the Northwest.

137. " some of the strongest work . . ." Cu, p. 143.

137. Her volume on Joe Meek. F. F. Victor: *The River of the West,* Hartford, Connecticut, 1870.

138. Ralph Keeler. BaE; BaS; *National Magazine,* Vol. 23, p. 65; OM, Vol. 12, pp. 188, 381; autobiographical articles in *Atlantic Monthly,* 1870–5; Keeler letters to Stoddard in Huntington Library; Alta, June 7, 1867, January 18, 1874; two scrapbooks in Bancroft Library. See also Walker, Franklin: " Ralph Keeler, Literary Vagabond," *Westways,* September 1935. Keeler disappeared mysteriously from a boat off the Cuban coast in 1874.

139. " stuffed hyena . . ." Quoted from Keeler, Ralph: *Vagabond Adventures,* Boston, 1870.

140. " The trance-dead . . ." Clipping from *Era* in Bancroft scrapbook.

141. " The pleasant ripple . . ." Quoted by Stoddard in *National Magazine,* Vol. 23, p. 65.

141. *Gloverson and His Silent Partners.* Eventually published in Boston, 1869. Mark Twain in his *Autobiography* (Vol. 1, pp. 154 ff.) tells amusingly of Keeler's excitement on discovering a copy of the book for sale in a book-store while the two were on a lecture tour in New England.

142. Prentice Mulford on the *Era*. Mu; MuS; articles in *Era* beginning October 8, 1865; autobiographical articles in OM. See also entries under Mulford, in note on p. 70.

143. "What a glorious land . . ." Mu, p. 261. Om, Vol. 4, pp. 89 ff., tells amusingly of Mulford's campaign.

144. "canned oysters . . ." Om, Vol. 2, pp. 556–62 is devoted to Mulford's culinary experiences in California.

144. "The retched maiden . . ." Era, January 14, 1866.

CHAPTER VI

VISITORS

General authorities: files of Era, 1863 to 1865.

Page 146. Miller on visit to *Era* office. Call, September 4, 1892.

146. Burton's visit to San Francisco. Burton, Richard F.: *The City of the Saints,* New York, 1862. In San Francisco from November 5 to November 15, 1860.

147. Theodore Winthrop. DAB; Winthrop, T.: *The Canoe and the Saddle,* 1863; Johnson, L. W.: *The Life and Poems of Theodore Winthrop,* 1884.

147. Joseph G. Baldwin. DAB; Ba (*California,* Vol. 7, p. 233); Good; *American Literature,* Vol. 2, p. 292.

148. Joaquin Miller's sojourn in San Francisco in 1863. See entries on Miller, in note on p. 82. Also Call, September 4, 1892, July 31, 1892. Miller's "Valedictory" in the Eugene City *Review* for February 14, 1863 establishes the date of his departure for San Francisco. Files of Era for 1863. Minnie Myrtle's lecture on her early married life are reported verbatim in Bul, September 25, 1872; Call, September 26, 1872. See also interview with Minnie Myrtle, Call, September 21, 1872. Another lecture, Bul, November 13, 1872. Letters of John Whittaker to Miller in 1863 in Huntington Library contain references to San Francisco experiences.

148. "Minnie Myrtle" Dyer. Cu; WagM; MiM; and lectures listed above.

148. "little lisping river . . ." Call, September 26, 1872.

148. "all the beautiful . . ." Ibid.

149. "He came to fall . . ." From "Even So," in Miller, Joaquin: *Songs of the Sierras,* London, 1871.

150. "the longest string . . ." Era, February 15, 1863.

150. Miller's contributions to the *Era*. Photostatic copies of all Miller items in the *Era* in 1863 are to be found in RicM.

150. " The Devil's Castle, or The Dark Covenant." Minnie Myrtle referred to this serial in her interview, Call, September 21, 1872. Whittaker, op. cit., refers to the serial in a letter to Miller dated October 25, 1863. I have not been able to find a file of the California *Police Gazette* for 1863. See also Call, September 4, 1892.

151. " Breathes there a miner . . ." Era, October 12, 1863.

151. " We will go . . ." Era, May 24, 1863.

151. " A man never becomes famous . . ." Call, September 26, 1872.

152. " Gay Frisco! . . ." From " Cape Blanco," Era, July 19, 1863.

152. Mark Twain's visit to San Francisco in 1863. CleR ; CleL ; CleW ; PaM.

152. " it is just like being in Main Street . . ." CleL, Vol. 1, p. 90.

152. " I fare like a prince . . ." CleL, Vol. 1, p. 92.

153. Mark Twain's trips across the Sierra. See CleR, Vol. 1, p. 142.

153. William Wright (Dan de Quille). Cu: CleW; PaM ; " Dan " in CleR. See also entries under Washoe, p. 92, and staff of *Territorial Enterprise,* p. 95. See Call, October 4, 1903 ; Era, May 4, 1864 ; Ex, March 19, 1893 ; and preface to CleW for accounts of Mark Twain's feud with Dan de Quille.

154. " a stewed chicken ghoul . . ." Era, July 30, 1863.

154. " No paper in the U. S. . . ." CleL, Vol. 1, pp. 91–2.

155. " Mrs. Hon. F. F. L. . . ." Era, September 27, 1863.

155. " tasteful tarantula . . ." Ibid.

155. " gorgeous bouquet . . ." Ibid.

156. " Dooney comes up fresh . . ." California *Police Gazette,* April 13, 1867.

156. " No sooner did Low . . ." Era, October 11, 1863.

157. " scarcely refined in character . . ." See PaM, Vol. 1, p. 243, for a discussion of this sketch, not named by title. " Those Blasted Children," as well as all other Mark Twain sketches to appear in the *Era,* is reprinted in CleW.

157. San Francisco in 1863. General references Hi, Hing, Ne, and files of Era.

158. Browne, Charles Farrar (Artemus Ward). Hing; CleR ; PaM; DAB; LyS; CrH; Ex, March 19, 1893; Ch, January 10, 1892; Era, November 1, 8, 15, 1863; (Browne, C. F.) *Artemus Ward's Panorama,* London, 1869.

159. " What will you take . . ." Era, October 18, 1863.

160. " The colonel chanced to be . . ." Hing, p. 83.

160. The article on Ward, Shakespeare, and spiritualism. Era, November 8, 1863; see also Hing, pp. 92 ff.

161. " of the vein of thought . . ." Era, November 15, 1863.

161. " Had Artemus appeared . . ." Era, December 27, 1863.

162. " The humor of audacious exaggeration . . ." Ibid.

163. Fitzhugh Ludlow. DAB; Parry; *Harper's Magazine,* Vol. 42, p. 139; Alta, July 19, 1863; Era, fall of 1863 and spring of 1864; Ludlow, Fitzhugh: *The Hasheesh Eater,* New York, 1857; Ludlow, Fitzhugh: *The Heart of the Continent,* Boston, 1870; autobiographical articles by Ludlow in *Atlantic Monthly,* Vols. 13, 14, and 15. For further detail see Walker, Franklin: " The Hasheesh Infant among the Argonauts," *Westways,* August 1935.

164. Twain on Ludlow. PaM, Vol. 1, p. 244.

164. Stoddard on Ludlow. StC.

164. Mock Trial. Account by Inigo in " Things," Era, November 22, 1863.

165. " the candid visitor . . ." Era, November 8, 1863.

166. Adah Isaacs Menken. DAB; Parry; RoT; LyS; PaM; Leman, Walter M.: *Memoirs of an Old Actor;* Falk, B.: *The Naked Lady; National Magazine,* Vol. 21, p. 477; Ex, March 19, 1893; Era, late 1863 and early 1864, also April 30, 1865; Call, July 31, 1892. Introduction to Menken, A.: *Infelicia,* Philadelphia, 1888.

167. " They are killing me . . ." Call, July 31, 1892.

167. Harte's " The Crusade of the Excelsior." The character of Mrs. Hurlstone was undoubtedly suggested by Menken. See SteH, p. 121. As this story was written long after Harte left San Francisco, naturally he took many liberties in drawing the character.

168. " Resurgam." Era, November 29, 1863. Many of Menken's poems which appeared in the *Era* while she was in the West had previously been printed in Eastern and Southern journals.

168. Swinburne's " Dolores " was written after Menken visited him in London. See Falk, op. cit., for an amusing account of that visit.

168. " Every curve of her limbs . . ." Stoddard in *National Magazine,* Vol. 21, p. 477.

168. " an idealized duality of sex . . ." Era, September 13, 1863.

169. For Webb on Menken see Era, August 30, 1863.

169. " Let a pure youth . . ." Call, August 28, 1864.

170. Menken on Whitman. Era, November 15, 1863.

170. Robert Henry Newell. DAB and entries under Menken. See also Era, April 24, 1864, October 2, 1864, January 8, 1865.

171. Ada Clare. Cu; DAB; Parry; LyS; *National Magazine,* Vol. 22, p. 637; Ex, March 19, 1893; Era, 1864; C, December 29, 1864.

173. Menken's Virginia City party. Described by Dan de Quille in Ex, March 19, 1893.

173. For reviews of Clare's appearance in *Camille,* see NL, December 31, 1864.

174. " the fairest and most accomplished lady . . ." Era, March 20, 1864.

174. " We doubt not . . ." Ibid.

174. " Miners developing their gold . . ." etc. Ada Clare's column started in the *Era* on March 20, 1864 and continued for several months.

174. " As a whole, I esteem . . ." Era, March, 27, 1864.

174. " But, as usual . . ." Cu, p. 23.

175. " Yes, they killed it . . ." Cu, p. 17.

CHAPTER VII

POLITE LITERATURE AND GHOSTS

General authorities: Hi, Cu, Ne, files of Era and C.

Page 178. Plans to start the *Californian.* See SteH, pp. 124 ff.; Era, November 8, 15, and 22, 1863.

179. The *Californian.* Much of the Harte and Twain material in C is republished in HoW.

179. " I have been engaged . . ." CleL, Vol. 1, p. 100.

179. " The Californian nearly bankrupted me . . ." Webb, p. 5.

180. Financial control of *Californian.* C, November 26, 1864; CleR, Vol. 1, p. 145.

181. " All the characters move about . . ." C, December 3, 1864.

181. Nom-de-plumes. " Podgers " was Richard S. Ogden; " Theophilus Potsherd," J. F. Bowman; " Ingle," Carrie S. Walters; " Black Annan," C. W. Stoddard; and " Meg Merrilies," Ina Coolbrith. See Coolbrith name card in California State Library.

182. "whether the individual . . ." C, November 25, 1865. Quoted in SteH, p. 151.

182. " outright offences against public decency . . ." C, December 2, 1865.

183. C. H. Webb on the *Californian.* See listings under Webb, note on p. 133.

183. " If we may not die . . ." Era, November 15, 1863.

184. Bret Harte on the *Californian.* SteH; files of C. For bibliography, see SteBH.

185. " This fable teaches us . . ." C, November 4, 1865.

185. " Question not the theology . . ." C, May 13, 1865.

185. " attenuated sentiment and moral pathos . . ." C, September 30, 1865.

186. " gradual decay of short story telling . . ." C, June 9, 1866.

186. " I had killed twenty-nine men . . ." C, May 12, 1866.

186. " The loss of his upper lip . . ." Ibid.

187. *Condensed Novels.* These parodies on contemporary novelists started in the *Era* and continued in the *Californian* as sketches by the *Californian's* Condensed Novelist. They were collected and appeared as Harte's first book, *Condensed Novels and Other Papers,* New York, 1867.

187. Mark Twain on the *Californian.* PaM; CleR; CleL; CleW; CleA; CleN; files of Era and C. Sketches reprinted in HoW.

188. " I take it all back . . ." Bul, October 31, 1863. See also Bul, November 3, 1863 for newspaper comments.

188. Mark Twain's duel. Call, May 28, 1864, June 2, 1864. See account in Benson, pp. 106 ff.

189. " a remarkably spirited and chatty little journal . . ." Hing. See also Ll.

189. " It was fearful drudgery . . ." PaM, Vol. 1, p. 257.

190. " His head was striking . . ." Pemberton, T. E.: *The Life of Bret Harte,* p. 73.

190. " He trimmed and trained and schooled me . . ." CleL, p. 182.

191. " Bret Harte was one . . ." Quoted in SteH, p. 171.

192. " There was but one . . ." C, October 22, 1864.

193. Mark Twain's notebook. Printed in CleN.

194. " proceed cheerlessly to scout . . ." C, March 18, 1865.

194. The Pound Package Jamestown Smoke Co. Prentice Mulford tells of this elaborate hoax in Mu, pp. 159 ff.

195. " a villainous backwoods sketch . . ." CleL, Vol. 1, p. 101.

195. " It hath a sow . . ." C, October 28, 1865.

196. " If I had you in the range . . ." Era, September 20, 1863.

196. " a chance to taste . . ." C, November 17, 1866.

196. " spitting on his shirt bosom . . ." C, December 2, 1865.

197. " The tradition goes that three clergymen . . ." C, May 13, 1865.

197. " And why shouldn't they shove . . ." Reprinted from the *Territorial Enterprise* in Era, January 21, 1866.

198. " radically a rather grave man . . ." BaS.

198. " The Moralist of the Main . . ." PaM, Vol. 1, p. 274.

198. " What you want is Morality . . ." C, August 25, 1866. In How, this is attributed to Mark Twain, probably erroneously, as it was but one of a series of bogus letters of application for the editorship.

198. Henry George on the *Californian*. GeG. Three articles discussed appeared in C, August 5, 1865, July 14 and 28, 1866.

201. Spiritualism. McCabe, Joseph: *Spiritualism;* Hardinge, Emma: *Modern American Spiritualism,* New York, 1870; Hing; Webb; Bul for January and February 1866; files of Era, particularly January 14 and 28, 1866; files of C.

202. Spiritualism Unmasked, by Miles Grant, San Francisco (n. d.).

202. " was a priestess . . ." StT, pp. 68–74. See also interesting letter from Stoddard to Mulford about Mrs. Cuppy in Stoddard notebook No. 7, dated February 17, 1885, in possession of Ed Grabhorn, San Francisco.

203. " Your hair commences growing long . . ." Era, June 17, 1866.

203. Mark Twain on spiritualism. CleW contains all of Mark Twain's San Francisco articles on spiritualism.

203. " I can remember . . ." Era, March 4, 1866.

204. " I'm not afraid . . ." Era, March 11, 1866.

204. Prentice Mulford and spiritualism. Information gained principally from his articles in the *Era* and later treatises in the White Cross Library (Boston and New York), written by Mulford in the late eighties.

206. " The Invisible in Our Midst." Era, November 28, 1869 to April 17, 1870. Some of these are reprinted in MuS.

206. " I am not particular . . ." MuS, p. 104.

206. Hermit in New Jersey. Mulford wrote a book about his experiences as a second Thoreau, entitled *The Swamp Angel,* Boston, 1888.

CHAPTER VIII

A RASH OF POETRY

General authorities: Cu; files of Era and C.

Page 207. Edward C. Kemble. See note on Kemble in *California Historical Society Quarterly,* Vol. 14, p. 80.

208. " The Emigrant's Dying Child." Era, May 1, 1853.

209. Edward Pollock. BaS; BaE; J. F. Bowman's introduction to Pollock's *Poems,* Philadelphia, 1876.

210. " Thoughts toward a New Epic." Pi, Vol. 2, pp. 65 ff.

210. " The air is chill . . ." PP, p. 28. Pollock holds the place of honor in both *Outcroppings* and *Poetry of the Pacific.*

211. " These were the flush days of the Comstock . . ." Article by Sam Davis, Ex, January 22, 1893.

213. The editing and reception of *Outcroppings.* " My First Book " in HaW; SteH; reviews in How; journals of the period.

215. " certain veiled libels and indecencies . . ." " My First Book " in HaW.

215. Harte's review of *Outcroppings.* C, December 9, 1865. Though unsigned, this series is attributed to Harte by Stewart. SteH, p. 133.

215. " Mr. Frank Bret Harte's long-promised and much talked of book . . ." NL, December 9, 1865. Quoted in SteH, p. 132.

216. " purp-stuff . . ." etc. Quoted by Harte in " My First Book," op. cit. A search through contemporary files reveals similar though not identical epithets. See Bul, December 21, 1865, January 17, 1866; DrCh, September 9, 1866; and C, December 15 and 23, 1865, January 20, 1866.

216. *Tailings: Rejections of California Verse.* C, December 23, 1865. This review is unquestionably by Harte, the *Californian's* Condensed Novelist.

216. " Lo! Where the orient hills . . ." Ibid.

217. " And through the valleys rose between . . ." Ibid.

217. Sam Brannan. Scherer, J. A. B.: *The First Forty-niner.* Also C, February 10, 1866.

218. Gottschalk on Sam Brannan. Gottschalk, Louis Moreau: *Notes of a Pianist,* p. 375. Gottschalk gives an amusing picture of San Francisco in the mid-sixties.

218. " the vexed question of who are the California poets . . ." Bul, January 17, 1866.

218. May Wentworth. See note on p. 136. Also Era, February 11, 1866, and Bul, January 17, 1866, for plans for editing PP.

219. " It must be remembered . . ." Preface to PP.

220. Soulé's " Labor." PP, p. 69.

221. " And in the lapse of countless ages . . ." " Poem," PP, p. 132.

221. Frank Soulé. One of the compilers of *The Annals of San Francisco.* Cu; DagS; Call, July 5, 1882; Alta, April 22, 1877.

221. William H. Rhodes. See note on p. 117.

221. " Strike! till the Unicorn shall lose its crown! . . ." Era, May 15, 1869.

223. Eliza Pittsinger. Cu; C, January 6, 1866; she is frequently called " The Prophetess " in contemporary reviews, e. g. Inigo in C, December 23, 1866.

224. " The toe of the Pope! . . ." Pittsinger, Eliza: *Bugle Peals,* San Francisco, 1882.

224. Ina Coolbrith. See references in note on p. 57 and files of C.

225. Rivalry between Twain and Harte. Raine Bennett in *Touring Topics,* November 1933, says that Ina Coolbrith told him of this feud.

225. " Fragment from an Unfinished Poem." PP, p. 343.

225. " Unrest." Bul, December 26, 1862.

225. " A Mother's Grief." In *Outcroppings.*

225. The loss of an infant child. No records of births and deaths were kept as early as 1860 in Los Angeles.

226. W. S. Kendall. Cu; Ch, December 15, 1872; Alta, January 20, 1876; *Pacific Monthly,* Vol. 18, p. 639; letters to C. W. Stoddard, Huntington Library.

226. " Oh were my soul as high as Jove . . ." C, December 14, 1867.

227. W. Frank Stewart. See note in DeS, p. 94.

227. John R. Ridge. See notes on page 45.

228. Harte's *The Lost Galleon.* But an adverse review, " A Plagiary Poet," echoed the *Outcroppings* feud. DrCh, December 30, 1867.

228. C. W. Stoddard. See authorities listed under notes for p. 73, particularly StC.

229. Stoddard's autograph album. The letters that Stoddard received for his autograph album were printed in " *Notable Autographs* " by Pourquoi, *the Californian* (San Francisco, 1880–2), Vol. 1, pp.

353–7, 528–36. These articles were to have formed a part of StC in event of publication.

230. " nearly every well-known name . . ." Quoted in StC.

230. One Stoddard collection. With the Coolbrith papers in the hands of Mr. Finlay Cooke, San Francisco.

230. " owlish air . . ." Quoted in StC.

231. " It is very clear . . ." Quoted in StC. For other reviews of Stoddard's *Poems,* see C, August 31, September 7 and 26, November 9, 1867.

231. " Perhaps the Sun is an egg of gold . . ." *Outcroppings,* San Francisco, 1886, p. 69.

232. " He has a woman's soul . . ." OM (n. s.), Vol. 51, p. 135. In this article Phillips states that Jack London called Stoddard " The love man."

232. His diaries. The diaries I have examined (see note on p. 73) contain most compelling evidence of Stoddard's epicene nature. See also StP for self-analysis on this subject.

233. " I laid my heart . . ." StT, p. 120.

233. Edward Rowland Sill. DAB; ParS; introduction to *Poetical Works,* Boston, 1906; Sill, E. R.: *The Hermitage and Other Poems,* San Francisco and New York, 1868; *U. C. Magazine,* May 1896.

233. " But I am tired . . ." *The Hermitage and Other Poems,* op. cit., p. 35.

234. " I know that Duty . . ." Quoted in ParS, p. 73.

234. " I wish I had more faith in men . . ." Quoted in ParS, p. 72.

234. " Pikes, fools, fools . . ." Quoted in ParS, p. 61.

235. " one's only companions . . ." Quoted in ParS, p. 26.

235. " Ah, give me back the clime I know . . ." " Eastern Winter," *The Hermitage and Other Poems.*

236. Reviews of *The Hermitage.* See C, November 30, 1867.

CHAPTER IX

THE TOWN CRIER

General authorities: Hi; NL; McWB; Ll; Fish.

Page 237. Ambrose Bierce. I have relied principally on McWB for biographical detail on Bierce. I have also consulted Starrett, V.: *Ambrose Bierce;* Gratten, C. H.: *Bitter Bierce;* De Castro, A.: *Portrait of Ambrose Bierce;* Neale, W.: *Life of Ambrose Bierce; Pacific Monthly,* March 1908; *American Mercury,* September 1925; files of C, OM, NL;

Ex, January 22, 1893; Ex, March 3, 1889; Bierce letters in Huntington Library.

239. Bierce's notebooks. Discussed and quoted in McWB, pp. 69 ff.

240. "Tell anybody anything . . ." Letter to Stoddard, San Rafael, California, November 13, 1871. Huntington, M. S., 10, 100.

240. "I intend, merely as a matter of duty . . ." NL, September 25, 1869.

241. "Basilica." C, September 21, 1867.

241. "A Mystery." C, November 23, 1867.

241. "Concerning Tickets." C, December 28, 1867.

241. "Female Suffrage." C, December 7, 14, 21, and 28, 1867.

242. "blanked fools who landed here . . ." *Century,* Vol. 36, p. 447.

243. "Hear the corrupt and ulcerated tongue . . ." DrCh, October 11, 1867.

243. James F. Bowman. StC; Bul, May 22, 1897; Call, April 30, 1882; Sacramento *Union,* May 1, 1882; Bul, May 8, 1870; Alta, May 8, 1870; files of Era, C, OM. *Annals of the Bohemian Club,* Vol. 1; C, September 28, 1867. Bowman is "Archer" in StP.

243. Mark Twain's letters from the Sandwich Islands. Collected by G. Ezra Dane and reprinted as *Letters from the Sandwich Islands,* San Francisco, 1937.

244. "The missionaries braved a thousand privations . . ." Sacramento *Weekly Union,* April 28, 1866.

244. "Few men of first class ability . . ." Ibid., June 23, 1866.

245. Harte's articles for the *News Letter.* The best of these were collected by G. R. Stewart and published in *Frontier,* Vol. 13, pp. 93 ff. Bibliography of Harte items in NL found in SteBH.

245. "California Madrigal." NL, March 30, 1867.

245. "The patients who most profit . . ." NL, July 13, 1867.

245. "only another evidence . . ." NL, February 23, 1867.

246. "Go back to your cowardly masters . . ." NL, March 23, 1867.

247. *Mazeppa.* BaS (W–38) on California Journalism contains a clipping dated June 22, 1866 describing the horsewhipping.

247. Edward Jump. See Alta, May 26, 1868; Call, July 3, 1892; Sacramento *Union,* April 21, 1883; Peters, H. T.: *California on Stone,* New York, 1935, p. 131.

247. T. L. Johns. Alta, January 10 and 13, 1875; *Figaro,* January 9, 1875; C, September 28, 1867.

247. " The *Alta* had rabies badly . . ." *Figaro* (San Francisco, 1865), July 1, 1874.

248. Frederick Marriott and the *News Letter.* Ll; Fish; BaS (W–38); San Francisco *News Letter and Wasp,* December 14, 1935; Bul, December 17, 1884; Peters, H. T.: *California on Stone,* New York, 1935, p. 174.

249. " Little Fred Marriott, Fly quickly . . ." C, April 22, 1865.

250. " It seems impossible for a man . . ." Bul, January 20, 1864.

250. " The Italians continue . . ." All Bierce quotations taken from the Town Crier department of NL in 1869.

CHAPTER X

THE OVERLAND MONTHLY

General authorities: Cu; Hi; files of OM.

Page 256. San Francisco magazines. I have found much interesting and valuable data in Bepler, D. W.: " A History of Early Magazines in San Francisco," a master's thesis in the University of California Library. Other detail in BaE; OM (n. s.), Vol. 12, p. 337; Greene, C. S.: *Magazine Publishing in California,* Library Association of California Publications #2 (May 1, 1898), and files of journals.

257. J. M. Hutchings. See notes on p. 27.

258. The Overland Monthly. All references are to the first *Overland Monthly,* sometimes called OM (o. s.). For material on its genesis and publication, see Cu; Fish; Ba, Vol. 38; SteH; OM, Vol. 15, p. 533; OM (n. s.), Vol. 12, p. 337, Vol. 32, pp. 4, 41, 66, and 72, Vol. 40, pp. 220 and 264, Vol. 60, p. 220; Bepler, op. cit.; Greene, op. cit.; Tassin, A.: *The Magazine in America.*

258. Account-books of *Overland Monthly.* In the University of California Library.

259. Anton Roman. SteH; Ch, June 22, 1903; DagS; articles above on OM. Roman was killed in a train wreck in 1903.

260. Noah Brooks. DAB; Ch, October 31, 1897, August 18, 1903.

260. William C. Bartlett. OM (n. s.), Vol. 32, p. 4; Bartlett, W. C.: *A Breeze from the Woods,* San Francisco, 1883.

260. " My only objection at that time . . ." Roman in OM (n. s.), Vol. 32, p. 72.

262. Bret Harte on the *Overland Monthly.* SteH; *Century,*

Vol. 36, p. 447; *McClure's Magazine,* Vol. 4, p. 44; *Pacific Monthly,* Vol. 18, p. 639.

264. "Well, he had a right to . . ." StE.

264. "an era replete . . ." Preface to *The Luck of Roaring Camp and Other Tales,* 1870.

265. "I will not trouble you . . ." J. C. McCracken in OM (n. s.), September 1902.

266. Joe Goodman's anonymity. This move on Goodman's part is revealed in a file of letters to the editor of the OM, deposited in University of California Library.

266. Harte's secretary. Josephine Clifford McCracken. See OM (n. s.), September 1902; and Cu, pp. 126 ff.

266. Charges against Harte. See letter from Phil B. Bekeart in Stewart notes on Harte (University of California Library) and article by Kendall in Ch, December 15, 1872, and DagS, Vol. I, p. 198.

267. Carmany's arrangements with Harte. SteH, p. 184; and HaL, p. 7.

268. "I can make here, by my pen . . ." Letter dated September 13, 1875, in file of OM letters in University of California Library.

268. The Golden Gate Trinity. SteH; StC; StE; *National Magazine,* Vol. 26, p. 315; *National Magazine,* June 1907; Coolbrith, I.: Introduction to *The Heathen Chinee* (Nash edition), San Francisco, 1934. Ina is Elaine in StP.

269. "And they added in language emphatic . . ." Coolbrith: Introduction to *The Heathen Chinee,* op. cit.

270. "And I could kiss, with longing wild . . ." From "Longing," OM, Vol. 1, p. 17.

271. "circling about him . . ." StP, p. 51.

271. Stoddard's experiences as an actor. StC; StP, pp. 55 ff.; *Argonaut,* May 25, 1878; articles by Stoddard on his ácting, *Atlantic Monthly,* Vol. 34, pp. 20, 168, 527. His first appearance was in *The Willow Copse* in Sacramento, March 12, 1868.

271. "This frugal repast . . ." *National Magazine,* Vol. 21, p. 378.

271. "Now you have struck it . . ." StC.

272. Stoddard's visits to Hawaii and Tahiti. StC; StP; StE; BaS; Ch, January 11, 1902; *Sunset,* September 1905; *Argonaut,* May 25, 1878; *National Magazine,* Vol. 22, p. 379; letters in *American Literature,* May 1933. Hearn's tribute to Stoddard's influence is expressed in a letter in the hands of Mrs. E. P. Van Sicklen, San Francisco.

272. Stoddard's championing of Father Damien. In *The Lepers of Molokai,* 1885. See also *U. C. Magazine,* Vol. 2, p. 272, and Oscar Lewis's preface to Stoddard's *Diary of a Visit to Molokai* for account of Stoddard's influence on Stevenson in connection with Father Damien.

274. Joaquin Miller visits San Francisco. In addition to sources listed in note on p. 82 see *Pacific Monthly,* Vol. 18, p. 639, and Miller and Stoddard letters in Huntington Library.

275. " Good fellows here but ignorant as asses . . ." Letter from Miller to Stoddard dated August 30, 1869, in Huntington Library.

275. " Without learning I was trying . . ." MiM, p. 216.

275. Specimens. This rare paper-covered volume is reproduced in full (by photostat) in RicM.

276. " a savage little letter . . ." So described in Miller's letter to Stoddard of October 30, 1869, in Huntington Library. Harte's letter is found in HaL, p. 8.

277. " and at such times . . ." OM, January 1870.

277. " the tricks and treachery of one-horse politicians . . ." Letter from Miller to his brother, March 19, 1870, printed in WagM, p. 62.

277. " Myrrh." *Oregon State Journal,* June 11, 1870.

278. " besides some nut brown beauty . . ." Undated letter from Miller to Stoddard, written presumably in August 1870, now in Huntington Library. This letter carries references to Ina Coolbrith and the photographs mentioned.

279. Articles in OM. Indexed in a folio in the Bancroft Library, Berkeley, by subject and by author.

281. " First, applause . . ." Cu, p. 158. On Gally, see also Fish.

282. Therese Yelverton. StI; Badé; Leman's *Memories of an Old Actor,* pp. 347 ff.; M. T. Yelverton (Longworth): *Teresina in America,* London, 1875.

282. John Franklin Swift. DagS, Vol. 3, p. 24; Sacramento *Union,* March 11, 1891, August 28, 1886; Stewart, W. M.: *Reminiscences,* p. 162; Parkinson, P. R.: *Pen Portraits,* p. 78.

282. William V. Wells. DAB; articles in OM.

CHAPTER XI

PRACTICAL LITERATURE

General authorities: Hi; BaE; Cu; files of OM.

Page 284. W. C. Bartlett on California literature. OM, Vol. 15, p. 533.

286. B. P. Avery. See notes on p. 27.

286. W. C. Bartlett. See notes on p. 260.

286. Clarence King. DAB; Good; OM (n. s.), Vol. 40, p. 355; BaL, p. 348; Adams, H.: *The Education of Henry Adams;* preface to King; Brewer, W. H.: *Up and Down California in 1860–64,* New Haven, 1930; Emmons, S. F.: *Biographical Memoir of Clarence King,* National Academy of Sciences, Biographical Memoirs, Vol. 6 (1909).

288. "There were scores of short stories . . ." Quoted in preface to King, p. 19.

288. "The mother was a bony sister . . ." From "Wayside Pikes," *Atlantic Monthly,* November 1871. Included in King.

289. "The rock was so steep . . ." From "The Descent of Mount Tyndall," *Atlantic Monthly,* July 1871. Included in King.

290. John Muir. DAB; Badé. Portrayed as Kenmuir in YZ. (For key to characters in YZ, see Badé, pp. 279 ff.)

293. "as a mouthpiece for a portion of my ice . . ." Quoted in Badé, p. 321.

293. "There is at least a punky spark . . ." Quoted in Badé, p. 272.

294. J. S. Hittell. See note on p. 27.

294. Josiah Royce. DAB; *Philosophical Review,* May 1916; Royce, Sarah: *A Frontier Lady,* New Haven, 1932; Royce, Josiah: *California,* Boston, 1886; and articles in OM, Vol. 14, p. 542, Vol. 15, p. 157. See also his California novel, *The Feud of Oakfield Creek,* Boston, 1887.

294. "I have learned . . ." Joyce, R.: *California,* p. 500.

294. Henry George. GeG and GeP, with notes on p. 78. Also Post, L. F.: *The Prophet of San Francisco,* New York, 1930; and Young, Arthur N.: *The Single Tax Movement in the United States,* Princeton, 1916.

295. "utter heathens . . ." GeG, Vol. 1, p. 194.

295. "Like a flash it came upon me . . ." Ibid., p. 210.

295. "Once, in daylight, and in a city street . . ." Ibid., p. 193.

296. "increase in population . . ." From "What the Railroad Will Bring Us," OM, Vol. 1, pp. 297–306.

298. "On uncultivated tracts of land . . ." GeP, p. 310.

300. "for the study of political economy you need . . ." GeG, Vol. 1, p. 278.

300. "A monkey with a microscope . . ." Ibid.

300. "the reverend gentleman . . ." GeP, p. 94.

301. " the event which, more than any other . . ." Quoted in Somervil, D. C.: *English Thought in the Nineteenth Century,* p. 207.

301. George's anticipation of Turner's thesis. See GeP, p. 350.

302. H. H. Bancroft. DAB; BaL; Fish; Ll; OM, Vol. 12, p. 283; *Southwest Review,* Vol. 17, p. 380; Ch, January 3, 1881; Ex, January 22, 1893; Morris, W. A.: " The Origin and Authorship of the Bancroft Pacific States Publications," *Oregon Historical Society Quarterly,* Vol. 4, pp. 287–364; Oak, Henry L.: *Literary Industries in a New Light,* San Francisco, 1893; Lewis, Oscar: " The Launching of Bancroft's *Native Races,"* the *Colophon* (n. s.), Vol. 1, p. 3.

302. The Bancroft Building. Ll, pp. 162 ff., pp. 294 ff.; BaL; Fish.

303. Bancroft's assistants. BaL; Morris, op. cit.; Oak, op. cit.

305. " Where are your college men? . . ." BaL, p. 150.

306. " Books! Books! . . ." Ibid., p. 172.

307. " Wherever I touched the continent . . ." Ibid., p. 295.

309. " reached sixteen pages . . ." Ibid., p. 313.

309. " never probably was a book . . ." Ibid., p. 361.

310. " the purely garret philosopher . . ." Ibid., p. 602.

310. " It was my ambition . . ." Ibid., p. 654.

310. " Let me die . . ." Ibid., p. 281.

312. Thomas Savage. See note on Bancroft's assistants, p. 303.

312. Francis Fuller Victor. Ibid.; also note p. 137.

313. " The work of my assistants . . ." BaL, p. 306.

314. Apportionment of writing of Bancroft histories. Morris, op. cit., has clearly demonstrated the origins of the history. See also Oak, op. cit.

314. " a purloiner of other people's brains . . ." *Salt Lake Tribune,* February 16, 1893.

314. Bancroft's prejudices. For an amusing attack on Bancroft, see the pamphlet *Proceedings of the Society of California Pioneers in Reference to the Histories of H. H. Bancroft,* San Francisco, 1894. The society expelled Bancroft as an honorary member because they felt he had blackened the names of a number of their members. Bierce, in Ex, January 22, 1893, sums up the popular charges against Bancroft.

FROM GOLD GULCH TO PARNASSUS

General authorities: Hi; Cu.

Page 317. " The dear, old book of travel . . ." OM, Vol. 1, p. 101.

317. J. Ross Browne. References in note on p. 29, particularly RoB.

318. " a quaint mixture . . ." BaS (California Authors, p. 2).

318. " The smallest steamboat . . ." Browne, J. R.: *Yusef,* New York, 1853, p. 55.

319. John Franklin Swift. See notes on p. 282.

319. Mark Twain's excursion on the *Quaker City.* PaM; CleL; CleI; *Century,* Vol. 57, p. 97.

320. " We do not know . . ." CleI, p. 338.

321. " a land which has groped . . ." CleI, p. 196.

322. " They say that the long-nosed . . ." CleI, p. 408.

323. " a great historical creek . . ." CleI, p. 188.

323. The *Alta California* letters. A cursory glance through these fifty-two letters (1867–8) suggests that a close textual comparison with *The Innocents Abroad* would prove interesting. OM, Vol. 1, pp. 18, 120, 209, 316, are sections which appeared with little change in *The Innocents Abroad.*

324. Joaquin Miller's London success. See references in notes on pp. 82 and 148, particularly StE; MiM; and Miller letters in Huntington Library. In addition, see OM, Vol. 6, p. 409, Vol. 7, p. 325; the *Independent,* some twenty articles on European experiences during 1874 and 1875; again, several articles in 1884 and 1885; Call, some twenty articles running at irregular intervals between November 27, 1892 and May 28, 1893; Bul, August 24, 1871, August 24, 1872; New York *Sun,* October 17, 1872; NL, January 13, 1872; New York *Sun,* November 20, 1871; San Francisco *Post,* February 8, 1872, January 25, 1875; OM (n. s.), Vol. 84, p. 216; *Argonaut,* February 16, 1878; *Gentleman's Magazine* (London), Vol. 9, p. 301; Hueffer, F. M.: *Memories and Impressions;* Reed, T. W.: *Life of Lord Houghton;* Hawthorne, J.: *Shapes that Pass;* Rossetti, C. G.: *Letters;* Rossetti, D. G.: *Letters;* Hare, Augustus: *The Story of My Life;* Hueffer, F. M.: *Ford Madox Brown;* Moore, I.: *Talks in a Library with Lawrence Hutton.*

325. " Here I met Tennyson . . ." Miller's lecture, reported in Bul, February 8, 1872.

325. " Swinburne said to me . . ." Ibid. See also Call, December 25, 1892.

326. " among the tombstones . . ." MiM, p. 15. This is from Miller's diary, printed in MiM.

326. " Cardinal Wolsey, Lord Byron . . ." OM, Vol. 6, p. 409.

326. " Boatswain's tomb . . ." Ibid.

327. " Aye, now, don't you know . . ." MiM, p. 25.

328. Miller's visit to Jean Ingelow. Call, January 22, 1893. Miller letters to Locker-Lampson in Morse collection. See also MiM, p. 26.

328. " It helps sell the poems, you know . . ." Hawthorne, J.: *Shapes that Pass,* p. 78.

329. " a lover of beasts and birds . . ." *Academy,* Vol. 2, p. 30.

329. " I rather disbelieved . . ." RicM, p. 38. See also MiM, p. 26; Call, November 27, 1892.

330. London reviews of *Songs of the Sierras.* Some of the more important were *Academy,* June 15, 1871; *Athenæum,* June 3, 1871; *Blackwood's,* October 1871; *British Quarterly,* January 1872; *Chambers's,* August 3, 1871; *Dark Blue,* Vol. 2, pp. 120, 607; *Fraser's,* Vol. 84, p. 346; *Gentleman's,* September 1871; *Saturday Review,* June 1871; *Westminster,* July 1871; *Dublin Review,* April 1874; *Dublin University Magazine,* January 1876.

331. " In heaven's name . . ." *Blackwood's Magazine,* Vol. 110, p. 430.

331. " I should now like to see Mr. Browning . . ." Letter from Miller to Locker-Lampson (1871), Morse collection.

331. " study it every day . . ." MiM, p. 46. MiM contains a detailed account of the Pre-Raphaelite dinner. Also Call, December 18, 1892.

332. Beale on Miller. See Bonsal, S.: *Edward F. Beale,* p. 284.

334. Prentice Mulford in Europe. In addition to references in note on p. 70, see Mulford's European correspondence in Bul, May 1872 to August 1874, in OM, 1872 and 1873.

334. " to advance by writing . . ." See biography in White Cross Library, #64.

335. " Here was congregated . . ." OM, Vol. 9, p. 371.

335. " to operate on . . ." Bul, January 3, 1874.

335. " Perhaps I have mistaken my vocation . . ." Quoted in PaM, p. 498.

336. Ambrose Bierce in London. McWB and Bierce letters to Stoddard in Huntington Library.

336. "my object in coming was to loaf . . ." Letter from Bierce to Stoddard, May 16, 1873, in Huntington Library.

338. Mark Twain in London. PaM; CleN; CleL; Huntington Library letters.

339. " I would a good deal rather live here . . ." Quoted in PaM, p. 470.

340. Stoddard in London. References in note on p. 73, particularly StE; *U. C. Magazine,* Vol. 2, p. 272, and correspondence for OM, 1873–5, and Ch, June 1874, ff.

341. 11 Museum Street. See Mulford in Bul, February to August 1874; Miller in Call, August 7, 1892; Stoddard in " Lodgings in Bloomsbury " in StE. For further comments on Josie see McWB, p. 109; WagM, pp. 259 ff.; and clippings in State Library on Mulford.

342. " I am glad you like Miss Allen . . ." Letter from Miller to Stoddard, dated Rome, November 3, 1873, in Huntington Library.

342. " about twenty-six . . ." See letter from Mark Twain to Mrs. Fairbanks, July 6, 1873, in Huntington Library.

343. "Among men he says little . . ." Moore, I. (editor): *Talks in a Library with Lawrence Hutton,* New York, 1911, pp. 357 ff.

344. " Joaquin Miller would have been thought . . ." Hare, A.: *The Story of my Life,* Vol. 4, p. 308.

344. "Americans . . . were . . ." Hawthorne, J.: *Shapes that Pass,* p. 146.

344. "implying a sort of religious . . ." *Rossetti Family Letters* (1908), p. 211.

346. " to tell him to his teeth . . ." *Athenæum,* August 30, 1873. For other discouraging reviews, see *Academy,* Vol. 4, p. 301; *Temple Bar,* Vol. 37, p. 396; *Saturday Review,* Vol. 35, p. 825.

347. Joaquin Miller's pink lady. She emerged as the principal character in Miller's autobiographical novel, *The One Fair Woman,* New York, 1876. Miller amusingly accused Henry James of getting his plot for *Daisy Miller* from this novel. See Call, October 30, 1892; StE, p. 229.

349. " For nearly all that is good . . ." *Argonaut,* February 9, 1878.

CHAPTER XIII

EPILOGUE

General authorities: SteH; PaM; McWB; GeG; WagM.

Page 352. The Bohemian Club. See *Pacific Monthly,* Vol. 18, p. 639; Parry; and *Bohemian Annals,* Vol. I (San Francisco), for accounts of the genesis of this club.

352. "It is my intention . . ." Quoted in McWB, p. 123.

352. Bowman. See notes on p. 243 and Henry Edwards's letters to Stoddard, in Huntington Library.

353. Johns. See notes on p. 247.

353. Kendall. See notes on p. 226.

353. "I have stated immediate cause . . ." From clipping on suicide in collection of Kendall's letters to Stoddard, in Huntington Library.

353. T. Arundel-Harcourt. See notes on p. 303 under Bancroft's assistants, and McWB, pp. 127 ff.

354. "Thus my friend . . ." Quoted in McWB, p. 128.

354. Ina Coolbrith. See notes on p. 57. Also Edwards's letters to Stoddard, in Huntington Library, and *Wasp-News Letter* (San Francisco), December 22–9, 1928.

356. "I grind out the old tunes . . ." Quoted in SteH, p. 263.

357. "How awfully glad I shall be . . ." Grabhorn Stoddard diary #6: October 24, 1884.

357. Stoddard's relics. See SteP; *National Magazine,* Vol. 21, pp. 304, 308; *Sunset,* Vol. 15, p. 503; OM (n. s.), Vol. 47, p. 374; *Oakland Tribune,* January 26, 1920.

358. "Those were the old days! . . ." CleL, Vol. 2, p. 773.

359. Miller's rain chant. See Sterling in *American Mercury,* February 1926; also *National Magazine,* Vol. 24, p. 19.

360. California Literary Society. I am indebted to Mr. Fulmer Mood for a detailed account of the meetings of the California Literary Society. See also *Touring Topics* (Los Angeles), November 1933. Miss Coolbrith lived until 1928.

360. Ella Sterling Cummins (Mighels). Cu; BaS. Mr. Mood has also furnished me with many memories of this very active member of San Francisco's literary group.

INDEX

o

AMERICANA LIBRARY

The City: The Hope of Democracy
By Frederic C. Howe
With a new introduction by Otis A. Pease

Bourbon Democracy of the Middle West, 1865-1896
By Horace Samuel Merrill
With a new introduction by the author

*The Deflation of American Ideals: An Ethical Guide
for New Dealers*
By Edgar Kemler
With a new introduction by Otis L. Graham, Jr.

Borah of Idaho
By Claudius O. Johnson
With a new introduction by the author

The Fight for Conservation
By Gifford Pinchot
With a new introduction by Gerald D. Nash

Upbuilders
By Lincoln Steffens
With a new introduction by Earl Pomeroy

The Progressive Movement
By Benjamin Parke De Witt
With a new introduction by Arthur Mann

*Coxey's Army: A Study of the
Industrial Army Movement of 1894*
By Donald L. McMurry
With a new introduction by John D. Hicks

Jack London and His Times: An Unconventional Biography
By Joan London
With a new introduction by the author